HERMENEUTICAL INQUIRY

Volume I: The Interpretation of Texts

ÆR

American Academy of Religion
Studies in Religion

Editors
Charley Hardwick
James O. Duke

Number 43
HERMENEUTICAL INQUIRY
Volume I: The Interpretation of Texts
by
David E. Klemm

HERMENEUTICAL INQUIRY.
Volume I: The Interpretation of Texts

by

David E. Klemm

Scholars Press
Atlanta, Georgia

HERMENEUTICAL INQUIRY
Volume I: The Interpretation of Texts

by
David E. Klemm

Library of Congress Cataloging in Publication Data

Klemm, David E., 1947–
  Hermeneutical inquiry.

  (AAR studies in religion ; 43)
  1. Hermeneutics — Religious aspects.
I. Title. II. Series: Studies in religion
(American Academy of Religion) ; no. 43.
BL41.K57 1986   200'1   86-13927
ISBN 1-55540-032-9 (v. 1 : alk. paper)
ISBN 1-55540-035-3 (pbk. : v. 1 alk. paper)

Printed in the United States of America
on acid-free paper

DEDICATION

To my parents—

Eugene Woods Klemm
Pamela Mawdsley Klemm

—with love and respect.

ACKNOWLEDGMENTS

I have selected the essays in this collection because they are either acknowledged classics in hermeneutics or representative of the best of the current hermeneutical thinkers. All of the essays or excerpts appearing here have been previously published elsewhere; they are reprinted here with permission. No alterations have been made in original texts unless noted.

Details of the original publication are as follows:

Friedrich D. E. Schleiermacher, "The Academy Addresses of 1829," in *Hermeneutics: The Handwritten Manuscripts* by F. D. E. Schleiermacher. Edited by Heinz Kimmerle. Translated with an Introduction by James Duke and Jack Forstman (Missoula, Montana: Scholars Press, 1977), pp. 175–214. Copyright 1977 by the American Academy of Religion; used with permission.

Wilhelm Dilthey, "The Development of Hermeneutics," in *Selected Writings* by Wilhelm Dilthey. Edited and translated by H. P. Rickman (Cambridge, London, and New York: Cambridge University Press, 1976), pp. 246–63. Copyright 1976 by Cambridge University Press; used with permission.

Rudolf Bultmann, "The Problem of Hermeneutics," in *Essays Philosophical and Theological* by Rudolf Bultmann. Translated by James C. G. Greig (London: SCM Press, Ltd., 1955), pp. 234–61. Copyright 1955 by SCM Press Ltd.; used with permission.

Martin Heidegger, "Language," Chapter VI in *Poetry, Language, Thought* by Martin Heidegger. Translated by Albert Hofstadter (New York: Harper and Row, Publishers, 1971). Copyright 1971 by Martin Heidegger; reprinted by permission of Harper and Row, Publishers, Inc.

Paul Tillich, "The Meaning and Justification of Religious Symbols," from *Religious Experience and Truth: A Symposium*. Edited by Sidney Hook. Copyright 1961 by New York University; used by permission of New York University Press.

Hans-Georg Gadamer, "The Universality of the Hermeneutical Experience," in *Philosophical Hermeneutics* by Hans-Georg Gadamer. Edited and

TABLE OF CONTENTS

PREFACE

Hermeneutical Inquiry is primarily intended for the student of religious studies who wishes orientation within the vast and difficult literature of hermeneutics. My aim is to provide an advanced introduction for such a student. The significance of this book lies in the fact that it presents hermeneutical inquiry in relation to the field of religious studies, rather than literary theory or philosophy. Within the field of religious studies, my general and specific introductions address not only students of religious thought but also the current participants in scholarly hermeneutical discussions.

I begin the volume with an extensive general introduction with four parts. In the first part, I describe the hermeneutical problem as one of encountering otherness; religious studies poses a heightened case in which we confront the otherness of ultimate concern and are challenged to understand, while allowing the other to remain other. In the second part, I describe the formation and historical development of the hermeneutical problem. I focus on the relation of hermeneutics to "premodernity," "modernity," and "postmodernity." In the third part, I present a systematic analysis of the structure of understanding from the standpoint of postmodern hermeneutical inquiry. In the fourth part, I present an original and constructive thesis. I argue that we can derive types of hermeneutical inquiry from the basic elements of the structure of understanding. By highlighting one or another element in the structure of understanding, hermeneutical inquiry takes the form of hermeneutical theory, practical philosophy, and speculative ontology. Moreover, I drive my systematic interpretation of the understanding process one step further. Theological hermeneutics, I argue, appears on the limits of each type of hermeneutical inquiry through the interpretive experience of "overturning." As a final step, I suggest a way of thinking beyond the three forms of theological hermeneutics to the one God who appears in the play of texts and existence as the "otherness of the other." My proposal of hermeneutical types, both theological and nontheological, has a pragmatic side to it. My theoretical construction provides a means for understanding apparently disconnected texts in hermeneutics as part of an encompassing whole. In the introduction, I intend, in other words, to show one possibility for conceiving the unity of hermeneutical inquiry.

Beyond my general introduction, this book consists of a collection of texts that, in my judgment, are fundamental to the study of hermeneutics from the standpoint of religious studies. These core works by Schleiermacher, Dilthey, Husserl, Heidegger, Bultmann, Gadamer, Ebeling, Tillich, Ricoeur, Habermas, Perrin, and Scharlemann each make an important contribution to hermeneutical discussion. For some, the selection of texts may appear to be too provincial. These texts are largely written by Protestant men from continental Europe. In defense of my selection, I acknowledge the important work currently underway by both Catholic thinkers and feminist critics. But for either of these enterprises, the texts gathered here are classics in the field. Historically, modern and postmodern hermeneutics were initiated by Protestant men in Europe. To acknowledge that fact is not to claim that others should stay away from the discussion, nor is it to suggest that hermeneutics should carry a denominational self-understanding. I make these texts more widely available in hopes that hermeneutical inquiry will become more open, critical, and accessible to all. Hopefully, an anthology of works from the 1980s will be much more universal in representing different standpoints and concerns.

The question that guides my selection of texts is, "What becomes of theology and religious thought when thinking is self-consciously hermeneutical?" In different ways, each of the texts selected for this anthology provides instances of hermeneutical thought as it bears on theology or religious thought. Some of the texts (which are essays or excerpts from larger works) are primarily concerned with the principles of hermeneutical thinking in general and only secondarily pertain to the matters of theology or religious studies. As classics in hermeneutical theory, these texts lay out the essential elements in the structure of hermeneutical inquiry as a new paradigm of reflection. Other texts included here are involved in the first instance with matters of religious or theological thought, perhaps with disclosing the meaning and being of the self or the "world of the text" in relation to God. These latter works are significant contributions to theology or religious thought that display the importance of hermeneutics for reflection on the nature of ultimate reality and selfhood. In my introduction to each selection, I shall outline the relation of the text to the history of hermeneutics, situate the text within the set of ideal types of hermeneutics, mention some of the major themes of the author, and summarize key points in the particular essay.

In addition to the essays and the introduction, the reader will find an extensive bibliography following the essays for further research.

I began my work as editor and author of the general and specific introductions to the essays in this volume at the request of Professor Charley Hardwick of The American University. As co-editor of the Studies in Religion Series for the American Academy of Religion and Scholars Press, he deserves my thanks for the support, encouragement, and assistance which he generously offered throughout the duration of this project. Professor James O. Duke of the Pacific School of Religion, the other co-editor of the

Studies in Religion Series, helped me enormously with suggestions for improvement. I wish to express my appreciation to him as well.

Special thanks are also due to The University of Iowa Foundation, which supported my research for the summer of 1983 under an Old Gold Grant. Brian Brandt, Dennis Bielfeldt, and Richard Severson served as proofreaders and bibliographers while working for me as research assistants engaged in their doctoral programs in religion at The University of Iowa. Sandra Herwig of the Office of Publications at The University of Iowa and Priscilla Stuckey-Kaufman, James O. Duke's editorial assistant, did a wonderful job of copy editing. Margaret Leahey, editor and reader extraordinaire, made many helpful suggestions to improve the text. I am grateful to all of the above named.

I want to mention how much I have gained from the rigorous and lively discussions I have had with my colleagues at the University of Iowa. Professors John Boyle and William Schweiker, colleagues in theology and ethics, are thought-provoking and helpful discussion partners. Professor Donald G. Marshall in the English Department is another major contributor to our "hermeneutical circle" at Iowa. Weekly conversations with Professors William Klink (Physics), Allan Megill (History), and Evan Fales (Philosophy) over matters hermeneutical and rhetorical have sharpened my thinking considerably. The graduate students in the School of Religion who challenge my thinking in the course "Methods and Theories in the Study of Religion" also deserve my thanks, as do my colleagues in that team-taught venture: Professors Robert D. Baird, J. Kenneth Kuntz, and William Schweiker.

No set of acknowledgments is complete without mention of the support and patience of my family: my wife Gretchen and our children Matthew, Hannah, and Stephen.

June 15, 1986
Iowa City, Iowa

INTRODUCTION

The student of religion faces no easy task. Wherever he or she turns, a strange face appears. Images from foreign cultures—Buddhist sages, Indian philosophers and yogis, tribal shamans, or any number of other examples—all present us with otherness. The religious expressions of alien forms of life break into our known world with the power of another reality. Scholarly attempts to explain the other are pale in comparison with the reality of what appears. The reality of other traditions challenges us to respond by *understanding* the other precisely as other. In responding to the presence of the other, we must come forward ourselves. We must understand ourselves. Neither task is easy: understanding religious meanings found in diverse cultures and understanding ourselves in the process.

And this double task is only the beginning. The two roots of our own religious past (the Judeo-Christian traditions of faith in the God of the Bible and the Greek philosophical traditions of thinking about the final ground of our experience of being) disclose visages of strangeness equal to those of alien cultures: the language of Jewish prophets; the New Testament parables of Jesus; Paul's testimonials to the life of faith; the dialogues of Plato; and the theological reflections of Augustine, Anselm, Aquinas, Luther, or Calvin, to name a few. The meanings of the Western religious and theological inheritance are all the more strange for their apparent familiarity as classics of our own tradition. For us, sons and daughters of the technological world, our own tradition speaks to us with the voice of otherness. How are we to understand religious myth and ritual or the expressions of philosophical dialogue, when our technological society runs in another direction?

Whether we look at non-Western or Western traditions, we see otherness. In response, we attempt to understand: to transform the strange into the familiar, to allow the familiar to be transformed by the strange. Although difficult, understanding is not impossible, for a *human* face appears in every case. What is human cannot be so alien as to defy understanding, we tell ourselves. But the special difficulty for us is that the religious reality, to which the faces of traditional ways of life give witness, is deeply and profoundly alien to us in the world of high technology and mass communication. We cannot merely dress the archaic in current designs, or clothe ourselves in handwoven fabric, and thereby increase our understanding of the other. And how much less would such a tactic work with regard to the otherness of the religious reality that myth, ritual, or theology embodies in its expressions. The religious traditions comprise not only other humans who ask to be understood. They include manifestations of the sacred reality or "Wholly Other" from which the heirs of modern life may be more deeply separated. The task of understanding is thus doubly difficult. We are no longer immediately attuned to the traditional forms of expression in myth, ritual, and theology; we are immersed in a world that grants little or no reality to the religious dimension of the traditions.

Another thought unsettles us. Not only do the traditional religious worlds and the reality of the sacred evoke misunderstanding. The foundations of the modern world also present us, at least in part, with the face of otherness. Unbounded optimism about the progress of science and technology and faith in the power of autonomous human reason to overcome ignorance and despair no longer strike us as expressions of a homecoming for the restless spirit. Have not the events of modern history thrown modernity into question? Is it so clear that modernity is an unqualified advance over the traditional worlds? I am not saying that the modern ideals are defunct or unworkable. My point is that we may not assume a common home in the modern ideals. Many of us confront the modern world as profoundly strange, as a reality from which we are estranged. The modern sphere, almost as much as the premodern, challenges us with the task of renewed understanding.

The encounters with otherness within religious studies point us to hermeneutics. By "hermeneutics," I mean the theoretical interest that focuses on the process of understanding meaning in signs and symbols. Interest in hermeneutics arises when we recognize a meaning in human expression and communication that beckons us to understanding and yet withholds the abundance of its sense. Hermeneutical inquiry begins with the advent of meaning: something in the world of a text or actual existence manifests an otherness, a doubleness of meaning. The image or thought is what it is—*and more*—for a second dimension of meaning is there and addresses us. We stand in its presence and are drawn into an event in which our response is called forth.

Hermeneutics has the task of allowing the meaning in texts and existence to speak again. Sacred scriptures, classic literature, and legal codes are texts that carry an intent to speak into a human situation. Because human situations change in unforeseeable ways, these texts call for hermeneutics to assist them in speaking again. The meanings that demand our understanding may be ritual gestures or significant actions within the social world. Here as well, hidden and disputed meanings must be brought to light. Hermeneutics functions as an aid to understanding meanings in texts and existence. Because the text or significant action cannot speak for itself and must be interpreted to speak at all, hermeneutics comes into play.

The hermeneutical problem of recovering the hidden meaning of a text or action has surfaced in an exemplary way in theology and religious thought. Modern hermeneutics arose as a general theory of understanding and interpretation within the religious context of translating meanings in the Bible and the theological tradition across the centuries into situations vastly different from those of the original hearers and readers. In encountering the otherness of religious traditions, a paradigm of the hermeneutical problem emerges. *Religious studies is fundamentally a hermeneutical discipline.* Increasingly, scholars are realizing this fact. Because religious thought must decipher signs and the presence of otherness appearing within them, hermeneutics is the first philosophy of the field of religious studies. By "first philosophy," I mean that hermeneutics provides the basic categories, principles, and norms for religious thought.

The hermeneutical essays collected here were chosen because of their applicability to the tasks of religious studies. But because religious studies presents a model of the hermeneutical problem, the significance of these texts is not limited to religious studies. Systematic inquiry into the general principles of hermeneutics may have arisen initially in theology, especially through the efforts of Friedrich Schleiermacher, but the hermeneutical problem is universal. Indeed, across the disciplines in American universities, we see the surfacing of hermeneutical inquiry and increased interest in the classic texts of hermeneutical theory.

The texts in this collection point out that Western thought in the modern age has overlooked the pervasive and distinct role of understanding. More than anyone else, Martin Heidegger reminds us that modern habits of thought have neglected the process of understanding. Modern thought has concentrated on the tasks of gathering reliable data and constructing adequate theories.[1] The activities of perception and formal thinking have consequently received special attention. But the activity of understanding, which is not reducible to either perceiving or formal thinking, has been left out of consideration. Hermeneutics restores attention to this forgotten dimension. It recovers an activity that is ever-present but taken for granted in premodern systems of meaning and is excluded from modern systems of analysis. The classics of hermeneutics are becoming a common literature for cross-disciplinary and cross-cultural discussion as problems of understanding appear within the various disciplines in which understanding was forgotten.[2]

[1] Martin Heidegger, "What Is Metaphysics?" in *Basic Writings*, ed. David Farrell Krell (New York: Harper and Row, Publishers, 1977), pp. 96–97.

[2] Hermeneutics has surfaced not only within religious studies as an important theoretical issue. In the natural sciences, social sciences, and humanities, hermeneutics has lately risen to a position of prominence. For a discussion of this development from a cross-disciplinary perspective, see Richard J. Bernstein, *Beyond Objectivism and Relativism: Science, Hermeneutics, and Praxis* (Philadelphia: University of Pennsylvania Press, 1983), especially pp. 1–49. For a

II. The Path to Contemporary Hermeneutical Inquiry

Hermeneutical inquiry into the nature and scope of understanding began in the early nineteenth century. Friedrich Schleiermacher, the first great theologian of the modern age, is also founder of modern hermeneutics. His general theory of understanding should be understood within the context of the demands of modern thought in contrast to premodern (precritical) thought. Wilhelm Dilthey, historiographer and philosopher of history at the end of the nineteenth century, expanded hermeneutical theory in order to answer certain critical questions that are typically modern. Confronting the strictures of modernity, Schleiermacher and Dilthey developed hermeneutical theory partly in order to justify religious forms of awareness and theological modes of thinking in a period in which religion and theology were under attack from modernity. Hermeneutical theory, then, is a child of modernity. To understand it, we must understand modern consciousness, at least insofar as religious thought and theology were transformed by modernity.

In the twentieth century, under the hand of Martin Heidegger, hermeneutics broke out of the confines of modern consciousness. Heidegger's hermeneutical philosophy marks one place among many within Western thought at which the modern gave way to a postmodern paradigm. After Heidegger, much of hermeneutical inquiry displays the characteristics of the postmodern. The essays in this volume, other than those by Schleiermacher and Dilthey, are expressions of the postmodern mode of thought and experience.

The terms *modern* and *postmodern* are difficult to pin down. But they are crucial for understanding the role hermeneutics plays for religious studies now. Moreover, we cannot understand either the presuppositions of modernity nor those of postmodernity without first grasping the premodern, against which modernity struggles, and toward which postmodernity has a reflexive and interpretive relation. Consequently, I shall stipulate what I mean by these three terms for purposes of this study.

I propose, therefore, to provide a sketch of three paradigms of thought and experience: premodern (or traditional, precritical), modern (critical), and postmodern (postcritical). These three paradigms, or deep structures of self-world relations, have corresponding cultural and institutional expressions. I outline these paradigms as heuristic devices or models to disclose common features of life and thought amid the diversity of human experi-

---

discussion of hermeneutics as one of three major strands of current German philosophy, see Rüdiger Bubner, *Modern German Philosophy,* trans. Eric Matthews (Cambridge: Cambridge University Press, 1981), pp. 11–68. For evidence of a turn from analytic philosophy to hermeneutics within American philosophical circles, see Richard Rorty, *Philosophy and the Mirror of Nature* (Princeton: Princeton University Press, 1979), especially pp. 315–94.

ence. They have no ontological status of their own. They will best serve their purpose if they evoke critical thought about their own validity, while showing some basic features of the changing landscape of cultural life.

I shall isolate the following features in each paradigm: (1) the grounding figure of the type; (2) the picture of the world that accompanies the type; (3) the system of images, practices, and thought that unfolds around the central figure; and (4) the fundamental relation of the self to the world characterizing the type. Highly selective in my accounts, I write for the reader of the essays presented herein rather than for an audience interested in problems other than those of hermeneutics in religious thought.

THE PREMODERN

The premodern is a vast category. It must unify many diverse religious and cultural forms. The modern did not receive its first expressions until the fifteenth and sixteenth centuries and was not incorporated more widely in social institutions until the seventeenth and especially the eighteenth centuries in Europe. Hence the premodern includes everything prior to and apart from the development of modernity in the West. This one paradigm encompasses all traditional social worlds, from tribal societies to high civilizations. Only severe restrictions of space can legitimate such broad lines of demarcation.

Apart from any other differences, however, the premodern worlds share a basic structure described by Mircea Eliade and Paul Ricoeur as a "sacred cosmos" and by Peter Berger and Thomas Luckmann as a "symbolic universe."[3] In the view of these writers, premodern worlds display several fundamental elements.

1. A hierophany, a manifestation of the sacred in the profane space and time of human experience, founds a symbolic world, a system of intersignifications or total context of meaningfulness. Through the hierophany, the world first stands out as a centered world oriented to absolute reality. A home and a purpose present themselves to the human community receiving the hierophany. Through its power and meaning, the inbreaking sacred manifests the real so convincingly that the human community tends not to distinguish between the appearing symbol of the sacred and the sacred reality itself.

2. The premodern picture of the world is that of a "sacred cosmos." A world has a center, an *axis mundi*, where the world is open to the transcendent beyond and where the sacred manifests itself in the extradivine, thus

---

[3]Mircea Eliade, *Sacred and the Profane: The Nature of Religion,* trans. Willard R. Trask (New York: Harcourt Brace & Company, 1959), p. 17. Paul Ricoeur, *The Symbolism of Evil,* trans. E. Buchanan (New York: Harper & Row, 1967), pp. 10–13. Peter L. Berger and Thomas Luckmann, *The Social Construction of Reality: A Treatise in the Sociology of Knowledge* (New York: Doubleday and Company, 1966), pp. 92–128.

founding the world. The world also has boundaries, beyond which is chaos or nothing. The human subject is imagined as part of the worldly sphere of objectivity, rather than in opposition to it. The subject is, therefore, an element within the objective whole. The picture of the world is a literal picture of how everything hangs together.

3. A system of myth and ritual legitimates the common view of the world.[4] Myth temporalizes the meaning of the central symbol, placing it into narratives (for example, myths of the creation of the world). Creation myths speak of events in a time before time and a place beyond earthly places.[5] They narrate how the temporal-spatial world, including the human community, came into being. Mythic events live on in the worldly sphere through ritual reenactment. Myth and ritual shape the context for all socially objectivated meanings.

According to Eliade, myths tell not only of the sacred origin but also of the destiny of the community.[6] Sacred myths speak of the acts of divine beings in setting the goals for human beings, the meaning of human suffering and trials, and the sequence of life stages through which every individual must pass. Myths intend the integration of individual and collective life within the sacred order of being. Individuals and cults internalize the mythological narrative, allowing it to shape their lives. The meanings of dreams, death, transitions in life from youth to adulthood, or the range of practices of the community (in farming, hunting, crafts of all kinds, customs, names of things, and so on) are intelligible either directly through the mythical narratives or indirectly in their light. Ritual reenactment of myth ensures the public, social status of the myth and enables the internalization of meaning. Because of public ritual, myths are not just stories but are scripts for performance. We learn through ritual performance that myth guides human action in the world.

Myths are stories of the divine and human encounters with the divine. These stories give rise to rudimentary or sophisticated theologies, metaphysics, and ethics. Theological thinking grows out of the discourse of mythic narrative of divine deeds, when people ask, "Who or what is the divine?" Such questions open thought to a level of reflection that extends beyond myth while remaining focused on its content. Myths also disclose what truly is and how what is came to be. Metaphysics, a body of thought about being as being, is thereby evoked by myth.[7] In addition, myths give models for human imitation. We are presented with exemplary types of human being and doing in myths. By disclosing in narrative form the proper ends of

---

[4]Berger and Luckmann, *The Social Construction of Reality*, pp. 99–103.
[5]Ricoeur, *Symbolism of Evil*, p. 18.
[6]See also Mircea Eliade, *Myth and Reality* (New York: Harper & Row, 1963), p. 5–6.
[7]Eliade, *Sacred and Profane*, p. 95.

human practices, myths set forth an account of human virtues for precritical ethical elaboration.[8]

4. Myth and ritual in the sacred cosmos of premodernity enable a fundamental mode of being that Eliade calls an existence "open to the world."[9] Existence is open when the central symbols of the sacred communicate their meaning to people and manifest an additional dimension to life. For the recipient of meaning through religious myth, life is lived on two planes—human and transhuman—because the symbols transfer meaning from the mundane sphere to the sacred sphere and back. If the myth of Odysseus enables people to understand their own lives as a journey back home requiring courage and patience, then it opens a relation to the world previously hidden. Through myth and ritual, the roles of family life, political organization, and other institutional orders are integrated into a comprehensive framework of interaction with and openness to the sacred power. According to Berger and Luckmann, through myth and ritual "the political order is legitimated by reference to a cosmic order of power and justice, and political roles are legitimated as representatives of these cosmic principles."[10] Individual biography is also sacralized by referring to the embeddedness of the story of the individual's life in the community.

The mythic order, the fountain of meaning from which thought arises, is not infallible. According to Berger, the symbolic order is "continually threatened by the presence of realities that are meaningless in its terms. The legitimation of the institutional order is also faced with the ongoing necessity of keeping chaos at bay."[11]

Both the strength and fragility of the premodern world lie in an identification beyond the superficial distinction of myth and reality, word and thing, sense and reference of language. As long as the sacred meaning of myth remains unquestioned and unquestionable in its self-evident reality and truth, the identity of the order of symbolic language and the order of reality is intact.

In premodern worlds, understanding is a social practice. Understanding takes place through identification with myth, symbol, and ritual. Symbols manifest their meaning directly in both the cosmos and social order at one and the same time. Symbolic meaning is both subjective and objective; no isolated subject is yet wholly distinguished from the objective meaning. Meanings narrated in myth and the meaning of the individual's life mirror one another; life is lived as reenactment of mythic stories.

Premodern thought shares in this structure of reenactment and participation. In premodern thought, no chasm exists between the self and reality.

[8]Alasdair MacIntyre, *After Virtue: A Study in Moral Theory* (Notre Dame: University of Notre Dame Press, 1981), pp. 204–5.

[9]Eliade, *Sacred and Profane*, pp. 162–213.

[10]Berger and Luckmann, *The Social Construction of Reality*, p. 103.

[11]Ibid.

Typically, forms or essences of things—universals—are abstracted from experience and are taken into the intellect. The essence is present in the intellect just as it is in the object. Both knower and known object come to their completion and perfection through the other. In knowing the whatness of natural realities, the self plays its proper role in the world: to become the self-awareness of the world. And in being known, the world comes into its being. The reflecting self is part of the whole that is reflected. Structures of thinking are not yet divided from structures of being. Thinking of being is an event within being, not the act of a separated subject.

My sketch of the premodern view of the world is necessarily simplistic. Let me attempt to give it some more content. Because the hermeneutical essays in this volume so often treat topics in Christian thought, I turn now to a brief consideration of the world of premodern Christianity.

1. The grounding image and sacred symbol of the Christian religion is the revelation of God in Jesus as Christ. The foundational myth of traditional Christianity portrays the uniqueness of God, Lord of creation, who revealed Godself in Jesus. Jesus was born of human flesh through Mary, suffered and died on the cross, and was raised bodily from the dead. His incarnation and resurrection are salvific; according to Christian belief, he will return at the end of time to judge the living and dead, and to raise believers to eternal life.

2. The picture of the world in traditional Christianity draws together two principal sources: Greek cosmology and the Bible.[12] Plato's *Timaeus* and Aristotle's *On the Heavens* are central texts for the former. The Bible does not present an explicit world picture, nor does cosmology belong to the gospel message. But theologians incorporated biblical data concerning creation, redemption, and last judgment into the Greek world picture.[13] In the Middle Ages, the Christian world picture, a composite of Greek and biblical views, was nearly universally accepted. According to N. Max Wildiers, a historian of theology and author of *The Theologian and His Universe*, it was "simply inconceivable that one would doubt the correctness of this picture which was . . . presented to him by the infallible authority of sacred Scriptures and confirmed by the great minds of antiquity."[14]

The world picture is one of a perfectly ordered cosmos. At the center of the cosmos, immovable, is the earth. Below its surface is hell. Above the earth are seven planetary spheres, which influence earthly events. Above the planetary spheres are three higher spheres yet, the lowest of which carries the fixed stars. And above all is heaven. The cosmos as a whole is spherical in shape, with planets moving in circular orbits. Within the whole, microcosm and macrocosm are attuned to each other. The whole order of

---

[12]N. Max Wildiers, *The Theologian and His Universe: Theology and Cosmology from the Middle Ages to the Present*, trans. Paul Dunphy (New York: Seabury Press, 1982), pp. 19–35.

[13]Ibid., p. 25.

[14]Ibid., p. 37.

creation, from lowest animals to angels, is perfectly and immutably ordered in a hierarchy by the Creator; the higher beings are naturally more powerful and influential than lower beings. The harmonious cosmos is apprehended as created for human habitation, yet at the same time humans view themselves as pilgrims on earth. The sheer fact that everything appears as created by God points humanity toward its true home with God in heaven.[15]

Martin Buber indicates how the picture of a sacred cosmos provided a dwelling place for humanity. According to Buber,

> The pattern of this image of the universe is a cross, whose vertical beam is finite space from heaven to hell, leading right across the heart of the human being, and whose cross-beam is finite time from the creation of the world to the end of days; which makes time's center, the death of Christ, fall coveringly and redemptively on the center of space, the heart of the poor sinner. The mediaeval image of the universe is built round this pattern. In it Dante painted life, the life of men and spirits, but the conceptual framework was set up for him by Thomas Aquinas.[16]

3. The system of images, concepts, and practices in traditional Christianity reflects the orderedness, balance, hierarchy, and harmony of the world picture. Medieval theology moves in systematically ordered wholes. Redemption is conceived as the restoration of the original world order: Christ canceled by his obedience the disruptive effects of the disobedience of the first man.[17] Church order mirrors the order of the cosmos: above all is Christ, from whom all goodness comes; his representative on earth is the pope, under whom bishops, clergy, monks, and finally the common faithful form a descending order. The feudal system also reflects cosmic hierarchy: the emperor or king stands at the summit above feudal lords, vassals (dukes, counts, barons, knights), and the commoners. The idea of order provides the rule of morality in social practices: actions consonant with the cosmic order of God are good; actions contrary to God's order are sinful.

4. Within Christian premodern religious thought, hermeneutical practice of understanding Holy Scripture reflects the self-world relation of "openness" to and participation in the sacred cosmos. The biblical text is not treated as an object for distanced analysis but as an occasion for disclosure of divine truth. In ancient culture and medieval traditions, the task of biblical interpretation is, in Paul Ricoeur's words,

> ... to broaden the comprehension of the text on the side of doctrine, of practice, of meditation on the mysteries. And consequently it is to

[15]Ibid., pp. 36–58.

[16]Martin Buber, "What Is Man?" in *Between Man and Man*, trans. Ronald Gregor Smith (New York: Macmillan, 1948), p. 129.

[17]Wildiers, *The Theologian and His Universe*, p. 71.

equate the understanding of meaning with a total interpretation of existence and of reality in the system of Christianity. In short, hermeneutics understood this way is coextensive with the entire economy of Christian existence. Scripture appears here as an inexhaustible treasure which stimulates thought about everything, which conceals a total interpretation of the world.[18]

Within this interpretive scheme, the Bible has both a literal sense and a spiritual sense. The latter is the inexhaustible but buried treasure that God intends for transmission and appropriation within a tradition of understanding. Why this emphasis on a spiritual sense of the Bible?

Consider Origen of Alexandria.[19] For Origen, the whole of the Bible, the Old Testament as well as the New, is the inspired word of God for the Christian. In this, he follows Philo, the Jewish thinker, and Clement, for whom "every expression, every word, and every letter has its meaning" for us here and now.[20] Where the literal meaning of the text is obscure, contradictory, unbelievable, and so forth, the text is beckoning you into the depth of its secrets. It is saying, "You are in the proximity of mystery and secrecy! Be on your watch for the hidden word of God!"

The Holy Scripture presents a stumbling block for understanding. But, as literary critic Gerald Bruns has put it, the obscurity is God's way of teaching secrets about spiritual events without "giving them away or betraying them as secrets—without demystifying the mystery."[21] Origen does not deny the literal or plain sense of Scripture, but he thinks that very little of spiritual significance is communicated in that way. More often, the mysteries are plainly communicated through allegory or symbol. Allegorical reading, for Origen, is not a method of interpretation in the modern sense of an analytic tool. As Bruns says, allegory is a form of spiritual life, a way of practicing philosophical contemplation. Discovery of divine teaching beyond the literal meaning is a gift from God for the purpose of deepening the faith of the church.

The point is that the premodern interpreter does not stand outside the text, testing the truth of the text as a collection of propositions about the

[18]Ricoeur, "Preface to Bultmann," in *The Conflict of Interpretations: Essays in Hermeneutics*, ed. Donald Ihde (Evanston: Northwestern University Press, 1974), pp. 384–85.

[19]See Robert M. Grant with David Tracy, *A Short History of the Interpretation of the Bible* (Philadelphia: Fortress Press, 1984), pp. 52–62. See also Gerald L. Bruns, "The Problem of Figuration in Antiquity," in *Hermeneutics: Questions and Prospects*, ed. Gary Shapiro and Alan Sica (Amherst: University of Massachusetts Press, 1984), pp. 147–64. For a more general discussion of writing and interpretation among the ancients, see Gerald L. Bruns, *Inventions: Writing, Textuality, and Understanding in Literary History* (New Haven: Yale University Press, 1982), pp. 17–59.

[20]Grant and Tracy, *A Short History of the Interpretation of the Bible*, p. 53.

[21]Bruns, *The Problem of Figuration in Antiquity*, p. 155.

world, but instead meditatively seeks to apply the meaning of the text to a concrete situation. This is possible because the whole of the text is God's word and hence bears the divine mystery. To interpret Scripture is to find more to say than the literal meaning by discovering still deeper meanings and to apply them to oneself. Allegorical interpretation is also possible in the premodern world of Christianity because the world described in biblical narrative, as the one and only world, includes any present age and reader. The reader is always already encompassed by the narrative, since he or she exists after the resurrection and before the second coming.

By referring to Origen, I have selected a hermeneutical extremist, a reader who carries allegory to the farthest limits. But what I have said about his method of reading applies across the late Patristic period and the Middle Ages. Of this period, Robert M. Grant, a historian of biblical interpretation, writes that "the most important and characteristic method of biblical interpretation . . . was not literal but allegorical."[22] And the medieval system of finding four meanings in every text—the literal, the allegorical, the moral, and the anagogical (or mystical)—was a refinement of a basic scheme of recognizing a literal and a spiritual sense. The characteristic of traditional Christian hermeneutics is precisely the openness of the reader to the spiritual sense beyond the literal.

At the time of the Reformation, a decisive change occurs within premodern hermeneutics. Luther delivered the Bible from the Latin of the priesthood to the vernacular of the common people. In addition, he proposed an appropriate hermeneutical principle. Luther's principle is, in the words of Hans Frei, that "the Bible is self-interpreting, the literal sense of its words being their true meaning, its more obscure passages to be read in the light of those that are clear."[23]

Luther's simplification of the task of hermeneutics signaled a reversal of the pattern of seeing secrecy as intrinsic to the divine word. In place of the multiplication of meanings, the reformers found univocity and clarity. According to Frei, "The literal or grammatical meaning, primary for Luther and Calvin, was for both men usually identical with the text's subject matter, i.e., its historical reference, its doctrinal content, and its meaningfulness as life description and prescription."[24] Although a decisive change, this turn was made within the premodern openness to God's word directly or indirectly manifest in Scripture. The more fundamental change, breaking the premodern paradigm, did not occur in the Reformation but in the Enlightenment period.

[22]Grant and Tracy, *A Short History of the Interpretation of the Bible*, p. 85.
[23]Hans W. Frei, *The Eclipse of Biblical Narrative: A Study in Eighteenth and Nineteenth Century Hermeneutics* (New Haven: Yale University Press, 1974), pp. 18–19.
[24]Ibid., pp. 23–24.

THE MODERN

A distinct paradigm of religious thought emerges when the autonomy of critique dominates Western culture. Both the Greek philosophical tradition and the Judeo-Christian religious tradition had included elements of critique within their visions of the sacred universe. Greek metaphysical thought developed critical questioning in asking, "What is being? the good? the beautiful?" Biblical law and prophecy presented a critique of idols in asking, "Is this the true God?" For neither, however, was critique the dominant element. Greek philosophy reflected critically on the whole of being. But it did not critique the givenness of the whole. Jewish and Christian faith undercut the claims of "divine" beings in the name of the one God. But it did not critique the givenness of God through the Bible.

The modern paradigm breaks away from the premodern with the appearance of a fully autonomous critical consciousness.[25] Modern criticism asserts its superiority over all restraints in asking, "How do I know that what is given to me or appears to me is in reality what it appears to be?" When directed to the sacred "givens" of religion and theology, this question presses to the center of the symbolic universe, for it cuts through the immediacy of symbolic consciousness by breaking the connection between expression and appearing reality. Critical consciousness thus makes the sacred power in the symbol vanish. Religious objects, texts, institutions, and pictures of the world lose their unquestioned authority and innocence when the historical and psychological processes infusing sacrality to the symbol are "exposed" and brought into the light.[26] The result of critical reflection is the desacralization of the world.

The relation between the modern paradigm and the premodern paradigm is a matter of vigorous debate. Agreement exists that the modern period in the West grew out of a Christian culture. But disputes rage concerning the connection between the modern world and the Christian tradition. Is the modern world a genuine achievement and completion of the premodern Christian tradition? Many important thinkers argue so, including Friedrich Gogarten, Ernst Troeltsch, and Karl Löwith. Or is modernism an independent power that grew on Christian soil, freed itself from its beginnings, and

---

[25]For a discussion of critical consciousness and its impact on religious consciousness, see Robert P. Scharlemann, "Critical and Religious Consciousness: Some Reflections of the Question of Truth in the Philosophy of Religion," in *Kairos and Logos: Studies in the Roots and Implications of Tillich's Theology*, ed. John J. Carey (Cambridge: North American Paul Tillich Society, 1978), pp. 74–95. For a treatise on critique, see Remy C. Kwant, *Critique: Its Nature and Function*, trans. Henry J. Koren (Pittsburgh: Duquesne University Press, 1965).

[26]This sentence is a paraphrase of Zwi Werblowsky in *Beyond Tradition and Modernity: Changing Religions in a Changing World* (London: Athlone Press at the University of London, 1974), p. 26.

produced a cultural and social world without debt to Christianity? Others, such as Hans Blumenberg and Zwi Werblowsky, would say so.[27]

However we interpret the relation between the traditional Western civilization and the modern world, the very presence of modernity renders the past problematic.[28] The modern offers a viable alternative to the premodern and thereby changes the situation. An unquestioned relation no longer exists between a symbolic system and the everyday world of practical life. Traditional forms of faith and the symbolic meanings of religion no longer are self-evidently at hand once the modern paradigm appears. Let me refer now to four features of modernism.

1. At the center of the modern paradigm is not the symbol of the sacred but what Hans Blumenberg, in *The Legitimacy of the Modern Age*, calls human self-assertion.[29] By "self" he does not mean the self of modern narcissism, nor the solitary "I" of twentieth-century existentialism, which is doomed or graced to create its own meanings to avoid despair, but the self determined by the universal law of reason. Reason is a natural principle enabling humans to judge the true from the false or the just from the unjust. Modern thought asserts itself when it submits traditional authorities to the laws of autonomous reason.

Descartes was instrumental in inaugurating the new age, because he discovered a foundation of certainty from which anything premodern could be challenged: the certainty that while thinking, "I am." The way to the new foundation is methodical doubt, which calls into question the reality of anything that appears. The truth of the whole of being can be cast in doubt. In any experience or thought, I can doubt whether my sense experiences are misleading me or whether I am otherwise deluded. Any claim to truth falls under the shadow of doubt. But I cannot doubt the "I" who "is" in the act of thinking. Whenever I think about my own thinking, regardless of what I am thinking about, "I am." The Cartesian *cogito* represents the birthplace of modernity, the detachment of the subject as the Archimedean point from which a new mode of existence is to be constructed.[30]

2. The world picture undergoes a complete revision in the modern age: from sacred cosmos to infinite universe. The revolution in scientific and metaphysical thought began in the late middle ages, with thinkers such as

[27]For a discussion of the debate and review of literature, see Harry J. Ausmus, *The Polite Escape: On the Myth of Secularization* (Athens, Ohio: Ohio University Press, 1982). The debate about the relation between modernity and Christian tradition is brought into focus in Robert M. Wallace, "Progress, Secularization and Modernity: The Löwith-Blumenberg Debate," in *New German Critique* 22 (Winter 1981): 63–79.

[28]Werblowsky, *Beyond Tradition and Modernity*, p. 14.

[29]Hans Blumenberg, *The Legitimacy of the Modern Age*, trans. Robert M. Wallace (Cambridge: MIT Press, 1983), p. 141 and p. 137.

[30]See Bruns, *Inventions*, pp. 63–87; Bernstein, *Beyond Objectivism and Relativism*, pp. 16–20; and Rorty, *Philosophy and the Mirror of Nature*, pp. 54–69.

Nicholas of Cusa (1401–1468). It accelerated, through the use of mathematics and telescopic observations, with Nicolaus Copernicus (1473–1543), Tycho Brahe (1546–1601), Johannes Kepler (1571–1630), Galileo Galilei (1564–1642), and Sir Isaac Newton (1642–1727).[31] By the late eighteenth century, the center, boundaries, and hierarchical order of the sacred cosmos were abolished by the advance of critical reflection. For the critical thinker, the earth was displaced from centrality and swallowed in infinite space. Heaven and hell were lost as physical places in the unlimited expanses. Why should critical thought postulate an end of space? Mathematics demands that we keep counting when imagining distances. Likewise, the temporal endpoints of creation and second coming of Christ are removed. Why should critical thought postulate a beginning or end of time? Do we not immediately ask what came before and comes after the beginning and end?

Moreover, the new mathematical physics uncovered laws with tremendous explanatory power. For example, the premodern picture of seven planets in spherical orbits around the earth was destroyed and replaced by a scheme of elliptical orbits around the sun. Newton was able to explain and predict planetary movement quite precisely, through the simple formula that bodies attract each other in direct proportion to their mass and in inverse proportion to the square of their distance apart.[32]

The modern world picture is one of an infinite, mechanistic universe governed by impersonal, deterministic laws. What does this world picture mean? First, it means, according to Buber, the loss of a home for human dwelling. Premodern humanity found a sense of security and belongingness in the concentric cosmos. But "Once the concept of infinity has been taken seriously a human dwelling can no longer be made of the universe."[33] No image of the world can be formed, for a photographic likeness of infinity is impossible. And no pretense can be made to live in a world ordered for human meaningfulness.

Second, just as humans lose their spiritual home, God in some sense becomes homeless. Consider the differing views concerning God's address. Pantheists, like Baruch Spinoza (1632–1677), deified the universe and distinguished within it two modes of being: God, the active side of naturing nature; and the world, the objective side of natured nature. Deists and rationalists, such as Newton, thought of God as architect of the universe, who has now removed Godself from the scene. They argued whether or not the architect upheld providence or or even cared about human conduct at all. Atheists and naturalists, such as Diderot, said belief in God is superfluous or harmful. The critical thinker must ask where, if anywhere, does God belong in the modern scheme of things?

[31]See Wildiers, *The Theologian and His Universe*, pp. 79–104.
[32]Ibid., pp. 99–100.
[33]Buber, "What is Man?" in *Between Man and Man*, p. 133.

The confusion wrought by disintegration of the Christian and metaphysical views of the world came into terrifying clarity in the writings of Blaise Pascal (1623–1662). Pascal grasped the real threat of the loss of the world picture to religious, moral, and social beliefs and institutions, when he wrote,

> When we behold the blindness and wretchedness of man, when we look on the whole dumb universe, on man without light, abandoned to his own devices and appearing as though lost in some corner of the universe, without knowing who has placed him there, what he is supposed to be doing, what will become of him when he dies, incapable of all knowledge, I am overcome by fear like a man who has been carried off during sleep and deposited on some terrifying desert island who wakes up without knowing where he is and without any means of escape. And I am amazed that people do not fall into despair over such a wretched state.[34]

The human is a mere reed in an infinite universe, though at least a *thinking* reed. He or she can at least become aware of finitude.

With meaningfulness threatened, detached knowledge offers a substitute vision of order. Philosopher Richard Bernstein refers to the "Cartesian anxiety" of the modern thinker who faces the dissolution of the Christian and metaphysical views of the world. He says, "Descartes leads us with an apparent and ineluctable necessity to a grand and seductive Either/Or. *Either* there is some support for our being, a fixed foundation for our knowledge, *or* we cannot escape the forces of darkness that envelop us with madness, with intellectual and moral chaos."[35] Hence I refer now to the task of epistemology for modernity.

3. Under the modern conditions, a new body of theoretical and practical tradition emerges. It was justified not by appeal to myth but by appeal to epistemology (the theory of knowledge). According to Rorty's reading of modern thought in *Philosophy and the Mirror of Nature*, philosophy becomes the discipline privileged to adjudicate truth claims made in the fields of science, morality, art, or religion. Philosophy holds its privilege because the thinking "I" presents the indubitable starting point for construction of a solid ediface of knowledge.

In Rorty's analysis, modern epistemology rests on the image of "the mind as a great mirror, containing various representations—some accurate, some not, and capable of being studied by pure, nonempirical methods."[36] Knowledge is accuracy of representation by the mental mirror. Philosophy is

---

[34]Blaise Pascal, *Pensées*, no. 693, quoted in Wildiers, *The Theologian and His Universe*, p. 111.

[35]Bernstein, *Beyond Objectivism and Relativism*, p. 18.

[36]Rorty, *Philosophy and the Mirror of Nature*, p. 12.

the construction of a general theory of representations or mental processes. It explains how knowledge of the objective world is possible. Epistemology establishes a permanent, ahistorical framework, a final court of appeal, for determining knowledge and rationality.

Just as premodern myth gives rise to premodern metaphysics, ethics, and theology, so the self-assertion of the modern age gives rise to tremendous successes in science and technology. Modern self-assertion expresses itself in a drive to bring the world under the control of human reason. Scientific and technological successes in turn evoke the notion of "progress," so crucial to the modern spirit. Tangible historical progress in raising the standards of living and in dispelling superstition justifies the self-assertion of the modern age.

The modern age saw replacement of monarchs and hierarchical systems of inherited privilege by liberal democracy. Political freedom was extended without necessarily destroying social unity. Economic liberalism was also a success. The so-called "free market" appeared to make greater amounts of goods available to everyone in society. The self-assertion of reason appeared to work through a hidden harmony of wills that made for progress, freedom, and tolerance.[37]

4. In contrast to the premodern openness to the world, which implies a sense of participation of the self in the world, the modern paradigm separates self from world. Descartes provided the basis for the subject-object split in his distinction between *res cogitans* and *res extensa* (minds and spatial objects). The "I" as thinking being, distinct from external objects and other minds, is the fixed point of modernism. The structure of knowledge is constructed on its foundations.

Understanding has no role to play within the epistemological framework of the subject-object split. Once a social practice of identification of the self with the symbols handed on through tradition, understanding falls into neglect with the rise of modernity. The model of the mind as mirror gives no hint of a participation of the knower in the known. Rather, the subject stands outside the object, which is always that about which the subject thinks. Symbols do not speak when treated as standing objects or translated into univocal propositions. Nor does modern epistemology hold that the mind takes universals into itself, as did premodern metaphysics. The modern subject inspects entities rather than taking the whatness of things into the soul or identifying with meanings in myth and ritual.

What happens to hermeneutics within the modern paradigm of thought? And how does modern hermeneutics relate to transformations in Christian theology and religious thought?

[37]For an intellectual history that embraces political, social, and economic outlooks, see Willson H. Coates, Hayden V. White, and J. Salwyn Schapiro, *The Emergence of Liberal Humanism: An Intellectual History of Western Europe* (New York: McGraw-Hill, 1970), passim.

As modern critical reflection reached maturity, theology was confronted with a crisis. By the end of the eighteenth century, the leading questions were, "Is theology possible? Does theology have a subject matter and a rationale for its existence? Or is theology, practiced either as biblical theology or philosophical theology, an illusion that has been unmasked by critical reflection?" These questions arose when critical thinking challenged the givenness of the foundations of theology. Prior to the end of the eighteenth century, the reality of God and the metaphysical world (or, in more religious language, eternal life in heaven), were absolutely self-given. The triumph of critical thought, however, forces us to ask whether the word *God* refers to anything at all and whether an eternal world exists.[38]

Two crucial developments in German thought during the eighteenth century brought on this crisis. The first was historical criticism of the Bible; the second was criticism of reason itself. Both had a profound effect on theology, and beyond that, on the Christian religion and the European spirit. Let me briefly consider each in turn, beginning with the impact of historical criticism.

For the sake of simplicity, I shall focus on Johann Semler (1725–1791), a pioneer in the application of historical-critical methods to the Bible. Prior to Semler, educated readers of the Scriptures assumed that God authored the real content of the Bible. Biblical revelation was an unchallenged authority. Semler dislodged this assumption. By analyzing the meanings, significations, and references of words within reconstructed historical contexts of authorship, Semler identified individual authors of the biblical books and showed how different books belonged to different social contexts and periods of history. Moreover, Semler showed how the guiding interests of the communities for which the authors wrote influenced the content of the text. In short, Semler tied the message of the biblical books to the interests and points of view of specific authors within particular historical situations.[39]

The upshot of such historical methods was the breaking of any literal identification of biblical texts with word of God. Historical criticism removed the warrant for saying the Bible as a whole was the work of a single divine author. In addition, no single work within the Bible could be identified as a direct revelation of God's truth to humans. Once the distinction is drawn between the human author and God, no historical reasons can reidentify the biblical text and word of God. So if I ask, for example, "Is Paul's letter to the Romans theologically true?" no answer can be given on historical grounds. But once the Bible is routinely read as a historical document, how can we speak of it as "revelation"?

Consider now the impact of rational criticism on theology. Here Im-

---

[38]For a general discussion, see Claude Welch, *Protestant Thought in the Nineteenth Century,* vol. 1, *1799–1870* (New Haven: Yale University Press, 1972), especially p. 59.

[39]Frei, *Eclipse of Biblical Narrative,* pp. 61, 64, 111–12, especially 161–62, and 246–48.

manuel Kant is the crucial figure. Prior to Kant, the fundamental assumption of the Western tradition was that humans possess some knowledge of God, because the human mind participates in the being of God when it intuits the highest principles of being: the good, the beautiful, and the true. The philosophical absolute was considered the ground, goal, and norm of human thinking and activity. Participatory intuition of first principles makes knowledge possible in the first place, since any act of knowing relies on prior acquaintance with the first principles. The metaphysical and theological traditions sometimes called the first principles "ideas in the mind of God." Acquaintance with the principles constituted natural knowledge of God.

Consequently, the basic question for the precritical tradition of natural theology was, "How much can the human mind know about God?" Kant's critical philosophy, however, reformulated the question. Kant asks, "How is it possible for us to know what we claim to know about God?" In other words, Kant's critique focuses on the possibility of knowledge itself. By what right can we claim to know something, especially when that "something" is God? Kant said we must first give a critique of reason itself, a test of the nature and limits of the rational faculty, before we can claim to know about such things as the immortality of the soul or the existence of God.

Kant's fundamental point is that human reason is limited and finite. Finitude pervades our human being, although we are tempted to transgress it. Clear limits exist to the human desire to know the realities of the soul, world, and God; natural theology violates those limits. When we move in the sphere of natural theology, we mistake movements in thought alone for reality. Hence we must question the possibility of knowledge about realities that transcend human experience.

At the heart of Kant's rational critique is the description of knowledge as a synthesis of two distinct kinds of representations, namely, concepts and (sensible) intuitions (or, departing from Kant's terminology, "perceptions"). We can claim knowledge when intuitions fall under concepts or when we are acquainted with the a priori formal conditions of the possibility for intuitions to fall under concepts. Such conditions include a priori intuitions (time and space) and a priori concepts (e.g., causality and substance). Thus knowledge of the natural world and knowledge about the necessary conditions making possible our knowing the natural world are justified.

But we must abandon claims to knowledge about the content of some important ideas, because they lack the requisite intuitions. In fact, ideas such as God or the immortal soul are among those displaying no intuitions. Although we must *think* the idea of God, because our thinking of particular and contingent things logically implies a universal and necessary being, a necessity of thinking cannot substitute for a givenness of intuitions. We have no intuitions of God or of the soul; nor is God or the soul a necessary condition for knowledge of those objects that we do intuit. Thus the ideas of God and the soul present the mind with a temptation to convert a necessary idea into a real object of knowledge. But such a conversion is not justified by the critique of reason.[40]

The Kantian critique of theology and metaphysics results in the death of the God of the philosophers, a crucial element in the emergent modern world picture. By the "death of God," I mean the inability of critical thought to assert the existence of God on rational grounds. It signals the loss of the ability to apprehend the truth of one's own being on the basis of a prior identity with the truth of being as a whole (God). The thinking "I" no longer belongs to the being of God. The imitation of God fails as the highest ethical ideal. The self no longer has its true home in the transcendent sphere of eternal life, for the rational faculty cannot know about such a transcendent sphere. The self now stands over against the natural and historical sphere of being as the solitary and autonomous originating point of reflection.[41]

Modern hermeneutics, especially in the work of Friedrich Schleiermacher, takes up both problems—the demise of the sacred Scriptures as self-evidently the word of God, and the collapse of natural theology as human participation through thought in the being of God. I shall speak about Schleiermacher's program in connection with the two selections from the writings of the founder of modern theology and hermeneutics in the collections to follow. At present, I shall simply say that Schleiermacher's response to the appearance of critique was to go beyond critique by accepting its full implications. Schleiermacher could not accept a retreat before critical thinking. His greatness lies in reworking the methods of theology and hermeneutics in light of the critical methods of modernity.

THE POSTMODERN

In large part, postmodernism arises out of the disillusionment with the modern ideals felt by European intellectuals after World War I. The postmodern disenchantment was subsequently distributed more thoroughly across the face of society after World War II (in Europe) and Vietnam (in the United States).

The testimonies to the shattering of an age are well known. For example, Karl Barth wrote of his horror at reading the names of his teachers, professors of theology, on a petition supporting the war policy of Kaiser Wilhelm II: "For me, at least, nineteenth-century theology no longer held any future."[42] Paul Tillich spoke of his loss of faith in modernity while serving as a chaplain

[40]Immanuel Kant, *Critique of Pure Reason*, trans. Norman Kemp Smith (New York: St. Martin's Press, 1929). For a useful guide to the critical philosophy, see W. H. Walsh, *Kant's Criticism of Metaphysics* (Chicago: University of Chicago Press, 1976), passim.

[41]See Georg Picht, "The God of the Philosophers," in *Journal of the American Academy of Religion* 48 (March 1980): 61–80.

[42]Barth is quoted in Heinz Zahrnt, *The Question of God*, trans. R. A. Wilson (New York: Harcourt Brace Jovanovich, 1969), p. 16.

on the front lines during World War I: "We are experiencing the most terrible catastrophes, the end of the world order . . . it is coming to an end, and this end is accompanied by deepest pain."[43] Summing up the sense of crisis in the passing of an age, Hans-Georg Gadamer wrote,

> With World War I a genuine epochal awareness emerged that welded the nineteenth century into a unit of the past. This is true not only in the sense that a bourgeois age, which had united faith in technical progress with the confident expectation of a secured freedom and a civilizing perfectionism, had come to an end. The end is not merely an awareness of leaving an epoch, but above all the *conscious withdrawal* from it, indeed, the sharpest rejection of it.[44]

The postmodern turn is the calling into question of the whole development of modern culture.

We can find the causes for disillusionment all around us. The intellectuals of the twentieth century have grown up in the midst of world wars, worldwide economic depression, the rise of totalitarian states in Italy, Germany, and Russia, unprecedented evil in Auschwitz, Buchenwald, and Dachau, the horrors of Hiroshima and Nagasaki, the Cold War, American or Soviet war power in Vietnam, Afghanistan, Central America, and elsewhere, starvation and hunger in the Third World, and the threat of nuclear war. At the same time, the tradition of moral and religious discourse that once permitted people to make sense of catastrophic events does not seem to have survived intact. In other words, the intellectuals of the twentieth century live in *our* world.

Postmoderns no longer take their intellectual orientation from the major figures of the Enlightenment or other modernist movements. As Allan Megill, a historian of modern and postmodern ideas, has argued at length in *Prophets of Extremity,* the important thinkers of our time are taking their orientation from the radical critics of Enlightenment—especially Nietzsche and Heidegger.[45] For many, a postmodern paradigm for thought has taken the place of the modern one. Zwi Werblowsky tells us what it means for religious thinkers in the twentieth century. The religious thinker is

> fully aware of living after Darwin, Marx, Freud, Weber, and Durkheim. He is also aware of living after Kant, Hegel, Nietzsche, Dostoyevski, and Kierkegaard. If he is committed to a religious tradition that possesses

---

[43]Tillich is quoted in Wilhelm and Marion Pauck, *Paul Tillich: His Life and Thought,* vol. 1: *Life* (New York: Harper & Row, 1976), p. 51.

[44]Hans-Georg Gadamer, "The Philosophical Foundations of the Twentieth Century," in *Philosophical Hermeneutics,* trans. and ed. David E. Linge (Berkeley and Los Angeles: University of California Press, 1976) pp. 107–29.

[45]Allan Megill, *Prophets of Extremity: Nietzsche, Heidegger, Foucault, Derrida* (Berkeley and Los Angeles: University of California Press, 1985), pp. 339–42.

Holy Scriptures, he also knows that he lives after Spinoza's *Tractatus* and after Wellhausen. Taking them all for granted, he asks where do we go from here? What symbolic systems and frameworks of understanding are available that could set our personal lives, embedded as they are in social contexts and institutions, into a coherent pattern of meaning? The big question is what is the role, if any, which specific traditions, that is to say the established forms of faith and the concomitant institutions of the great religious cultures, can play in creating, re-creating, salvaging, catalyzing or infusing universes of meaning that would somehow fit the condition of man and society?[46]

While critical of modernity, postmodern thought is nonetheless deeply indebted to the ideals of the modern age. For example, the Enlightenment represents, among other things, a self-assertion on behalf of *truth beyond superstition and above conflicting opinions*. Modern thinkers typically submit for criticism what is taken as self-evident. And they do so in the name of truth. The postmodernist continues to exercise human freedom and the power of critique on behalf of the search for truth. But the postmodernist is more likely to see truth served by divesting oneself of the conviction that we possess unshakeable foundations on which to adjudicate claims to truth. Nonetheless, postmodernist hermeneutics considers itself answerable to the norm of truth through criticism. In that sense, the postmodern is the continuation of the modern.

But important differences exist between the modern and postmodern. For instance, postmodern thinkers do not suppose that construction of theories is free of hidden interests, as did many modern thinkers. Radical critique has unmasked the pretenses of the Enlightenment quest for knowledge. Frameworks of meaning are constructed within historical languages by the language-using community. Preconceptions, or "biases" and "prejudices," provided by the historical community, color every theoretical construction. Pointed questions and interests guide the most objective program of historical research; they cannot help but influence results. Chastened by the recognition that every project has limiting preconditions, postmodern consciousness includes reflexive awareness of one's own finite standpoint and interests.

Postmodern thinkers consciously reject the modern paradigm; yet the postmodernist feels increasingly caught up in the products of modernity, especially technology and bureaucracy. Postmodern consciousness struggles against the spiritual decline of the modern West. But it must carry on within what Werblowsky calls the "Space Age of high-speed and fully-automated mechanical technologies, as well as of high-speed and fully-automated nonmaterial information systems and microcircuitries; the world of shrinking distance and quick transportation in which nevertheless thousands die of

---

[46]Werblowsky, *Beyond Tradition and Modernity*, p. 19.

hunger every day."[47] The paradox of the postmodern is the appearance of reflexive consciousness within burgeoning bureaucracy and anonymity. The postmodern thinker must live in the tension of this paradox.[48]

What, then, are the characteristics of the postmodern?

1. At the center of the postmodern paradigm is neither the manifestation of the sacred nor rational self-assertion, but the linguistic event of dialogue. The life of conversation structures the postmodern paradigm. Whereas the premodern appearance of the sacred presents an objective reality to which the subject belongs, and the self-assertion of the modern paradigm presents a neutralized subject, whose projects transform the world, the event of dialogue in language cannot be located on the "objective" or "subjective" side of a subject-object model. Language is the middle and medium of the event of dialogue between a self and another.[49]

2. The postmodern world picture is neither the image of the sacred cosmos nor the loss of that image. It is rather the image that there is no image of the whole of things. We imagine that we have no image of the universe in which we can see ourselves as intimately belonging or from which we see ourselves as ultimately excluded. If "Cartesian anxiety" is related to the loss of world in the modern period, the postmodern mode of existence is marked by acceptance of the erasure of the literal world picture. The imagelessness, and hence anonymity, of the world itself becomes a powerful symbol of the whole.[50] For the postmodern, the whole is not represented as an image to vision or sight, but is disclosed in language or word. Indeed, the postmodern thinkers hold it as axiomatic that only through language do we have anything like a world.

3. In *Philosophy and the Mirror of Nature,* Richard Rorty analyzes the postmodern system of thought as hermeneutical and edifying, rather than epistemological and systematic (as is modern thought). (Note that Rorty does not use the terms *modern* and *postmodern* and might very well object to them.) Rorty means that postmodern thought attempts to find "new, better, more interesting, more fruitful ways of speaking" rather than polishing the mirror of epistemology.[51]

For the postmodernist, epistemological theories of mental representation cannot hope ultimately to distinguish true from false pictures of

---

[47]Ibid.

[48]See the powerful essay by Thomas J. J. Altizer, "The Anonymity of God," in *Total Presence: The Language of Jesus and the Language of Today* (New York: Seabury Press, 1980), pp. 19–36, for a discussion of the theological implications of current anonymity.

[49]The classic text about the linguistic event of dialogue is Hans-Georg Gadamer, *Truth and Method,* trans. Garrett Barden and John Cumming (New York: Seabury Press, 1975). See p. 345 for the reference to language as "the middle ground in which understanding and agreement concerning the object [*die Sache,* or what is spoken about] takes place between two people."

[50]Wildiers, in *The Theologian and His Universe,* p. 60, says, "Even the absence of a coherent and generally accepted worldview can in a way act as a 'world picture.'"

[51]Rorty, *Philosophy and the Mirror of Nature,* p. 360.

objective reality. "Objective" reality is always already interpreted through linguistic, hence social, preconceptions. Heidegger formulated this postmodern insight as follows: everything that we understand, in word, text, gesture, or action, is approached through anticipations (or preunderstanding). These anticipations direct our questions to the other. They make understanding of the other possible. They situate understanding within the horizon of anticipations that are historically effective here and now. Heidegger calls this phenomenon the hermeneutic circle. Because of it, all understanding is potentially and essentially a dialogue rather than a monological mirroring of reality.[52]

Understanding is a dialogue with the "other." And just as in conversation, the subject matter directs the dialogue. The event of understanding is best displayed in a conversation where two people are drawn by their discussion of something to mutual recognition. Strangely, the other of dialogue may include oneself as well as the conversation partner or text. The otherness of oneself appears in conversation with another insofar as the speaker or reader as "I" becomes aware of his or her own hidden preconceptions or anticipations during the conversation. This occurs through listening to what the text or other person is saying about the subject matter and by allowing what is said to call one's preconceptions into question by criticizing their appropriateness for this situation.

4. The postmodern self-world relation is neither immediate openness to the sacred nor is it differentiation between subject and object, although it participates in both. The postmodern thinker relates reflexively to each of the other possibilities. He or she focuses now on the content of symbolic understanding and now on the results of critical reflection. The back and forth movement between participation in meaning and objectifying critique can sometimes suggest new, "postcritical" interpretations. By virtue of being able to recall the direct meaning in light of the critical view, the postmodernist can mediate the symbolic consciousness through the critical. Ricoeur calls this relation the "second naiveté."[53] It is not a direct relation to meaning, as are both the openness or naiveté of the premodern and the critique of the modern. It is an interpretive relation to each of the two direct relations. The task of the second naiveté is to translate the meaning given to the openness of precritical consciousness into postcritical ontological or theological concepts that have been worked out in full awareness of the modern critical program.

The reflexive "I" of the postmodern consciousness is not the universal "I" of modernity, unaware of its own situatedness. The reflexive "I" recognizes that it always begins with prejudgment, and it self-consciously enters into the precritical mode by responding directly to symbolic under-

---

[52]See the excerpt from Heidegger's *Being and Time* in the readings included in this volume.
[53]Ricoeur, *Symbolism of Evil*, p. 352.

standing in "sympathetic imagination." It thereby approaches texts by respecting the original, immediate meaning of the symbol. (*Original* in this context means "what I first understand through the symbol," not "what the original audience understood.") But the reflexive "I" also brings the tools of critical thought to bear on the symbolic understanding. The creative act of interpretation finds new meanings and new things to say about the text by letting the text speak into the new situation. Postmodern hermeneutics rests on the wager that the "I" can reappropriate meanings in texts and actions by translating its understanding into postmodern concepts. Ricoeur puts it this way:

> Thus hermeneutics, an acquisition of "modernity," is one of the modes by which that "modernity" transcends itself, insofar as it is forgetfulness of the sacred. I believe that being can still speak to me—no longer, of course, under the precritical form of immediate belief, but as the second immediacy aimed at by hermeneutics. The second naiveté aims to be the postcritical equivalent of the precritical hierophany.[54]

The postmodern situation profoundly alters the shape of hermeneutics in theology and religious thought. Many of the essays in this collection will illustrate how this is so. Because I will explain the postmodern views of understanding in the next sections of this introduction, I will comment now only in the most rudimentary way on their impact within religious thought.

Two points stand out as the most crucial aspects of current religious hermeneutics. We will see both of them repeated at various places in the following pages.

First, religious and theological language is symbolic through and through. The postmodernist sees symbols *as* symbols rather than as literal manifestations of the divine or preconceptual objects of belief. Postmodernist hermeneutics is put into play through the ability of religious symbols to disclose something about what it means to be human in relation to the divine. Its task, of course, is to interpret what religious and theological language is all about.

Second, postmodern hermeneutics stresses the kerygmatic quality of religious symbols and texts. Religious language has the capacity on occasion to enable and to impart that which it depicts. Recognition of the enabling power of symbols shows the respect that postmodern religion has for the premodern openness to the divine. These two features distinguish any contemporary program of hermeneutics from its modern forebears.

Behind postmodern hermeneutics is a philosophical description of the nature of understanding. To it, I now turn.

[54]Ibid.

III. The Nature of Understanding

A central claim of postmodern hermeneutics is that understanding has been forgotten. Like a misplaced house key or pen, something we rely on and notice only when it is missing, understanding is "here somewhere," although momentarily hidden. The simile is helpful only to a point, however, for understanding is not a tool for our use in life, like a house key or a pen, but rather the fundamental mode of our being in the world. As humans, we are always already understanding ourselves, our world, and God as the ground of self and world. If understanding has been lost or misplaced, the resulting condition is more like amnesia or forgotten identity than frustration over a broken or lost tool. Understanding is more basic to our humanness than our use of tools. Indeed, understanding makes possible our use of tools and, beyond that, our social life and its cultural expressions.

Postmodern hermeneutics also claims to have brought understanding out of hiddenness and into the light. How does understanding appear? What are its leading characteristics? These are immensely difficult and complex questions. The essays that follow will assist us in coming to an understanding of understanding. In what immediately follows, I present a brief analysis of the activity of understanding, one that is shared by the postmodern hermeneutical thinkers represented in this collection. I focus on four overlapping elements in understanding: temporality, linguisticality, dialogue, and appropriation. The essays in this collection have more to say on these topics, but I hope that this lightning-flash sketch provides a preliminary grasp.

Understanding As Activity

Hermeneutics is the theoretical interest in understanding. Understanding occurs as an event in time. Because understanding is an activity and not a self-sufficient object, describing it will involve comparing it to other related activities. Robert P. Scharlemann, an important theologian who has contributed two essays to these volumes, gives us some assistance in this matter. In his book *The Being of God*, Scharlemann focuses on understanding in relation to other similar activities. Following Scharlemann's terminology, I shall here consider understanding as an activity that is distinct from, but related to, conceiving and perceiving, abstract thinking and concrete experiencing.[55]

Conceiving is the activity of forming abstract thoughts, universal notions that can be applied to many entities. *Perceiving* is the activity of noticing singular entities that are given to the senses for experience. Each of these is

---

[55]For a further discussion, see Robert P. Scharlemann, *The Being of God: Theology and the Experience of Truth* (New York: Seabury Press, 1981), p. 47.

a basic form or structure of relating to the world. Although understanding cannot be reduced to either conceiving or perceiving, it is typically overlooked in descriptions of human knowledge of the world. We tend to think that we can explain knowledge by referring only to perceiving and abstracting. Empiricists often purport to account for human knowledge from sense data and the rules of logic alone. But what is left out of such modern epistemological accounts is the more elusive, and more basic, activity of *understanding*—the activity of connecting our thinking with our experiencing of reality. We cannot account for the connections we make between thinking and experiencing without broaching the independent domain of understanding.

The acts of perceiving, conceiving, and understanding are incredibly complex. Put into the most elementary terms, they can be described as follows. In perceiving a singular thing, I see or hear or feel *that* thing. In conceiving something, I abstract a notion of *what* the thing is. In understanding a thing, I connect the experience and thought by responding to the object as a sign that carries a meaning. Understanding is the process that synthesizes the perceiving (experiencing) on one side and thinking on the other.

For example, if I see my friend on the other side of the street, and he is waving at me in a certain way, I perceive the whole gesture. Taking the gesture as a sign, I connect it with the thought of anger (if I see the gesture as a "waving away" as if to say, "I've had it with you; go away!") or the thought of welcome (if I see the gesture as a "beckoning" as if to say, "Hello, what's up?"). Understanding is the process by which the concrete percept—the physical reality as a sign—is connected with abstract thought to render meaning. How do we make this connection between the perceived thing and the thought? In what way does understanding synthesize experience with reflection? Simply put, the answer is through images or figures of speech. Let me try to explain how this is so by referring to understanding as an activity.

Understanding involves three elements. First, we have the *meaning* that is understood, a connection between the abstract notion and the concrete experience. Second, we have the *activity* of understanding, the bringing together of notion and the experience. Third, we have the "*I*" or agent of the act: "I" understand this reality as that notion. In understanding, a meaning is discovered *on* the thing by the "I."

Heidegger, in the excerpt from *Being and Time* included in volume two, describes the synthesis of perception and conception in some detail. According to Heidegger, understanding means seeing something *as*, or "in terms of," something else. Something given to experience is taken not merely as brutely there, but as something more. Heidegger calls this the "hermeneutical *as*." The understood meaning has the structure of this *as* that. Heidegger argues that the hermeneutical "*as*" is in a certain important sense more basic than either the percept or concept, because the "as" is a figure or image that structures our first perception of the object and guides our abstracting of it. The understood meaning is initially an image in terms of which we see this (percept) as that (concept). The activity of understanding concretizes the concept and universalizes the percept. It effects both sides by connecting them.

Let us return to a simple example to clarify these terms. With my physical eyes, I see a singular thing: a person. Through abstract thought, I call this person "my friend." Understanding is the activity of connecting my experience of this person with my notion of a friend. In this case, understanding is rooted in the relation I have to the other person. Over time, the image I have of the relationship enables me to say of him, "He is my friend." Perhaps this example seems too value laden to work as an illustration. After all, ascribing friendship to a relationship seems to imply a valuation of that relationship and not merely a description of how a thought and an experience are joined together through understanding.

Take a more value-neutral example: If I see a two-legged creature and think "a person," the connection between the percept and the concept is made by means of an image of a person in general. That image makes possible the connection between what I see and what I think. In this case, I perceive something particular (that thing), I think something universal ("person"), and I understand that thought and percept belong together on the basis of an image. The image is in the first place what I understand. It is neither a thought nor a percept, but an understood meaning. Whether we see this creature as a person or this person as a friend, we combine thought and percept in terms of an image that is understood.

Kant referred to the hermeneutical phenomenon of understanding in his discussion of the transcendental image, although he used different terminology. According to Kant, our knowledge of objects presupposes three phases of the cognitive activity. First, sensibility receives a series of intuitions (*Anschauungen*) by virtue of sense organs. Second, understanding (caution: what Kant means by "understanding" is here called conception) orders the intuitions through applying concepts. Third, the transcendental imagination makes possible the combination of concepts and intuitions. For Kant, knowledge of an object presupposes a synthesis of concepts and intuitions. Without both of these, we cannot claim knowledge. But Kant argues that because sensibility (or, here, perception) and understanding (or, here, conception) are different and discontinuous, there must be a third thing, intermediate between the two and homogeneous with each, by which to combine them. This third thing is the transcendental image.[56] It is a *generalized* image of an object, and so it fits the abstract quality of the concept. Yet, as a *singular* image, it fits the concrete quality of intuition.

[56]Kant, *Critique of Pure Reason*, B177, p. 314.

Kant's transcendental image plays the role of the hermeneutical "as" for Heidegger: the image "in terms of" which I see this "as" that. This means that the Kantian transcendental imagination marks the place of what recent hermeneutics calls understanding.

Understanding is intrinsically temporal, since it involves producing images that synthesize thought and experience. Connecting percept and concept requires time. But there is a more significant sense in which understanding is temporal. Heidegger spells this out in terms of mediating past, future, and present. Let me briefly consider the temporal modes of understanding.[57]

According to Heidegger, the "I" always finds itself in a situation to which it is answerable. Heidegger names this belongingness to a situation *Befindlichkeit*. It is the name for the ontological dimension of our life that is attuned to being through mood or feeling. Mood, for Heidegger, does not designate a mere affect, but a fundamental mode of being in which we find ourselves in a particular place and endowed with a certain voice. All understanding involves being attuned to a particular situation. What this means for hermeneutics is that understanding always speaks out of the past that in part makes us who we are. We cannot set aside the history and location of our own voices in understanding.

Understanding is also oriented to the future. The activity of understanding involves projecting images from the particular situation into the future. The projection of images throws forward possibilities for understanding. When I understand this person as my friend, I imagine a possibility for future realization. The projection of future possibility has two sides: I imagine the other person as becoming my friend in time, and I imagine myself as becoming something new in time.

Present acts of understanding involve the mediation of past into future. We grasp the possibilities of the situation by projecting new meanings in the future from the horizon of meanings that have reached us from the past. And likewise, we understand the meanings of the past by grasping history in terms of new possibilities for understanding. Understanding is always a temporal activity of mediation: a translating of past into present in light of the future, an opening of the future from the present as grounded in the past. Understanding is thus not so much an activity that an "I" does to an object or other person. It is rather an ongoing temporal event of mediating past and future through the present. Understanding does not stand apart from the movement of history but is the fundamental temporal activity making historical experience possible. And each act of understanding is an event in the ongoing life of a historical tradition.[58]

---

[57]Martin Heidegger, *Being and Time*, pp. 383–400.

[58]Gadamer's term for this is *effective historical consciousness (wirkungsgeschichtliche Bewusstsein)*. See *Truth and Method*, p. 305.

UNDERSTANDING AS LINGUISTIC

One vital element in contemporary hermeneutics is Heidegger's claim that understanding is thoroughly a linguistic process. For postmodern hermeneutics, language is the medium through which both our abstract thinking and our concrete experiencing assume definite shape. The basic linguistic unit of the understanding process is the sentence. In the sentence, we bring together percept and concept while still holding them apart.[59]

In a sentence like "This is a house," language is the medium for the separation and conjunction of a singular percept ("this") and a general concept ("house"). We see the object as what is generally conceived as a house. We understand the connection that is semantically marked by the copula ("is"). We do not see that connection, nor do we have a concept of it. To say we understand it is to say that we grasp the sense in the object by expressing the meaning in a sentence. Understanding makes its appearance in linguistic expression.

To dwell in a linguistic world and to understand the self and the other are two sides of the same activity. To mediate past and future in present acts of understanding is a linguistic process. The effect of the past on our present situation is concretized in the language we speak. Our language is historically stamped by past speakers and the mediation of their meanings into changed circumstances. And our future is linguistically projected and imagined; we open a vision of a transformed world by opening new meanings in language. Language is the medium of understanding, just as water is the medium of swimming. In it, we find the traces of past experience and future possibility.

The linguistic medium of understanding grants us a relation to the whole of being. By producing images through which we connect thought and experience, we are not primarily related to discrete meanings. Relations to particular meanings are possible because we have, in our use of language, a relation to the whole of being itself. Whatever is, or is not, is sayable. And in our capacity to speak, we are connected to whatever is, has been, and may be. To dwell in a linguistic world is to be in the openness of being and nonbeing. The mystery of understanding is one with the mystery of being addressed by a word that is the center of language, the point of our openness to being itself.[60]

The temporality of understanding, which merges with its linguisticality, points out both the finitude and reflexivity of being human. In understanding, we move in the finite sphere of situation and project, of past and future, of language received and transformed, of traditions spent and self-renewing. But this finitude is not a prison house of confinement and monologue. The

[59]Ricoeur, *Interpretation Theory*, pp. 6–8.
[60]Gadamer, *Truth and Method*, pp. 415–16.

understanding process is fundamentally open to the other in its finitude. The openness of understanding means that the "I" who speaks and understands always moves beyond himself or herself to mediate meaning. Linguistic being is essentially dialogue.

UNDERSTANDING AS DIALOGUE

Understanding begins with a response to something that appears as a sign of something else. Someone addresses me; a text interests me; an event happens to me. In responding to the meaning of what appears, I understand what the person, text, or event says to me. Even misunderstanding is a diminished form of understanding that can be corrected through conversation. In the nature of the case, understanding is a dialogue with the other. My response to any such meaning-bearing sign initiates a dialogue of question and answer, or give and take. An interaction unfolds between myself and the other person, text, or event that claims my attention.

Understanding as dialogue involves an exchange of voices. Like any good conversation, good will must be present between speakers in order for the dialogue to take place. Respect for the other provides the openness necessary for the other to take an active role in the dialogue. Without an openness to hear the other and to be changed by what is said, a reprimand or a quarrel or a shouting match may occur—but not a genuine dialogue. This is as true of reading texts or experiencing events as it is of conversations with another person.[61]

Understanding as dialogue is undermined if I focus my attention directly on the other person as a person, or text as a text, or event as an event. For dialogues happen when the participants are both responding to the subject matter about which they are speaking. The give and take, question and answer, or genuine conversation is not so much an exchange between the two speakers as it is between the speakers and the topic of conversation. The theme or subject matter of conversation draws me into the dialogue and sustains my interest. And the conversation seems to take on a life of its own when the theme evokes understanding and discloses something about the situation in which the speakers find themselves. Conversations take on a living quality when the topics discussed are understood as belonging to the situation in which I stand, even when they confront me with an otherness or strangeness because I had not anticipated them.

Openness to the viewpoint of the other and deference to the spirit of dialogue are essential ingredients in understanding. Without either one, no genuine conversation occurs. Understanding is that elusive experience of being drawn outside myself into what Martin Buber calls the region of the "between." Between "I" and "you" (even if the "you" is a text or an object

[61]Ibid., pp. 321–25.

with presence), understanding finds its dwelling place: we are at home in the world of meaning.[62]

UNDERSTANDING AS APPROPRIATION

Understanding as dialogue opens the "I" to "you" in the region of meaning between partners. The dimension of meaning is an open region of discovery. There, I am led to think further about the topic at hand by taking seriously what the other has to say. But I am also led to think further about my own prejudices and assumptions. In every conversation, I express myself along with the subject matter under discussion. Engaging in open dialogue through understanding, I encounter myself along with the topics of concern. Language, the medium of understanding as dialogue, is a two-way street. Through it, I respond to new meanings. In responding, I become myself and am aware of becoming myself. Understanding is thus a reflexive activity: it is openness to the other and openness to the self. I understand the other and thereby understand myself. Let me explain how this is so.

Recall that the linguistic activity of understanding is a mediation of past and future: I project new possibilities into the future from the past that has determined my situation here and now; I grasp the meaning of the past in light of my vision of a possible future. The situatedness and temporality of understanding means that I never understand as a disembodied and neutral "subject." My understanding of new meanings always proceeds from a horizon of meanings sedimented in language and inherited from the past. The set of meanings handed on from the past constitutes a tradition. Belonging to a tradition means that I do not begin from nowhere, without an advance idea of whatever might enter my world of familiar meanings. Because I have a tradition, I can respond to otherness and place the unfamiliar into a familiar context of meanings. Without prejudices (or "preconceptions," literally, prejudgments), I would be helpless to understand.

Religious symbols, images of the world, impressions of human nature, meanings from narratives of all kinds (history, myth, fairy tales, children's stories, proverbs, and so forth), philosophical and theological ideas—any of these may be sources of prejudices in the sense of a preunderstanding that belongs to my situation. Preunderstandings may be invaluable aids to understanding in all kinds of situations. For example, confronted with a friend fearing for his life, I may be enabled to understand because of my vague familiarity with stories about characters who met fear with courage. But preunderstandings may also prevent my understanding. For example, faced with a person needing help, I may be unable to offer it because he or

[62]Martin Buber, *I and Thou*, trans. Walter Kaufmann (New York: Charles Scribner's Sons, 1970), p. 168.

she is of a different race. I may have learned to distrust "those people" through stories and distortive images.

The all-too-obvious and painful misunderstanding caused by false prejudices led modernist thought in the Enlightenment to reject "prejudice" altogether.[63] To be rational meant to be free of prejudice. Postmodern hermeneutics has discovered, however, that prejudice-free rationality is impossible. We cannot avoid bringing ourselves and our past into the activity of understanding. What is crucial is not whether we have prejudices; we do. It is whether our prejudices have been questioned and tested for their authenticity. Do they enable genuine understanding or block it?

How do I critique my own prejudices? Hermeneutics answers: not by introspection, but by opening oneself to the other in dialogical understanding. In following a conversation with a text or person, I am impelled by the fundamental issue or concern animating the conversation. I question further the direction for thought opened up by the dialogue. This "questioning further" allows the text or other voice to place my preunderstandings into question. In following the topic as it is played out in conversation, I let my initial understanding be checked and reversed by the emerging meanings.[64]

Without a self-critical questioning of prejudices, texts and other voices remain mute and I remain unchanged. All understanding proceeds under the will to submit oneself to the meaning of the text, to allow oneself the openness of self-understanding. Modernist hermeneutics thought that it was one thing to understand the meaning of a text and another thing to apply it to oneself or "appropriate" it. But this is mistaken. Every act of understanding already is an appropriation, an act of making the meaning into one's own meaning. For we cannot help but to include the self in the activity of understanding. Only "I" can understand; and when understanding happens, appropriation of meaning happens as well. The task of hermeneutics is not to distinguish understanding from appropriation. It is to ask, "Which meanings, texts, symbols, figures really do have something to say to me? How should I appropriate them?"[65]

IV. TYPES OF HERMENEUTICS

Earlier in this introduction, I defined hermeneutics as a theoretical inquiry into understanding. Now, I wish to be somewhat more specific about the relation of hermeneutics to understanding. Many different versions of hermeneutical inquiry exist. The essays assembled here are not all of the same type. They do not all have the same purposes. I propose systematically

---

[63]Gadamer, *Truth and Method*, pp. 241–44.

[64]For a fine discussion of understanding in Gadamer and the reversals of preunderstandings, see Donald G. Marshall, "Reading as Understanding: Hermeneutics and Reader-Response Criticism," in *Christianity and Literature* 33 (Fall 1983): 37–48.

[65]Gadamer, *Truth and Method*, pp. 274–78.

to distinguish basic types of hermeneutics in order to sort out the similarities and differences among the essays in this collection. A typology of hermeneutics will provide us with a compass both for identifying the intention of each essay and for conducting further research. My thesis is that distinct types of hermeneutics may be distinguished on the basis of the different possible relations of hermeneutical inquiry to the activity of understanding. Let me be very clear, however, about the limits of any typology of hermeneutics.

When we look at actual writings in the field of hermeneutics, we find that some fall rather neatly into the types I describe below. For example, the writings of Schleiermacher conform to hermeneutics as "theory of interpretation." Other writings will participate in more than one type. For instance, Hans-Georg Gadamer's writings appear to belong both to hermeneutics as "practical philosophy" and to hermeneutics as "speculative ontology." This overlapping is to be expected. The various types I construct here are not necessarily separate and distinct; we might best think of them as phases or moments in a single enterprise. Paul Ricoeur's writing, for example, appears to make use of all four types as phases of a single hermeneutical project. The fact that one author may incorporate more than one version of hermeneutics into his or her writings does not damage the heuristic power of the typology, which provides us with some categories and leading questions to ask about any hermeneutical efforts.

I call understanding a first-order activity, because it is by its very nature direct and immediate. Understanding is always going on; we are already engaged in understanding. By contrast, interpretation is one step removed from the primary event of understanding: interpretation is the cultivation of understanding. When we interpret, we elaborate, critique, and adjust our understanding. I take interpretation, then, to be a second-order activity directed to the first-order activity of understanding. Hermeneutics is the theoretical approach to understanding. Strictly speaking, it is a third-order activity directed to the interplay of understanding and interpretation. It provides norms and standards for conducting and evaluating interpretations of understanding.

In constructing a typology of hermeneutics, I begin with the primary act of understanding. I offer a simple linguistic model of that activity. When understanding occurs, we might acknowledge it by saying, "I understand what you say." This sentence expresses the fact that *I understand a meaning* that a person, text, or event expresses. Three elements stand out in this model: the understood meaning, the activity of understanding, and the "I" who understands. For my model sentence to display three elements, I shorten it to read "I understand you." By "you," however, I mean "what you say . . . ; the subject matter about which you express yourself." The three elements of this structural model of understanding are thus displayed in each of the parts of the sentence: subject, verb, and object. Let "I understand you," then, serve as the model of understanding.

My suggestion is that four types of hermeneutics may now be derived from the three elements in the model of understanding. If this is so, we can grasp why hermeneutical inquiry appears in the four forms it does and we can trace each of the versions back to the structure of understanding from which they emerge. My thesis, in other words, purports to locate the principle of order in the multiple voices of hermeneutical inquiry. I shall itemize the four types of hermeneutics and indicate how each one represents a permutation of the basic structure of understanding.

1. Hermeneutics becomes *theory of interpretation* when the focus of inquiry is on the meaning understood ("you"). It primarily asks about the intention of the author or what the original audience understood; it seeks invariant meaning.

2. Hermeneutics becomes *practical philosophy* (ethics) when the focus of inquiry shifts to the activity of understanding ("understand"). It primarily asks about the meaning of the understanding process as the basic way humans interact with themselves and their world; it seeks authentic human life.

3. Hermeneutics becomes *speculative ontology* when the focus of inquiry shifts again to the subject of understanding ("I"). It primarily asks about the meaning of being itself as this is reflected in the understanding "I"; it seeks to understand the whole of being.

4. Hermeneutics becomes *theology* when the whole structure of understanding is overturned within any of the three types. It primarily asks about the depth dimension of understood meanings, the understanding process, and the whole of being; it seeks to understand appearances of the divine.

I shall explain each of these briefly so that my proposed typology may function as an interpretive device for understanding the essays to follow in this collection.

HERMENEUTICS AS THEORY OF INTERPRETATION

Modern hermeneutics first appears as theory of interpretation. This is the version that Schleiermacher presents and that Dilthey develops. It is no accident that hermeneutics initially assumes this form. Understanding is a form of consciousness, and consciousness is in the first place directed outward to its object and is oblivious to itself. Only under special conditions does consciousness turn back on itself in reflexivity. So it makes sense that hermeneutics, as theoretical reflection on understanding, orients itself first to the understood meaning and grants the objectivity of that meaning a privileged position.

Theories of interpretation are called for only when problems of interpretation arise. As long as understanding is unimpeded and interpretation is relatively noncontroversial, a general theory of interpretation is beside the point. In Western religious thought, the rise of modernity symbolized in the power of critique prompted the formation of a general theory of hermeneutics. Prior to historical and rational critique, the Bible and the classic works of theology were assumed to carry religious meaning. Of course, controversies arose about the interpretation of the meaning. But the religious meaningfulness of the central texts, rituals, and institutions was not in dispute. That situation changed when modernity developed its critique. The power to dislodge self-evident meanings given in the religious tradition broke the immediacy of traditional understanding. It became necessary to develop a theory that could reconstruct the meaning of precritical texts in light of the modern critique. And since the power of critique affects all ancient texts and not simply this or that one, a general theory of interpretation was called for.

Hermeneutics as theory of interpretation displays three typical features. Each of these places this version of hermeneutics within the modern paradigm. Theories of interpretation are not extinct in the twentieth century, however. Modern and premodern forms of thought and life continue to exist alongside the emerging postmodern forms. The postmodern thinkers divest themselves of these elements, of course. But for many current writers, as for the nineteenth century thinkers, the goals of modernist theory still stand.

Hermeneutics as theory of interpretation starts with the postulate that texts have a definite and objective meaning. In part, this reflects the interest behind such theories: retrieval of lost meaning from a text that once disclosed the core of a community's self-understanding. In the case of an authoritative text (such as the Bible, a classic in literature, or a legal text) that once conveyed a norm for understanding, but has lost its self-evident meaning, a theory of interpretation must back up any attempt to reclaim the meaning under new conditions. The text becomes a focus for interest, as interpreters try to articulate its meaning and thus save the text from meaninglessness or ambiguity. The meaning must be objective in the sense that it resides in the text as an ideal object to be recovered by the interpreter. For this type of project, meaning is not the subjective construction of the interpeter; it is objective and self-identical.

Theories of interpretation may settle the question of the meaning of the text in any number of ways. Most typical is the claim that the author's intention is the single meaning of the text. Current theorists of interpretation, such as E. D. Hirsch, Jr., and Emilio Betti, argue that validity in interpretation demands unchanging and definite meaning; for if meaning changes in different contexts or is indefinite, then interpretation is a free-for-all.[66] This, they claim, is a disaster; especially when it comes to norma-

---

[66]E. D. Hirsch, Jr., *Validity in Interpretation* (New Haven: Yale University Press, 1962); Emilio Betti, *Teoria Generale della Interpretazione*. Betti has translated his two-volume treatise into German: *Allgemeine Auslegungslehre als Methodik der Geisteswissenschaften*. An English

tive texts that supply values and direct action for a community. They argue
that if meaning is defined as the author's intention, valid interpretation can
be assured at least in principle. In this case, we can say the meaning of the
work is unchanging and definite although the significance of the text may
indeed vary with changing contexts.

Hirsch's theory of interpretation continues the tradition of nineteenth-
century hermeneutics. Both Schleiermacher and Dilthey postulate objective
meaning and identify it with the author's intention. There may be differences, however, between Hirsch and his nineteenth-century predecessors
on the notion of intention. In his book on hermeneutics, philosopher David
Hoy claims that Schleiermacher and Dilthey rely on a psychological sense in
which intention is a private meaning in the author's mind, whereas Hirsch
defends a linguistic sense in which intention is a verbal and shareable
meaning.[67] In each case, however, the theory of interpretation attempts to
isolate the author's meaning as the objective meaning of the text.

Objective meaning may also be located in the intention of the text, as
opposed to that of the author. Paul Ricoeur, among others, thinks that
referring to the author's conscious intent is neither always possible nor
always helpful. Rather, Ricoeur argues, texts have an objective sense, but it
is located in the formal structure of the text itself.[68] The structure of the
text—we might call this the system of relations internal to the text—gives the
reader a clue for deciphering what the text is about.[69] This formulation of the
objective sense—shared by structuralists and new critics—avoids focusing
on the author and genuinely makes meaning immanent in the text itself. But
it is an alternative within the framework of hermeneutics as theory of
interpretation, rather than a proposal that breaks with this version of
hermeneutics.

Once hermeneutics as theory of interpretation places its interest in
objective meaning, interest in methodology follows. For if a definite meaning is to be found in the text, then we require a set of rules to apply when
interpreting texts and evaluating the interpretations of others. Wherever the
discussion in hermeneutics turns to methodology, which is bound to happen
once objective meaning is the focus, we are in the realm of hermeneutics as
theory of interpretation.

Moreover, epistemology also becomes a necessary item on the agenda of

---

translation is being prepared by Susan Noakes. A portion of the whole text is available in
Hermeneutics: Questions and Prospects, edited by Gary Shapiro and Alan Sica, pp. 29–53. Josef
Bleicher summarizes Betti's position in *Contemporary Hermeneutics: Hermeneutics as Method,
Philosophy, and Critique*, (London: Routledge & Kegan Paul, 1980), pp. 27–94.

[67]David Couzens Hoy, *The Critical Circle: Literature, History, and Philosophical Hermeneutics* (Berkeley and Los Angeles: University of California Press, 1982), p. 29.

[68]Ricoeur, *Interpretation Theory: Discourse and the Surplus of Meaning* (Fort Worth: Texas
Christian University Press, 1976), p. 80–88.

[69]See Ricoeur's essay in this volume: "What Is a Text?"

theories of interpretation. To postulate an objective meaning is to determine the interpreter's relation to the text as a cognitive relation. The interpreter approaches a text just as a nineteenth-century scientist approached nature—as a detached subject who investigates an independent object. Understanding is taken as a mode of knowing. Obviously, this means that the justification of the proposed methods of interpretation must be epistemological. The theory must account for the possibility and limitations of understanding objective meanings.

HERMENEUTICS AS PRACTICAL PHILOSOPHY

Hermeneutics appears in a new version as practical philosophy when interest shifts from the understood meaning to the activity of understanding. By speaking of a shift of interest, I do not imply that this version loses interest in the text. Hermeneutics as practical philosophy is always guided by the topic of discourse, by what is said in a text. So hermeneutics in this version does not lose sight of the meaning presented by the text. However, in this context, the meaning presented by the text is understood as the outcome of an interaction between the interpreter and the text. Meaning is internal to the act of understanding the text; it is a historical event of dialogue rather than a reproducible mental act. Understanding performs the meaning in this version of hermeneutics; it does not merely reconstruct it. By emphasizing understanding as constructive performance, interest shifts to the activity itself. What does it mean that we reenact meaning differently when seeking the same? What kind of beings are we, who must reinterpret on our own what has been handed on to us from the past? These are the questions that lead to hermeneutics as practical philosophy. With the answer that we are temporal and historical through and through, hermeneutics as practical philosophy approaches the postmodern paradigm of thought and experience.

Recall the three characteristics of hermeneutics as theory of interpretation: such theories are objectivist, methodological, and epistemological. Hermeneutics as practical philosophy presents three contrasting characteristics: meaning is *contextual;* understanding is figured as *practical wisdom;* and justification of understanding is sought through an *ontology of human existence* or philosophical anthropology. Let me discuss these three features.

Prompting the shift from theory of interpretation to practical philosophy is the postmodern recognition of the temporality of the interpreter. Modern hermeneutics as theory of interpretation already recognizes the temporality or historicity of the texts it studies. The Bible, for example, is understood by modern hermeneutical theory to occupy a different historical horizon from that of the interpreter. Hermeneutics as theory of interpretation takes on the task of reconstructing the objective meaning of the text in its own context. The task of reconstruction, however, neglects the historicity of the interpreter. The postmodern thinker sees that every historical reconstruction of objective meaning bears the distinctive imprint of the specific historical situation from which the interpreter approaches the text. Hermeneutics as practical philosophy concedes that no objective point of view on the meaning or author's intention is possible, because that meaning must be brought into the interpreter's system of values and meanings. The meaning of the text will be differently shaped in different contexts.[70]

Hermeneutics as practical philosophy shifts its goal from reconstructing an objective pregiven meaning to creative participation in an ongoing conversation and "handing on" from past to present. Let us say, then, that this version of hermeneutics turns from objectivism to contextualism. This does not imply that meanings are somehow not "objective," but are mere subjective constructs. Contextualism in hermeneutics repudiates the dichotomy between objective and subjective meaning as inadequate. By contrast, postmodern contextualism holds that meaning is both subjective and objective. Meanings are mediated by language as objective realities distinct from the subject who understands. But part of the objectivity of meaning is its capacity to be mediated into a new situation where subjects understand differently. Thus certain elements of meaning diminish and fade away and other elements arise within the new linguistic context. But within a relatively stable and abiding context of understanding and interpretation, meanings are identifiable and repeatable.

In this view, texts are no longer repositories of objective meaning so much as they are potentialities for recontextualizing meaning. Understanding is no longer a mode of knowing, but a dialogical activity that defines our finitude as humans and makes openness to meaning possible. Furthermore, understanding is seen not as one type of activity among others, but as the fundamental historical current in which humans have their being in the world. Consequently, in discerning what it means to understand and to interpret normative texts, we discern what it means to be human at all. Hermeneutics, the theory of understanding and interpretation, must become a global philosophy of human being. Such a philosophy sets the disclosure of authentic humanness as its goal, by spelling out the norms for genuine understanding. Such a program may be called practical philosophy or ethics. It proposes to teach us what it authentically means to be human through the practice of understanding.

As practical philosophy, hermeneutics drops its focus on methodology in favor of a path of learning and practical wisdom. Gadamer links hermeneutics to Aristotle's practical philosophy in that understanding may be likened

---

[70]See Hoy's discussion of hermeneutical contextualism in *The Critical Circle*, pp. 68–72. Richard J. Bernstein argues that hermeneutical contextualism is not a version of what we ordinarily take to be relativism or subjectivism. See *Beyond Objectivism and Relativism*, p. 114, pp. 165–69.

to *phronesis* or practical wisdom. For that reason, it would be helpful to review Gadamer's understanding of Aristotle's distinction of *phronesis* from both *episteme* and *techne*.[71] *Episteme*, or scientific knowledge, is cognition of unchanging universals whose truth may be formally demonstrated. *Phronesis*, the form of reasoning appropriate to practice, is different from and similar to *episteme*. Like *episteme*, *phronesis* is related to truth. But unlike knowing in science, practical reason deals with changing situations to which the thinker belongs. Practical wisdom is not cognition of universals but the ability to mediate between the universal element (the good) and the particular situation at hand. Success in practical reasoning rests on the ability to discriminate the good in this situation, to deliberate on possibilities, and to choose.

Techne, or technical know-how, is a form of reasoning that produces a certain product. Like practical wisdom, *techne* applies to concrete situations and the practices appropriate to them. But unlike practical wisdom, which humans are always obliged to use, *techne* is learned and can be forgotten. Moreover, whereas *techne* has a particular product as an end, *phronesis* aims at the happiness of a whole lifetime insofar as one comes to embody the good. And finally, *techne* demands no understanding of other humans, unlike ethical reasoning, but only of the materials which are to be fashioned into a work.[72]

Gadamer's point is that hermeneutics yields practical wisdom rather than either scientific knowledge or technical know-how. The chief task of hermeneutics is to recover the meaning of our authentic being as humans by considering the ethical dimension of our understanding. The chief goal of hermeneutics is to take on practical wisdom.

Hermeneutics as practical philosophy also drops its reference to epistemology as a means of justifying its methods. For justification, it turns to the ontology of human existence. The classic text for description of what it means to be human is Martin Heidegger's *Being and Time*.[73] In that work, Heidegger announces a turn from hermeneutics as theory of interpretation to hermeneutics as an interpretation of Dasein (Heidegger's term for the kind of being that we humans display). In the excerpts from Heidegger in this collection, we shall become familiar with his description of understanding as the fundamental possibility for being human. Crucial for hermeneutics as practical philosophy are Heidegger's descriptions of the openness of Dasein

[71]Hans-Georg Gadamer, "The Problem of Historical Consciousness," in *Interpretive Social Science: A Reader*, ed. Paul Rabinow and William M. Sullivan (Berkeley and Los Angeles: University of California Press, 1979), pp. 103–60, especially pp. 135–45. See also Gadamer, *Truth and Method*, pp. 278–89.

[72]In Aristotle, see Book 6 of *Nicomachean Ethics*, trans. Martin Ostwald (Indianapolis: Bobbs-Merrill, 1962), pp. 146–73.

[73]A second, and less formidable, "ontology of human existence" is Paul Ricoeur, *Fallible Man*, trans. Charles Kelbley (Chicago: Henry Regnery, 1965).

to its own most authentic possibilities to be itself through the moods of joy, boredom, anxiety, and courage. For Heidegger, hermeneutics is basically concerned with the recovery of our genuine and authentic being from fallenness and inauthenticity. In both Heidegger and Gadamer, we see hermeneutics appear as practical philosophy.

HERMENEUTICS AS SPECULATIVE ONTOLOGY

Yet a third version of hermeneutics appears when theoretical interest brings the subject into the forefront of concern. Let me begin my description of the third version by drawing some contrasts with the first two.

I proposed that the first version of hermeneutics, theory of understanding, focuses on the object of understanding: it aims to isolate the objective meaning of a text, constructs methods for doing so, and justifies them by referring to epistemology. Then I suggested that the second version of hermeneutics, practical philosophy, finds its point of reference in the activity of understanding: it focuses on the event of understanding as a fusion of contextual horizons, follows the path of practical wisdom, and grounds its norms in an ontology of Dasein or philosophical anthropology. Now I submit that the third version of hermeneutics, speculative ontology, orients itself to the agent of understanding: it leads us back to the *linguisticality of human understanding,* which *speculatively discloses the structure of being itself,* and enables a *hermeneutic ontology.*[74]

If hermeneutics as speculative ontology orients itself to the agent of understanding, how does it direct us back to linguisticality? To understand this, we must recall the project of hermeneutics as practical philosophy. The aim of practical philosophy is to live well: to become an authentic self and to retrieve one's true being from inauthenticity. This presupposes that the "I," the agent of understanding, is initially not itself.

Indeed, Heidegger says in *Being and Time* that, "It could be that the 'who' of everyday Dasein just is *not* the 'I myself.'"[75] For the most part, the human being has "fallen away [abgefallen] from itself as an authentic potentiality for being itself and has fallen into the 'world.' "[76] The world into which the "I" has fallen is the world of the "they" (*das Man*). Rather than being a self as "I," responsible for its own decisions and future, Dasein loses itself in public opinion or the anonymity of group identities: "We take pleasure and enjoy ourselves as *they* take pleasure; we read, see, and judge about literature and art as *they* see and judge; likewise we shrink back from the 'great mass' as *they* shrink back; we find 'shocking' what *they* find

[74]The basic reference for hermeneutics as speculative ontology is Gadamer's *Truth and Method,* pp. 397–447.

[75]Heidegger, *Being and Time,* p. 150.

[76]Ibid., p. 220.

shocking."[77] Thus the agent of understanding is not normally the "I myself." The impersonal "they" has taken the place of "I myself." Understanding is not something that "I" do for the most part, but is something "they" do for me.

Hermeneutics as practical philosophy responds to the call of the authentic "I" as it beckons us out of inauthenticity and fallenness. According to Heidegger, the possibility of grasping existence as something "I" understand, and of reclaiming the "I" from "they," presents itself through anticipating of the "end" of my life in death. For death is the possibility for me to be that finalizes my past, cuts off my future, and invades my present. Anticipation of death provides the perspective from which "I" may see my life in its whole and conclusive meaning. By appropriating this possibility of death, I may seize the perspective from which to take responsibility for my life. In that way, death may bring me back to the self that is "I myself," the self that is called on to construct a meaningful whole by caring for others and the world.

In brief, an authentic self is not a given for human understanding. When we turn to the agent of understanding, we turn not to "I myself" but to "they." Authentic selfhood is the goal and gift of genuine understanding. From where does it come?

According to Heidegger, the source of the call for authenticity is precisely from the self as "I." In alienation from myself as "I," I hear my own authentic being calling me in fallenness and prompting the decision whether or not to be myself.[78] But this call does not beckon through introspection or analysis. "I" am always the subject or agent of reflection or understanding. In the nature of the case, "I" cannot reflect on the "I"; for that would make the subject into an object, hence no longer subject. So what does it mean to assert that the call comes from the "I"? Where do "I" appear as a caller to authenticity? According to Heidegger's later thought, the "I" appears through my understanding of linguistically mediated meanings. Poetry, religious symbols, and so forth, present me with the "I." In understanding the meanings given to me for interpretation, I respond to the "I." In other words, the call comes from the linguisticality of understanding.

Understanding always occurs through language. Language is the medium of understanding in that language determines the meaning understood, the act of understanding, and the subject of understanding. The linguisticality of understanding means the activity of understanding always occurs as the historical movement of a linguistic tradition. The historical meanings of a linguistic community are reembodied in the time of understanding, interpretation, and appropriation.

As a participant in a language community, I am inseparably a part of the

---

[77]Ibid., p. 164.
[78]Ibid., p. 317.

language I use. The central meanings of the language are already a part of my being; I already belong to them. One of the central meanings is that of the authentic self. What it means to be "I myself" is already manifest in the tradition to which I belong. Myth, poetic symbol, ritual, narrative, philosophy, and theology present me with figures of a potentiality to be myself. They do not say, "Let me take the burden of existence from you." Images of authentic selfhood say, "Let me disclose your own authentic selfhood. This is something you can be on your own, within your own situation." In our Western tradition, the images of Jesus as Christ and Socrates are root symbols of authentic selfhood from which a multiplicity of expressions and interpretations have grown.

In sum, reflecting on the subject of understanding leads us to the linguisticality of all understanding. We fundamentally belong to language and tradition. Through this belongingness, we are directed toward images of selfhood. As participants in language, we are not passive recipients of meaning from a given linguistic system, however. We must bring forth meaning in our own lives. But we do this by mediating past and future as part of an ongoing language process. Our deepest efforts to do so are successful when they are open to receive the gift of meaning from the tradition. In such instances, to use Heidegger's phrase, "language speaks" and confers meaning and identity on us.[79] If receiving a gift is effortless, and becoming oneself is difficult; then appropriation of one's "I myself" through language and tradition is the graceful coming together of strenuous effort and effortlessness.[80]

The second step in describing hermeneutics as speculative ontology takes us from the linguisticality of understanding to the speculative structure of language. The term "speculation," as used in hermeneutics especially by Gadamer, does not mean idle reflection on what transcends empirical experience, nor does it mean risky investment in hopes of fast and sizable profits. Rather, the meaning is closer to the Latin *speculum* or "mirror." To speculate is to meditate or ponder on something that appears in a mirror and would otherwise be hidden from view.[81]

When Gadamer speaks of the speculative structure of language, he means that language is like a reflecting surface or medium of manifestation. It allows something otherwise hidden to appear. We have already seen how language allows the "I" to appear. In uttering the word "I," what is meant by the word appears, even if the appearance is not genuinely "I myself" but is

---

[79]Martin Heidegger, *On the Way to Language*, pp. 81, 88, 124.

[80]For a discussion of the conjunction of activity and passivity, see Buber, *I and Thou*, p. 62.

[81]The metaphor of mirroring is used differently here than it is in Rorty's *Philosophy and the Mirror of Nature*. In his use of the word, Rorty refers to the ability of the mind to represent accurately what lies outside it. That is not the speculative sense of meditating on what appears in a mirror and would otherwise be hidden. For a further discussion of the meaning of speculation, see Gadamer, *Truth and Method*, p. 423.

"they." And in speaking a language and receiving its central meanings, the "I" of authenticity appears as a power for appropriation. Without language, we could not know or show who "I" am.

Moreover, language is the manifestation of the world and ultimately of being itself. "World," here, does not mean the same thing as "physical environment." World is, rather, the context of meaningfulness that makes possible communication and understanding among humans.[82] World is the shared region of the "between" in which human institutions, relationships, and cultural expressions all have their being. Language manifests world in the sense that it allows shared understanding to come forth. This is not to say that language is a tool by which we designate the structure of the world. Hermeneutics opposes any instrumental view of language. Rather, language discloses world because the world is linguistic in its structure. World is a common ground for shared meanings. It appears linguistically.

Beyond the reference to world, the speculative structure of language allows being itself to appear. Our use of language in dialogue—participating in a shared world—always discloses a relation to being as such.[83] The relation is speculative, because we do not first have a relation to being, which is subsequently put into words. It is not that being as reality stands over against human subjects, who deploy words to get at objective reality. The linguisticality of understanding means that being appears in our linguistic disclosure of self and world. And the speculative structure of language means that our meditation on being does not transcend actual experience, but has an empirical "given" for interpretation: language embodies being; being is manifest in language.

Robert Scharlemann suggests that being is manifest in language in two ways. First, when we understand a sentence (or some other unit of language), being is manifest as meaning. Second, when we follow the meaning of the sentence to its referent (what the sentence is *about*), being is manifest as reality. The referent is extralinguistic, but it appears in language as the reality it is.[84]

For example, consider our everyday use of the English verb "to be." All verbs imply the verb "to be," because anything that "runs" or "dreams," and so on, also "is." In forming and understanding sentences, such as "John is a true friend," *being appears as meaning* in the connection between the subject and the predicate. If someone then asks, "Is that one John?" and I answer (truly), "Yes," *being appears as reality* on "John" in the connection between percept and thought. In each case (the appearance of being first as meaning and second as reality), the activity of understanding is open to

[82]Heidegger, *Being and Time*, pp. 91–95, 114–22.

[83]Gadamer, *Truth and Method*, pp. 414–15.

[84]The appearance of being as meaning and reality is analyzed by Scharlemann in *The Being of God*, pp. 23–24, 48.

being as a connection of particularity and universality. The linguisticality of understanding allows being to appear. This means that whereas we *think* universals and *perceive* particulars, we *understand* being (as the connection between universals and particulars).

These simple examples point out that being can appear both as the meaning of a sentence and as the connection between a name and a percept. But in these limited acts of being, we also have appearances of being itself—the ongoing process of connecting and total context of interconnectedness that constitutes meaningful reality. In these limited acts of understanding, we glimpse the universal understanding process in which each of us participates. Language discloses and makes possible the understanding of being that is always going on.

Do we ever see the whole of being all at once? Such a possibility must rely on a limited appearance of being taking on universal significance, thereby becoming a symbol of being. The symbol of being would have to present what is always going on in a unified image that could evoke a sense of the whole. Given the linguisticality of understanding, perhaps one symbol of being is "word," for it presents the medium in which the whole appears and without which being could not be.

How, then, are we to think the notion "being itself," if hermeneutics as speculative ontology is to advance a third step to a formulated meaning of being? Hermeneutics answers that we cannot think of being itself as a clear concept. The linguisticality of understanding means that being always appears here (as meaning or reality) and now (in a particular situation and context). Linguistic communities are historical. So are languages. No concept or symbol of being can abide as a permanent sign of being. The meaning of being is that no word conditioned by context can forever name the unconditioned dimension of being. Yet being does come to language, and contexts of meaning and reality are relatively stable and enduring. The temporality of language and understanding does not mean that speculative ontology is meaningless. It means that the meaning of being is bound up with time. Perhaps the best expression coined to name the meaning of being in hermeneutics is "being as . . . ."[85] *Being* is being *as* this manifestation of being. Being is not separate from its manifestation nor identical to it, for the conditioned meaning or reality that initially gives voice to the unconditioned may lose its power to do so. And conversely, new meanings or realities may appear that do disclose the whole of being symbolically. Gadamer likens this to the Platonic idea of the beautiful, which radiates through the particulars that manifest it and is never exhausted by its appearances.[86]

---

[85]See the essay by Scharlemann in this volume: "Being 'As Not'."
[86]Gadamer, *Truth and Method*, pp. 435–47.

Hermeneutics as Theology

The fourth version of hermeneutics is theological hermeneutics. It is different from the other three types in at least one important respect. With each of the other three, I derived the type from one of the three elements in the linguistic model of understanding: "I understand you." I connected the theory of interpretation to a preponderant interest in the objective meaning. I related practical philosophy to the theoretical focus on the understanding process. And finally I unfolded speculative ontology through turning to the subject of understanding. In contrast to those three, I do not refer theological hermeneutics to any one element in the structure. Rather, I suggest that hermeneutics appears as theology when the unconditioned depth of the structure breaks through the structure itself. Let me try to explain.

Understanding is the basic activity of relating the self to reality. The structure of understanding includes subject, act, and other. By engaging in understanding, the self is open to the other, to being in its appearance as meaning or reality. The three-term structure of understanding is a dynamic structure of interrelated elements: the subject is conditioned by the act in which it engages and the other being which it understands; likewise, the act of understanding is conditioned by the subject and other being; and so also, the other being is conditioned by the subject and act. The whole structure is temporal and dynamic—a structure of openness.

At the "depth" of the structure is the unconditioned unity of the three elements. The post-Kantian tradition of philosophical theology refers to the depth as the "unconditioned" unity of thinking (or here, understanding) and being. The unconditioned is the shared subject matter of ontology and theology. The classic statement "God is being itself" formulates the identity of God and the depth of the basic self-world structure. The metaphor of depth indicates the elusiveness of the unconditioned to formal thought, while it points us to the location of the unconditioned in relation to the elements of the structure of understanding. Theologians also use the terms *prius* of the subject-object split and *final ground and abyss* of self-world relations to refer symbolically to the unconditioned.

Tillich's theology provides us with the clearest and most useful guide to the relations of structure and depth in hermeneutics, or so I would argue. In what follows, I shall take my bearings from Tillichian theology and his interpretation of "God is being itself," although I do not woodenly follow Tillich.[87] I choose Tillich in part because the two sides of his method of correlation—analysis of human existence and interpretation of religious symbols—are mainstays for postmodern theological hermeneutics. His positions on both sides are represented by essays in this collection, and I shall discuss them later. Another reason for focusing on Tillich is that he avoids

---

[87]Paul Tillich, *Systematic Theology*, vol.1, *Being and God*, p. 235.

two common mistakes in thinking theologically about the topic that concerns us now: the relation between structure and depth of understanding.

The first error that Tillich avoids is to treat the unconditioned reality— God—as a supernatural being dwelling outside the world of time and space. This leads to the insuperable problems facing metaphysics in a postmetaphysical world of thought. For Tillich, the term "depth" does not refer to such a supernatural entity or metaphysical object. This is the position of supernaturalism or metaphysical theology.[88] It is unacceptable to hermeneutical theology as I have described it.

The second error from which Tillich steers clear is to identify the depth or final ground—God—with the identity of subject, activity of understanding, and other being *within the whole structure of understanding*. This is a more subtle error. It overlooks what Tillich calls the "abyss" separating the depth from the structure, or what Kierkegaard and Barth call the "infinite qualitative distinction" between God and world (depth and structure). God is entrapped within the structure of the whole and lacks freedom over against the structure. This is the position of idealism.[89] It too is untenable on the grounds of hermeneutics.

For Tillich, God is the depth of the structure of understanding as both ground and abyss. As ground of the whole, God is the ultimate source, sustaining power, and goal of the universal process of understanding. But these terms cannot be taken literally. As abyss of the whole structure of understanding, God cannot be caught in a definition, literal picture, or reflection on the whole. God *appears* in the dynamic process of selves understanding other beings. But God appears as what is *other than* any literal sense of God: namely, as the manifestation, word, or symbol of God.

In the postmodern paradigm of thought and experience, for which Tillich offers a theological road map, God *breaks into* the structure of a self understanding another self (or any other stand-in for a self, such as a text). Breaking into the structure, God appears as a sign for interpretation, not as a self-sufficient object or absolute synthesis. Hence hermeneutics becomes a crucial dimension of postmodern theology.

How should we understand theological hermeneutics in contrast to the other three types of hermeneutics? My thesis is that theological hermeneutics is the theoretical interest in the way we understand and interpret God's breaking into the structure of understanding. In the nature of the case, the depth of this structure—God—appears in all three elements of the structure as their ground and abyss. Since I have derived three types of hermeneutics from the three elements of understanding, I turn now to look at how God may appear in each of these types. The overarching point is that hermeneutics becomes theological when the depth of the structure of understanding

---

[88]Robert P. Scharlemann, *Reflection and Doubt in the Thought of Paul Tillich*, p. 29.
[89]Ibid.

breaks into the subject matter of any one of the other types of hermeneutics. When this happens, theological hermeneutics "overturns" the nontheological type of hermeneutics.[90] In each case, what distinguishes the theological from the nontheological type of hermeneutics is the appearance of God overturning the normal subject matter of hermeneutics. Let me specify this notion with regard to the three types of hermeneutics. To do so, I shall make use of Robert Scharlemann's analysis of the three ideas of God in the Western Christian tradition.[91] My proposal is that each of these ideas of God may be related to a type of hermeneutics.

THEOLOGICAL OVERTURNING OF THEORY OF INTERPRETATION

In hermeneutics as theory of interpretation, objective meaning is the focal element. The objective meaning is variously described as the author's intention (available through reconstruction and reexperiencing) and the intention of the text (available through analysis of formal properties of the text).

In interpreting most texts or actions, we search for the author's intention by aiming at understanding the purposes and "idea in mind" of a human author. For example, in writing a history paper on the unification of Germany by Bismarck, I may attempt to grasp the meaning of certain events by understanding the decisions made by Bismarck in terms of his purposes and thoughts about the whole question of German unity. The hermeneutical effort would be to grasp the individuality of Bismarck by reconstructing his intentions.

Searching for the formal structure of a text is different. Here one searches for linguistic patterns within a text. For example, in Lévi-Strauss's analysis of the myth of Oedipus, "units of meaning" are identified in the narrative and expressed in sentences. By grouping the units of meaning and noting the relations among the groups, Lévi-Strauss discovers a formal structure. Ricoeur adds another step to this procedure: the formal structure in turn signifies a meaning, the intention of the text.

Theory of interpretation provides the epistemological grounds for showing that understanding of objective meaning is possible and for justifying the methods for interpretation. It is "overturned" by the theological depth when it encounters a meaning that cannot be integrated into the system of interpretation. For example, if a text claims divine authorship or speaks in the name of God, efforts to discern authorial intention reach an unsurpassable limit. More specifically, in *Fear and Trembling*, Kierkegaard's reading of the biblical story of the divine command of Abraham to sacrifice Isaac

---

[90]See the essay in volume two of this collection by Scharlemann: "Being Open and Thinking Theologically."

[91]Scharlemann, *The Being of God*, pp. 57–60.

shows the limitations of human understanding in facing the dictates of a hidden God. The normal process of understanding the intentions of another are overturned when Abraham hears the horrible command of God.

In these cases and others (such as Bonaventure's interpretation of the book of nature), an objective meaning appears for understanding that simultaneously overturns the possibility of understanding and brings the limits of understanding into view. The idea of God that most directly connects to the appearance of the unconditioned as objective meaning is that of the *supreme being:* God as someone or something possessing divine properties.[92] God is thought of as a supreme and transcendent being who is strictly speaking not an entity or a person but the incomprehensible power of being itself.

THEOLOGICAL OVERTURNING OF PRACTICAL PHILOSOPHY

Consider the second type of hermeneutics: practical philosophy. In this case, the chief concern is the process of understanding, construed as the fundamental human activity of discerning authenticity within changing situations. Understanding is a dialogical process resembling practical wisdom, rather than scientific knowledge or technical know-how. The task of hermeneutics here is to recognize and articulate one's own authentic being through encountering the other in text and existence.

The theological depth of understanding appears within this type when the figure of authenticity becomes an enabling symbol for my appropriation and not simply a sketch or picture of the authenticity from which I am alienated. The difference lies in whether I am merely *shown* my authentic nature through a text or am *empowered* to become myself through the appearing symbol. The first possibility resides within the structure of understanding as practical wisdom; the second overturns it. No longer merely a matter of understanding, it is an instance of grace as enablement. The overturning here refers to the reversing of what is impossible for me.

Ordinarily, I may be able to recognize what I should do or become in this situation of life, but I may be unable to actualize it on my own. For instance, I may face a situation in which I am called on to act with courage. Let's say that some political refugees are being moved through my city and I am asked to put them up, at great risk to myself as well as to them, until further arrangements can be made. Let's say as well that I think it to be morally imperative that I consent. If so, I may understand that courage is demanded here; but I may be capable only of fear. A theological depth overturns my understanding if, in view of a certain symbol, I am encouraged to do the true thing, so that I am able freely to take the risk and to become

[92]Scharlemann discusses the first idea of God as supreme being in *The Being of God* on pp. 60–64 and 94–110.

authentic. If the symbol enables me to become myself by donating the power to do so, it is the appearance of God overturning the structure of practical wisdom.

In Bultmann's classic essay, "New Testament and Mythology," he ascribes this quality to the kerygma of Jesus as the Christ.[93] That the symbol enables one to be true is the test of its being a symbol of God.

The idea of God that illuminates the overturning of hermeneutics as practical philosophy is different from the first version of hermeneutics. It is not the idea of a supreme being but the idea of a *symbol of God*.[94] A theological symbol makes the being of God perceptible. It manifests the being of God by bringing about the authentic unity of self, activity, and other being. The symbol of God does not show what God is in any literal sense; it manifests what it means for God to be God and it makes appropriation of that meaning possible. For Tillich, what it means for God to be God is to be a living God by overcoming the threat of nonbeing. If so, then symbols that enable the individual courageously to overcome the appearances of nonbeing in guilt, fate and death, and meaninglessness, are symbols that manifest what it means for God to be God and empower a mode of being in faith.

THEOLOGICAL OVERTURNING OF SPECULATIVE ONTOLOGY

The third version of hermeneutics is speculative ontology. It appears when theoretical interest centers on the agent of understanding and uncovers the role of language and tradition. Language is the "true agent" in the sense that language speaks to and through the "I" of understanding. When language speaks, "I" understand. And insofar as language is the medium of being, interpretation of the being of language is interpretation of being as such. What is true about language as such is true about being as such. Hermeneutics becomes fundamental ontology.

My suggestion at this level is that the overturning of speculative ontology occurs when the activity of being, revealed through the depth of language, is traced to a hidden agent. Language is an event, ultimately the event of being. Through language the whole of being "is." The structure of being is disclosed in the activity of language. Being makes its appearance through the linguistic activity. Hermeneutics as speculative ontology articulates the structure of being through inquiry into the being of language. But who or what is the agent of the universal activity of the coming-into-being through language? Only the activity, not the agent, is visible to us in the linguistic process.

[93]Rudolf Bultmann, "New Testament and Mythology," in *New Testament and Mythology & Other Basic Writings*, ed. and trans. Schubert M. Ogden (Philadelphia: Fortress Press, 1984), p. 39.

[94]Scharlemann discusses the symbol of God in *The Being of God*, pp. 78–84 and 134–52.

If a text or event makes the hidden agent appear as the depth of the linguistic structure of being, then, I propose, we have the theological overturning of hermeneutics as speculative ontology. The theological depth appears in this version as the agent of the power of being. The agent is distinct from the activity of being: it is the agent of the activity, the one whose doing is "to be."

The idea that clarifies the agent of the universal linguistic activity of being is that of God as the *one agent in the many acts of being*. "God" names the one whose being is "to be." Scharlemann puts it this way: "On this reading 'God is' has the same kind of validity that 'light shines (*lux lucet*)' has . . . . 'To be' is what God, as God, does. Light cannot but *lucere*, and God cannot but *esse*."[95] When a text or event manifests this one agent, the depth of understanding appears in a third version.

An example of such an overturning occurs in Martin Buber's *I and Thou*. For Buber, the structure of being is the dialogue of I and you ("Ich und du"). God is not identical to the structure, but is the one "You" in every finite you. God is the "eternal you" or one agent in the many.[96] God never appears directly to our gaze or thought as the eternal you. God always appears, so to speak, indirectly, through an "otherness." Amid the otherness, God does appear. When we are drawn into the presence of a you—in our relations to nature, to the tradition and the spiritual beings inhabiting it, and to our other humans—so that the whole of being is concentrated into a unified act of I and you; we are brought into the presence of the eternal you, the hidden agent of all being. In Buber's words,

> In every sphere, in every relational act, through everything that becomes present to us, we gaze toward the train of the eternal You; in each we perceive a breath of it; in every You we address the eternal You, in every sphere according to its manner. All spheres are included in it, while it is included in none. Through all of them shines the one presence.[97]

So, too, does a single presence, as Buber puts it, shine through all three forms of theological overturning. I summarize my thesis concerning theological hermeneutics by addressing that point.

Earlier in this introduction I claimed that the hermeneutical problem arises when we encounter otherness and respond with understanding. Hermeneutics is the theoretical interest focusing on the understanding of unfamiliar meanings. It has the task of allowing the otherness of meaning to

[95]Scharlemann discusses God as the one agent in the many acts of being in *The Being of God*, pp. 64–78 and 111–34.
The quotation is on page 58.
[96]Buber, *I and Thou*, p. 123.
[97]Ibid., p. 150.

address our concerns through text or existence, while letting the other remain other. Furthermore, I proposed that the elementary structure of understanding has four elements: 1) the content of understanding (the meaning or intention communicated by the other), 2) the activity of understanding, 3) the agent of understanding, and 4) the depth of the three-termed structure. A paradigm sentence for the three-termed structure is "I understand you."

I extended my argument by claiming that when theoretical interest centers on the first element of the primary phenomenon, the content of understanding, we have hermeneutics as theory of interpretation; when we focus on the second element, the activity of understanding, we have hermeneutics as practical philosophy; and when we concern ourselves with the third element, the subject of understanding, we have hermeneutics as speculative ontology. Three basic types of hermeneutics refer to the three primary elements in a unitary phenomenon of understanding. The appearance of the fourth element, the depth of the unitary structure, signals the turn from philosophical to theological hermeneutics. With respect for this turn, I claim that the depth of the structure of understanding appears in the interpretive experience of "overturning." When a primary form of understanding (and thus a hermeneutical type) reaches a limit and is undercut by the manifestation of an infinite depth of meaning, the form of understanding is overturned. A philosophical reflection gives way to a theological one in view of the appearing depth. If philosophical hermeneutics engages in critical understanding and appropriation of otherness, then theological hermeneutics involves the critical interpretation of the otherness of otherness.

We deal here with a theological pattern of double negation, which points beyond itself. Initially, the appearance of otherness addresses our understanding; otherness negates the self (while preserving it) by opening the self to a new meaning. Philosophical hermeneutics reflects this. But in some texts or interpretive experiences, a depth of meaning appears. The depth overturns that appearing otherness (while preserving it) by opening it to an infinite dimension of meaning. Theological hermeneutics reflects this second negation, the overturning of otherness. What appears initially as other is overturned as not other, but an expression of the ultimate unity and solidarity in the being of things, in spite of differences. The otherness of the other is a figure of the unity within the diversity of being, which is seen as issuing from a common source and aiming at a common end.

Theological depth appears in theory of interpretation as a divine author or intention, overturning human authorship and intention. The idea of God clarifying this appearance of depth is the theistic idea of God as supreme being. Theological depth appears in practical philosophy as the empowering of authentic selfhood, overturning inauthenticity. The idea of God clarifying this appearance of depth is God as the symbol of God. Theological depth appears in speculative ontology as the hidden agent of the universal activity of being in language. The idea of God clarifying this depth is God as the one agent in the many acts of being. But in each case we understand "God as . . .".

Just as the three elements of the understanding process are interrelated, so, I claim, are these three ideas interrelated. Stated separately, they are abstractions from actual texts and actual events of understanding in which they may flow into one another and refuse to be kept separately. But all three may be considered symbols of the "otherness of the other," the divine that appears while remaining hidden in appearance. Unlike the dialectical theologians of the 1920s, I do not propose that God as the "wholly other" appears only as the negation of everyday forms of understanding and correlative hermeneutics. I suggest that God appears and that we can critically and tentatively discern the events of divine overturning: God appears in texts, when inscriptions of divine intention point us to the source and goal of all intentions. God appears in understanding texts and existence, when we come to be the ones we are authentically through symbols of the depth of meaning. God appears as the living agent of openness in the conversation of humankind, when the activity of being a self in the world of other selves manifests a higher subjectivity (as the playing of a game may show a hidden subject).

The otherness of the other appears through the overturning of familiar forms of understanding. It discloses the limits and depths of the forms of understanding and the hermeneutical types constructed on them. The appearance of the otherness of the other points us to the one God of theology, but it does not press us into a single theological language or a single idea of God. Theological hermeneutics points us to the unity of the divine in relation to human understanding, but it preserves the pluralism of theological and religious discourse. As I understand it, theological hermeneutics discloses the hiddenness of the divine in the manifestness of linguistic understanding. The naming of God in our understanding of texts and existence shows us God as what is other than God but a manifestation of God.

In sum, I have argued that in understanding texts and existence, God may appear in three ways: (1) as divine intention or the otherness of the authorial or textual intention, (2) as empowerment of authentic existence or the otherness of inauthentic existence, or (3) as the one in the many or the otherness of the many events that happen. Divine manifestations appear on what is other than the understanding self, but they show themselves as what is other than the other—the otherness of the other. This hermeneutical naming of God as the depth of meaning points out the unity of the content of theological thinking without imposing unity on the act of theological thinking. It celebrates the diversity of theological discourses while pointing to the unity of the divine.

In conclusion, I submit that the highest task of theological hermeneutics is to think beyond the play of the differences among these ideas to the one God who appears through the various types of hermeneutical inquiry. To do so is an expression of our human freedom, an interpretation of our ultimate concern, and an action on behalf of human solidarity which preserves human difference. It is one thing to spell out a task for theological thinking. It is another thing to think responsively to the overturnings of texts and existence in ever new situations that call for understanding. I hope that the classic essays included here will assist our hermeneutical efforts.

INTRODUCTION TO SCHLEIERMACHER'S "ACADEMY ADDRESSES"

Friedrich Schleiermacher (1768–1834) is best known today as the father of modern Protestant theology. During his lifetime, however, the theologian was also known as a preacher, classical philologist, Plato translator, and permanent secretary of the Berlin Academy of Sciences. His magnum opus, *The Christian Faith* (1821–22, 1831), is a meticulously worked out Christian dogmatic theology. It presents Christianity as an individual version or configuration of the original and religious "feeling of absolute dependence." Schleiermacher's theology is thoroughly modern because it reconstructs Christian dogma with reference to this primordial experience of an immediate awareness that precedes and unites both knowing and doing. By so tracing theological statements back to their ground in experience, Schleiermacher was able to create a dogmatic system that was critically sound and epistemologically respectable. His theology established the *Wissenschaftslichkeit* of the discipline and presented a viable alternative to supernaturalists.

Born the son of a Reformed army chaplain who converted to the Moravian Brotherhood, Schleiermacher attended the Moravian school at Niesky (1783–85) and the Moravian seminary at Barby (1785–87). Repelled by the narrow thought at the seminary, Schleiermacher nonetheless remained committed to the subject matter of theology and devoted to the authentic form of Moravian Christian piety. In 1787, he went on to study theology at the University of Halle, where he would eventually teach theology from 1804 until Napoleon disbanded the university in 1807. In 1810, he was called to the University of Berlin, where he remained for the rest of his life, serving both as professor of theology and pastor at Trinity Church. Since he was enormously respected, Schleiermacher's funeral in Berlin (1834) was attended by 20,000 to 30,000 people (according to the estimate of Leopold von Ranke).

`Schleiermacher is also credited with initiating fully modern hermeneutical inquiry. Obviously, he was not the first modern thinker to reflect in an orderly way about the problem of interpretation. But he is responsible for raising the problem of hermeneutics to universal scope. Prior to Schleiermacher, theory of interpretation was discussed by classical philologists and biblical exegetes, among others. But in each case, the theory was constructed to serve specific practical applications either in the classics of Greco-Roman antiquity or in the sacred Scriptures of Judeo-Christian tradition. No general theory of interpretation existed, only loose collections of rules and principles tied to specific texts. By elevating the problem of *understanding as such* to a theoretical level, Schleiermacher opened a new chapter in the history of hermeneutics.

Schleiermacher did not consider hermeneutics as a theoretical tool to sharpen our understanding of particular texts. On the contrary, he thought that hermeneutics should assume that misunderstanding, not understanding, usually occurs. Understanding is the goal, not the starting point, of hermeneutics. By assuming initial misunderstanding, he therefore provoked the universalization of hermeneutics. For it meant that interpretations must be measured against a theoretical norm of what it means to understand anything at all, rather merely against classical interpretations from the tradition. Since no such abstract norm of understanding had been articulated, Schleiermacher took on the theoretical tasks of working out a normative description of understanding and spelling out methods to avoid misunderstanding.

The universalizing of hermeneutics as a theory of understanding was consistent with the critical spirit of Kant's philosophy. Just as Kant had turned attention from the contents of knowledge to the conditions of the possibility of knowledge, so Schleiermacher turned discussion from the meaning of texts to how understanding the meaning of texts is possible. Only then can the problem of working out appropriate methods be addressed. With Schleiermacher, a genuinely modern hermeneutical theory makes its appearance.

In universalizing the problem of understanding, Schleiermacher elevated hermeneutics from its previous status of a theoretical aid within the study of ancient languages to an autonomous theoretical discipline. This was possible because problems encountered in understanding ancient texts are not essentially different from difficulties involved in understanding a friend in conversation. Both concern understanding the meaning of linguistic and gestural signs. The problem of hermeneutics is one of grasping meaning in discourse; hermeneutics therefore assumes the reader's familiarity with the historical language of the discourse in question. But hermeneutics has its own principles and methods apart from the particular subject matter or the traditional interpretations of the discourse in question.

The universality of the problem is rooted in the identity and difference of language and thought. There is no thought without discourse, according to Schleiermacher. Thought is formed and communicated through word. And reciprocally, word is the bearer of thought. Concretely, the reciprocity of thought and word means that I cannot form a thought, much less communicate one to another person, without finding the word or expression appropriate to it. This interdependence of thought and word signals a point of identity between them. Yet the same thought may be put into different expressions in one or many languages. For example, any number of expressions may be chosen to say "I am hungry"—some of them more fitting to the situation than others, of course. This detachability of thought from word indicates the difference between them.

For Schleiermacher, the hermeneutical problem appears precisely in the identity and difference between expression and thought. Since the *telos* or goal of discourse is to communicate thought and feeling, and since we ordinarily misunderstand discourse, the aim of interpretation must be to reproduce the thought that gave rise to the expression in the first place. Hermeneutics serves the task of reconstructing the author's intention in discourse. As any interpreter knows, that task is not easy—particularly when we are far removed from the situation in which the original expression bore the thought.

The model Schleiermacher proposes for successful understanding is the direct and immediate understanding that sometimes occurs among friends. In what he calls "significant conversations," the immediate presence of the speaker and the commonality of a shared life sometimes make it possible "to understand a series of thoughts as a moment of life which is breaking forth, as one moment set in the context of many others." Even sophisticated interpretation of ancient texts should aim for the same immediacy and directness of understanding. Hermeneutics should explain both how such understanding is possible and how it can be achieved.

Schleiermacher never placed hermeneutical theory at the top of his agenda as a critical thinker, however. As a theologian, New Testament exegete, and translator of Plato, the topic of hermeneutics arose naturally in the course of his work. But he wrote no book or systematic treatise on hermeneutics. He left only a series of writings that were not intended for publication. The early edition of these writings compiled by Friedrich Lücke has been replaced by the critical edition of Heinz Kimmerle (1959). It contains *Aphorisms* from 1805 and 1809, a draft of a paper from 1809 to 1810, a lecture compendium from 1819, marginal notes from 1828, and the two addresses to the Berlin Academy (reprinted here) from 1829.

In spite of the occasional nature of the writings, several key themes of Schleiermacher's hermeneutics are clearly evident in the two academy addresses that have been reprinted in this volume. First, hermeneutics is called for whenever "one encounters something strange in the way thoughts are being expressed in speech . . . ." The thought is to be made familiar by reproducing the original act of generating it. In that way, we "understand the text first as well as and then even better than its author."

Second, since thought is expressed in discourse, the object of interpretation—the linguistic expression—has a twofold reference: to the objective meaning in the context of the entire language and to the specific thought in the entire life of the author.

Third, the combination of language and thought in discourse demands in turn the combination of two tasks of interpretation: *grammatical inter-pretation,* which focuses on the common language itself, and *technical* or *psychological interpretation,* which tries to understand the author's individual style as the way she or he sets experience and thought into language.

Fourth, both comparative and divinatory methods are necessary for grammatical and psychological interpretation. Comparative methods place individual expressions in larger linguistic contexts in order to see how the individual thereby takes on specific meanings. Divinatory methods reproduce the author's experience of combining thoughts and images into a whole. In practice, grammatical interpretation gives greater emphasis to comparative techniques; psychological interpretation favors divinatory techniques. But full understanding requires employing both of these operations on both the grammatical and psychological sides of interpretation. Higher understanding is achieved when both sides are worked out and brought into agreement.

Behind each of these themes is the "uncontestable principle" on which hermeneutical rules are based: the whole of a discourse is understood from its parts, and the parts are understood from the whole. Understanding is a movement of mediation between part and whole, singularity and generality. Interpretation, or methodical understanding, consciously places parts and wholes in relation. With respect to the grammatical task, words are understood in the larger contexts of sentences, which are themselves understood in contexts of paragraphs, and so forth through larger wholes such as chapters, books, bodies of literature, genres, languages, and ultimately the infinity of thought. With respect to the psychological task, each work is understood in the context of the unfolding of the author's life as a whole. Both within the grammatical and psychological tasks, and between them, understanding moves back and forth between part and whole.

The *style* of a written work mediates between the psychological and grammatical sides of interpretation. The schooled grasp of an author's style relies equally on psychological insight into the unique way the author combines his or her thoughts and experiences and on grammatical analysis of the relation of the author's use of language to the received usages within the same genre or other sphere of literature. The ideal interpreter approaches a sense of the author's style through both routes and avoids one-sidedness. Such balanced treatment safeguards the objectivity of the author's intention while assuring access to his or her inner life.

By taking "significant conversation" as the model of understanding, Schleiermacher's hermeneutics relates its theoretical formulations back to a ground in living communication. Hermeneutics is a theory of understanding that takes the communication existing between friends as a standard for more sophisticated reflections on human texts. And just as Schleiermacher himself showed a genius for understanding and interpreting texts, he was skilled personally in the art of friendship—a true connoisseur of the human spirit.

One peculiarity of the "Academy Addresses" is that throughout they make reference to Friedrich Ast, author of *Grundlinien der Grammatik, Hermeneutik, and Kritik* (1808) and to Friedrich August Wolf, author of *Darstellung der Altertumwissenschaft nach Begriff, Umfang and Zweck*, in the journal *Museum der Altertumswissenschaft* (1808). Ast was a student of Friedrich W. J. von Schelling; for him the basic aim of understanding is to grasp the spirit of Greek antiquity and Christianity. The discernment of the spirit is possible only by taking hold of the whole view of life expressed in individual works. Ast's skills tended to be divinatory. Most importantly, Ast operated with a conception of the part-whole dialectic that Schleiermacher would also adopt. Wolf was the more scholarly of the two; he tended to the comparative techniques. He lacked an intuitive vision of the whole that could give insight into the unique way the author connects thoughts. Schleiermacher's own position is worked out with reference to their views. The attentive reader of the addresses should have no difficulty in separating Schleiermacher's theory from his comments about Ast and Wolf.

THE ACADEMY ADDRESSES OF 1829:
ON THE CONCEPT OF HERMENEUTICS, WITH REFERENCE TO F. A. WOLF'S INSTRUCTIONS AND AST'S TEXTBOOK
(1829)

Friedrich Schleiermacher

THE FIRST ADDRESS
AUGUST 12, 1829.[1]

Many, perhaps most, of the activities which make up human life may be carried out at one of three levels. One level is almost spiritless and entirely mechanical; the second is based on a wealth of experiences and observations; and the third is artistic in the true sense of the term. It seems to me that interpretation, too, is marked by these three levels, at least insofar as the word "interpretation" refers to understanding all foreign or strange speech. The first and lowest level we encounter daily, in the market place and in the streets as well as in many circles of society, wherever people converse about common topics in such a way that the speaker always knows almost immediately and with certainty what the other will respond, and language is tossed back and forth as a ball. Most of the time we seem to operate at the second level. This sort of interpretation is practiced in our schools and universities and in the commentaries of philologians and theologians, the two groups who have worked this field most extensively. The treasure of instructive observations and references found in their works adequately attests that many of them are true artists of interpretation. Even so, juxtaposed to this wealth of information we often find instances where difficult passages are given wild and arbitrary explanations and where some of the most beautiful passages are carelessly overlooked or foolishly distorted because of the interpreter's pedantic lack of sensitivity. But when a person who is not himself proficient in such matters is called upon to interpret, he needs, in addition to these treasures, a primer with a solid methodology that not only presents the fruits of masterful studies but also presents in reputable scientific forms the total range and foundations of the method. This is all the

[1]The editor of the Addresses has written in the margin: "Read in the plenary session on August 13, 1829—Jonas." On the different datings from Schleiermacher and Jonas, cf. Kimmerle's introduction to *Hermeneutics: The Handwritten Manuscripts* (Missoula, Montana: Scholars Press, 1977), pp. 24–25.

more necessary when that person is supposed to introduce inquisitive youth to the art of interpretation and to direct them in it. Consequently, for my own sake as well as for that of my audience, when I began to lecture on hermeneutics I searched for the best treatment of the method. But my search was in vain. Neither the numerous theological compendia—though many of them, such as Ernesti's book, are considered products of sound philological study—nor even the few purely philological essays on interpretation offered more than compilations of individual rules extracted from the researches of the masters.[2] Moreover, although these rules were sometimes clear, frequently they were quite ambiguous; and although they were now and again arranged in a helpful fashion, at other times the arrangement was unsatisfactory. I had high expectations when Fülleborn's philological encyclopedia, based on Wolf's lectures, was published.[3] But the few references to hermeneutics in it did not amount even to a sketch of a general hermeneutical theory. And since this work was directed specifically to the literature of classical antiquity, just as most handbooks are designed specifically for the study of the Holy Scriptures, I found myself no more content than before.

The essays mentioned in the title of this address are the most significant ones to appear since that time. Because Wolf is one of the best minds among us, and one of our most independent and creative philologians, and because Ast is trying to develop a philosophically-oriented philology, it would seem all the more instructive and useful to combine the strengths of both. Thus I thought it appropriate to follow their lead and to relate my own ideas about the task of interpretation to theirs.

Wolf intentionally avoids structuring his essay in a systematic form. This may be because he always takes care to avoid even the slightest hint of pedantry, preferring to leave to others the laborious and rather banal task of putting together the remarks he strews about so gracefully and elegantly, or it may be because he does not consider such a structure suitable for a lead article in a general journal that advances no systematic position of its own.[4] Ast, in contrast, considers a systematic form essential, and at the outset he asserts that no theory can be communicated scientifically without philosophical support.[5] Nonetheless, since Wolf assures us that he intended the contents of his essay to serve as an introduction for a philological encyclopedia, we may assume that he had thought through his statements with this

[2]In the history of Protestant theology since Flacius, *Clavis scripturae sacrae*, hermeneutical texts were published again and again.

[3]G. G. Fülleborn, *Encyclopaedia philologica* (Bratislava, 1798). Schleiermacher refers here to the 2nd edition, ed. D. J. Kaulfuss (Bratislava, 1805). See especially *Pars prima* I. *Grammatica*, II. *Critica*, III. *Hermeneutica*.

[4]The essay by Wolf opened the journal *Museum der Altertumswissenschaft*, ed. F. A. Wolf and Philip Buttmann, p. 79, n.1.

[5]See Friedrich Ast, *Grundlinien der Grammatik, Hermeneutik und Kritik*, (Landshut, 1808) pp. iii–viii.

purpose in mind, and we are justified in believing that his own theory is contained in this essay.[6]

Wolf puts together grammar, hermeneutics, and criticism as preparatory studies that provide entry to the philological disciplines per se, as the organon of the science of antiquity.[7] Ast, however, attempts to treat these same three disciplines as an appendix to his as yet unpublished outline of philology.[8] The two men are not so far apart. Even Ast's view, although he is not very clear about how the appendix is related to the main work, certainly means that his exposition of philology has led him to see the necessity of treating all three disciplines scientifically. No one would dare to deny that grammar, criticism, and hermeneutics are closely related, as these men maintain. But I would like to focus on hermeneutics, leaving the other two aside for the moment.

Certainly the works of classical antiquity, as masterpieces of human language, are the most excellent and worthy subject with which the art of interpretation normally has to deal. But it is undeniable, too, that many scholars have worked on other texts with great success, especially on the Christian Bible, which is not such a rich source for philologians. Were an encyclopedia for the study of these texts to be constructed, then without question hermeneutics, along with several other preparatory studies, would constitute an organon for Christian theology.[9] If, then, hermeneutics is important for Christian theology in the same way as it is for classical studies, then neither theological nor classical hermeneutics represents the essence of the matter. Rather, hermeneutics itself is something greater out of which these two types flow. To be sure, only these two, classical philologians and philological theologians, have contributed to our discipline. Juristic hermeneutics is a different matter. In the main it is concerned only with determining the extent of the law, that is, with applying general principles to particular cases which had not been foreseen at the time the principles were formulated.

Ast could almost induce me to assert that hermeneutics should be restricted to these two areas of study. For at the very beginning of his outline, where he describes the task of understanding, he leads us up to the very

---

[6]See Friedrich August Wolf, "Darstellung der Altertumswissenschaft nach Begriff, Umfang, Zweck und Wert," in *Museum der Altertumswissenschaft* ed. by F. A. Wolf and Philip Buttman (Berlin, 1809) pp. 3–6.

[7]Ibid., pp. 34–41. The term "organon" is found on p. 35.

[8]In "Zur Frühgeschichte der romantischen Hermeneutik," p. 438, n. 21, Patsch has noted that Schleiermacher evidently was not familiar with Ast's *Grundriss der Philologie*, which was published in Landshut in 1808, the same year as the *Grundlinien*.

[9]In his *Brief Outline of Theology* (1811, 1830), Schleiermacher drafted a theological encyclopedia. In addition to hermeneutics, Schleiermacher presents higher and lower criticism, knowledge of language, and mastery of the historical milieu as the organon of "exegetical theology," which is itself of fundamental importance for theology as a whole. (Cf. second edition, #110-146).

height of the unity of spirit and concludes that all our cultural activities are directed toward the unification of the Greek and Christian life. Thus hermeneutics, too, is directed to these two alone.[10] And if hermeneutics introduces, on the one hand, the science of antiquity and, on the other hand, Christian theology, then both studies would be carried out in the spirit of their unity. Moreover, there would be justification for hermeneutics to deal both with oriental texts, which represent the common point of origin for classical and Christian studies, and with romantic literature, which is clearly close to the unity of the two. Were oriental and romantic literature regarded as self-contained spheres in the way classical philosophy and Biblical studies are, we would require four hermeneutics, each constructed in a distinctive manner to serve as the organon for its particular discipline. Then, however, there would have to be a still higher organon common to all four.

Now although I want to ascend to this higher sphere, I am afraid of Wolf's shadow. In the few sentences he devotes to hermeneutics Wolf laments that this theory is by no means complete, and he notes that several investigations remain to be be undertaken before it can be established. These investigations do not lie on such dizzy heights, but in quite moderate zones. They deal with the meanings of words, the senses of sentences, and the coherence of statements. Yet at the same time he states, as a consolation, that this incompleteness is not too damaging, since the results of these investigations would contribute but little to awaken the talent of the interpreter or to enhance his intellectual ability. Then, as a warning, he refers to the distinction he makes between the type of theories advanced by the ancients, which actually facilitated a task (in this case, the task of interpretation), and those theories to which we moderns are inclined, which become engrossed in abstruse accounts of the nature and bases of the art and so fail to be of any practical value.[11] I fear he was referring to the distinction with which I began. In that case the purely scientific theory is one that will be of no use; the only useful theory is the one that offers an orderly collection of philological observations. Yet, on the one hand, it seems to me that this collection of observations requires something more in order that we may determine the extent to which the rules should be applied. The "modern" kind of theory certainly supplies that. On the other hand, I think that this "modern" kind, even though it deals only with the nature and bases of an art, will always exercise some influence on the practice of that art. But since I do not want to endanger the applicability of the theory, I prefer to leave the speculative guides to their soaring and follow the practical one.

These leaders explain above all (although only parenthetically and without much emphasis) that hermeneutics is the art of discovering with

[10]Ast, *Grundlinien*, pp. 167–171.
[11]Wolf, "Darstellung," p. 37.

necessary insight the thoughts contained in the work of an author.[12] And this next assertion salvages much of what I had hoped to gain by following the more speculative guides: Hermeneutics does not apply exclusively to classical studies, nor is it merely a part of this restricted philological organon; rather, it is to be applied to the works of every author. Therefore, its principles must be sufficiently general, and they are not to be derived solely from the nature of classical literature. Ast makes me uncomfortable with such a well-formulated statement, but even so I must try to draw its component parts together.

He begins with the concept of something foreign which is to be understood. Now, to be sure, he does not state this concept in its sharpest form. If what is to be understood were so completely foreign to the one trying to understand it that there was nothing in common between the two, then there would be no point of contact for understanding at all.[13] But I conclude that the concept holds in a relative sense. It then follows that, just as hermeneutics would be unable to begin its work if what is to be understood were completely foreign, so there would be no reason for hermeneutics to begin if nothing were strange between the speaker and hearer. That is, understanding would always occur immediately upon reading or hearing, or it would be already given in a divinatory manner, and understanding would take place by itself.

I am quite content to restrict the application of hermeneutics to the area between these two extremes. But I must also admit that I want to claim this entire area for it, meaning that wherever one encounters something strange in the way thoughts are being expressed in speech, one is faced with a task which can be solved only with the help of a theory, presupposing of course some common point between the speaker and the one who is to understand.

My two guides, however, restrict me at several points. The one states he is interested only in understanding authors, as though the same problems do not arise in conversation and direct speech. The other wants to restrict what is "foreign" to something written in a foreign language, and, more specifically, to works marked by genius [*Werke des Geistes*] a sphere even narrower than that of authors in general.[14] But we can come to learn a great deal from works which have no outstanding intellectual content, for example, from stories narrated in a style similar to that normally used in ordinary conversation to tell about minor occurrences, a long way from artistic historical writing, or from letters composed in a highly intimate and casual style. Even such cases as these present equally difficult tasks for the work of hermeneutics. Moreover, I submit that Wolf's view is really not much different than Ast's, and were I to ask him whether such authors as

---

[12]Ibid.

[13]Ast, *Grundlinien*, pp. 167–68.

[14]See Wolf, "Darstellung," pp. 34–35; Ast, *Grundlinien*, pp. 173–174.

newspaper reporters or those who write newspaper advertisements are to be treated by the science of interpretation, he would not give me a very friendly response. Although many of these materials are such that there can be nothing foreign between the author and the reader, there are exceptions, and I cannot understand why these strange elements can or must be made intelligible in some way other than more artistic writings. Further, there are other cases (epigrams, for example, that are not significantly different from newspaper articles) which are impossible to differentiate into two classes, or two different methods or theories. Indeed, I must reiterate that hermeneutics is not to be limited to written texts. I often make use of hermeneutics in personal conversation when, discontented with the ordinary level of understanding, I wish to explore how my friend has moved from one thought to another or try to trace out the views, judgments, and aspirations which led him to speak about a given subject in just this way and no other. No doubt everyone has such experiences, and I think they make it clear that the task for which we seek a theory is not limited to what is fixed in writing but arises whenever we have to understand a thought or series of thoughts expressed in words.

Nor is the hermeneutical task restricted to a foreign language. Even in our native language, and without considering the various dialects of the language or the peculiarities of a person's speech, the thoughts and expressions of another person, whether written or spoken, contain strange elements. Indeed, I readily acknowledge that I consider the practice of hermeneutics occurring in immediate communication in one's native language very essential for our cultured life, apart from all philological or theological studies. Who could move in the company of exceptionally gifted persons without endeavoring to hear "between" their words, just as we read between the lines of original and tightly written books? Who does not try in a meaningful conversation, which may in certain respects be an important act, to lift out its main points, to try to grasp its internal coherence, to pursue all its subtle intimations further? Wolf—especially Wolf, who was such an artist in conversations, but who said more by intimation than by explicit statement, and even more by innuendo—would not deny that these were being understood by his listeners in an artistic way, so that he could count on the audience always knowing what he meant. Should the way we observe and interpret experienced, worldly-wise and politically shrewd persons really differ from the procedure we use with books? Should it be so different that it would depend on entirely different principles and be incapable of a comparably developed and orderly presentation? That I do not believe. On the contrary, I see two different applications of the same art. In the one application certain motives are more prominent, while others remain in the background; and in the others the relationship is just the reverse. In fact, I would go even further and assert that the two applications are so closely related that neither can be practiced without the other. To be specific, however, and to deal with matters which are most similar to the interpretation of written works, I would strongly recommend diligence in interpreting significant conversations. The immediate presence of the speaker, the living expression that proclaims that his whole being is involved, the way the thoughts in a conversation develop from our shared life, such factors stimulate us, far more than some solitary observation of an isolated text, to understand a series of thoughts as a moment of life which is breaking forth, as one moment set in the context of many others. And this dimension of understanding is often slighted, in fact, almost completely neglected, in interpreting authors. When we compare the two, it would be better to say that we see two parts rather than two forms of the same task. To be sure, when something strange in a language blocks our understanding, we must try to overcome the difficulty. But even if we do come to understand this strange element, we may still find ourselves blocked because we cannot grasp the coherence of what someone is saying. And if neither approach is able to overcome the difficulty, the problem may well go unsolved.

To return then to the explanations we mentioned above, I must first lodge a protest against Wolf's claim that hermeneutics should ascertain the thoughts of an author with a necessary insight.[15] I do not mean to suggest that I consider this demand too stringent. To the contrary, for many cases it is not too stringent at all. Yet I am afraid that by stating the task in these terms, many cases for which this formulation of the problem is simply not appropriate would be passed over, and I do not want them to be overlooked. There are, of course, many instances in which one can prove that a given word in its context must mean "this" and nothing else, although such proof is difficult to find without recourse to those investigations into the nature of word-meanings which Wolf, perhaps too summarily, has rejected. And, taking up a position somewhere outside of this circle, one may put together a number of these elementary proofs in order to arrive at a satisfactory proof of the sense of a sentence. But how many other cases there are—and they are crucial for interpreting the New Testament, especially—where a necessary insight is impossible, and interpreters come to equally probable meanings according to their points of view. Even in the field of criticism it often happens that some know no other way to oppose the result of a thorough investigation than to claim that some other meaning is still "possible." Of course, in the long run such remonstrances do not accomplish very much, but until each and every such possibility has been definitively eliminated, there can be no talk of a necessary insight. And if we go further and remember how advisable it is to undertake the difficult task of establishing the coherence of thoughts in the larger sections of the text, and to ascertain the hidden supplements of, as it were, lost intimations, then understanding is not only, as Wolf portrays it, a matter of collating and summarizing minute

[15]See Wolf, "Darstellung," p. 37.

historical moments. Rather it becomes sensitive to the particular way an author combines the thoughts, for had those thoughts been formulated differently, even in the same historical situation and the same kind of presentation, the result would have been different. In the such cases we may be fully convinced of our view, and it may even be convincing to our contemporaries who are engaged in similar studies. Nonetheless, it would be futile to try to pass this account off as a demonstration. This is not said to disparage such studies, but in this area, especially, we may cite the otherwise rather paradoxical words of a distinguished scholar who has only recently been taken from us: an assertion is much more than a proof.[16] Moreover, there exists a completely different sort of certainty than the critical one for which Wolf is praised, namely, a divinatory certainty which arises when an interpreter delves as deeply as possible into an author's state of mind (*Verfassung*).[17] Thus it is often the case, as the Platonic rhapsodist admits, though quite naively, that he is able to offer an outstanding interpretation of Homer, but frequently cannot shed light on other writers, whether poets or prosaists.[18] For, provided the knowledge is available to him, an interpreter can and should show himself to be equally competent in every area related to language and to the historical situation of a people and of an age. Yet, just as in life we are most successful in understanding our friends, so a skillfull interpreter is most successful in correctly interpreting an author's process of drafting and composing a work, the product of his personal distinctiveness in language and in all his relationships, when the author is among those favorites with whom he is best acquainted. For works of other authors, however, an interpreter will content himself with knowing less about these things; he will not feel ashamed to seek help from colleagues who are closer to them. In fact, it might be maintained that the entire practice of interpretation is to be divided as follows. One class of interpreters deals more with the language and with history than with personalities, granting equal consideration to all of the authors who write in a given language, regardless of the fact that the authors excel in different areas. A second class of interpreters, however, deals primarily with the observation of persons, regarding the language merely as the medium by which persons express their history and as the modality within which they exist. Thus each interpreter limits himself to that writer who is most readily understandable to him. This description may well be accurate except that writers of the latter group come less frequently to public attention because their work is less susceptible to polemical discussions, and they enjoy the fruits of each other's labors in quiet contentment. Still, several passages

---

[16]According to Patsch, "Zur Frühgeschichte der romantischen Hermeneutik," Schleiermacher is referring to Friedrich Schlegel, who died January 12, 1829.

[17]See Wolf, "Darstellung," pp. 240–241.

[18]See Plato, *Ion*, 530c–531d.

indicate that Wolf has by no means completely overlooked this side of interpretation, but, at least in part, has taken into account that certainty which we have described as more divinatory than demonstrable. It is worthwhile for us to investigate one of these places more closely.

In his *Compendium* Ast presents grammar, hermeneutics and criticism together as correlated disciplines without adding anything else as related knowledge. But we have no way of comprehending how they are interrelated because he relegates them to an appendix.[19] Wolf, however, does not consider these three alone sufficient for an organon of the science of antiquity, but adds to them fluency in style and the art of composition, which, because it includes poetry, involves classical meter.[20] At first glance this is very surprising. For my own part I would have been content to have understood the fluency in ancient styles of writing—and in the case of the languages of antiquity this is the only aspect of composition we are discussing—as the mature fruit of long-term studies in the science of antiquity. For one must have lived just as fully and vigorously in the ancient world as in the present, and one must be keenly aware of all the forms of human existence and of the special nature of the surrounding objects at that time, in order to excel in weaving such graceful patterns based on set formulae and to form in Roman and Hellenistic ideas works which can affect us deeply even today, and to reproduce these in the most ancient way possible. How then can Wolf demand such art from us as the admission fee, so to speak, to the shrine of the science of antiquity? And by what honest means are we supposed to obtain it? Assuming there is no magical way, I see no other than that of tradition and that of adopting a procedure that is, fortunately, not merely imitative, but also divinatory—methods that would ultimately lead to fluency as the fruits of study. This path leads us in a kind of circle, for we cannot gain a style of writing Latin—for which we must know Greek as well—in the same immediate way as those who, by virtue of having Latin and Greek as their native languages, developed their stylistic fluency from their immediate existence and not from such studies as these. Nor had I expected Wolf to demand a knowledge of meter. It seemed to me that this was one of the more specialized aspects of the science of antiquity rather than an essential part of the ancient theory of art. It had as much to do with the science of orchestration as with the science of poetry, and the theory of prose rhythm and declamation which was drawn from it represents the whole development of the national temper as shown in the character of artistic movements.

But let us put meter aside, for regardless of what is involved in one's fluency in ancient composition, the true key to this Wolfian research is the following: Wolf does not require this fluency directly for the specialized disciplines of the science of antiquity, but for hermeneutics, that is, for

[19]See n. 8 above.
[20]Wolf, "Darstellung," pp. 42–44.

gaining a correct and complete understanding in the higher sense of the term. And although he does not especially emphasize it, it is obvious, with respect to both criticism and meter, that his entry to the shrine of the science of antiquity is founded on two steps. The lower step is grammar, in his view the foundation of hermeneutics and criticism, and the fluency of style. The higher step is hermeneutics and criticism. Now just as Wolf sets forth his grammar in great detail and not in the elementary way which we could use with beginning students, so, too, we may be certain that by fluency of style he is not referring to the Latin exercises done in our high schools, which are skilled imitations and applications of grammatical knowledge. But since it is also certain that only a person who had worked through the entire literature of antiquity could perform the actual operation which the ancients did in the two languages in a free and individual fashion, is it perhaps possible that this great scholar is referring to something other than a knowledge of the various forms of presentation, their limits and possibilities, which is acquired by actual practice?[21] And this other element is of great influence on that less demonstrable aspect of the art of interpretation which is oriented toward the internal intellectual activity of an author. Herewith a new understanding of this side of interpretation is opened to us, and surely Wolf had it in mind, even though he did not give it much emphasis at the beginning of his exposition.[22]

In essence, then, the matter is as follows. When we view, on the one hand, the different forms of outstanding oratorical art and, on the other hand, the different types of style used for scientific and commercial activities which have developed in a language, it is evident that the entire history of literature is divided into two contrasting periods, the characteristics of which may later reappear simultaneously, but only in a subordinate fashion. The first period is that in which these forms are gradually developed; the second is that in which they predominate. And if the task of hermeneutics is to reproduce the whole internal process of an author's way of combining thoughts, then it is necessary to know with as much certainty as possible to which of these two periods he belongs. For if an author belongs to the first period, he was creating purely from his own resources, and from the intensity of his production and his linguistic power we may conclude not only that he produced a distinctive work, but that to a certain extent he originated a new type of work, which persists in the language. The same thing may be said, although not in such strong terms, about every author who especially modified these forms, introduced new elements in them, or founded a new style in them. However, the more a writer belongs in the second period and so does not produce the form but composes work in forms which are already established, the more we must know these forms in order

[21]Ibid., pp. 36–37.
[22]Ibid., pp. 42–44.

to understand his activity. Even in the initial conception of a work, an author is guided by the established form. Its power affects the arrangement and organization of the works, and its particular laws close off certain areas of language and certain modifications of ideas, and opens up others. Thus the power of the form modifies not only the expresssion, but also—and the two can never be fully separated—the content. Consequently, an interpreter who does not see correctly how the stream of thinking and composing at once crash against and recoil from the walls of its bed and is diverted into a course other than it would have taken by itself cannot correctly understand the internal movement of the composition. Even less can he ascertain the author's true relation to the language and to its forms. He will not become aware of how an author may have more fully and forcefully expressed the images and thought which inspired him had he not been restricted by a form which in many respects conflicted with his personal individuality. He will not know how to assess correctly an author who would not have ventured very far into a genre had he not stood within the protective and guiding power of a form, for a form may aid as well as limit an author. And of the two kinds of authors he will not sufficiently appreciate the one who, rather than struggle with a form, is stimulated just as freely by an existing form as if he had just produced it himself. This insight into an author's relationship to the forms imbedded in his literature is such an essential aspect of interpretation that without it neither the whole nor the parts can be correctly understood. There is no doubt, of course, that Wolf is right to maintain that an interpreter cannot "divine" correctly unless he himself has experienced how an author can work within the given limits and rules which exist in a language and how he may struggle against them.[23] And though here as elsewhere the comparative operation is set over against the divinatory, it cannot replace it completely. For how are we to find a point for beginning the comparative operation if it is not given by a proper search? And it is for this reason that meter is to be considered, since the emphasis on the syllables of a poetical composition is essentially a matter of choosing expressions and since the position of the thoughts is conditioned by the form. And it is in the influence which this exercises on their work that the different relations to the clearest passages are to be found. Yet in all the languages with which we are dealing here the relationship between the content and the form during the process of composition is essentially and in the main the same. And so I would not insist as strongly as Wolf that the training necessary for interpretation must be acquired solely from practice in the ancient languages.[24] Were that necessary, I would not be able to understand why the Roman language was able to supplant the Greek.

I want to underscore here a consideration about the character which

[23]Ibid.
[24]Ibid.

these exercises will always display when we apply ourselves to the thoughts in the literature of a given language, because several significant conclusions are to be developed from what has been written above. We must always remember that whenever we practice this art, we must remain conscious of both methods, the divinatory and the comparative. This rule is so universal that, on the one hand, we can regard an immediate understanding, in which no particular mediating activities can be detected, as a temporarily indistinguishable combination and interaction of the two methods and, on the other hand, we can see that even the most complex applications of the art of interpretation involve nothing other than a constant shifting from the one method to the other. In this interaction the results of the one method must approximate more and more those of the other. Otherwise, very few satisfactory conclusions can be gained. This distinction between the more grammatical aspect, which aims at understanding the discourse in terms of the totality of language, and the more psychological aspect, which aims at understanding the discourse in terms of a continuous production of thoughts, is based on the following premise. Just as both methods are necessary to obtain complete understanding, so every combination of the one method will be supplemented by further applications of the other.

We must ask, then, whether these two methods apply to both the grammatical and technical aspects of interpretation, or whether each method is appropriate for only one aspect? For example, when Wolf, on the basis of the role he assigns to meter and fluency in composition, tries to argue that only a comparative procedure can be used for the more psychological aspect of interpretation, is he implying that the other, more grammatical aspect, must be furthered by the divinatory method? His essay does not provide us with a direct and definitive answer to this question. But his investigations into the meanings of words and the senses of sentences, although not organized in a very helpful fashion, evidently have to do only with the grammatical aspect of interpretation and require a comparative method.[25]

An examination of the task itself leads to the same conclusion. All grammatical difficulties are overcome by a comparative operation alone, by repeatedly comparing what is already understood with what is not yet understood, so that what is not understood is confined within even narrower bounds. And, on the other side, the finest fruit of all esthetic criticism of artistic works is a heightened understanding of the intimate operations of poets and other artists of language by means of grasping their entire process of composition, from its conception up to the final execution. Indeed, if there is any truth to the dictum that the height of understanding is to understand an author better than he understood himself, this must be it. And in our literature we possess a considerable number of critical works which have

[25]Ibid., p. 37.

performed this task with good success.[26] But how is such success possible except by a comparative procedure which helps us gain a thorough understanding about where and how an author has gone beyond or lagged behind others, and in what respects his kind of work is related to or different from theirs? Nonetheless, it is certain that the grammatical side of interpretation cannot dispense with the divinatory method. For whenever we come upon a gifted author (*genialer Autor*) who has for the first time in the history of the language expressed a given phrase or combination of terms, what do we want to do? In such instances only a divinatory method enables us rightly to reconstruct the creative act that begins with the generation of thoughts which captivate the author and to understand how the requirement of the moment could draw upon the living treasure of words in the author's mind in order to produce just this way of putting it and no other. But here, too, our conclusions will be uncertain unless the comparative operation is applied to the psychological aspect.

Therefore, we must answer the question before us as follows. If our first reading of a text does not immediately give us a certain and complete understanding, then we must employ both methods in both aspects—though naturally in varying degrees according to the difference of their objects— until the result approximates as nearly as possible that of immediate understanding. We surely must accept what I have said about one class of interpreters inclining more to the psychological and another to the grammatical aspect. We know that many a virtuoso in grammatical interpretation gives scant attention to the internal process of combining thoughts in one's mind and feeling. And, vice versa, there are fine interpreters who reflect about the special relationship of a text to its language only minimally and then only in those rare cases when they are forced to consult a dictionary. If we take this into account and apply it equally to the two methods, we must conclude that just as we can regard immediate and instantaneous understanding as having arisen in either way, thus directing our attention to the author's creativity or to the objective totality of the language, so we can regard the successful completion of a more artful method in interpretation in these same terms. We can now say that all of the points of comparison, for the psychological as well as for the grammatical aspects, have been brought together so perfectly that we no longer need to consider the divinatory method and its results. We can then add that the divinatory operation has been conducted with such thoroughness and precision that the comparative method is rendered superfluous. Likewise, the internal process has been made so transparent by the divinatory and the comparative methods that, since what has been intuited is a thought, and there is no thought without words, the entire relationship between the production of the thoughts and its

[26]Here the basic hermeneutical principle of the "psychological" interpretation of "composition" is interpreted as an inner "process."

formation in language is now fully and immediately evident. But the reverse would also be true.

Yet, even as I am dealing here with the completion of the operation, I am driven back almost involuntarily to the very beginning in order to encompass the whole within these two points. This very beginning, however, is the same as when children begin to understand language. How, then, do our formulae apply to these beginnings? Children do not yet have language but are seeking it. Nor do they know the activity of thinking, because there is no thinking without words. With what aspect, then, do they begin? They do not yet have any points of comparison, but they acquire them gradually as a foundation for a comparative operation that, to be sure, develops remarkably fast. Are we not tempted to say that each child produces both thinking and language originally, and that either each child out of himself by virtue of an inner necessity engenders them in a way that coincides with the way it had happened in others or gradually as he becomes capable of a comparative procedure he approximates others. But in fact this inner movement toward producing thoughts on one's own, although initially stimulated by others, is the same as that which we have called "the divinatory." This divinatory operation, therefore, is original, and the soul [*die Seele*] shows itself to be wholly and inherently a prescient being [*ein ahndendes Wesen*]. But with what an enormous, almost infinite, power of expression does the child begin! It cannot be likened to later developments, nor to anything else. The two ways must be grasped simultaneously as essentially one, since each supports the other, and only gradually are the two distinguished, as the language objectifies itself by fixing particular words to objects and to images which themselves become increasingly clear and certain. But at the same time the act of thinking is able—how should I say—to use these in order to reproduce them, or to reproduce them in order to grasp them. These first activities of thinking and knowing are so astonishing that it seems to me that when we smile at the false applications which children make of the elements of language they have acquired—and to be sure often with all too great consistency—we do so only in order to find consolation or even to take revenge for this excess of energy which we are no longer able to expend.

Viewed in this light, whenever we do not understand we find ourselves in the same situation as the children although not to the same degree. Even in what is familiar we encounter something that is unusual in the language, when a combination of words does not become evident to us, when a train of thought strikes us as odd, even though it is analogous to our own, [or] when the connection between the various parts of a train of thought or its extension remains uncertain and hovers unsteadily before us. On such occasions, we can always begin with the same divinatory boldness. Therefore, we ought not simply contrast our present situation to those immense beginnings in childhood, for the process of understanding and interpretation is a whole which develops constantly and gradually, and in its later stages we must aid each other more and more, since each offers to others points of comparison and similarities which themselves begin in this same divinatory way. This is the gradual self-discovery of the thinking self. But, just as the circulation of blood and the rhythm of breathing gradually diminish, so the soul, too, the more it possesses, becomes more sluggish, in inverse proportion to its receptivity. This is true of even the most active people. Since each person, as an individual, is the not-being of the other, it is never possible to eliminate non-understanding completely. But although the speed of the hermeneutical operation diminishes after its early stages, a more deliberate movement and a longer duration of each aspect enhance this process.

Finally there comes that period when hermeneutical experiences are collected and become guidelines—for I prefer to call them this rather than rules. A technical theory, however, cannot develop, as should be obvious from what I have said, until we have penetrated the language of an author in its objectivity and the process of producing thoughts, as a function of the life of the individual mind, in relationship to the nature of thinking. For only in these terms can the way thoughts are combined and communicated and the way understanding takes place be explicated in a fully coherent fashion.

Yet in order to clarify fully the relationship between these two operations, we must give due attention first to a notion which seems to give Ast the advantage over Wolf, although until we fully determine the form of hermeneutics from it, it seems to be more a discovery than an invention. This is the notion that any part of a text can be understood only by means of an understanding of the whole, and that for this reason every explanation of a given element already presupposes that the whole has been understood.[27]

THE SECOND ADDRESS
OCTOBER 29, 1829.

The hermeneutical principle which Ast has proposed and in several respects developed quite extensively is that just as the whole is understood from the parts, so the parts can be understood only from the whole. This principle is of such consequence for hermeneutics and so incontestable that one cannot even begin without using it.

Indeed, a great number of hermeneutical rules are to a greater or lesser extent based on it. Each word has a certain range of meanings, but what part of this range occurs in a given passage and what parts are excluded are determined by the other parts of speech in the sentence and especially by those parts of speech most closely or organically related to it. This means that the word is understood both as a part of a whole range of meanings and as a special meaning with a given context. This is the case for words that have a

---

[27]Ast, *Grundlinien*, pp. 171–72.

variety of so-called meanings, words that are capable of different levels of meaning, and words that are emphasized to varying degrees.

Accordingly, the rule that a word which occurs twice in the same context should be explained the same way in both instances is sound, for it is improbable that an author would have used the word differently in the two instances.[28] This rule, however, holds only under the condition that the sentence in which the word occurs the second time can legitimately be considered a part of the same context. In certain circumstances an author will use a word differently in a new context, just as he would in another work. So, if the meaning a word has the first time determines the meaning it has in its second appearance, the part is understood from the whole, for the explanation depends on our certainty that this section of the text is, with reference to the word in question, a whole. Likewise, the proper way to treat parallel instances of a word is to select only those passages that provide a similar context for explaining the word in question. That is, they represent parts of the same whole. Insofar as this is not certain the resulting explanation will be questionable.

Although this account is quite intelligible—and it could be confirmed by additional examples—it is still difficult to decide how far one should go in applying this rule. Just as the word in a sentence is a particular and a part, so, too, is the sentence in the larger context of a text. Consequently, we very easily get completely mistaken ideas [*Vorstellungen*] from sentences that have been extracted from their context and inserted into another as snippets or as sayings. The use of such citations is so common that it is only astonishing that trust in them has not become universal. Of course, it is another matter entirely with statements that may be appropriately used as aphorisms. Even so, taken in isolation, these, too, always seem quite vague, and their precise meaning comes from the context into which they are introduced. Actually, much of their special charm is due to their ability to enrich such a variety of contexts, and though they more easily stand alone because of their aphoristic form, the context modifies their meaning each time they are used.

To proceed a step further, this rule may be applied to combinations of sentences. No doubt this is the reason, for example, that we Germans are so often accused of not understanding persiflage, which always extends through a series of sentences. Such a misunderstanding is the author's fault when he fails to provide any indicators and the serious reading seems altogether adequate; but it is the reader's fault when he overlooks the clues present in the text and fails to discern how this set of sentences is related to the whole.

Yet the problem is by no means limited to such instances as persiflage.

---

[28]See Johann August Ernesti, *Institutio Interpretis Novi Testamenti,* first edition (Leipzig, 1761) pt. I, sec. 1, chap. 1, #4-5.

Wherever the understanding of a series of sentences and their interconnection is in question, one must first and foremost know the whole to which they belong. Indeed, since this case, too, can be traced back to the original principle, the principle must hold universally. In fact, every highly coherent set of sentences is governed by a dominant concept, though the way this concept "governs" the text will vary according to the type of work. This concept, just as a word in a given sentence, can be fully determined only when it is read in its context. That is, any set of sentences, large or small, can be understood correctly only in terms of the whole to which it belongs. And just as the shorter sets of sentences are conditioned by larger sets, so, too, these larger sets are conditioned by still larger ones. Thus the obvious conclusion is that any part can be completely understood only through the whole.

When we consider the task of interpretation with this principle in mind, we have to say that our increasing understanding of each sentence and of each section, an understanding which we achieve by starting at the beginning and moving forward slowly, is always provisional. It becomes more complete as we are able to see each larger section as a coherent unity. But as soon as we turn to a new part we encounter new uncertainties and begin again, as it were, in the dim morning light. It is like starting all over, except that as we push ahead the new material illumines everything we have already treated, until suddenly at the end every part is clear and the whole work is visible in sharp and definite contours.[29]

We cannot quarrel with Ast when he tries to overcome this constant backtracking and beginning anew by advising us to begin with a presentiment of the whole. But how are we to gain such a presentiment?[30] Of course, if we limit our task to written works, as both Wolf and Ast apparently intended, it is possible to gain such a presentiment. Prefaces, which are seldom given in oral presentations, are more helpful than mere titles. Moreover, we demand that certain types of books present summaries of the sections and tables of contents, not only to allow readers to locate particular points easily but even more to provide them with an overview that enables them to see how the work is structured and to identify these key words which govern the various parts. The more help of this kind we have, the easier it is to follow Ast's advice. And even when such aids are entirely missing, if only the text is before us, we can resort to that practice, so distasteful to look at, of thumbing through the pages of a book before reading it in earnest. If one is lucky or has a knack for this sort of thing, it may be of considerable use in compensating for the lack of help from the author. Nonetheless, when I think of the people of antiquity, I am almost ashamed to say such a thing. They were condemned to use the same rules of

[29]Ast, *Grundlinien*, pp. 186–87.
[30]See note 14 above.

understanding as we, but they knew nothing of such aids or tricks. Indeed, some of the most outstanding prose works were so composed that such aids were not only omitted but would have been disdained and the unavoidable external divisions of the work were not related at all to the actual organiza-tion from which a presentiment of the whole could be gained. In poetic works anything hinting of such aids is almost laughable. Finally, there are still a few among us who are sufficiently noble to let others read to them, and they do not thumb through the pages, nor are they helped by tables of contents. How, then, are we supposed to arrive at this presentiment of the whole without which an understanding of the parts is impossible? We must try to answer this question in the most general way.

It must first be said that not every text is a whole in the same sense. Some texts are only loose series of statements. In these cases understanding a particular part in terms of the whole is not possible at all. Other texts are only a loose succession of smaller units. In these cases particular points must be understood from the units of which they are a part. Which of these is the case with a given discourse or text depends on the genre to which it belongs, and of course even within a given genre there are numerous gradations. One author will develop his work in strict adherence to the specifications of a genre, whereas another will be extremely flexible in the use of those specificatons. Our first inkling of how an author deals with a genre is gained from our general acquaintance with the author and his way of writing. In the case of speeches which are not available to us in written form and can be heard only once, our provisional grasp of the whole cannot extend beyond what we can gather from our general knowledge of the genre and from our acquaintance with the speaker and his habits, unless the speaker himself gives us an overview of what he is going to say. If we are not familiar with a given genre and with the speaker we must draw our conclusions about the whole from the way the speaker accents and constructs the material and the way he develops it as he proceeds. Even when a provisional grasp of the whole is not possible, we may still come to understand the whole from the parts. Such an understanding, however, will necessarily be incomplete unless we remember the parts clearly and are able, once the entire speech has been delivered, to refer back to them in order to understand them more precisely and more fully from the whole. Consequently, the difference between oral and written statements disappears, because in dealing with the former our memory supplies all of the information that the written form alone seemed to insure. Thus, as Plato said long ago, we need to write only to make up for defects in our memory, a vicious circle, since writing arises from the corruption of the memory and further corrupts the memory.[31]

It follows from what I have said that for both speeches and written texts our initial grasp of the whole is only provisional and imperfect. It is, as it

---

[31]See Plato, *Phaedrus* 276d and 277c–278b.

were, a more orderly and complete way to thumb pages, but it is adequate and equal to the task only so long as we do not encounter anything strange and understanding takes place by itself, that is, where no hermeneutical operation is performed consciously. In all other cases, however, we must shift from the ending back to the beginning and improve our initial grasp of the work by starting all over again. The more difficult it is to grasp how the entire text has been organized, the more we will develop our conception by working on the parts. The richer and more significant the parts are, the more we will develop our conception by means of a view of the whole in all its relations. To be sure, almost every work contains certain parts that cannot be fully understood in relation to the overall organization of the text because they, as it were, lie outside of the textual organization and so can be called secondary thoughts. They could just as easily occur in another text as in this one, and were they developed as major thoughts they might require an entirely different type of work. But to some degree at least these secondary thoughts, as freely expressed convictions of the author, though determined by a momentary occasion, do constitute a whole, not so much in relation to the genre of the work as to the individuality of the author. Therefore, they contribute less to our understanding of the text as a living and organized expression of the language than as a creative moment of the author.

Just as those texts in which the whole is evident from the parts or in which, given even the faintest outlines of the whole, the parts can be surmised offer the most simple task for determining the relationship between the whole and the parts, so the most difficult ones are those great works of the creative spirit, whatever their form and genre, each of which in its own way is organized in infinite detail and at the same time is inexhaustible in each of its parts. Every solution to the task of understanding appears to us as only an approximation. Our understanding would be complete only if we could proceed with such works as we do with those we have designated as minimal in this respect, that is, if we could solve the problems of the organization of the whole and the parts at least in a relatively similar way. If we reflect on this, we certainly find a powerful reason why Wolf demands a skill in composition as an almost indispensable condition for the interpreter as well as for the critic.[32] For it may be well nigh impossible in this task to substitute a large selection of analogies for the divinatory method, which is awakened mainly by one's own productivity.

Yet, not content with the range of the task as previously described, Ast shows us a way to raise it to a still higher power, and this way is not to be disdained. Just as a word relates to a sentence, a sentence to a section, and a section to a work as a particular to a totality or a part to a whole, so, too, every speech and every text is a particular or part that can be completely

[32]Wolf, "Darstellung," pp. 42–44.

understood only in relation to a still larger whole.[33] It is easy to see that every work represents just such a particular or part in two respects. First, each work is a part of the sphere of literature to which it belongs, and together with other works of similar merit it forms a body of literature. This body of literature helps one to interpret each work with reference to the language. Second, each work is also a part of the author's life, and together with his other acts it forms the totality of his life. Thus it is to be understood only from the totality of the person's acts, inasmuch as it is of influence upon his life and is in keeping with it. There will always be a considerable difference— though greater or lesser depending on how the work was created—between a reader who acquires an understanding of the work in the way I have described and a reader who has accompanied the author throughout his entire life up to the appearance of the work. This latter reader, far more than the former, has a clearer and more definite view of how the author's personality steps forward in the course of the work as well as in each of its parts. A similar distinction may be made between that reader and one who is acquainted with the entire circle of related literature and can therefore assess in an entirely different way the linguistic values of the various parts and the technical aspects of the entire linguistic complex. Thus whatever is said about the smallest part of a work may be applied to the entire work, for it, too, is part of an ever larger whole.

Even after we have revised our initial concept of a work, our understanding is still only provisional, and a text is placed in entirely different light when, after reading through all of the literature related to it and after acquainting ourselves with other, even quite different, works by the same author and, as much as possible, with his entire life, we return to the work in question. Thus, if we are to understand the various parts of a work in terms of the whole, tables of contents and schematic overviews cannot take the place of reworking our initial conceptions or turning back from the ending to the beginnings. This procedure is indispensable, both because it enables us to free ourselves from reliance on the opinions of others, which can mislead us before we are able to detect their flaws, and because none of these aids is perspicuous enough to arouse in a lively way the divinatory talent, which is most important.

Likewise, when it is a question of understanding a work from both the related literature and the total activity of the author, substituting prolegomena and commentaries for these procedures will be of little avail. Usually, a study of related works only helps up to see what the author has used, and vice versa, and only a knowledge of the author himself, his acts and his relationships, enables us to see what importance they may have had on the work. Thus such study helps us only to deal with the part and not at all with the whole. A vivid and reliable characterization of the author, which

[33]Ast, *Grundlinien*, pp. 178–184.

draws on his entire life or a morphology of the genre which compares entire groups of texts in order to gain a comprehensive understanding of those groups which perhaps were first brought in relation to a given author or genre by this work itself, would not be appropriate to deal with the specific character and intent of this work.

Although these statements seem to express the highpoint of the demand that we understand the parts from the whole, we would not want to forget what was said still earlier. Although it was mentioned only in passing, you will recall the statement that there are two classes of interpreters who can be distinguished by their procedures. The one class directs its attention almost exclusively to the linguistic relations of a given text. The other pays more attention to the original pyschic process of producing and combining ideas and images.

At this point we can see with special clarity the difference in talents. Linguistically-oriented interpreters try to comprehend a work by grasping how it is related to similar works of the same type. They focus on the forms of composition which arise from the nature of the language and of the common life which develops and is bound together with language. Thus the individual and personal elements which emerge here are those which have become most universal, and so these elements receive least attention. The other interpreters, however, want to determine from a composition what kind of person the author is. To do this they identify themselves as much as possible with the moments of creativity and conception which break into the fabric of the author's everyday life like higher inspirations. They seek a vivid insight into every facet of the parts that may illuminate the process of creation, including secondary thoughts which were of no consequence for the idea of the work, in order to evaluate properly how the whole process of composition is related to the author's existence or how the author's personality develops itself in representations. Of course, for such interpreters the relation to the language mentioned above recedes into the background.

Full understanding requires both of these operations, and no interpreter can fully understand if he leans so much to one side that he is completely unable to make use of what the other side offers. An interpreter in the latter class who wanted only to dabble in linguistic matters would make many mistakes, no matter how much he might love to understand the author and no matter how much he might guard against imputing intentions to the author which the author did not have in mind, as such interpreters tend to do. The more significant the author was for the development of the language, the more errors would be committed. In our field of interest we have to call such an interpreter by a name that has been used, not without appropriateness, in the sphere of artistic productivity—I take this generally to include the poet and speaker and even the philosoper as well as the artist: he is a "nebulist." Or consider an interpreter of the other type, even one who ascertains how a work is related to others of its genre with such precision that, not satisfied with discerning sharp comparisons and juxtapositions, he also has a profound grasp of their significance. Because such an interpreter does not see the whole man in the work and does not participate in his life, indeed is incapable of doing so, he cannot avoid what we call "pedantry." Since it is easier to use the works of others to compensate for one's own deficiencies than to acquire for oneself techniques for which one has no aptitude, it seems that those who scale the mountain that rises before us from the one side are less valuable as interpreters in their own right than as resources for others. And we might advise all those who want to be interpreters to work at both sides, even at the expense of virtuosity at either, in order to avoid one-sidedness.

Since we have distinguished these two sides of our enterprise from the outset and have found, in connection with then, two methods, the divinatory and the comparative, we need now to inquire how the two are related to the higher level of understanding. Earlier, when we were limiting our discussion to a given work, we saw that both operations were necessary for each side, for the grammatical as well as for the psychological. But now, on account of particular problems with the language, we have to deal not only with passages from other texts, but with a whole sphere of literary production. At the same time, our concern is no longer merely to discover what developed from the author's original, creative conception of a work, but thoroughly to consider how it actually developed from the unity and total context of this particular life.

Thus it may seem that these two methods are no longer given equal weight. If, once again, we pursue both sides of our task to their conclusions, the one side seems so underdeveloped and thin in comparison with the other that it would seem completely improper to give it a place equal to the other in a new hermeneutics. To confine ourselves to classical antiquity, which remains the primary field for the art of hermeneutics, we see that we know so little about the life and existence of so many of the most important authors that we always wonder how much we can trust them. Outside of their works themselves, does our knowledge of Sophocles and Euripides supply us even the most limited explanation for the differences in their compositions? Or take such well-known men as Plato and Aristotle. Does what we know of their lives and relationships explain even in the most minimal way why the former took one course in philosophy and the latter another, or to what extent they may have reconciled their differences in writings no longer available to us? Indeed, is there any other ancient whom we know as well as Cicero? He is, I believe, the only man of antiquity for whom we have a treasury of personal letters, as actual documents of his personality, entirely distinct from his major works. If we turn now to the production of the distant and hazy Orient, how is it possible to think of trying to distinguish the forms of particular human beings in order to illumine their works by reference to the special way in which their inner life [*Gemüth*] developed? The harvest of such material is sparse even for those earlier witnesses in our own land that we have only recently begun to study scientifically. It is only as we approach our own era and restrict ourselves to the European scene we know so well and where we all stroll, as it were, in the same hall that it seems possible to undertake this mode of treatment with sufficient resources for a reasonable degree of success.

Moreover, how trivial this method looks in comparison to the other one! The latter method always leads us to further material, and just when we think we have mastered all the literature related to a given work we find another piece, a part of the same great whole, that promises an even better measuring rod and an even more certain result. The former method, however, always restricts us to the narrow confines of an individual's life, and the most we can expect from our taxing, multifarious effort is a clear picture of this person's life. Nonetheless, even the finest historical reconstruction which we undertake in order to comprehend better a work of some author will achieve true excellence not merely because it clarifies the work in question but also because it enriches our own lives and the lives of others. Such enrichment is sublime, and it should be added to our consideration of works so that we do not produce trivialities which demean ourselves and our scientific labor. Thus a knowledge of a given person as such is not the aim of this side of our task, but a means of enabling us to master the author's activities and so of leading us to an objective consideration of his way of thinking. There can be no doubt that people in classical antiquity were no less concerned with the author as a person, and we must presume that the original readers could come to an understanding that we can only envy because we no longer possess the resources for it. This much, however, is certain from these remarks: in the psychological task we cannot avoid giving greater emphasis to divination, for it is entirely natural for people to construct for themselves a complete image of a person from only scattered traces. But we cannot be too careful in examining from every angle a picture that has been sketched in such a hypothetical fashion. We should accept it only when we find no contradictions, and even then only provisionally. But no one who neglects this side of the hermeneutical task can do justice to a work, for whether a work is integral to an author's intellectual life or is occasioned merely by special circumstances, whether it is a prelude to some greater work or a polemic, is of greatest import to the interpreter.

The other method is by its very nature predominately comparative. Only by taking a number of works together and observing their similarities and differences can one form a general picture of the genre and ascertain how the work in question is related to the genre. But even so there is originally a measure of divination in the way one poses the question about a work, and until the interpreter has determined fully the work's place in the overall group to which it belongs he should not fail to leave a certain field of play for the divinatory method.

If it is a mistake, though I do not think it is, to assign both of these tasks
to the interpreter, then it is my fault alone, for my guides do not accept this
view any more than they accept what I said earlier. Indeed, I must
acknowledge that I have conceived the comparative side of the task differently than Ast. Although he wants to understand a work as a whole from a
larger context, the body of literature in which the work is included is for him
both too unwieldy and too restrictive to serve as that context. Since he
confines himself to classical literature, he advances the formula that a work
should be understood out of the spirit of antiquity. This formula could be
viewed as an abbreviation of the methods which I have presented. For this
spirit would be that which commonly dwells in all productions of the same
time, and it is identified by abstracting from the works of a given type
whatever is distinctive to each individual work. But Ast specifically objects
to this procedure. He argues that this spirit need not be collected and
constructed from various works, but that it is already given in each individual
work since each work of antiquity is only an individualization of this spirit.[34]
I do not contest that it is present in each text, but I doubt that it is
recognizable without considerably more effort. We begin to see the difficulty
if, in dealing with one of Demosthenes's speeches, I want to posit in addition
to the spirit of antiquity the Hellenic spirit, and then also the spirit of
Athenian oratorical eloquence, and then also the particular spirit of
Demosthenes and, above all, the characteristics of the era and the special
occasion of his speech, as the "body" to which it belongs. And if I add to this
the observation that the spirit of antiquity is to be found not only in a certain
type of written works but also in the graphic arts and who knows where else,
this formula seems to break out of the specific limits of hermeneutics
entirely, for hermeneutics deals only with what is produced in language.
Ast's formula will surely fail to accomplish its goal.

If we reflect for only a moment on the procedure that some time ago we
frequently based on just this statement, namely, the use of the technical
language of one sphere in an entirely different sphere, then no one will deny
that, even if such formulae are not a mere game founded on a sound view,
they lead only to ruinous vagueness and indecision. Nor can I absolve Ast of
these faults in the application of his theory. For when I read in this
connection that the idea, as the unity which encompasses a life, both as its
variety and form and as an absolute unity (the reverse would state the case
better), then I find myself in a fog.[35] Such vagueness is not propitious for
theory that demands clarity. Everyone must grant that up to the point just
described the level our interpretations have achieved is a notable step
toward rightly conceiving the spirit of a people and of a time from the way
language is used. Moreover, a theory developed from these observations

[34]Ibid., pp. 171, 176–77, 182.
[35]Ibid., pp. 188–90.

receives substantial confirmation when studies in other areas of intellectual productivity yield similar results. But I do not wish a venture in the opposite direction and try to comprehend the particular by such general hypotheses, nor do I wish to suggest that such a procedure would still belong to hermeneutics.

This leads me to another point. Ast distinguishes three kinds of understanding: historical, grammatical, and an understanding of spirit. To be precise, the understanding of the spirit is itself twofold, directed toward both the spirit of the individual author and the spirit of classical antiquity as a whole. Thus he actually distinguishes four kinds of understanding. Taking his list of three, however, he speaks of the third as the highest and claims that it penetrates the other two.[36] It could therefore be supposed that he actually intended to point to the two stages of interpretation that we have disclosed in exploring the formula that the particular can be understood only from the whole. But this supposition remains at best highly uncertain. For if he considers the twofold understanding of the spirit to be the higher one, and grammatical and historical understanding to be the lower, such that they occupy a single stage over against the understanding of the spirit and penetrated by it, why does he not put them together and simply differentiate between the lower and higher kinds of understanding? But the fact of the matter is that he also speaks of a threefold hermeneutics, hermeneutics of the letter, of the sense, and of the spirit, and this tripartite division is irreconcilable with my supposition.[37] This distinction of a threefold understanding of a threefold hermeneutics rests on the fact that to him the understanding of speech is not the same as interpretation, for interpretation is to him the development of what has been understood.[38] This view, and many have advocated it before Ast, only confuses the issue. By the term "development" he means nothing other than the presentation of the genesis of understanding, the communication of the way understanding has been attained. Interpretation, then, is distinguished from understanding only as articulated speech from internal speech, and something else would be introduced for the purpose of communication. Thus interpretation could occur only as the application of the general rules of eloquence without, however, adding anything to the contents or altering anything in the text. Wolf also knows nothing about this matter and defines hermeneutics as merely the art of

---

[36]Ibid., p. 177.

[37]Ibid., pp. 191–92.

[38]Ibid., pp. 184–85. From the beginning Schleiermacher criticized the distinction between understanding (*intelligere*) and interpretation, especially explanation (*explicare*). The distinction goes back to Augustine, *De Doctrina Christiana* (396/426). In Books 1–3 Augustine deals with understanding the teaching (*Lehre*) of Christianity and in Book 4 he deals with the restatement (*Wiedergabe*) of what has been understood. This distinction was generally accepted until Wolf (*Darstellung*, p. 37) and Schleiermacher.

discovering the meaning of the text.[39] Were we to grant Ast his distinction, a threefold hermeneutics would follow only to the extent that there would be that many ways of developing the understanding. But his instructions do not point toward this, nor are they developed in this sense, insofar as they are developed at all. Just as little, however, do they agree with his three modes of understanding. Because the hermeneutics of the letter, which explains the words and content, deals with historical and grammatical understanding, the hermeneutics of the sense and the spirit are both included in the understanding of the spirit. To be sure, this is twofold, but these two hermeneutics cannot be distinguished in this way because the one pertains exclusively to the spirit of the individual author and the other to the spirit of classical antiquity. The hermeneutics of sense deals only with the meaning [*Bedeutung*] of the letter in the context of a particular passage. On the other hand, both procedures offer an explanation of the spirit in each passage, so in the end nothing seems to harmonize.

This alone is clear: the explanation of words and contents are not themselves interpretation but only elements of it, and hermeneutics begins with the determination of meaning, although to be sure by means of these elements. Further, no explanation, that is, no determination of meaning, is correct unless it is supported by an examination of the spirit of the author and the spirit of classical antiquity. For only a person in a disturbed state of mind speaks or writes against his own spirit, and, were one to insist on an explanation of an ancient writer that stands in clear contradiction to the spirit of antiquity, one would have to prove that the author was a mongrel in his spirit. Ast himself says as much when, discussing the explanation of the sense, he argues that whoever fails to grasp the spirit of an author is unable to uncover the true meaning of particular passages and that a proposed meaning is true only when it is in harmony with that spirit.[40] Thus, although Ast divides his hermeneutics into three types, he actually offers us only a single hermeneutics, the hermeneutics of the sense, because the hermeneutics of the letter is not yet hermeneutics and the hermeneutics of the spirit, insofar as it is not encompassed by the hermeneutics of the sense, lies beyond the scope of hermeneutics altogether.

On this issue we must stand with Wolf, adding only that in order to apply this technique fully to a text we must not only explain the words and the content, but comprehend the spirit of the author as well. Wolf himself admits as much, perhaps inadvertently, when he distinguishes interpretations into grammatical, historical, and rhetorical.[41] By grammatical interpretation he means the explanation of words, and by historical the explanation of the content. But he uses rhetorical in the same sense as we use aesthetic today.

[39]Wolf, "Darstellung," p. 37.
[40]Ast, *Grundlinien*, pp. 194–95.
[41]Wolf, "Darstellung," p. 37.

Consequently, rhetorical interpretation would in fact be hermeneutics only with reference to the particular artistic genre, and it would include only a portion of what Ast calls the understanding of spirit, namely, those art-forms determined by the spirit of classical antiquity. In any case he would have had to add a "poetic" interpretation to rhetorical in order to exhaust what we mean by aesthetic. Consequently, were he to attend also to the individual or special spirit of the author, his hermeneutics would yield five different kinds of interpretation. However correct this view may be, I would have to protest against a formulation of the hermeneutical task that makes grammatical and historical interpretations seem to be special and distinct in themselves. Theologians have already combined these two in order to strengthen a good case against a bad one, and they make use of the phrase "grammatical-historical interpretation." Although in and of itself this is right, the phrase is used in opposition to dogmatic and allegorical interpretions, as if these represented independent types of interpretation, regardless of whether or not they are justified.[42]

Ast succumbs to a similar mistake when he distinguishes a simple meaning and an allegorical meaning, thereby leaving the impression that an allegorical meaning is a second and additional meaning.[43] But if a passage was intended to be allegorical, then the allegorical meaning is the only one and the simple one. The passage has no other meaning at all, and that meaning is understood historically. If a passage was intended to be allegorical, then by positing the allegorical meaning as a second one, the interpreter would not be reproducing the actual meaning of the words at all, because he would not be attributing to them the meaning they have in their context. And the reverse would be the case were he to give an allegorical explanation to a passage that was not intended to be taken allegorically. If the interpreter does this deliberately he is no longer engaged in interpretation but in practical application; if he does it unintentionally, his explanation is simply false, and we have enough of those already—and they, by the way, are caused by this same mistake. One would be equally justified to invent a mystical interpretation for Masonic and other such formulae and then to distinguish the mysterious meaning from the simple one. Then when we recall that some time ago a philosopher presented us with a moral meaning in addition to the dogmatic, for which the same conditions pertain as for the allegorical, we can only hope that the right position had been reached by the

---

[42]The extension of grammatical interpretation to dogmatic interpretation and allegorical interpretation was developed by the humanistically educated theologian Hugo Grotius, and, on the Catholic side, Richard Simon. In these, the historical context for interpretation was included from the beginning. One can speak of grammatical-historical interpretation in the sense of a strict application of historical methods and of an opposition to dogmatic and allegorical interpretations with J. S. Semler. Schleiermacher wants to overcome the frontal opposition between different kinds of interpretation.

[43]Ast, *Grundlinien*, pp. 196–97.

person who recently invented a panharmonic interpretation.[44] He surely intended nothing other than that in a correct interpretation all the various themes must concur in one and the same conclusion.

All these innovations seem to stem from the belief that there are various kinds of interpretation from which interpreters can freely choose. But were that so, it would no longer be worth the effort to speak or write. Unfortunately, it is abundantly clear that these various interpretations have had a deleterious influence on hermeneutics. Since they grow out of the chaotic conditions of the discipline, we may be sure they will not disappear until hermeneutics assumes the technical form it is due and, starting from the simple fact of understanding by reference to the nature of language and to the fundamental conditions relating a writer and reader or a speaker and hearer, develops its rules into a systematic, self-contained discipline.

[44]The idea of a "moral interpretation" is obvious in enlightenment philosophy. It is introduced in Semler's hermeneutics (cf. *Abhandlung von freier Untersuchung des Canons*, 1:23). Kant advances it in *Die Religion innerhalb der Grenzen der blossen Vernunft*, 2nd edition (Königsberg, 1794), p. 161. The "inventor" of panharmonic interpretation cannot be identified.

INTRODUCTION TO DILTHEY'S
"THE DEVELOPMENT OF HERMENEUTICS"

Wilhelm Dilthey (1833–1911) cannot be easily situated in any single intellectual discipline. His work eludes simple characterization because of both its scope and methodology. However, a theoretical preoccupation persists through Dilthey's writings: What, he asked, is the theoretical foundation of the human sciences (*Geisteswissenschaften*)? How is knowledge possible in these fields of study? In addition to his role as metatheoretician (he called his work "philosophy of philosophy" at one point), Dilthey made significant contributions to European cultural life as a historian, psychologist, philosopher (having written in ethics, aesthetics, epistemology, and pedagogy), and literary critic. Richly suggestive, his writings have influenced the shape of philosophy of history, theory of the human sciences (*Geisteswissenschaften*), and hermeneutics.

Wilhelm Dilthey was born in 1833, within two years of the deaths of Friedrich Hegel (1831) and Schleiermacher (1834). His intellectual formation was deeply rooted in the great period of German idealism; major influences on Dilthey included Kant, Fichte, Hegel, Schelling, and Schleiermacher. By the time Dilthey was writing, idealism was no longer acceptable. Dilthey saw that idealism had valiantly attempted to revive metaphysics after its death in the Kantian critique. But the attempt, he thought, had failed. The absolute of speculative idealism was in the end a metaphysical construct that transcends possible experience. Dilthey was also opposed to the rising positivism and empiricism of the late nineteenth century, with their joint demand that the natural sciences provide the model of knowledge for all human thought, including the human sciences and social sciences. Dilthey's task could be construed as the attempt to secure a theoretical foundation for the human sciences that would neither succumb to metaphysics (as did idealism) nor restrict meaning to empirical explanation (as did positivism and empiricism).

Dilthey's university studies began in theology at Heidelberg (1852–1853) and Berlin (1854–1856). But he did not remain in theology, although his father and grandfather were Reformed ministers. After 1856, his studies at the University of Berlin branched out to include a number of fields, especially the history of thought. His dissertation was on Schleiermacher's ethics (1864). Dilthey took lifelong inspiration from Schleiermacher; he wrote the standard biography of Schleiermacher and an analysis of his philosophical and theological systems. In 1866, Dilthey joined the philosophy faculty at the University of Basel; he went on to teach at Kiel (1868), Breslau (1870), and Berlin (1882–1907). In many ways, he was the consummate German professor. Erudite beyond belief, a prodigious worker, and committed researcher, he routinely questioned the practicality of his own ideas.

Martin Heidegger explicitly acknowledged Dilthey's influence on his thought. Many other major intellectual figures have likewise credited Dilthey as a formative factor in their thought: Max Weber, Karl Jaspers, Ernst Cassirer, Ernst Troeltsch, Max Scheler, Georg Simmel, Karl Mannheim, Rudolf Bultmann, Alfred Schütz, Hans-Georg Gadamer, and Paul Ricoeur, among others. For most, Dilthey's ideas were provocative rather than directly adaptable for their own uses. Dilthey's thought seems perennially to be exploratory and preparatory. No systematic order governed the whole, and thus his thought sometimes appears to lack precision. But several important and focal ideas dominate the *Gesammelte Schriften* of Dilthey, and I shall summarize them here.

First, according to Dilthey, the natural sciences study outer appearances that are given to the senses, while the human sciences focus on expressions of "inner reality directly experienced in all its complexity."[1] Furthermore, our "inner reality" (*Erlebnis*) or immediate experience of a self relating to its world and, through it, to itself, is ordered to reflection. Inner lived experience is prereflective but nonetheless permeated with awareness through feeling and understanding. In other words, the immediate experience of being in the world is intrinsically meaningful and aware of the matrix of meaning. Thinking is embedded in and generated by life itself. This primordial thinking process may be called understanding. More specifically, understanding is the elementary activity of "recognizing a mental state from a sense-given sign by which it is expressed."[2] We understand a text or an utterance when we trace a linguistic expression both forward to the clarifying contexts of meaningfulness that determine the meaning, and backward to the experience that produced it as an intention. This process "extends over the whole of life and relates to any kind of speech or writing."[3] The main point is that understanding, as prereflective awareness of meaning, is already active in life itself.

Second, Dilthey thought that the process of understanding has common characteristics in all its diverse settings. A child first learning language and a scholar translating ancient Hebrew into a modern language share a single process of understanding. This process is rule-governed: expressions refer both to cultural systems of meaning (Hegel's "objective spirit") and to inner

---

[1] Wilhelm Dilthey, "The Development of Hermeneutics," p. 93 below.
[2] Ibid, p. 94.
[3] Ibid., p. 103.

experience. Understanding gleans both references and coordinates them. In a word, understanding is always a grasp of the individual consciousness by means of larger patterns of intelligibility. Understanding is a transposition into the other, a reconstruction of the intentional act, *in its proper cultural and linguistic context.*

Third, understanding is possible because of two central conditions of life: (1) Humans share a *common nature* as historical and expressive beings. Dilthey says, "The same human spirit speaks to us from stone, marble, musical compositions, gestures, words and writings, from actions, economic arrangements and constitutions, and has to be interpreted."[4] (2) Humans express their thoughts in *language,* which enables reconstruction of a historical setting different from one's own. Linguistic and cultural contexts have a stabilizing affect on individual expression and make it possible to "reproduce an alien life" in one's own thoughts. This means that hermeneutics, the theory of interpretation of written expressions, can be developed as a philosophical foundation for the human sciences. A full analysis of understanding is called for, in order to make interpretation systematic and to work out the methodology of the study of human culture. Just as Kant provided a critique of pure reason to demonstrate how natural science is possible, Dilthey aims at a critique of historical reason to show how human science is possible. Hermeneutics is to be the epistemology of the *Geisteswissenschaften.*

In each of these three ideas, we see both the pervasive influence of Schleiermacher on Dilthey as well as Dilthey's attempt to extend the hermeneutical theory of Schleiermacher. Schleiermacher's hermeneutics echoes in Dilthey's emphasis on the twofold reference of expressions to inner psychological life and to cultural contexts, in Dilthey's focus on the single identity of the understanding process in its many appearances, and in Dilthey's interest in spelling out the conditions of the possibility of understanding with reference to the human spirit and its possession of language.

Although Dilthey is massively indebted to Schleiermacher, he does not merely repeat Schleiermacher's program. Dilthey argues for broadening hermeneutics into the context of the epistemology, logic, and methodology of the human studies. Dilthey extends Schleiermacher's notion of hermeneutics for use in the debate over the justification of knowledge in the study of human expressions. His reworking of hermeneutics into a general method for human studies remains within the framework of a modern theory of interpretation, however. Dilthey's thought is characteristically objectivist (he is interested in protecting the validity of interpretation), methodological (he wants to prescribe rules for valid interpretation), and epistemological (he intends to legitimate interpretation by showing how it is possible).

The Dilthey essay I have chosen for this volume, "The Development of

---

[4] Ibid., p. 94.

Hermeneutics," does not spell out his own program of hermeneutics so much as it makes a case for the revival of hermeneutics in continuity with Schleiermacher. Written in 1900, this essay marks a transition in Dilthey's thought from his earlier attempts to secure the theoretical foundations of the human sciences in a descriptive psychology to his later attempts to do so through hermeneutics.

The essay begins with an argument that the human sciences, which in the nature of the case must always focus on unique human expressions and events, are grounded in the process of understanding—the recognition of inner content from signs received by the senses. Knowledge of the individuality of other people proceeds by way of understanding their expressions of inwardness through language. Moreover, knowledge of one's own individuality—of oneself as an "I"—likewise proceeds not by way of introspection but through an understanding of one's own externalizations of selfhood and through a comparison of one's own expressions with those of others. Objectivity in the grasp of human individuality depends on methodical interpretation of the expressions of inner life in language. Through the ages, rules of interpretation have been formulated to direct interpretation. The debate about rules of interpretation has given rise to hermeneutics, which Dilthey defines as "the methodology of the interpretation of written records."[5]

Next, Dilthey provides a valuable history of the rules of hermeneutics from the time of the Greeks. He traces the independent development of classical and biblical hermeneutics, focusing first on Aristotle, Alexandrian philology, and the Stoics; and second on the contest between the theological schools of Alexandria and Antioch, the reformation of biblical interpretation in the sixteenth and eighteenth centuries, and the culmination of the process in Schleiermacher. Dilthey concludes the essay by summarizing those central elements of Schleiermacher's theory on which further development of hermeneutics depends.

[5]Ibid., p. 95.

THE DEVELOPMENT OF HERMENEUTICS
(1900)
Wilhelm Dilthey

In a previous work I have considered how to describe the process by which individual works of art, in particular of poetry, are produced. Now we must ask if it is possible to study individual human beings and particular forms of human existence scientifically and how this can be done.

This is a question of the greatest significance, for our actions always presuppose the understanding of other people and a great deal of human happiness springs from empathy with the mental life of others. Indeed, philology and history rest on the assumption that the understanding of the unique can be made objective. The historical sense based on this assumption enables man to recapture the whole of his past; he can look across all the barriers of his own age at past cultures and increase his happiness by drawing strength from them and enjoying their charm. While the systematic human studies derive general laws and comprehensive patterns from the objective apprehension of the unique, they still rest on understanding and interpretation. These disciplines, therefore, like history, depend for their certainty on the possibility of giving general validity to the understanding of the unique. So, from the beginning, we are facing a problem which distinguishes the human studies from the physical sciences.

No doubt the human studies have the advantage over the physical sciences because their subject is not merely an appearance given to the senses, a mere reflection in the mind of some outer reality, but inner reality directly experienced in all its complexity. Here we are not considering what difficulties, arising from the way in which this reality is experienced, obstruct objective apprehension but a further problem that inner experience of my own states can never, by itself, make me aware of my own individuality. Only by comparing myself to others and becoming conscious of how I differ from them can I experience my own individuality. However, Goethe is, unfortunately, right when he notes how difficult it is to gain this most important of our experiences, and how imperfect our insight into the extent, nature and limit of our powers always remains. We are mainly aware of the inner life of others only through the impact of their gestures, sounds and acts on our senses. We have to reconstruct the inner source of the signs which strike our senses. Everything—material, structure, even the most individual features of the reconstruction—must be supplied by transferring it from our

own lives. How, then, can an individually structured consciousness reconstruct—and thereby know objectively—the distinct individuality of another?
What kind of process is this which steps so strangely into the midst of the
other cognitive processes?

We call the process by which we recognize some inner content from
signs received by the senses understanding. This is how the word is used
and a much-needed, fixed psychological terminology can only be established when every firmly coined, clearly and usefully circumscribed expression is used by writers consistently. Understanding of nature—*interpretation naturae*—is a figurative expression. Even awareness of our own state of
mind cannot properly be called understanding. It is true I may say: I can't
understand how I could do that; I don't understand myself any longer. But
then I mean that an expression of my nature which has been externalized
confronts me as something alien that I cannot interpret or else that I have got
into a state at which I gaze astonished as if it were foreign to me. Understanding is the process of recognizing a mental state from a sense-given sign
by which it is expressed.

Understanding ranges from the apprehension of childish patter to
understanding *Hamlet* or the *Critique of Pure Reason*. The same human
spirit speaks to us from stone, marble, musical compositions, gestures, words
and writings, from actions, economic arrangements and constitutions, and
has to be interpreted. This process of understanding must always have
common characteristics because it is determined by common conditions and
means of its own, and remains the same in its basic features. If, for example,
I want to understand Leonardo[1] I must interpret actions, pictures and
writings in one homogeneous process.

Understanding shows different degrees which are, to start with, determined by interest. If the interest is limited so is the understanding. We listen
impatiently to some explanations if all we want to know about is one point of
practical importance and are not interested in the inner life of the speaker. In
other cases we strain to get inside a speaker through every facial expression
or word. But even the most strenuous attention can only give rise to a
systematic process with a controllable degree of objectivity if the expression
has been given permanent form so that we can repeatedly return to it. *Such
systematic understanding of recorded expressions we call exegesis or
interpretation.* In this sense there is also an art of interpreting sculptures or
pictures. F. A. Wolf called for a hermeneutic and critique in archaeology.
Welcker[2] advocated it and Preller[3] tried to develop it. But Preller emphasized that such interpretations of non-verbal works depended on explanations from literature.

[1]Leonardo da Vinci, 1452–1519.
[2]F. G. Welcker, German classical scholar, 1784–1868.
[3]L. Preller, German philologist, 1809–1861.

Because it is in language alone human inwardness finds its complete, exhaustive and objectively comprehensible expression that literature is immeasurably significant for our understanding of intellectual life and history. The art of understanding therefore centers on the *interpretation of written records of human existence.*

Therefore, the exegesis—and the critical treatment inseparably linked with it—of these records formed the starting-point of philology. This is essentially a personal skill and virtuosity in the treatment of written records; any interpretation of monuments or historically transmitted actions can only flourish in relation to this skill and its products. We can make mistakes about the motives of historical agents, but the work of a great poet or explorer, of a religious genius or genuine philosopher can only be the true expression of his mental life; in human society, full of lies, such work is always true and can therefore—in contrast to other permanent expressions—be interpreted with complete objectivity. Indeed it throws light on the other artistic records of an age and on the historical actions of contemporaries.

This art of interpretation has developed just as slowly, gradually and in as orderly a way as, for example, the questioning of nature by experiment. It originated and survives in the personal, inspired virtuosity of philologists. Naturally it is mainly transmitted through personal contact with the great masters of interpretation or their work. But every skill also proceeds according to rules which teach us to overcome difficulties and embody what can be transmitted of personal skill. So the art of interpretation gives rise to the formulation of rules. The conflict between such rules and the struggle between different schools about the interpretation of vital works produces a need to justify the rules and this gives rise to hermeneutics, which is *the methodology of the interpretation of written records.*

Because it determines the possibility of valid interpretation by means of an analysis of understanding, it penetrates to the solution of the whole general problem with which this exposition started. Understanding takes its place beside the analysis of inner experience, and both together demonstrate the possibility and limits of general knowledge in the human studies in so far as it is determined by the way in which we are originally presented with mental facts.

I shall document this orderly progress from the history of hermeneutics, by showing how philological virtuosity arose from the need for deep and valid understanding. This gave rise to rules which were purposefully organized and systematized according to the state of scholarship in a given period, and finally an assured starting-point for making these rules was found in the analysis of understanding.

1

Systematic interpretation of poets developed as a required part of education in Greece. Clever play with interpretations and criticism of

Homer and other poets was popular wherever Greek was spoken during the age of Greek Enlightenment. A more firm foundation was laid when the interpretations of the Sophists and rhetorical schools was related to rhetoric. For this contained—applied to eloquence—a more general theory of literary composition. Aristotle, the great classifier and analyst of the organic world, of states and literary works, taught in his *Rhetoric* how to dissect the whole of a literary work into its parts, distinguish literary forms and recognize the effects of rhythm, period and metaphor. The definitions of the elements of effective speech such as example, enthymeme, sentence, irony, metaphor and antithesis, are assembled even more simply in the *Rhetoric for Alexander*.[4] Aristotle's *Poetics* deals quite specifically with the way the nature and purpose of poetry and its different types determine their inner and outer form.

The art of interpretation and its systematization took a second important step in Alexandrian philology. The literary heritage of Greece was collected in libraries; textual revisions were made and the results of critical work were recorded by means of a refined system of signs. Spurious writings were eliminated and complete inventories made. Philology as an art of textual revision based on intimate linguistic understanding, higher criticism, interpretation and evaluation had come into existence as one of the last and most characteristic creations of the Greek spirit which was powerfully motivated, from Homer onwards, by joy in human speech. The great Alexandrian scholars also began to be conscious of the rules contained in their inspired technique. Aristrarch[5] worked on the consciously formulated principle of establishing Homeric usage strictly and comprehensively, and of basing explanation and textual emendation on it. Hipparch[6] deliberately based his factual interpretation on a literary-historical investigation when he pointed to the sources for the *Phenomena*[7] of Aratos and interpreted the poems accordingly. It was the ingenious handling of the principle of analogy, according to which a canon of usage, a range of ideas, the inner consistency and aesthetic value of a poem was ascertained (and what contradicted it eliminated) which made it possible to recognize spurious poems in the transmitted body of Hesiod's poems, to eliminate many lines from Homer's epics and to judge the last section of the Iliad and part of the penultimate and the whole of the last section of the Odyssey as of more recent origin. The application of moral-aesthetic canons by Zenodot[8] and Aristarch emerges clearly from the following argument by Atethesen,[9] i.e., *si quid heroum vel deorum gravitatem minus decere videbatur* ("If anything pertaining to

[4]*Rhetorica ad Alexandrum*, formerly ascribed to Aristotle, now considered spurious.
[5]Alexandrian grammarian of the third century B.C.
[6]Hipparchus, Greek astronomer of the second century B.C.
[7]A poem by Aratos who was a Greek astronomer and poet of the third century B.C.
[8]Zenodotus of Ephesus. Head of the library at Alexandria, fourth century B.C.
[9]Fourth century B.C.

heroes or gods seems less befitting to their dignity"). Aristrarch also relied on
Aristotle.

Methodological consciousness about the right procedures of interpretation was strengthened by the reaction of the Alexandrian school against the
philology of Pergamon. This conflict of hermeneutic trends proved of
significance for world history because it reemerged—in a new situation—in
Christian theology. Two great historical views about poets and religious
writers are conditioned by it.

From the Stoics, Krates of Malos[10] imported allegorical interpretation
into the philology of Pergamon. This form of interpretation was influential
for a long time because it eliminated the conflict betweeen religious texts
and an enlightened world view. This is why it was almost indispensable for
the interpretation of the Vedas, Homer, the Bible, and the Koran—a skill as
necessary as it is pernicious. But it was also based on a deeper view of poetic
and religious creation. Homer is a visionary and the contradiction between
deep insights and sensuously coarse ideas in his work can only be explained
by treating the latter simply as a poetic means of presentation. So allegorical
interpretation originated when this relation was understood as a deliberate
enfolding of a spiritual meaning in images.

2

If I am not mistaken, this conflict recurs under altered circumstances in
the struggle between the theological schools of Alexandria and Antioch.
Their common assumption was, of course, that an inner connection between
prophecy and fulfillment linked the Old and New Testaments because this
was implied by the use of prophecies and examples in the New Testament.
Starting from this presupposition the Christian church found itself in a
complicated position *vis-à-vis* its opponents as regards the interpretation of
its Holy Writ. If the logos-theology was to be applied to the Old Testament,
the Church had to maintain an allegorical interpretation where the Jews
were concerned, but where the Gnostics[11] were involved it had to limit the
allegorical method. Following in the footsteps of Philo,[12] Justin[13] and
Irenaeus[14] tried to establish rules for limiting and managing the allegorical
method. In this same struggle with Jews and Gnostics, Tertullian [15] takes up
the procedure of Justin and Irenaeus but, on the other hand, develops
fruitful rules for better interpretation which, alas, he does not always follow
himself. The contrast found fundamental expression in the Greek church.

[10]Greek philologist of Pergamon, second century A.D.
[11]A religious school of the first century A.D.
[12]Philo the Jew, Alexandrian philosopher, 20 B.C.–A.D. 40.
[13]Religious writer and martyr of the second century A.D.
[14]Religious writer, A.D. 140–200.
[15]Christian apologist, A.D. 165–220.

The school of Antioch explained its texts strictly according to grammatical-historical principles. The Antiochian Theodorus[16] saw the Song of Songs simply as a wedding song. Job was for him merely the poetic rendering of a historical tradition. He rejected the titles of the psalms and refuted the direct reference to Christ of a sizeable part of Messianic prophecies. He did not assume a double meaning of the texts but only a higher connection between the events. In contrast to this, Philo, Clement[17] and Origen[18] distinguished a literary and spiritual meaning of the texts.

From this struggle the first worked out hermeneutic theories we know of originated. This is a further step in the development of interpretation into hermeneutic through which it became scientific. According to Philo κανόνες ("rules," "criteria") and νόμοι τῆς ἀλληγορίας ("laws of allegory") are already applied in the Old Testament and have to be assumed as underlying his interpretation. On this Origen in the fourth book of his work Περὶ ἀρχῶν ("On Principles") and Augustine in the third book of De Doctrine Christiana based a coherently presented hermeneutic theory. These were opposed by two, unfortunately, lost hermeneutic works of the Antiochian school: Diodoros' Τίς διαφορὰ θεωρίας καί ἀλληγορίας ("What is the difference between theory and allegory?") and Theodoros' De Allegoria et Historia Contra Originem.

3

Interpretation and its systematization have entered a new stage since the Renaissance. Language, conditions of life and nationality separated it from classical and Christian antiquity. In contrast to what it was once in Rome, interpretation thus became transposition by means of grammatical, factual and historical studies into an alien mentality. This new philology, polymathy and critique had frequently to deal with mere reports and fragments. So it had to be creative and constructive in a new way. Philology, hermeneutic and critique therefore entered a higher stage. We have voluminous hermeneutic literature from the next four centuries. There were two strands because classical and Biblical writings were powerful influences to be absorbed. The classical-philological systematization described itself as *ars critica*. Its works—eminent among them those of Scioppius[19] and Clericus[20] and the incomplete one of Valesius[21]—contained a methodology in their first part. Innumerable essays and prefaces were *de interpretatione*. But the final putting together of hermeneutics we owe to Biblical interpretation. The first

[16]Ecclesiastical historian, A.D. 393–458.
[17]Clement of Alexandria, religious writer, second to third century A.D.
[18]Father of Christian theology, A.D. 185–254.
[19]K. Scioppius (or Schoppe), religious controversialist from Prague, 1576–1649.
[20]J. Leclerc, Arminian theologian, 1657–1736.
[21]H. Valesius, French ecclesiastical theologian, 1603–76.

significant and perhaps most profound of these writings was the *clavis* (*"The Key"*) of Flacius.[22]

Here, for the first time, the essence of the rules of interpretation discovered so far was linked into a system of teaching, based on the postulate that valid understanding was possible through the systematic use of these rules. Flacius became conscious of this fundamental point of view, which, in fact, dominates hermeneutics through the struggles of the sixteenth century because he had to fight on two fronts. Both the Anabaptists and the Catholicism of the Counter-Reformation maintained that the holy scriptures were obscure. In opposing this, Flacius learned especially from Calvin's[23] exegesis which frequently referred from interpretation back to its principles. The most urgent business of a Lutheran of the period was to refute the then newly-formulated Catholic doctrine of tradition. The right of tradition to determine interpretation could in the quarrel with the Protestant principle of interpretation only be justified by the assumption that no sufficient and valid interpretation could be elicited from the Biblical writings themselves. The Council of Trent, in session from 1545 to 1563, dealt with this question from its fourth session onwards; in 1564 the first authentic edition of its decrees appeared. Later, some time after Flacius, Bellarmine,[24] the exponent of Tridentine Catholicism, attacked the comprehensibility of the Bible most incisively in a pamphlet of 1581 and tried to prove the need for tradition to supplement Holy Writ. In the context of these controversies, Flacius embarked on proving the possibility of valid interpretation hermeneutically. In his struggle to accomplish this task he became conscious of methods and rules which earlier hermeneutics had not elicited.

If the interpreter encounters difficulties in his text there is a sublime aid for overcoming them at hand—to place them into the context of vital Christian religious experience. As we would say, rather than expressed as dogma, the hermeneutic value of religious experience is only one example of the principle that every interpretation contains as one of its factors reference to the factual context. Beside this religious principle of interpretation there are also rational ones. The first of these is grammatical interpretation. It was Flacius who was also the first to grasp the significance of the psychological or technical principle of interpretation according to which an individual passage must be interpreted in terms of the aim and composition of the whole work. He was the first to use methodically the insights of rhetoric about the inner units of a literary product, its composition and effective elements for technical interpretation. Melanchthon's[25] transformation of Aristotle's rhetoric had prepared the ground for him. Flacius himself is

[22]M. Flacius, Lutheran theologian, 1520–1575.
[23]J. Calvin, 1509–1564.
[24]R. Bellarmine, theologian and controversialist, 1542–1621.
[25]1497–1560.

conscious of having been the first to use methodically the help to be gained from context, aim, proportion and the consistency of individual parts or links in determining the definite meaning of passages. He sees the hermeneutic value of these aids in the general perspective of the methodology. "Everywhere else too the individual parts of a whole become comprehensible through their relation to the whole and the other parts." He traces the inner forms of a work back to its style and the factors by which its impact is achieved and subtly characterizes the styles of Paul and John. It was a great step forward though confined by the limits of the rhetorical point of view. For Melanchthon and Flacius every literary work is created and can be understood according to rules. It is like a logical automaton dressed in style, images and tropes.

The formal deficiencies of his work were overcome in Baumgarten's[26] hermeneutic. A second, great theological-hermeneutic movement emerges in this. Through Baumgarten's *News from a Library in Halle* not only Dutch interpreters but English free-thinkers and anthropological interpreters of the Old Testament became known in Germany. Semler[27] and Michaelis[28] developed their ideas through personal contact with him and through participation in his work. Michaelis was the first to apply a consistent, historical view of language, history, nature and law to the interpretation of the Old Testament. Semler, the forerunner of the great Christian Baur, shattered the unity of the New Testament canon, set the correct task of understanding every individual work against its background, and then linked these writings into a new unity based on the lively historical apprehension of the original Christian conflicts between Judeo-Christianity and the more loosely organized Christians. In preparing for a theological hermeneutic he based the whole discipline with down-to-earth decisiveness on two points, interpretation from linguistic usage and interpretation from historical circumstances. With this exegesis was liberated from dogma and the grammatical-historical school founded. Ernesti's[29] subtle and careful spirit produced in his *Interpres* the classical work of this new hermeneutic. Schleiermacher still read it and developed his own hermeneutic from it. But even this step forward occurred within fixed limits. In the hands of these interpreters the composition and thought structure of every work of an age dissolves into the same threads: the locally and temporally conditioned circle of ideas. According to this pragmatic view of history human nature is uniform in its response to religion and morality and only *externally* limited by local and temporal factors. Human nature is unhistorical.

Until then classical and Biblical hermeneutics developed indepen-

---

[26]A. Baumgarten, German philosopher, 1714–1762.
[27]J. S. Semler, German philosopher, 1724–1762.
[28]J. D. Michaelis, German Protestant theologian, 1717–1791.
[29]J. A. Ernesti, German Lutheran theologian, 1707–1791.

dently. But should they not be considered as applications of a general hermeneutic? The Wolfian Meier[30] took this step in his attempt at a general hermeneutic. He conceived the idea of his discipline in the most general terms—he wanted to draft the rules which are to be observed in every interpretation of signs. But the book shows once more that one cannot invent new disciplines from the standpoint of architectonics and symmetry. This only produces blind windows through which no one can look. An effective hermeneutic could only emerge in a mind which combined virtuosity of philological interpretation with genuine philosophic capacity. A man with such a mind was Schleiermacher.

4

The background for his work was provided by Winkelmann's interpretation of works of art, Herder's congenial empathy into the spirit of ages and people, and the philology orientated towards the new aesthetic of Heyne,[31] Friedrich August Wolf[32] and his disciples. One of these, Heindorf,[33] was closely linked to Schleiermacher by their common interest in Platonic studies. All this combined in Schleiermacher with the procedure of German transcendental philosophy which reaches behind what is given in consciousness to the creative capacity which, working harmoniously and unconscious of itself, produces the whole form of the world in us. From the combination of these elements his own particular art of interpretation and the definitive founding of a scientific hermeneutic originated.

Until then, hermeneutics had at best been an edifice of rules, the parts of which—the individual rules—were held together by the aim to achieve a valid interpretation. It had separated the functions which combine in this process into grammatical, historical, aesthetic-rhetorical and factual exegesis. From the philological virtuosity of many centuries it had crystallized the rules according to which these must function. Now Schleiermacher went behind these rules to the analysis of understanding, i.e. to the comprehension of the purposive act itself and from this comprehension he deduced the possibility of valid interpretation, its aids, limits, and rules. But he could only analyze understanding which is a reshaping or reconstruction on the basis of its relationship to the process of literary creation. He recognized the imaginative consideration of the creative process through which a vital literary work originates as the basis for appreciating the process by which we understand the whole of a work from its written signs and from this the purpose and mentality of its author.

[30]G. F. Meier, German philosopher, 1718–1777.
[31]G. G. Heyne, German classical scholar, 1729–1812.
[32]F. A. Wolf, German classical scholar, 1759–1824.
[33]L. F. Heindorf, German philologist, 1774–1816.

But to solve the problem set he needed a new psychological-historical view. We have traced the relation in question from the connection between Greek interpretation and rhetoric as a methodology of a special kind of literary production. But the conception of both processes always remained a logical-rhetorical one. The categories according to which this methodology proceeded were always: production, logical connection, logical order and then a clothing of this logical understanding of a literary product with style, tropes, and images. Now quite new concepts for the understanding of a literary product came into use. It assumes the existence of a unitary and creatively active capacity which, unconscious of its doing and shaping, receives the first stimulus for its work and then develops it. Receptivity and creativity cannot be separated. Individuality is all-pervasive right to the fingertips and individual words. Its highest expression is the outer and inner form of a literary work. Such a work meets with the insatiable desire (of the reader) to supplement his own individuality through contemplation of that of others. Understanding and interpretation therefore are constantly alive and active in life itself, but they are perfected by the systematic interpetation of vital works and the unity they were given in the author's mind. This was the new conception in the special form it assumed in Schleiermacher.

One of the further conditions for this great enterprise—a general hermeneutic—was the development of a *philological* hermeneutic in terms of the new psychological-historical views by Schleiermacher and his friends. German intellectual life, in the persons of Schiller, Wilhelm von Humboldt, and the brothers Schlegel had just turned from poetic production to the understanding of the historical world. It was a powerful movement and Böckh, Dissen,[34] Welcker, Hegel, Ranke and Savigny were influenced by it. Friedrich Schlegel became Schleiermacher's guide in the art of philology. The concepts which guided him in his brilliant works on Greek poetry, Goethe and Boccaccio were: the inner form of the work, the development of the author and the articulated whole of literature. Behind his individual achievements of philolgical reconstruction lay the plan for a science of criticism, for an *ars critica* which was to be based on a theory of literary creativity. How close this plan was to Schleiermacher's *Hermeneutic* and *Critique*!

Schlegel also initiated the plan of a Plato-translation. In it he developed the new technique of interpretation which Böckh and Dissen then applied to Pindar. Plato must be understood as a philosophic artist. The goal of interpretation is the unity between the character of Platonic philosophizing and the artistic form of the Platonic works. Here philosophy is still alive, rooted in conversation; its literary presentation is only an aid to memory. So it must be dialogue, and so stylized in form that it forces us to recreate the living context of thought. At the same time the strict unity of Plato's thought

[34]G. L. Dissen, German philologist, 1784–1837.

requires that each dialogue should continue earlier, and prepare later themes, thus spinning together the threads of the different parts of the philosophy. If one follows the relation between the dialogues, their connection, which discloses Plato's central intention, emerges. According to Schleiermacher only by grasping this methodically-developed context does a real understanding of Plato emerge. Compared with this, ascertaining the chronological sequence of his works is unimportant, though the order may coincide. Böckh could say in his famous review that this masterpiece made Plato accessible to philology for the first time.

But in Schleiermacher's intellect philological virtuosity was combined for the first time with a philosophic capacity of genius. He was specifically trained in transcendental philosophy which was the first to provide adequate means for stating the problem of hermeneutics in general terms and solving it. This was the origin of a general discipline and methodology of interpretation.

Schleiermacher sketched the first draft of it, based on his reading of Ernesti's *Interpres*, in the autumn of 1804 because he wanted to use it as the start of his course of exegetic lectures in Halle. We have the hermeneutic which thus resulted only in a very ineffective form. It was strengthened by a disciple of Schleiermacher from the Halle period, Böckh, in the magnificent section of his lectures on philosophic encyclopedia.

I select from Schleiermacher's hermeneutic the statements on which further development seems to depend.

All interpretation of literary works is merely the methodical development of the process of understanding, which extends over the whole of life and relates to any kind of speech or writing. The analysis of understanding is, therefore, the basis for making interpretation systematic. But this can only be done in the analysis of literary productions. The system of rules which determines the means and limits of interpretation can only be based on the relation between understanding and creation.

The possibility of valid interpretation can be deduced from the nature of understanding. There the personalities of the interpreter and his author do not confront each other as two facts which cannot be compared: both have been formed by a common human nature and this makes common speech and understanding among men possible. Here Schleiermacher's formal expressions can be further explained psychologically. All individual differences are, in the last resort, conditioned not by qualitative differences between people but by differences of degree in their mental processes. By transposing his own being experimentally, as it were, into a historical setting, the interpreter can momentarily emphasize and strengthen some mental processes and allow others to fade into the background and thus reproduce an alien life in himself.

On the logical side this process is one of coming to know a whole context from only partially defined signs by making use of existing grammatical, logical and historical knowledge. Expressed in logical terminology this aspect of understanding consists of the combination of induction, application or general truth to a particular case and comparison. It would also be necessary to ascertain the precise nature of the above logical operations and how they combine.

Here we encounter the general difficulty of all interpretation. The whole of a work must be understood from individual words and their combination, but full understanding of an individual part presupposes understanding of the whole. This circle is repeated in the relation of an individual work to the mentality and development of its author and it recurs again in the relation of such an individual work to its literary genre. In practice Schleiermacher solved this problem most beautifully in his introduction to Plato's *Republic*; in the postscripts to his exegetic lectures there are other examples of this procedure. He started with a survey of the structure, comparable to a superficial reading, tentatively grasped the whole context, illuminated the difficulties and halted thoughtfully at all those passages which afforded insight into the composition. Only then did interpretation proper begin. Theoretically we are here at the limits of all interpretation; it can only fulfil its task to a degree; so all understanding always remains relative and can never be completed. *Individuum est ineffable* ("The individual is not definable").

Schleiermacher rejected the division of the exegetic process into grammatical, historical, aesthetic and factual interpretation which he found established. These distinctions merely indicate that grammatical, historical, factual and aesthetic knowledge must be present at the beginning of interpretation and can influence every one of its procedures. In the process of interpretation itself we can only distinguish two aspects to grasping an intellectual creation through linguistic signs. Grammatical interpretation proceeds from link to link to the highest combinations in the whole of the work. The psychological interpretation starts with penetrating the inner creative process and proceeds to the outer and inner form of the work and from there to a further grasp of the unity of all his works in the mentality and development of their author.

Here we have reached the point from which Schleiermacher developed the rules of interpretation in a masterly fashion. His theory of inner and outer form is fundamental and his drafts for a general theory of literary creation which was to form the methodology of literary history were particularly profound.

The final goal of the hermeneutic procedure is to understand the author better than he understood himself; a statement which is the necessary conclusion of the doctrine of unconscious creation.

To summarize, understanding only becomes interpretation which achieves validity when confronted with linguistic records. When we consider the philological procedures of hermeneutics and the justification for it we may—rightly—not think very highly of the practical value of such a discipline compared with the living practice of Fr. A. Wolf. But it seems to me that it has, beyond its use in the business of interpretation, a second task which is indeed its main one: it is to counteract the constant irruption of romantic whim and sceptical subjectivity into the realm of history by laying the historical foundations of valid interpretation on which all certainty in history rests. Absorbed into the context of the epistemology, logic and methodology of the human studies, the theory of interpretation becomes a vital link between philosophy and the historical disciplines, an essential part of the foundations of the studies of man.

INTRODUCTION TO BULTMANN'S
"THE PROBLEM OF HERMENEUTICS"

Rudolf Bultmann (1884–1976) stands in line with Schleiermacher and Dilthey as a major figure of hermeneutical thought. He brings theology to the threshold of postmodern hermeneutics. Bultmann was long associated with the University of Marburg (active from 1921–1951, professor emeritus until his death). In fact, Bultmann's presence was largely responsible for turning Marburg into a world center for New Testament studies. As a New Testament scholar, Bultmann's achievements may be said to be equal to any and second to none. But, remarkably, Bultmann was also a theologian of enormous influence.

As readers of Bultmann know, he did not compartmentalize New Testament scholarship and theology. He used his technical skills in New Testament historical criticism to determine what the Christian texts are trying to say to their readers. And for him, that task required knowing both what the texts said in their original settings and how that meaning can be translated into a historically conscious and scientifically shaped world. In carrying out his project, Bultmann displayed the historical-critical skills of the New Testament exegete, the philosophical practice of existential analysis (as taught by Heidegger), and the rhetoric of dialectical theology in its formulations of the being of God as "wholly other." By today's standards, he was an extraordinary thinker of astonishing breadth.

Bultmann came to the hermeneutical problem by radicalizing historical criticism, that is, by asking questions about the fundamental presuppositions of both doing New Testament scholarship at all and understanding the subject matter of theology. Taking the historicity of humanity and faith seriously, Bultmann turned to Heidegger's philosophy of human existence for the technical terminology with which to talk meaningfully about human thought, action, and faith. He says in his "Autobiographical Reflections," "I have endeavored throughout my entire work to carry further the tradition of historical-critical research as it was practiced in 'liberal' theology and to make our recent theological knowledge the more fruitful as a result."[1] Heidegger's insights into the temporal structure of understanding (see Volume 2 for an entry by Heidegger from *Being and Time*) allowed Bultmann to do this. But he was also influenced by the critique of liberal

---

[1]"Autobiographical Reflections of Rudolf Bultmann," in *The Theology of Rudolf Bultmann*, ed. Charles W. Kegley (New York: Harper & Row, 1966), pp. xix–xxv, p. xxiv.

theology offered by Karl Barth, Friedrich Gogarten, Paul Tillich, and the other dialectical theologians of the 1920s.

Karl Barth dominated the theological scene in the 1920s and 1930s. But with the publication of "New Testament and Mythology" in 1941, Bultmann became the leading theological voice in Germany. What did Bultmann say in that famous essay? I think it would be helpful to review briefly some of the central points in that essay insofar as they will help us grasp his hermeneutical theory.

In "New Testament and Mythology," Bultmann addresses the fundamental problem for interpreting the New Testament. The problem is how we can understand the New Testament, since its language and world view are mythological through and through. The New Testament appears to be irrevocably obsolete for those who occupy the world view of modern science. Consider, for example, the New Testament's mythical cosmology. It describes a three-storied universe with heaven above, hell below, and the earth at the center. Earth is a battleground in a cosmic struggle between the angelic forces of God and the demonic forces of Satan for the possession of the human soul. Today, descriptions of demons and angels, virgin birth, and bodily resuscitations, as well as the other mythical figures, have been antiquated by modern science. This provokes a crisis. Is the New Testament merely mythology, and thus on a par with other prescientific myths? Or does it contains a nonmythological meaning that we can appropriate today within the scientific world view?

Bultmann's argument is that myths generally express an understanding of human being in the world. Myths express the human feeling of dependence on a power that transcends them, a power evident in their activity and suffering. Myths, however, speak of this power in terms of tangible objects and forces, such as worldly powers or the acts of gods. The terms of the myth thus belie the human recognition that the purpose of life lies not within this world but beyond it. The discrepancy between the realistic imagery of myth and the insight into the human condition expressed through the imagery prompts criticism of the mythological language. Like other mythological texts, the New Testament invites or, more strongly, demands demythologizing. The text itself raises the question of what is meant by the mythological framework. The question is: How is it possible to interpret the nonmythological intention of the New Testament? Bultmann's answer is that Heidegger's existential hermeneutics provides the key for interpretation of the New Testament. Heidegger's thought finds special application in New Testament interpretation, because the New Testament and Heidegger similarly understand the meaning of human existence.

According to Bultmann, Heidegger teaches us that interpretation should be focused on the subject matter of the text. In the case of religious and poetic texts, such as the New Testament, the subject matter concerns the *mode of existence* or manner of self-understanding presented in the text.

Moreover, Heidegger has provided a terminology with which to make sense out of human existence. Heidegger's analysis of the two modes of human existence—authenticity and inauthenticity—bears directly on the meaning of the New Testament. For Heidegger's understanding of human existence as being in the world (Dasein), who can either gain itself in authenticity or lose itself in inauthenticity, is precisely the understanding of existence expressed in mythological terms by the New Testament. So the task of demythologizing becomes one of applying the existential analysis of Heidegger to the New Testament. Once the form of life that is the subject matter of the text is extricated from its mythological package, the New Testament is again able to speak to us. But what does it say? Consider the following features of the New Testament, in Bultmann's understanding of it.

The New Testament tells us that human existence originates and has its purpose outside the physically present world. Paul, for example, claims that to pursue security within the physically present world is illusory; we become enslaved if we try to secure our own existence through the world. Faith, for the New Testament, is a decision "I" make to entrust myself to the grace of God that breaks into the world. Faith frees the self from worldly powers of fear and desire; it frees for service to others. The New Testament thus presents two basic types of human existence: first, understanding oneself as having to secure one's existence in the world; and second, understanding oneself as trusting in an invisible and liberating power that comes to the self from outside. This much is evident simply by applying Heidegger's analysis of existence to the New Testament.

Bultmann's appropriation of Heidegger is not uncritical, however. Bultmann thought that Heidegger's *Being and Time* and the New Testament do indeed express the same basic understanding of human existence. But he held that they are nonetheless different in at least two crucial respects. First, in Heidegger, existence is always understood in terms of its openness to being itself. In the New Testament, however, existence is exposed to the God who addresses humans and demands decision. The reality of God, not simply being itself, is a basic element in the New Testament. And for Bultmann, God cannot be reduced to the totality of the universe, even being itself. God is more than being itself: being itself points to the being of God as the hidden agent of the activity of being.

Second, Heidegger thinks that insight into the meaning of human existence can save the self from fallenness into the world. In other words, Heidegger confuses the mere recognition that human existence may be won or lost with the actual power to win it authentically. Mere existential insight cannot save humans from sin or inauthenticity, however. The New Testament knows this, although Heidegger in *Being and Time* apparently did not. Hence the view that faith (or authenticity) is obtained through grace is also an element of the New Testament that Heidegger leaves out of his account of human existence.

As Bultmann understands it, the nonmythological intention of the New Testament is precisely to convince us that the New Testament offers a power that can deliver the self from bondage to the powers of the world. This power is the kerygma, the grace of God that enables faith. Faith is an event that happens to the self through the kerygma; it is manifest in readiness to accept existential anxiety. To receive the power of faith is resurrection, in that it is freedom from sin and death and freedom for divine love. Because the New Testament has the capacity to donate the power of faith, the New Testament is not merely myth but kerygma. Whereas all religious texts may be demythologized, only the New Testament presents a power of salvation in and through its language. Heidegger gives us the technical terminology by means of which the New Testament can be understood existentially. The kerygmatic power of the text, however, is neither myth nor interpretation of the mode of existence expressed in myth; it is a gift of God that imparts the faithful existence depicted in myth and deciphered in interpretation.

"The Problem of Hermeneutics" was written nine years after the famous "New Testament and Mythology." In this essay, Bultmann conceives his hermeneutical project as carrying forward the tradition of Schleiermacher and Dilthey. Bultmann applauds the shift that Schleiermacher made to focus on the understanding process as it actually occurs for deriving hermeneutical rules and purposes. And he affirms the extension Dilthey gave to Schleiermacher's program, especially in questioning how knowledge of individuality in history is possible through understanding. But unlike Schleiermacher or Dilthey, both of whom remain thoroughly modern thinkers, Bultmann develops the idea of the historicity of human expressions. In his words, this insight involves appeal to the fact that "all literary documents are historically conditioned by the circumstances of time and place."[2] With recognition of the historicity of thought embedded in language, Bultmann opens the way toward a postmodern theological hermeneutics.

The difference between Dilthey's modern hermeneutics and Bultmann's postmodern version can be glimpsed through Bultmann's emphasis on *interest*. Dilthey, following Schleiermacher, held that to understand a text from the past requires reconstructing the historical meaning by reproducing the psychical processes of the author. Reconstruction is possible, in Dilthey's view, because the common human nature between author and expositor enables the transposition of the interpreter into the mental processes of the author. Contrary to Dilthey, Bultmann claims that what makes understanding possible is the interpreter's relation in his or her life to the subject matter of the text—that which the text says. For Bultmann, the emphasis shifts from reconstruction and empathy to interest in the subject matter. An interest in what the text has to say motivates the interpretation and gives it its line of inquiry.

[2]Rudolf Bultmann, "The Problem of Hermeneutics," p. 115 below.

According to Bultmann, Schleiermacher and Dilthey missed the fact that interpretation always involves formulating a question, which aims at some objective. Thus an interpretation has presuppositions in that it is governed by a *prior understanding* of the subject. Such a prior understanding is a necessary condition of interpretation, for it makes entry into the text possible in the first instance by establishing the purpose of the inquiry. The purpose of the inquiry is dependent in turn on the interest of the inquirer. Schleiermacher and Dilthey had focused attention on the individuality of the author and the ability of the inquirer to transpose herself or himself into the mental life of the other. But the crucial condition of interpretation that eluded their sight is the life relationship of the inquirer to the subject matter expressed in the text. Interpretation of a text from the past is possible not because of empathy with the mental life of the author but because of the inquirer's interest in the subject matter and prior understanding of it.

The inquirer's interest in a text may be naive or sophisticated. And it may or may not focus directly on the subject matter of the text. For instance, interest might center on the historical context that produced the work, which is read as a source for understanding that context (as is often the case with historical narratives). In contrast, interest might be focused on the thought of the author (as is often the case in reading philosophical texts). Or, interest might be in the aesthetic style of the work. Again, interest might be in the genuine possibilities of human being expressed in the text (especially in religious and poetic works). When Dilthey spoke of increasing one's individuality—becoming oneself—through interpretation, he should have realized that what is crucial is not the otherness of the author but the claim made on the inquirer by the possibilities of human being revealed in the text.

What does this transformation of hermeneutics mean for the problem of objectivity in the human sciences? Is knowledge of the individual possible through interpretation? In Bultmann's view, the kind of knowledge enjoyed in the natural sciences is not possible. For the natural scientist, knowledge is explanation of observed regularities in nature, verified through experimental prediction. Such knowledge is achieved by carefully neutralizing the inquirer's standpoint, so that in principle anyone may reproduce the same experimental results. The situation in the human sciences is different from those in the natural sciences, however.

Historical phenomena are different from natural ones in part because of the different *interests* of the situated inquirer. Knowledge in the human sciences refers to the results of inquiry that are methodically arrived at and validated by argument and discussion. The human standpoint of the inquirer cannot be completely neutralized; experimental results cannot be reproduced at will. The humanist must, of course, silence personal wishes about the outcome of inquiry. But the inquirer does not extinguish individuality, ignoring the claim made on her or him by the text. Historical texts in the broadest sense are only allowed to be historical phenomena when their claims are heard and they touch their readers. For the humanist, in Bultmann's words, "The 'most subjective' interpretation is in this case the 'most objective'; that is, only those who are stirred by the question of their own existence can hear the claim which the text makes."[3]

Bultmann's point about the role of the inquirer had been missed by Dilthey and Schleiermacher. Their program of psychological empathy implicitly attempts to neutralize the subjectivity of the inquirer so as to approximate the objectivity of the natural scientist. For Dilthey and Schleiermacher, the inquirer should leave himself or herself behind in order to enter into the alien life of the author, there to reproduce the mental processes as they originally occurred. According to Bultmann, Schleiermacher and Dilthey here failed to realize the historical situatedness of the inquirer. By pointing out the role of interest and the prior understanding of the subject matter as a precondition of understanding and interpretation, Bultmann instituted a shift toward a postmodern hermeneutics in theology. But Bultmann made only modest headway in this postmodern turn. As the reader of this essay will see, Bultmann lacked a reflection on language as the medium of historically situated understanding. This places Bultmann in the position of gatekeeper to the postmodern paradigm, which will focus on the linguisticality of understanding.

Bultmann expresses himself as a theologian in the final section of this essay. Here his discussion partner is Karl Barth. Recall that Barth thought that we deflect our interest from the word of God as announced in Scripture when we focus on the process of understanding. In opposition to Barth, Bultmann claims that even in the case of the encounter with the word of God, we cannot avoid the problem of understanding. Indeed, Bultmann would say that especially in the case of the word of God we cannot avoid hermeneutics. For if God breaks into our historical existence, there to encounter us and to transform our intentions, we cannot avoid some preunderstanding of what historical existence is all about and what faith as a life relation is all about. Hearing the word of God implies understanding, and hermeneutics inquires into understanding.

[3]Ibid., p. xx.

THE PROBLEM OF HERMENEUTICS[1]
(1950)

Rudolf Bultmann

I

According to Wilhelm Dilthey, hermeneutics, that is, the "technique of understanding expressions of life set in written form," always draws attention to itself only "in the *context* of a great historical movement." Such a movement, in fact, makes the "understanding of the individual historical being" and so the "scientific knowledge of the individual, and indeed of the great forms of individual human being in general" a pressing concern of science.[2] If today we stand "in the context of a great historical movement," the motives for broaching the problem of hermeneutics would thus be established. And, in fact, this discussion forms with historical tradition an essential piece of reflection on the self, which is, of course at the same time a reflection on the "great forms of individual human being."

The problem with which hermeneutics is concerned is, according to Dilthey, this question: "Is such a knowledge (that is, of the great forms of individual human being) possible, and what means do we have for attaining to it?" Or, more definitely, the question "whether our understanding of the individual can be given general validity." "How can an individuality come to possess an unfamiliar, individual expression of life, bestowed on it through the senses, as a generally valid, objective understanding?"[3] Thus it is the question of the possibility of attaining to *objectivity in understanding individual human being*, namely, of the past. This question is basically an inquiry into the possibility of understanding historical phenomena at all, in so far as they are testimonies to individual human being: thus hermeneutics would be the science of understanding history in general. In actual fact Dilthey confines hermeneutics to the interpretation of "constantly fixed expressions of life," that is, of the monuments of civilization, and so primarily

---

[1]The German original was published in *Zeitschrift für Theologie und Kirche* 47 (1950): 47–69.

[2]Wilhelm Dilthey, *Die Entstehung der Hermeneutik* (1900), published with the supplements from the manuscripts in vol. 5 of the *Gesammmelte Schriften* (1924), pp. 317–383. The quotations given above are from pp. 332–3 and 317. This article is reprinted in this collection under the title "The Development of Hermeneutics."

[3]Ibid., 317, 334.

of literary documents, alongside which, however, the works of art are also of material importance.[4]

II

From the time of Aristotle *hermeneutic rules* were developed for the interpretation of literary texts—rules which have become traditional and are followed throughout as a foregone conclusion.[5] As Aristotle already saw, the first requirement is the *formal analysis* of a literary work with reference to its structure and its style.[6] Interpretation has to analyse the composition of the work, and to understand the individual from the whole, and the whole from the individual elements. The idea that every interpretation moves in a hermeneutic circle arises in this. As soon as the interpretation of ancient or

---

[4]Ibid., 319.

[5]The representation of hermeneutics which is expressed in the pregnant article by G. Heinrici in vol. 7 of the *Realencyclopädie für protestantische Theologie und Kirche* (1899), pp. 718–750, is limited to a consideration of the development of the traditional hermeneutic rules. The same thing applies to Fr. Torm's *Hermeneutik des Neuen Testaments* (1930), while Er. Fascher, in *Vom Verstehen des Neuen Testaments* (1930), tries to get beyond this without, of course, in my (Bultmann's) opinion getting a clear idea of the way to do so. In his great work *Das Verstehen*, 3 volumes (1926, 1929, 1933), Joachim Wach has sketched out the "main features of a history of hermeneutical theory in the nineteenth century"; an extraordinarily careful stocktaking with a reserve which is in my opinion far too great in regard to the position he himself takes up—one which might illuminate history from the critical standpoint. The hermeneutic principles, too, which he outlines in the *Journal of Biblical Literature* 55 (1936): 59–63, are just the old hermeneutic rules, augmented only by the "necessity of psychological understanding"—by which he manifestly intends that Schleiermacher's requirement should be given recognition, but without its further development in accordance with the lines suggested by Dilthey. Even his article "Verstehen" in *Religion in Geschichte und Gegenwart* V (1931): 1570–1573, is still—understandably enough—too sketchy. Fritz Buri gives a critical analysis in which he discusses hermeneutic problems in Protestant theology of the present day in the *Schweizerische Theologische Umschau, Festgabe für Martin Werner zum 60. Geburtstag* (1947). I find myself in agreement with him in the same way, in his struggle for the critical historical comprehension of Scripture, as I am in his refusal to accept a "pneumatic, suprahistorical comprehension of Scripture" and what is called theological hermeneutics, by virtue of which a "christological" exegesis of the Old Testament is carried on. His failure to understand my essays correctly is certainly seen in the fact that hitherto I have not made a clear distinction between the scientific comprehension of Scripture and obedience with regard to the kerygma, according to him. But above all it is due to his failure to grasp the distinction between *existentiell* and existential; he speaks of my attempt at an *"existentielle Exegese"*—at which I can only register a protest. He quotes my statement from *Offenbarung und Heilsgeschehen* (1941), p. 41, that the mythology of the New Testament is to be interpreted existentially (*"existential" zu interpretieren sei*), but writes it as *existentiell*!

Translator's note: "existential" is used normally as the general term applied to the principles of existentialist philosophy (so far as that is not a contradiction in terms!), whereas *existentiell* has reference to particular situations that are handled in a way compatible with or in agreement with these principles. The equivalents "ontological" and "ontical" have been suggested by English-speaking writers as covering this distinction.

[6]See Dilthey, *Gesammelte Schriften*, 5 (1924), p. 321, and for what follows, pp. 321ff.

foreign-language texts becomes topical, the requirement of an interpretation in *accordance with the rules of grammar* comes to mind. Already with the Alexandrians the requirements of grammatical knowledge of the language is supplemented by that of knowledge of the author's individual linguistic usage, so that a criterion was gained, for example, for deciding questions of genuineness in the interpretation of Homer. With the development of historical work in the Age of Enlightenment, the question of the individual linguistic usage of the author was developed into the inquiry *into the linguistic usage of the particular period of the text.* But hand in hand with the insight into the historical development of language goes knowledge of historical development in general, and so knowledge of the fact that all literary documents are *historically conditioned* by the circumstances of time and place; and knowledge of this must be accounted from now on the presupposition of every proper interpretation.

Philology is the science which has for its object the interpretation of literary texts, and which for this purpose makes use of hermeneutics. However, in its development it is obvious that hermeneutics as the art of scientific understanding is in no way adequately defined by the traditional hermeneutic rules. Harald Patzer has recently shown how philology, which in the first instance makes use of the science of history for the purpose of interpretation, gradually finds its way into the service of the science of history, and so becomes a branch of the science of history for which the texts are only "testimonies" or "sources" from which an historical picture—that is, a past age—is to be reconstructed.[7] This is an understandable process, as a circle also exists, of course, between philological and historical knowledge. But the result was simply that philology lost its real subject matter, the interpretation of texts for the sake of understanding them. But the more profound reason for this development is this: the task of understanding them was not grasped at a deep enough level, and seemed capable of being sufficiently discharged in the observance of those hermeneutic rules—the insight into the *process of understanding,* for which Schleiermacher once strove, was lost.

For Schleiermacher had already seen that a real understanding cannot be attained simply by the observance of hermeneutic rules. "Psychological" interpretation must be added to that governed by them—which in his terminology we call "grammatical." He sees that the composition and unity of a work cannot be understood only by the categories of a formal logical and stylistic analysis. The work must rather be understood as the life-moment of a particular man. To the comprehension of the "external form" must be joined that of the "internal form," which is, he would say, the subject not of

---

[7]Harald Patzer, "Der Humanismus als Methodenproblem der Klassischen Philologie," *Studium Generale* 1 (1948): 84–92.

an objective, but of a subjective, "intuitive" interpretation.[8] Hence interpreting is a "copying," a "modelling" in its live relationship to the process of literary production itself. Comprehension becomes its "own reproduction of the live nexus of thoughts."[9] But such "reproduction" is possible because "the personalities of the interpreter and his author do not confront each other as two facts which cannot be compared." Rather it is that both have been formed on the basis of human nature in general and by this social life of men is made possible for purposes of speech and understanding.[10] Dilthey appropriates these ideas to himself, and tries to clarify them further: "All individual differences are, in the last resort, conditioned not by qualitative differences between people but by differences of degree in their mental processes. By transposing his own being experimentally, as it were into a historical setting the interpreter can momentarily emphasize and strengthen some mental processes and allow others to fade into the background and thus reproduce an alien life in himself." The conditioning of understanding "lies in the fact that nothing can appear in an unfamiliar, individual form of expression which was not also contained in the quality of living that comprehends it." And that can be interpreted in this way: "Exegesis is a work of personal art, and its most consummate execution is conditioned by the mental make-up of the exegete; and so it rests on *affinity*, intensified by a thoroughgoing communion with the author—by constant study."[11]

Schleiermacher's conception of understanding naturally stands in an historical connection with Winckelmann's "interpretation of works of art" and with Herder's "congenial empathy into the spirit of ages and peoples."[12] It is orientated to the interpretation of philosophical and literary texts. But does it also hold good for other texts? Are we to suppose that the interpretation of a mathematical or medical text arises from the consummation of the psychical processes which have been taking place in the author? Or do we only understand the inscriptions of the Egyptian kings telling of their deeds of war, or the ancient Babylonian and Assyrian historical and chronological texts, or the epitaph of Antiochus of Commagene or the *Res Gestae Divi Augusti*—do we understand them only on the basis of their translation into the inner, creative process in which they arose?

No, it would appear! And "no," in actual fact, in so far as the interpretation is thereupon removed from the sphere of understanding the contents *directly* mediated by the texts, and so of understanding their mathematical or

---

[8]Apart from Dilthey, cf. especially Wach, *Das Verstehen*, I (1926), pp. 83ff., 102ff., 143, 148–9.

[9]The formulations appended to Dilthey's *Charakteristik, Gesammelte Schriften*, 5 (1924), pp. 327–28, 335.

[10]Dilthey, Ibid., p. 329; Wach, *Das Verstehen*, I (1926) p. 141. Schleiermacher finds the foundation for the intuitive procedure in the fact that every man, apart from the fact that he himself is a peculiar being, has a "receptiveness" (*Empfänglichkeit*) in regard to all other men.

[11]Dilthey, *Gesammelte Schriften*, 5 (1924), pp. 329, 334, 332.

[12]Dilthey, Ibid., pp. 326–7.

medical knowledge or what they have to say about facts and processes in the world's history. But that is probably precisely the primary interest of those who read such texts. Naturally they can also be read in another interest, as for example the interpretation of those inscriptions by George Misch makes clear.[13] That is, as the "expressions of life" as forms of individual, historical being, whether as the expressions of the life of individual persons, or as expressions of the "life-spirit" or understanding of being of particular epochs. It is obvious, therefore, that the view of Schleiermacher and Dilthey is one-sided, in so far as it is guided by a particular formulation of the question.

A comprehension—an interpretation—is, it follows, *constantly orientated to a particular formulation of a question, a particular "objective."* But included in this, therefore, is the fact that it is never without its own presuppositions: or, to put it more precisely, that it is *governed always by a prior understanding of the subject,* in accordance with which it investigates the text. The formulation of a question, and an interpretation, is possible at all only on the basis of such a prior understanding.[14]

The subject in relation to which Dilthey investigates the texts is "life"— that is, "historical," personal life, which has taken shape in the texts as "constantly set expressions of life": the "psychical life" which is to be brought to our objective knowledge by interpretation, on the basis of "expressions in the shape of sensory data perceptible to the senses." But this is not the only subject to which interpretation can be limited: and so, too, the process of understanding characterized in this interest may well not be the only one which can be accomplished in an interpretation. Rather will the process of understanding be different, according as the purpose of the interpretation is determined.

It is manifestly not enough to say that it is determined in accordance with the nature of the texts, that is, according to the subject directly expressed in the text from time to time, or the leading interest at any given time. For all texts can, in fact, be understood in accordance with Dilthey's formulation, that is, as documents of "historical," personal life. What we have to go on, first of all, is of course the fact that the investigation of the texts is orientated to the subject which is spoken of in them and directly mediated by them. I will, for example, interpret a text on the history of music in the

---

[13]Georg Misch, *Geschichte der Autobiographie,* I (1907).

[14]The formula, that the comprehension of the author and his work is the real aim of exegesis (Hermann Gunkel, *Monatsschrift für die kirchliche Praxis* (1904): 522), is right in so far as it rejects the view that the exegesis is or may be governed by dogmatic or practical interests. Otherwise it tells us absolutely nothing about the problem of hermeneutics. For this is where the problem really begins! What comprehension of the author is intended—a psychological one, or a biographical one, perhaps?—and so on. And how is the work to be understood—as a problem in an historical light, or aesthetically, and so on?

light of the question of what it contributes to my understanding of music and the history of music, and so on.

III

The formulation of a question, however, arises from an interest which is based in the life of the inquirer, and it is the presupposition of all interpretations seeking an understanding of the text which is to be interpreted, and forms the link between the text and its expositor. So far as Dilthey *characterizes the relationship between author and expositor* as the conditioning factor for the possibility of comprehension of the text, he has, in fact, laid bare the presupposition of all interpretation which has comprehension as its basis. For this conditioning factor holds good not just for the special formulation of Schleiermacher and Dilthey, but for every interpretation which cannot ever be effected merely by following the traditional "hermeneutical rules." It is simply a question of determining this presupposition more exactly. Instead of reflection on the individuality of author and expositor, on their psychical processes and on the spiritual make-up or intellectual consanguinity of the expositor, it requires consideration of the simple fact, that *the presupposition for understanding is the interpreter's relationship in his life to the subject which is directly or indirectly expressed in the text.*[15] The interpretation is effected not by the fact that the individuality of the expositor and that of his author stand over against each other as two facts that do not admit comparison with one another, but by the fact that they both have the same relation in life to the subject which is under discussion and so is open to inquiry (that is, to the extent to which they have such a relation), because (and so far as) they stand in the same context of living experience. This relationship to the subject, with which the text is concerned and so with reference to which the text is being investigated, is the presupposition of comprehension.[16] Just for this reason it is also under-

[15]This idea is manifestly what is intended in the "idealistic metaphysics of comprehension, as a result of which historical comprehension is only possible on the basis of an identity of the human mind in its various objectivizations, and of these with the absolute mind" (Buri, Ibid., p. 25). But J. Chr. K. von Hofmann has seen what is the decisive factor in his own way, when he says that biblical hermeneutics does not seek to represent itself as an independent and self-contained science, but has as its presupposition hermeneutics in general; that it does not, however, consist simply in the application of this to the Bible, but assumes the existence of a relation to the contents of the Bible [*Biblische Hermeneutik* (1880), p. 1ff.]. On Hofmann, see Wach, *Das Verstehen*, II (1929), pp. 365, 369–70.

[16]In this sense, too, the "intellectual consanguinity" demanded of the historian is understood in Wilhelm von Humboldt, Boeckh and especially Droysen. On this, see Hildegard Astholz, *Das Problem "Geschichte" untersucht bei Johannes Gustav Droysen* (1933); she quotes among other things this characteristic sentence of Droysen's: "Every man is indeed a historian. But the man who makes history his vocation has something to do which is of human concern to a special degree (p. 97f.)."

standable that every interpretation is guided by a particular purpose; for a question which has some kind of orientation about it is only possible on the basis of the conditions of a context of living experience. And in the same way it is understandable for this reason, that every interpretation incorporates a particular prior understanding—namely, that which arises out of the context of living experience to which the subject belongs.

This fact can clearly be illustrated by consideration of *the process of translation from a foreign language*, that at the back of every interpretation there lies a relationship in life to the subject with which the text is concerned, and so the subject about which the investigation of the text is concerned. The meaning of this process is, as a rule, only concealed by the fact that knowledge of the ancient languages of our cultural sphere is transmitted to us by tradition, and need not be acquired afresh. Knowledge of a foreign language can only be acquired afresh (assuming texts in several languages are not available) when the objects (things, relations, etc.) designated by the words are familiar—familiar from use and wont. An object or a relation which is simply meaningless in the context of my life, in my environment, and in the way I lead my life, is also incomprehensible and untranslatable in its linguistic nomenclature—or can only be understood and translated in such a way that a word is chosen for the thing concerned which describes it in regard to external appearances, as for example the rendering of the *churunga* of the Australian aborigines by "boomerang."[17] Observation of the custom, as far or to such an extent as this is comprehensible, can lead to further variance, so that *churunga* can be described as "a potent magical instrument," as the idea of magical instruments is comprehensible to me from the context of my own life. Fundamentally the same process is, therefore, present when texts are given in or by means of pictorial representations, which for their part can be understood from the context of one's own life. In actual fact the child's understanding and learning to speak also takes place in close conjunction with his becoming familiar with his environment, and his intercourse with others, in brief, in the context of his life.

Interpretation, therefore, always presupposes a living relationship to the subjects which are directly or indirectly expressed in the text. I only understand a text dealing with music if and in so far as I have a relationship to music (for which reason many parts of Thomas Mann's *Doktor Faustus* are incomprehensible to many readers) and I only understand a mathematical text if I have a relationship to mathematics, and an historical representation in so far as historical life is familiar to me—in so far as I know from my own life what a state is, and what life in a state and its potentialities are—or a novel, because I know from my own life what, for example, love and friendship, family and vocation, are—and so on. It is just because of this that

---

[17]Nathan Söderblom, *Das Werden des Gottesglaubens* (1916), p. 41ff.

much literature is a closed book to many people, according to their age and education.

Of course my living relationship to a subject may be a quite naive and unreflective one, and in comprehension or interpretation it can be brought into the conscious mind and clarified. It may be superficial and generalized, and it may be deepened and enriched, modified and corrected by understanding the text. In any case a living relationship to the subject concerned is presupposed, and this knowledge eliminates in advance false problems such as the question of the possibility of understanding the being of "alien souls." This is simply given in common relationship of author and expositor to the subject concerned at any given time. Dilthey maintains that the "a common human nature" is a condition for the possibility of understanding, and therefore that "nothing can appear in an alien, individual form of expression which would not also be found in the living experience containing it." This could be further defined by saying that a condition for expositor is the fact that the expositor and author live as men in the same historical world, in which "human being" occurs as "being" in an environment, in understanding intercourse with objects and our fellow-men. And, of course, an integral part of that understanding intercourse is to be found in our inquiries, our problems, our struggles and our sufferings—both in joy and in ascetic withdrawal from the world.

IV

Interest in the subject motivates the interpretation and gives it its way of formulating the question—its line of inquiry. The orientation of the interpretation is not problematical, when guided by inquiry into that particular subject, the imparting of which is the intention of the text itself; thus, for example, the interpretation of a mathematical text or one on the theory of music, where I want to derive knowledge about mathematics or music from it. And it is the same with the interpretation of a narrative text, where I want to get to know what is narrated in it—thus, for example, the interpretation of chronicles, but also of Herodotus or Thucydides, where I do not want to get to know anything further than the historical relationships and occurrences reported by them. The same applies, for example, in the case of a hellenistic saga which tells, it is true, of fictitious occurrences, but which I read as an entertaining story. In the former instances we have historical instruction, in the latter case we have entertainment as the object of comprehension. In all these instances the formulation of the inquiry is quite naive; it becomes plain in its peculiarity when it is a question of understanding a poetical text of some standing—Homer's, for example; that is, if such texts can be read not as poetry but simply as narrative—which is indeed to a great extent the case to begin with, just as works of plastic art are investigated by naive and especially child observers from this point of view: "What story do they tell?"

And indeed plastic art does have this significance in part, as illustrative art, say in the "illuminated" manuscripts of the Bible, or in the cycles of mosaic work, as in the Cathedral of Monreale. And fundamentally it is the same thing when in the modern world a Goethe album, let us say, is published with illustrations of the life of Goethe.

But, of course, the subject soon gets more complicated: for the naive investigation of the texts does not long survive the stage of childhood, even although this never loses its right as the inquiry into what the text is directly seeking to impart. Naive investigation continues to hold sway especially in regard to *scientific texts*, which seek to transmit knowledge directly. For then, too, when the investigation goes on to understand the texts as witnesses of the history of the science concerned, a prior understanding of what they transmit directly in the way of knowledge is not to be excluded. And indeed the interest in the history of mathematics, for example, normally remains orientated to mathematical knowledge itself, and so to the subject intended in the texts concerned, and does not subordinate its interpretation to an alien interest, let us say to the interest of civilization—this is illustrated, for example, by the fact that the historian of this kind can ignore for his part the history of mathematics, as Jacob Burckhardt does in his *Kultur der Renaissance*. The object becomes different when scientific texts are read as testimonies to the history of science.

A similar modification occurs in the interpretation of *narrative and especially historical texts*: and in a twofold way—(1) in that they are not read primarily as testimonies for what they record, but as testimonies of their own time, from which their record comes. It is then not what is recorded but the recorder that is of primary interest. This can still be initiated within the intention of the recorder, in so far as the historical knowledge of the recorder provides us with the criterion for the understanding of his work. (2) When the historical text is interpreted as a testimony for the history of history, or of the science of history. In this the intention of the text is left entirely out of the question, for it does not seek to inform science about history, but to narrate history itself. It is now itself incorporated in history and is no longer interpreted as the medium of historical knowledge, but rather as its object.

But what is the position with regard to the *novel*? Even the naive reader doubtless reads not merely with curious interest in what is happening; and in the tension of getting to know what is going to happen there lies more than just curiosity; there lies, in fact, inner sympathy with the fate of the hero, into whose position the reader transposes himself. He does not take cognizance of the situation. He takes part in the experience: he is deeply moved—his frame of mind is actually affected, and his passions are aroused. And is not the author's intention indeed fulfilled only by this?

This way of looking at things is, in fact, the appropriate one with regard to the *works of genuine poetry*. They lay themselves open to sympathetic understanding, as Aristotle already makes clear in his own way, by his teaching of fear and pity as the effect of tragedy. And they lay open to such sympathetic understanding *human being in its possibilities as the possibilities that belong specifically to the one who understands.*

But it is not just appropriate understanding and the effects of poetry which are released in it, but the effect of *art* in general, which is of this kind. If we may designate the beautiful as "what is true in the realm of the visible,"[18] and if we can conceive of what is "true" in a radical sense as the laying bare of human being—laid bare by art as the power to show what is true in what is beautiful—then it holds good to say that the interpreter should understand the *possibilities of man's being* revealed in poetry as also in art.

If in poetry and art the "true" is presented to our view, and if it is here in its proper sphere in the comprehension that has been won, then it is the subject of philosophy as an object of reflective and speculative thought. Hence if the interpretation of *philosophical* texts is to be a really comprehending one, it must itself be concerned by the investigation of truth—in other words, it can only go on in discussion with the author. Only those understand Plato who philosophize with him. Interpretation lacks understanding if it investigates the text in accordance with dogmatic propositions considered as the result of scientific research, and if in consequence it takes the text in question as the "source" of a particular stage in the history of philosophy, and thus sees this history as an event which lies in the past, instead of revitalizing it for the present. For it is indeed no abandonment of real philosophical understanding to describe the history of philosophy, but it has to happen in such a way that the understanding of its history becomes the understanding of philosophy itself, as the problems connected with an understanding of "being," and so the "self," become clear.

The real aim of interpretation had to be rediscovered for the texts and monuments of poetry and art, of philosophy and religion, after it had been suppressed by the formulation which became dominant in the age of what we call the *historical school.* Dilthey's efforts and his harking back to Schleiermacher serve just this purpose. In a different way, *the texts and monuments were understood as "sources,"* under the hegemony of the historical school—mostly as sources from which the picture of a past age or of a period of time is to be reconstructed. They were interpreted as testimonies to an historical epoch or as links or stages in an historical process, and in this it does not fundamentally matter in what way the historical process was understood, whether as political or social history, as the history of the human spirit or as the history of civilization in the broadest sense of the term.

It is not as if texts and monuments could not be understood as *"sources"* too, and indeed must be so understood. And, in fact, there are even texts which only merit the rank of sources being accorded to them, in accordance

[18]Patzer, Ibid., p. 90.

with their content. The "classical" texts and monuments are to be distinguished from them, even if the frontiers cannot be clearly defined. If we are to interpret such documents as sources, they must nevertheless be always understood in the sense of their specific purpose—at least to begin with: and they are often so understood in an unreflective, superficial way. For example, if Plato is to be used as a source for the civilization of Athens in the fifth century, there must be some means of understanding the content of his work, if he is to serve as a source at all. However, the question directed to him as to a document of the history of civilization side-steps its own actual concern, and can with difficulty descry this in its totality and in its profundity: the formulation of the inquiry which takes the text as a source is, then actually justified in the service of a true interpretation. For every interpretation moves of necessity in a circle: the individual phenomenon is on the one hand comprehensible on the basis of its age (and environment) and on the other hand is itself a precondition to making this comprehensible. The understanding of Plato from his age stands in the service of a real interpretation of Plato and belongs to the sphere of those traditional hermeneutic rules.

Other forms of investigation developed in the period of the historical school in accordance with their authentic meaning do, analogously, serve the purposes of true comprehension, like (let us say) Heinrich Wölfflins's "interpretation on the basis of the history of style of works of art," or the numerous examinations carried out on the *history of types and motifs* in literature as in the plastic arts. Of course all such investigations can also conceal the real question in interpretation. The same thing holds good for *the formal analysis, made from the point of view of aesthetics*, of works of literature and art; when it is achieved, real comprehension is not as yet attained, but it can doubtless be prepared for by such analysis as, say, in Karl Reinhardt's book on Sophocles and in Paul Friedländer's work on Plato.[19] When we compare the interpretations of Michelangelo's *Last Judgement* by Jacob Burckhardt and by Graf Yorck von Wartenburg, as Karl Löwith has compared them,[20] we can see how different the interpretation of the same work of art can be, according as it is guided by interest in the form or by interest in the content of the work. And Erich Auerbach in his book *Mimesis* has a quite masterly way of making the formal analysis of works of poetry fruitful for the interpretation of their content.[21]

[19]Karl Reinhardt, *Sophokles* (2nd Edn., 1943); Paul Friedländer, *Platon, II: Die Platonischen Schriften* (1930). I may mention also Reinhardt's lectures and essays, which appeared in 1948 under the title *Von Werken und Formen*.

[20]*Theologische Rundschau*, N.F.II (1930): 44–46. *Theologische Rundschau*, N.F.II (1930): 44–46.

[21]Erich Auerbach, *Mimesis: Dargestellte Wirklichkeit in der abendländischen Literatur* (1946). In his *Bildnisstudien* (1947), Ernst Buschor attempts to make the stylistic analysis of what

Real comprehension of poetry and art, as of works of philosophy and religion is, as we have seen, orientated, according to Dilthey, to the *inquiry into the understanding of one particular existence in history*, and to this formulation of the question all historical documents may—as has also been shown—be subordinated. Can we grasp this intention of interpretation even more definitely and more aptly? The intention has already been modified in such a way that it amounts to illustrating *the possibilities of man's being* which are revealed in poetry and in art—and the same thing goes for philosophical and religious texts. My endeavor is to make this even clearer.

In an essay on J. J. Winckelmann's *Griechenbild*,[22] Fritz Blättner has contrasted very instructively the *intentio recta* and the *intentio obliqua* in the survey of religious works of art. The former presupposes the faith of the spectator, who sees in the work of art a representation of the divine reality in which he believes, as something objective; it sees the work of art not as a work of art at all; and for its need, an oleograph of the Madonna would, for example, serve the same purpose as a painting of Raphael or a Pietà by Michelangelo. On the one hand the *intentio obliqua* does not inquire into the objective meaning of the work of art, and for it, it is all one "whether an Apollo or a Saint Sebastian stand before our eyes; whether a Christ or a Moses or a slave was objectively intended: it inquires into the "humanity," into the "spirit from which the work of art proceeded, and a testimony to which it was."

This change took place with Winckelmann: he arrived at "the view which perceives, behind what is objectively intended and said, the spirit, the genius of the creator and of his race and which draws out of its experience of this what it feels to be the essential thing in the work." In the same way, too, the great philologists Friedrich Ast and August Boeckh inquired into the "spirit" of antiquity in general on the basis of which the individual work must be understood.[23] It is the mode of understanding which was developed by Herder and which gained the mastery in the romantic movement. This approach can, of course, also be linked with the historical school, as Winckelmann discovered the epochs in the history of Greek art; in considering that the sequence of these epochs conformed to laws, he could even be regarded as a forerunner of Oswald Spengler. In the period of National Socialism such a formulation of the inquiry was carried to absurd lengths—characterized, of course, by the biological view—but in its fundamental idea it is also alive in the essays on the hisory of art by Hermann

---

we may perhaps call an existential interpretation serviceable, though hardly in categories which are adequately clear.

[22]Fritz Blättner, "Das Griechenbild J. J. Winckelmanns," *Jahrbuch Antike und Abendland* 1 (1944): 121–132.

[23]See Wach, *Das Verstehen*, I (1926), pp. 106, 185.

Grimm, whose object it was to write a history of the artistic imagination of the race.[24]

This approach is, of course, right in a relative sense, and the relativism which is peculiar to it (which may have its background in a pantheistic belief in the divine which is in everything human) need not become predominant or reach conscious expression—as in the case of Winckelmann. The spirit which he saw taking shape in Greek art was the signal representation of the human spirit in general, on which man at all time has to model himself.

Dilthey's endeavour is manifestly to find his way out of the ultimately aesthetic approach of romanticism. He is, of course, still caught up in it when he sees the interest in the "feeling after strange states of the soul" (*Nachfühlen fremder Seelenzustände*) as lying in the happiness arising out of this, and when he speaks of the "enchantment" which that man enjoys who gazes beyond all the limitation of his own age into the civilizations of the past. But such a man does not only enjoy the enchantment; he also "appropriates for himself the power of the past." In that the person who understands "finds the history of the soul in all history," he "supplements" by a comprehending contemplation his own individuality, and learns "to come to himself in an understanding way."[25] In such sentences, however, it is clear that real understanding does not arise from the satisfying contemplation of an alien individuality as such, but basically from the possibilites of human being which are revealed in it, which are also those of the person who understands, who makes himself conscious of them in the very art of comprehension. Real understanding would, therefore, be *paying heed to the question posed in the work which is to be interpreted, to the claim which confronts one in the work*, and the "fulfillment" of one's own individuality would consist in the richer and deeper opening up of one's self (that is, out of one's incomplete, inert self which is always falling into the danger of persistent devotion to the status quo) by the work.[26]

It may be that Graf Yorck saw more clearly than Dilthey when he says in defining his position against Ranke's writing of history: "Heaven and earth are one and the same in history if anywhere." For behind that lies the view that the understanding of history does not lie in aesthetic contemplation but is a religious process, because the reality of history does not become visible at all for the spectator who is not personally involved in it. "Ranke is a great

[24]See Reinhardt Buchwald's foreword to the essays by Hermann Grimm, which appeared under the title *Deutsche Künstler.*

[25]The formulations according to Dilthey, *Gesammelte Schriften,* V (1924), pp. 317, 328, and according to the essay by Fritz Kaufmann, "Geschichtsphilosophie der Gegenwart," *Philosophische Forschungsberichte* 10 (1931): 109–117.

[26]See Kaufmann, Ibid., pp. 54–5, in the discussion with Simmel on personal relationship to what happens in history. On the perception of the claim of history in the case of Droysen, see Astholz, *Das Problem "Geschichte" untersucht bei J. G. Droysen (1933),* p. 106, and pp. 120–21 on comprehension as a function proper to life and as an act.

magnifying glass for which the things which have disappeared cannot become realities."[27] Yorck's words show how historical understanding is the perception of the claim of history, and is critical self-examination: "Michelangelo preached the renaissance of ethics with the most potent bias, in the Sistine Chapel. The mute, simple crosses scratched by Christians in the stones of the Mamertine prison found expression through Luther. If there is anything more potent than Michelangelo's *Last Judgment,* it is those crosses, points of light in a subterranean sky, the symbol of the transcendence of the consciousness."[28]

The problem of comprehension has been brought into decisive clarity by Heidegger's demonstration of understanding as something existential, and by his analysis of interpretation as the development of understanding, but above all by his analysis of the problem of history and his interpretation of the historical nature of existence.[29] Following up Heidegger's ideas, Fritz Kaufmann has given us a critical survey of the philosophy of history in the present day, from which the significance of a comprehending interpretation of historical documents springs clearly to view.[30]

VI

Now let us draw the threads together. The presupposition of every comprehending interpretation is a *previous living relationship to the subject,* which directly or indirectly finds expression in the text and which guides the direction of the inquiry. Without such a relationship to life in which text and interpreter are bound together, inquiry and comprehension are not possible, and an inquiry is not motivated at all. In saying this we are also saying that every interpretation is necessarily sustained by a certain *prior understanding* of the subject which lies under discussion or in question.

From the interest of the subject arises *the nature of the formulation of the inquiry, the direction of the investigation,* and so the hermeneutic principle applying at any given time. The direction of the investigation may be identical with the purpose of the text, and the latter then directly mediates the subject into which inquiry is made. But it may also arise from interest in the circumstances which may become apparent in all possible

---

[27]*Correspondence between Wilhelm Dilthey and Count Paul Yorck von Wartenburg 1877–1897* (1923), p. 60.

[28]Ibid., p. 120.

[29]Martin Heidegger, *Sein und Zeit* (1927), especially sections #31 and #32. On Heidegger, see Fritz Kaufmann, *Philosophische Forschungsberichte* 10 (1931): 118ff.

[30]See Kaufmann, Ibid., p. 41: "the understanding of an historical context of life is the understanding of how human life *(Dasein)* at one time understood or misunderstood its own problems, and stood up to them or fled from them." See also Droysen in Astholz, *Das Problem "Geschichte" untersucht bei J. G. Droysen* (1933), p. 121.

phenomena of life and consequently in all possible texts. The direction of the investigation then does not coincide with the purpose of the text, and the text mediates the subject under investigation indirectly.

The object of interpretation can therefore be supplied, for example, by the interest in the *reconstruction of the context of past history*—in political history, in the history of the problems and forms of social life, in intellectual history, in the history of civilization in its widest reaches; and in this, interpretation will always be determined by the view the interpreter has of history in any case.

The object of interpretation can be established by the *psychological interest*, which subjects the texts, let us say, to a formulation of the question in terms of individual, race, or religious psychology—that is, the question of the psychology of poetry, of technique, etc. In all these cases the interpretation is guided by a presupposed prior understanding of psychical phenomena.

The object can be given by the *aesthetic interest*, which subjects the texts to a formal analysis, and investigates a work as a work of art in relation to its structure, its "external" and its "internal" form. The aesthetic interest may be linked up with a romantic, religious interest, but it may also go no further than a consideration of style.

Lastly, the object of interpretation can be established by *interest in history as the sphere of life in which human existence moves*, in which it attains its possibilities and develops them, and in reflection upon which it attains understanding of itself and of its own particular possibilties. In other words, the object can be given by the inquiry into "human being" as one's own "being." The texts lying nearest to hand for such investigation are those of philosophy and religion and poetry: but fundamentally all texts (like history itself) can be subjected to it. Such an investigation is always guided by a *prior understanding* of "human being"—by a particular understanding of existence, which may be very naive, but from which in general in the first instance the categories develop, which make an investigation possible—for example, the question of "salvation," of the "meaning" of personal life, or of the "meaning" of history, of the ethical norms of action, the order of human community life, and such like. Without such a prior understanding and the questions initiated by it, the texts are mute. It is of no value to eliminate the prior understanding: on the contrary, it is to be brought into our consciousness and critically tested in our understanding of the text—it is to be put to the test; in short, it is valid in the investigation of the text to allow oneself to be examined by the text, and to hear the claim it makes.

In such a view the answer is also found to the dubious question *whether objectivity in the knowledge of historical phenomena, objectivity in interpretation, is attainable.* If the concept of objective knowledge is taken from natural science (in which, moreover, it may also have become problematical today in the traditional sense), then it is not valid for the comprehension of historical phenomena; for these are of a different kind from those of nature. They do not exist as historical phenomena at all, without the historical subject which comprises them. For facts of the past only become historical phenomena when they become significant for a subject which itself stands in history and is involved in it; only when they have something to say; and that they only do for the subject which comprehends them. Of course, it is not as if this subject can affix a meaning to them in accordance with subjective inclination, but so that they take on a meaning for those who are linked up with them in their life in history. In a certain sense their own future therefore belongs to the historical phenomenon, a future in which this is shown for the first time in its true nature.

It would be a mistake to say that every historical phenomenon is significant in many directions. For even if, naturally, it may be exposed without defence to the arbitrary nature of interpretation in accordance with inclination, it nevertheless has basically one meaning for scientific comprehension. It may indeed be true, however, that every *historical phenomenon is many-sided and complex*; it is subject to diverse formulations of the question, whether in the realm of intellectual history, of psychology, or of sociology, or whatever it may be, in so far as it only arises out of the historical link of the interpreter with the phenomenon. Every formulation of this kind leads to unambiguous, objective understanding, if the interpretation is methodically carried out. And naturally it is no objection that genuine comprehension forms itself in discussion, out of the conflict of opinions. For the simple fact that every interpreter is confined within his subjective capacity has no fundamental relevance.

Knowledge gained methodically is an "objective" knowledge, and that can only mean a knowledge appropriate to the subject, when this has found its way into a particular formulation of the inquiry. To call the formulation itself "subjective" is absurd. It may be so called when we take cognizance of the fact that it must naturally be selected at any given time by a "subject." But what do we mean here by "selected"?[31] The formulation certainly does not arise as such out of individual preference, it arises from history itself. The history of each phenomenon, corresponding to its complex nature, presents different aspects—that is, gains significance or, better, makes a claim in several directions. And in history each interpreter, to correspond with the motifs at work in the multifariousness of life in history, attains that formulation of the question in which the phenomenon has something to say specifically to him.

The demand that the interpreter must silence his subjectivity and extinguish his individuality, in order to attain to an objective knowledge is, therefore, the most absurd one that can be imagined. It is sensible and right

---

[31]In so far as it is not a question of the embarrassed and fortuitous choice of the subject for a dissertation.

only in so far as we mean by it that the interpreter must silence his personal wishes with regard to the outcome of the interpretation—let us say, the wish that the text should confirm a particular (dogmatic) opinion or should supply instructions which can be utilized for practical purposes—which, of course, was and is often enough the case in the history of exegesis. It is true enough that a lack of presuppositions with regard to the results is also demanded axiomatically and uncompromisingly for interpretation—as for all scientific research. Otherwise this demand absolutely misjudges the nature of real comprehension. For the latter presupposes *the utmost liveness of the comprehending subject, and the richest possible unfolding of his individuality.* Just as the interpretation of a work of poetry and of art can only be a success for those who allow themselves to be touched by it, so the comprehension of a political or sociological text can only be such for those who are stirred by the political and social life. The same thing, finally, holds good for that comprehension to which Schleiermacher and Dilthey orientate their hermeneutic theory, and which may be designated as the comprehension of historical phenomena in the ultimate and highest sense; and of the interpretation which investigates the texts with reference to the possibilites of human being as of one's own being. The "most subjective" interpretation is in this case the "most objective," that is, only those who are stirred by the question of their own existence can hear the claim which the text makes. The monuments of history "speak to us out of the depths of reality, which have produced them, only when we ourselves, from our own readiness for experience, know of problems, of ultimately unsurmountable want and jeopardy, which constitute the ground and the abyss of our being-in-the-world."[32]

VII

The interpretation of bibical writings is not subject to conditions different from those applying to all other kinds of literature. In the first place the old hermeneutic rules of grammatical interpretation, formal analysis, and explanation on the basis of the conditions of the historical periods are indisputably valid. It is clear, then, that here, too, the presupposition for comprehension is the connection of text and interpreter, which is found on the life relationship of the interpreter—on his previous relationship to the subject, which is passed on by the text. A presupposition for comprehension here, too, is a prior understanding of the subject.

Today this assertion meets with the *contradiction* that the subject about which the Holy Scriptures, and especially the New Testament, speak is the action of God, of which there can be absolutely no prior understanding, as the natural man does not have a previous relationship to God, but can only

[32]Kaufmann, Ibid., p. 41.

know of him through the revelation of God, that is, to be precise, by his action.

This contradiction is only apparently right. For man, of course, can have just as little a prior understanding of God's action becoming a reality in an event, as he can of other events taken as events. Before I hear of the death of Socrates from what has been passed on from one generation to another, I can know of nothing of him—and just as little as of the murder of Caesar or of Luther's nailing up of his theses. But in order to understand these events as historical events and not as mere random occurrences, I must certainly have a prior understanding of the historical possibilities within which they gain their significance and so their character as historical events. I must know what a life is for philosophical inquiry, what makes occurrences into political events, what possibilities there are in the Catholic and Protestant attempts at self-understanding, in which human being stands as "being" making its decision for itself. (It will hardly be necessary to remark that this knowledge naturally need not be an explicit one.)

In the same way the *comprehension of records about events as the action of God* presupposes a prior understanding of what may in my case be termed the action of God—let us say, as distinct from man's action, or from natural events. And if this is countered by saying that neither can man know who God is before his manifestation, nor, consequently, what God's action may be, then we have to reply that *man may very well be aware who God is, namely, in the inquiry about him.* If his existence were not motivated (whether consciously or unawares) by the inquiry about God in the sense of the Augustinian *"Tu nos fecisti ad Te, et cor nostrum inquietum est, donec requiescat in Te"* ("Thou hast made us for thyself, and our heart is restless until it rests in thee"), then neither would he know God as God in any manifestation of him. In human existence an existentiell knowledge about God is alive in the form of the inquiry about "happiness," "salvation," the meaning of the world and of history; and in the inquiry into the real nature of each person's particular "being." If the right to designate such inquiries as the inquiry about God can be attained only from belief in the manifestation of God, the phenomenon as such is the relation of the matter to the manifestation.

Existentiell knowledge about God exists in *some kind* of explicit form, when it gains conscious expression. For example, if it is consciously expressed in the question "What must I do to be saved?" (Acts 16.30), then in it some kind of notion of "salvation" is presupposed. The inquiry directed at the New Testament must be prepared for a correction of the notion it brings with it in hearing what the New Testament has to say. However, it can only receive such a correction if the basic intention of the inquiry, as comprised in the concept of "salvation," coincides with the intention of the answer given in the New Testament.

Now at least for scientific exegesis, it is decisively a question of the relevant interpretation of the inquiry, and that means, at the same time, the *relevant interpretation of human existence*. To work this out is a matter for human reflection—concretely, the task of philosophical, or existential analysis of human being. It is axiomatic that such work is not the prerequisite for paying simple heed to what the New Testament says—which is directed directly towards an *existentiell* understanding of the self, and not towards an existential knowledge. The case is different, however, when it is a question of scientific interpretation of Scripture. It takes its orientation from the inquiry into the understanding of human existence which finds expression in the Scriptures. Hence it has to concern itself with the relevant concepts in which human existence may be spoken of. These lie in the life relationship of the exegete to the subject expressed in Scripture, and they include a prior understanding of the subject. It is a mistake to think we can understand a word of the New Testament without such a prior understanding and the concepts which emanate from it, if it is to be understood as the Word of God. The interpreter requires critical reflection on the relevant concepts if he does not seek to read the biblical writings as a compendium of dogmatic pronouncements, or as "sources" for the reconstruction of a section of past history, or to study a religious phenomenon or the nature of religion in general, or to know the psychological course and theoretical objectivization of religious experiences; and if, on the contrary, he wishes to make Scripture itself speak as a power which has something to say to the present, to present-day existence. If the object of interpretation is designated as the inquiry about God and the manifestation of God, this means, in fact, that it is the inquiry into the reality of human existence. But then interpretation has to concern itself with the abstract facets of the existential understanding of existence.

VIII

Karl Barth rejects the view that a theological proposition can only be valid when it can show itself to be a genuine component part of the Christian understanding of *human* existence.[33] Here we have only to discuss this in so far as theological propositions are interpretations of scriptural pronouncements, in so far, therefore, as Barth contests my demand for an existential interpretation of Scripture. He does it in the following terms (in connection with words related to the principal propositions of the Christian confession of faith): "They (these propositions) are doubtless all related to human existence. They make possible and give a foundation to the Christian understanding of them, and so they also become—in an altered form— definitions of human existence. But they are not so originally. Originally they define the being and the activity of the God who is *different* from man

[33]Karl Barth, *Die Kirchliche Dogmatik*, III/2 (1948), p. 534.

and who *confronts* man: of Father, Son and Holy Ghost. And so for that reason they are not reducible to propositions about the inner life of man."

The last sentence betrays complete misunderstanding of what existential interpretation, and the meaning attached to "existence" in it, is. This is not the "inner life of man" at all, which can be brought under observation while setting aside what is different from it and what it encounters (whether environment, fellow-man or God)—say from a view which has to do with the psychology of religion, but at all events not from an existential one. For the latter seeks to contemplate and to understand the real existence (in history) of man, who exists only in a living connection with what is "different" from him—only in encounters. And existential analysis is concerned with the relevant abstract sphere in which that might occur. Barth obviously orientates his views of it on a concept of anthropology taken from Feuerbach, and ascribes this to Wilhelm Hermann, instead of seeing that Hermann is struggling (even if he does so with an inadequate body of abstract categories) to comprehend human being as "being-in-history."

We must demand of Barth that he give an account of his body of abstract categories! He concedes to me, for example, that the resurrection of Jesus is not an historical fact which can be established by the means at the disposal of historical science. But from this he thinks it does not follow that it did not *happen*: "Can *such* history, too, not really have taken place as history, and can there not also be a legitimate recognition of *such* history, which certainly for reasons of good taste we will abstain from calling an 'historical fact,' and which the historian in the modern sense may by all means call 'saga' or *Legende*, because it, in fact, shuns the means and methods together with with the tacit presuppositions of this historian?"[34]

My question is, what does Barth understand by "have taken place as history" and "history"? What kind of events are those about which it can be said that they "have really taken place as history in time far more certainly than everything which the 'historian' can establish as such?[35]" It is perfectly clear that Barth is interpreting the pronouncements of Scripture by means of an imported body of abstract categories. What is the origin and meaning of this apparatus of abstract thought?

Further: what kind of way of "endowing with faith" is it, if faith is to be brought over against the assertion of events which are said to have taken place as history in time and history, yet cannot be established by the means and methods of historical science? How do these events come into the believer's field of vision? And how is such faith distinguished from a blind acceptance involving a *sacrificium intellectus*? In what sense is Barth appealing to an imperative of truthfulness, which is of a higher or different kind from that forbidding us to consider anything true, which contradicts the

[34]Ibid., p. 535.
[35]Ibid., p. 535f.

truths actually presupposed in the understanding I have of the world—the understanding which is the guide for all my activity.[36] What elements, then, did the mythical picture of the world contain? It is a picture which, certainly, we need not adopt as a totality, but from it we may appropriate something by an eclectic process.[37] The purpose of my existential interpretation of myth is precisely to inquire into the possibility of a valid meaning for the mythical picture of the world, and in this I am trying to proceed methodically, while in the case of Barth I can perceive only arbitrary assertions. What, then, is his principle of selection?

Manifestly in Karl Barth's sense, Walter Klaas[38] holds up against me this proposition: "Whoever allows Scripture alone to be the criterion and yardstick of preaching [where do I dispute that?], whoever holds the work of the prophets and apostles to be foreordained and repeats it, as he has responsibly heard it, is carrying out the interpretation of Scripture." Such words merely show that the man who pronounces them has still not got the perspective of the problem of interpretation of the Scriptures at all. The exegete is to "interpret" Scripture, after he has responsibly "heard" what Scripture has to say! And how is he to "hear" without *understanding*? The problem of interpretation is precisely that of understanding!

[36]Ibid., p. 536f.

[37]Ibid., pp. 536–37.

[38]Walter Klaas, *Der moderne Mensch in der Theologie Rudolf Bultmanns* (1947), p. 29. This is a relevant and understanding contribution to the discussion. It is only to be regretted that the author has manifestly not understood the meaning of *Entmythologisierung* as a hermeneutic principle, and does not understand the distinction between existential and *existentiell* comprehension.

INTRODUCTION TO HEIDEGGER'S "LANGUAGE"

Martin Heidegger's first published work, *Being and Time,* would alone have assured Heidegger's place in the philosophical pantheon. Volume 2 of this collection contains the crucial excerpt on understanding, along with a discussion of its place in the hermeneutical tradition. I refer the reader of the upcoming essay, "Language," to the second volume, especially if *Being and Time* is not a familiar work. For in that earlier work of 1927, Heidegger coined the notion of a "hermeneutics of existence," which is presupposed by the present essay.

Breaking from the modernist assumptions, and taking Bultmann and others with him, the Heidegger of *Being and Time* questioned Dilthey's view that hermeneutics finds its genuine identity as the theory and methodology of the human sciences and thus is analogous to the theories of explanation appropriate to the natural sciences. Heidegger did not merely challenge particular topics in Dilthey's theoretical construction, while leaving uncriticized the modernist assumptions of objectivism, methodologism, and justification through epistemology. Rather, Heidegger called into question the fundamental conception of modernist hermeneutics; he transformed the identity of hermeneutics by exposing the ontological foundation of modern hermeneutical theory.

For Heidegger, the questions of modern hermeneutics, such as "How do we understand texts?" or "How is understanding possible?" are important but derivative questions. The way we answer them depends on our answers to more basic questions, such as "What is the mode of being of Dasein, the one whose being is to understand? What does the being of Dasein disclose about the meaning of being as such?" The question about the meaning of being, as interpreted through the being of human understanding, was for Heidegger the primary hermeneutical question. With this reformulation of the question behind hermeneutical inquiry, hermeneutics advanced beyond the problematic that preoccupied Dilthey. Under Heidegger's hand, hermeneutics was transformed from a theory of textual interpretation into practical philosophy and speculative ontology.

After the Second World War, something astonishing happened. Heidegger once again broke onto the philosophical scene in a way that would exercise a world-wide influence. As Otto Pöggeler put it, "Heidegger succeeded Heidegger."[1] The later thought of Heidegger is difficult and cryptic. I cannot hope to give even a hint of the corpus as a whole. But I do want to indicate some of the issues, crucial to hermeneutics, that Heidegger raises in the essay presented here. I shall begin, however, with brief reference to Heidegger's reflections on language in *Being and Time*.

In *Being and Time*, Heidegger raises anew the forgotten question of the meaning of being. Our ontological amnesia may be demonstrated by referring to paradigm sentences, such as "The sky is blue," or "I am happy." Ordinarily, when we reflect on our understanding of such sentences, we focus first on the particular entity denoted by the subject term ("the sky," "I") and then on the universal quality or state of affairs named by the nominative predicate ("blueness," "happiness"). Forgotten is the connection between particular and universal, a connection indicated grammatically by the copula ("is"). Being refers, in fact, both to the *connection* of percept and concept, particular and universal, and to the enactment of the connection, the act of connect*ing*. In the region between the givenness to experience of particulars and the abstract intelligibility of universals, being "is."

In Heidegger's existential analysis of Dasein, the enactment of being— the connecting process by which beings come to be—is described with reference to the primordial modes of Dasein's being (*existentials*), called understanding and mood. Dasein finds itself here, attuned to the world and in a mood, and it projects possibilities for itself to be. The attuned understanding is temporal activity, thus historical. Moreover, the primordial connecting activity is articulated in discourse (*Rede*), a third and co-original *existential* alongside understanding and mood. Language is explained existentially, as the structure of Dasein's being that articulates the intelligibility of experience. Language is rooted in the openness to the world that constitutes the being of Dasein.

In Heidegger's later reflections on language, represented by the classic essay to follow, Heidegger no longer focuses on Dasein as the locus of language. Instead, Heidegger reverses the the customary view of the initiative behind language from "Dasein speaks" to "Language speaks." Language is no longer primarily a human activity, namely, the expression of thought and feeling for purposes of communication. Rather, language is the address of being itself, the appearance and concealment of being as such. Interpretation thus deals most primordially with the possibility of entering into dialogue with the speaking of being in its address to Dasein. Joseph Kockelmans puts it as follows. In his later writings, Heidegger

> gave up the idea that Dasein "has" language and defended the view that Dasein is merely the place where language speaks. Language is no

[1]Otto Pöggeler, "Heidegger Today" in *Southern Journal of Philosophy* 8, (1970): 280.

longer just a tool, but it itself speaks, and man's speaking is merely a response to its speaking, a response which presupposes that Dasein must learn to hear and listen to what the language of Being has to say.[2]

The overarching theme of the later writings is the linguisticality of being. The emergence of being is tied to the origin of language. The primordial "saying" of language is understood as the advent of being itself. As Heidegger elsewhere wrote, language is the "house of being," it is being itself appearing historically as word.

What we find in this essay is a second Heideggerian transformation of hermeneutics. In *Being and Time*, Heidegger inaugurated ontological hermeneutics as the "interpretation of Dasein." Dasein is disclosed as interpretive or hermeneutical in its being, and as such Dasein is open to the meaning of being (which it preunderstands). In "Language," being itself as language gathers and distinguishes world and things (being and beings). The being of language is the expression precisely of the identity and difference between world as a totality of meaning and things in their distinctness. Language is the mediating of the identity and difference of the single activity of being and the many things that "are." Interpretation is the meditative, even poetic, process of listening and giving voice to the linguistic (and hence finite) appearance of being. Being is primary over human intention; not human thought but being is what enters language.

"Language" was given as a lecture in October 1950 and reprinted in *On the Way to Language* (*Unterwegs zur Sprache*) in 1957. Again quoting Kockelmans's fine study of Heidegger, the strategy employed by Heidegger is to take the interpretation of Trakl's poem "A Winter Evening" "as an occasion to explain the manner in which Being as language, by addressing and hailing Dasein, lets the difference come forth which in turn makes it possible for world and thing to come-to-pass."[3]

The lecture begins with Heidegger speaking of the nearness of language to humanness—"Language belongs to the closest neighborhood of man's being."[4] The proximity of language is evident in the fact that when we try to define the essence of language, we have no place outside of language from which to objectify it. Something essential to language is lost when we formulate the essence of language, even in the self-evidently successful view of speech as the audible expression and communication of human feelings and thoughts. Hence Heidegger takes up another standpoint concerning language. He entertains the view that language has a divine, not a human, origin.

This view brings the figurative and symbolic aspects of language to the

---

[2]Joseph Kockelmans, *The Truth of Being: Reflections on Heidegger's Later Philosophy* (Bloomington: Indiana University Press, 1984), p. 147.

[3]Ibid., p. 152.

[4]Martin Heidegger, "Language," p. 141 below.

foreground; Heidegger decides to let some primal symbols of language speak on their own. In this way, language will announce its own essence; the one reflecting need no longer seek vainly for a position outside of language as an object of reflection. To the end of letting language express its own essence for thought, he selects the Trakl poem, "A Winter Evening." A philosophical contemplation follows, undertaken as a close reading of what is said in the text. Heidegger's reading is characteristically eccentric. He does not present a formal analysis of the poem in the style of literary criticism, although he does articulate the structure of the poem. In contrast to any formalism, Heidegger's reading holds itself accountable to what is said in the poem itself. He claims not to break the poem down through formal methods, but to have listened to what the poem says.

Heidegger's interpretation of "A Winter Evening" hinges on understanding the relation between the imagery in the poem and language. The poem describes a winter evening. In the first stanza, events outside a house are depicted: snow falls on the window; the vesper bell tolls. Inside, a table is set. Here, language bids things to come into a presence that is also an absence: the images are present as meanings to the reader, but are not physically present. The linguistic appearance of these imagistic "things" presents the world, because things are called into the "fourfold" structure of world as sky and earth, mortals and divinities. In the second stanza, language initially calls to mortals who wander on wayward courses. For errant mortals, who also appear within the fourfold world, the world ("being") appears as the tree of graces, source of the fruit that falls to us unearned.

In the first two stanzas, the relation between one and many, world and things, is announced. Because world grants things, and things bear world, world and thing (being and beings) interpenetrate each other. They share a middle in which they are one, and across which they are two. This middle of world and things is called the "dif-ference." The dif-ference both holds apart and conjoins. It is not a third thing in addition to world and things, nor is it a distinction between two regions of being. Rather, the dif-ference is the identity and difference of world and things. It appears as the speaking of language itself, the creative medium and ground of the identity and difference of world and things.

In the third stanza, language bids the middle, the threshold or dif-ference of world and thing. In hailing the dif-ference, language speaks. And what it announces is the emerging of duality out of unity. The *process* of differentiating is a unity; the *content* of differentiating is the differentiated, the fall into duality. Hence the image of dif-ference is the threshold that pain has turned to stone. Pain adheres to dif-ference insofar as difference always signals loss of unity. But the duality in dif-ference also abides as a sign of unity. The pain of finite language illuminates the wholeness of being: conditioned words bespeak being in spite of their limitations. The dif-ference is shown as bread and wine upon the table—image of the fruits of heaven and earth, gifts from divinities to mortals.

At the end of the third stanza, which bids the dif-ference, the speaking of the poem becomes the peal of stillness. The poem is over, but language speaks on. And mortals? For their part, they speak insofar as they can listen and respond to the speaking of language, the call of being itself.

LANGUAGE
(1950)

Martin Heidegger

Man speaks. We speak when we are awake and we speak in our dreams. We are always speaking, even when we do not utter a single word aloud, but merely listen or read, and even when we are not particularly listening or speaking but are attending to some work or taking a rest. We are continually speaking in one way or another. We speak because speaking is natural to us. It does not first arise out of some special volition. Man is said to have language by nature. It is held that man, in distinction from plant and animal, is the living being capable of speech. This statement does not mean only that, along with other faculties, man also possesses the faculty of speech. It means to say that only speech enables man to be the living being he is as man. It is as one who speaks that man is—man. These are Wilhelm von Humboldt's words. Yet it remains to consider what it is to be called—man.

In any case, language belongs to the closest neighborhood of man's being. We encounter language everywhere. Hence it cannot surprise us that as soon as man looks thoughtfully about himself at what is, he quickly hits upon language too, so as to define it by a standard reference to its overt aspects. Reflection tries to obtain an idea of what language is universally. The universal that holds for each thing is called its essence or nature. To represent universally what holds universally is according to prevalent view, the basic feature of thought. To deal with language thoughtfully would thus mean to give an idea of the nature of language and to distinguish this idea properly from other ideas. This lecture, too, seems to attempt something of that kind. However, the title of the lecture is not "On the Nature of Language." It is only "Language." "Only" we say, and yet we are clearly placing a far more presumptuous title at the head of our project than if we were to rest content with just making a few remarks about language. Still, to talk about language is presumably even worse than to write about silence. We do not wish to assault language in order to force it into the grip of ideas already fixed beforehand. We do not wish to reduce the nature of language to a concept, so that this concept may provide a generally useful view of language that will lay to rest all further notions about it.

To discuss language, to place it, means to bring to its place of being not so much language as ourselves: our own gathering into the appropriation.

We would reflect on language itself, and on language only. Language itself is—language and nothing else besides. Language itself is language. The understanding that is schooled in logic, thinking of everything in terms of calculation and hence usually overbearing, calls this proposition an empty tautology. Merely to say the identical thing twice—language is language— how is that supposed to get us anywhere? But we do not want to get anywhere. We would like only, for once, to get to just where we are already.

This is why we ponder the question, "What about language itself?" This is why we ask, "In what way does language occur as language?" We answer: *Language speaks*. Is this, seriously, an answer? Presumably—that is, when it becomes clear what speaking is.

To reflect on language thus demands that we enter into speaking of language in order to take up our stay with language, i.e., within *its* speaking, not within our own. Only in that way do we arrive at the region within which it may happen—or also fail to happen—that language will call to us from there and grant us its nature. We leave the speaking to language. We do not wish to ground language in something else that is not language itself, nor do we wish to explain other things by means of language.

On the tenth of August, 1784, Hamann wrote to Herder:[1]

> If I were as eloquent as Demosthenes I would yet have to do nothing more than repeat a single word three times: reason is language, *logos*. I gnaw at this marrow-bone and will gnaw myself to death over it. There still remains a darkness, always, over this depth for me; I am still waiting for an apocalyptic angel with a key to this abyss.

For Hamann, this abyss consists in the fact that reason is language. Hamann returns to language in his attempt to say what reason is. His glance, aimed at reason, falls into the depths of an abyss. Does this abyss consist only in the fact that reason resides in language, or is language itself the abyss? We speak of an abyss where the ground falls away and a ground is lacking to us, where we seek the ground and set out to arrive at a ground, to get to the bottom of something. But we do not ask now what reason may be; here we reflect immediately on language and take as our main clue the curious statement, "Language is language." This statement does not lead us to something else in which language is grounded. Nor does it say anything about whether language itself may be a ground for something else. The sentence, "Language is language," leaves us to hover over an abyss as long as we endure what it says.

Language is—language, speech. Language speaks. If we let ourselves fall into the abyss denoted by this sentence, we do not go tumbling into emptiness. We fall upward, to a height. Its loftiness opens up a depth. The

---

[1] Johann Georg Hamann, *Schriften VII*, ed. F. Roth and G. A. Wiener (Berlin: G. Reimer, 1821), pp. 151 ff.

two span a realm in which we would like to become at home, so as to find a residence, a dwelling place for the life of man.

To reflect on language means—to reach the speaking of language in such a way that this speaking takes place as that which grants an abode for the being of mortals.

What does it mean to speak? The current view declares that speech is the activation of the organs for sounding and hearing. Speech is the audible expression and communication of human feelings. These feelings are accompanied by thoughts. In such a characterization of language three points are taken for granted:

First and foremost, speaking is expression. The idea of speech as an utterance is the most common. It already presupposes the idea of something internal that utters or externalizes itself. If we take language to be utterance, we give an external, surface notion of it at the very moment when we explain it by recourse to something internal.

Secondly, speech is regarded as an activity of man. Accordingly we have to say that man speaks, and that he always speaks some language. Hence we cannot say, "Language speaks." For this would be to say: "It is language that first brings man about, brings him into existence." Understood in this way, man would be bespoken by language.

Finally, human expression is always a presentation and representation of the real and the unreal.

It has long been known that the characteristics we have advanced do not suffice to circumscribe the nature of language. But when we understand the nature of language in terms of expression, we give it a more comprehensive definition by incorporating expression, as one among many activities, into the total economy of those achievements by which man makes himself.

As against the identification of speech as a merely human performance, others stress that the word of language is of divine origin. According to the opening of the Prologue of the Gospel of St. John, in the beginning the Word was with God. The attempt is made not only to free the question of origin from the fetters of a rational-logical explanation, but also to set aside the limits of a merely logical description of language. In opposition to the exclusive characterization of word-meanings as concepts, the figurative and symbolical character of language is pushed into the foreground. Biology and philosophical anthropology, sociology and psychopathology, theology and poetics are all then called upon to describe and explain linguistic phenomena more comprehensively.

In the meantime, all statements are referred in advance to the traditionally standard way in which language appears. The already fixed view of the whole nature of language is thus consolidated. This is how the idea of language in grammar and logic, philosophy of language and linguistics, has remained the same for two and a half millennia, although knowledge about language has progressively increased and changed. This fact could even be adduced as evidence for the unshakable correctness of the leading ideas about language. No one would dare to declare incorrect, let alone reject as useless, the identification of language as audible utterance of inner emotions, as human activity, as a representation by image and by concept. The view of language thus put forth is correct, for it conforms to what an investigation of linguistic phenomena can make out in them at any time. And all *questions* associated with the description and explanation of linguistic phenomena also move within the precincts of this correctness.

We still give too little consideration, however, to the singular role of these correct ideas about language. They hold sway, as if unshakable, over the whole field of the varied scientific perspectives on language. They have their roots in an ancient tradition. Yet they ignore completely the oldest natural cast of language. Thus, despite their antiquity and despite their comprehensibility, they never bring us to language as language.

Language speaks. What about its speaking? Where do we encounter such speaking? Most likely, to be sure, in what is spoken. For here speech has come to completion in what is spoken. The speaking does not cease in what is spoken. Speaking is kept safe in what is spoken. In what is spoken, speaking gathers the ways in which it persists as well as that which persists by it—its persistence, its presencing. But most often, and too often, we encounter what is spoken only as the residue of a speaking long past.

If we must, therefore, seek the speaking of language in what is spoken, we shall do well to find something that is spoken purely rather than to pick just any spoken material at random. What is spoken purely is that in which the completion of the speaking that is proper to what is spoken is, in its turn, an original. What is spoken purely is the poem. For the moment, we must let this statement stand as a bare assertion. We may do so, if we succeed in hearing in a poem something that is spoken purely. But what poem shall speak to us? Here we have only one choice, but one that is secured against mere caprice. By what? By what is already told us as the presencing element of language, if we follow in thought the speaking *of language*. Because of this bond between what we think and what we are told by language we choose, as something spoken purely, a poem which more readily than others can help us in our first steps to discover what is binding in the bond. We listen to what is spoken. The poem bears the title:

A Winter Evening

Window with falling snow is arrayed,
Long tolls the vesper bell,
The house is provided well,
The table is for many laid.

Wandering ones, more than a few,
Come to the door on darksome courses.

Golden blooms the tree of graces
Drawing up the earth's cool dew.

Wanderer quietly steps within;
Pain has turned the threshold to stone.
There lie, in limpid brightness shown,
Upon the table bread and wine.

The two last verses of the second stanza and the third stanza read in the first version (Letter to Karl Kraus, December 13, 1913):[2]

Love's tender power, full of graces,
Binds up his wounds anew.

O! man's naked hurt condign.
Wrestler with angels mutely held,
Craves, by holy pain compelled,
Silently God's bread and wine.

The poem was written by Georg Trakl. Who the author is remains unimportant here, as with every other masterful poem. The mastery consists precisely in this, that the poem can deny the poet's person and name.

The poem is made up of three stanzas. Their meter and rhyme pattern can be defined accurately according to the schemes of metrics and poetics. The poem's content is comprehensible. There is not a single word which, taken by itself, would be unfamiliar or unclear. To be sure, a few of the verses sound strange, like the third and fourth in the second stanza:

Golden blooms the tree of graces
Drawing up the earth's cool dew.

Similarly, the second verse of the third stanza is startling:

Pain has turned the threshold to stone.

But the verses here singled out also manifest a particular beauty of imagery. This beauty heightens the charm of the poem and strengthens its aesthetic perfection as an artistic structure.

The poem describes a winter evening. The first stanza describes what is happening outside: snowfall, and the ringing of the vesper bell. The things outside touch the things inside the human homestead. The snow falls on the

[2]Georg Trakl, *Die Dichtungen*, ed. Kurt Horwitz (Zürich: Arche Verlag, 1946). This poem, "Ein Winterabend," may also be found in *Die Dichtungen*, 11th edition (Salzburg: Otto Müller, 1938), p. 124. The letter to Karl Kraus may be found in *Erinnerung an Georg Trakl: Zeugnisse und Briefe* (Salzburg: Otto Müller, 1959), pp. 172–73.—Translator.

window. The ringing of the bell enters into every house. Within, everything is well provided and the table set.

The second stanza raises a contrast. While many are at home within the house and at the table, not a few wander homeless on darksome paths. And yet such—possibly evil—roads sometimes lead to the door of the sheltering house. To be sure, this fact is not presented expressly. Instead, the poem names the tree of graces.

The third stanza bids the wanderer enter from the dark outdoors into the brightness within. The houses of the many and the tables of their daily meals have become house of God and altar.

The content of the poem might be dissected even more distinctly, its form outlined even more precisely, but in such operations we would still remain confined by the notion of language that has prevailed for thousands of years. According to this idea language is the expression, produced by men, of their feelings and the world view that guides them. Can the spell this idea has cast over language be broken? Why should it be broken? In its essence, language is neither expression nor an activity of man. Language speaks. We are now seeking the speaking of language in the poem. Accordingly, what we seek lies in the poetry of the spoken word.

The poem's title is "A Winter Evening." We expect from it the description of a winter evening as it actually is. But the poem does not picture a winter evening occurring somewhere, sometime. It neither merely describes a winter evening that is already there, nor does it attempt to produce the semblance, leave the impression, of a winter evening's presence where there is no such winter evening. Naturally not, it will be replied. Everyone knows that a poem is an invention. It is imaginative even where its seems to be descriptive. In his fictive act the poet pictures to himself something that could be present in its presence. The poem, as composed, images what is thus fashioned for our own act of imaging. In the poem's speaking the poetic imagination gives itself utterance. What is spoken in the poem is what the poet enunciates out of himself. What is thus spoken out, speaks by enunciating its content. The language of the poem is a manifold enunciating. Language proves incontestably to be expression. But this conclusion is in conflict with the proposition "Language speaks," assuming that speaking, in its essential nature, is not an expressing.

Even when we understand what is spoken in the poem in terms of poetic composition, it seems to us, as if under some compulsion, always and only to be an expressed utterance. Language is expression. Why do we not reconcile ourselves to this fact? Because the correctness and currency of this view of language are insufficient to serve as a basis for an account of the nature of language. How shall we gauge this inadequacy? Must we not be bound by a different standard before we can gauge anything in that manner? Of course. That standard reveals itself in the proposition, "Language speaks." Up to this point this guiding proposition has had merely the function of warding off the ingrained habit of disposing of speech by throwing it at once among the phenomena of expression instead of thinking it in its own terms. The poem cited has been chosen because, in a way not further explicable, it demonstrates a peculiar fitness to provide some fruitful hints for our attempt to discuss language.

Language *speaks*. This means at the same time and before all else: *language* speaks. Language? And not man? What our guiding proposition demands of us now—is it not even worse than before? Are we, in addition to everything else, also going to deny now that man is the being who speaks? Not at all. We deny this no more than we deny the possibility of classifying linguistic phenomena under the heading of "expression." But we ask, "How does man speak?" We ask, "What is it to speak?"

> Window with falling snow is arrayed
> Long tolls the vesper bell.

This speaking names the snow that soundlessly strikes the window late in the waning day, while the vesper bell rings. In such a snowfall, everything lasting lasts longer. Therefore the vesper bell, which daily rings for a strictly fixed time, tolls long. The speaking names the winter evening time. What is this naming? Does it merely deck out the imaginable familiar objects and events—snow, bell, window, falling, ringing—with words of a language? No. This naming does not hand out titles, it does not apply terms, but it calls into the word. The naming calls. Calling brings closer what it calls. However this bringing closer does not fetch what is called only in order to set it down in closest proximity to what is present, to find a place for it there. The call does indeed call. Thus it brings the presence of what was previously uncalled into a nearness. But the call, in calling it here, has already called out to what it calls. Where to? Into the distance in which what is called remains, still absent.

The calling here calls into a nearness. But even so the call does not wrest what it calls away from the remoteness, in which it is kept by the calling there. The calling calls into itself and therefore always here and there—here into presence, there into absence. Snowfall and tolling of vesper bell are spoken to us here and now in the poem. They are present in the call. Yet they in no way fall among the things present here and now in this lecture hall. Which presence is higher, that of these present things or the presence of what is called?

> The house is provided well,
> The table is for many laid.

The two verses speak like plain statements, as though they were noting something present. The emphatic "is" sounds that way. Nevertheless it speaks in the mode of calling. The verses bring the well-provided house and the ready table into that presence that is turned toward something absent.

What does the first stanza call? It calls things, bids them come, Where? Not to be present among things present; it does not bid the table named in the poem to be present here among the rows of seats where you are sitting. The place of arrival which is also called in the calling is a presence sheltered in absence. The naming call bids things to come into such an arrival. Bidding is inviting. It invites things in, so that they may bear upon men as things. The snowfall brings men under the sky that is darkening into night. The tolling of the evening bell brings them, as mortals, before the divine. House and table join mortals to the earth. The things that were named, thus called, gather to themselves sky and earth, mortals and divinities. The four are united primally in being toward one another, a fourfold. The things let the fourfold of the four stay with them. This gathering, assembling, letting-stay is the thinging of things. The unitary fourfold of sky and earth, mortals and divinities, which is stayed in the thinging of things, we call—the world. In the naming, the things named are called into their thinging. Thinging, they unfold world in which things abide and so are the abiding ones. By thinging, things carry out world. Our old language calls such carrying *bern, bären*— Old High German *beran*—to bear; hence the words *gebaren*, to carry gestate, give birth, and *Gebärde*, bearing, gesture. Thinging, things are things. Thinging, they gesture-gestate-world.

The first stanza calls things into their thinging, bids them come. The bidding that calls things calls them here, invites them, and at the same time calls out to the things, commencing them to the world out of which they appear. Hence the first stanza names not only things. It simultaneously names world. It calls the "many" who belong as mortals to the world's fourfold. Things be-thing—i.e., condition—mortals. This now means: things, each in its time, literally visit mortals with a world. The first stanza speaks by bidding the things to come.

The second stanza speaks in a different way. To be sure, it too bids to come. But its calling begins as it calls and names mortals:

Wandering ones, more than a few . . .

Not all mortals are called, not the many of the first stanza, but only "more than a few"—those who wander on dark courses. These mortals are capable of dying as the wandering toward death. In death the supreme concealedness of Being crystalizes. Death has already overtaken every dying. Those "wayfarers" must first wander their way to house and table through the darkness of their courses; they must do so not only and not even primarily for themselves, but for the many, because the many think that if they only install themselves in houses and sit at tables, they are already bethinged, conditioned, by things and have arrived at dwelling.

The second stanza begins by calling more than a few of the mortals. Although mortals belong to the world's fourfold along with the divinities, the earth and sky, the first two verses of the second stanza do not expressly call the world. Rather, very much like the first stanza but in a different sequence, they at the same time name things—the door, the dark paths. It is the two remaining verses that expressly name the world. Suddenly they name something wholly different:

> Golden blooms the tree of graces
> Drawing up the earth's cool dew.

The tree roots soundly in the earth. Thus it is sound and flourishes into a blooming that opens itself to heaven's blessing. The tree's towering has been called. It spans both the ecstasy of flowering and the soberness of the nourishing sap. The earth's abated growth and the sky's open bounty belong together. The poem names the tree of graces. Its sound blossoming harbors the fruit that falls to us unearned—holy, saving, loving toward mortals. In the golden-blossoming tree there prevail earth and sky, divinities and mortals. Their unitary fourfold is the world. The word "world" is now no longer used in the metaphysical sense. It designates neither the universe of nature and history in its secular representation nor the theologically conceived creation (*mundus*), nor does it mean simply the whole of entities present (*kosmos*).

The third and fourth lines of the second stanza call the tree of graces. They expressly bid the world to come. They call the world-fourfold here, and thus call world to the things.

The two lines start with the word "golden." So that we may hear more clearly this word and what it calls, let us recollect a poem of Pindar's: *Isthmians* V. At the beginning of this ode the poet calls gold *periosion panton*, that which above all shines through everything, *panta*, shines through each thing present all around. The splendor of gold keeps and holds everything present in the unconcealedness of its appearing.

As the calling that names things calls here and there, so the saying that names the world calls into itself, calling here and there. It entrusts world to the things and simultaneously keeps the things in the splendor of world. The world grants to things their presence. Things bear world. World grants things.

The speaking of the first two stanzas speaks by bidding things to come to world, and world, to things. The two modes of bidding are different but not separated. But neither are they merely coupled together. For world and things do not subsist alongside one another. They penetrate each other. Thus the two traverse a middle. In it, they are at one. Thus at one they are intimate. The middle of the two is intimacy—in Latin, *inter*. The corresponding German word is *unter*, the English *inter-*. The intimacy of world and thing is not a fusion. Intimacy obtains only where the intimate—world and thing—divides itself cleanly and remains separated. In the midst of the two, in the between of world and thing, in their *inter*, division prevails: a dif-ference.

The intimacy of world and thing is present in the separation of the between; it is present in the dif-ference. The word dif-ference is now removed from its usual and customary usage. What it now names is not a generic concept for various kinds of differences. It exists only as this single difference. It is unique. Of itself, it holds apart the middle in and through which world and things are at one with each other. The intimacy of the difference is the unifying element of the *diaphora*, the carrying out that carries through. The dif-ference carries out world in its worlding, carries out things in their thinging. Thus carrying them out, it carries them toward one another. The dif-ference does not mediate after the fact by connecting world and things through a middle added on to them. Being the middle, it first determines world and things in their presence, i.e., in their being toward one another, whose unity it carries out.

The word consequently no longer means a distinction established between objects only by our representations. Nor is it merely a relation obtaining between world and thing, so that a representation coming upon it can establish it. The dif-ference is not abstracted from world and thing as their relationship after the fact. The dif-ference for world and thing *disclosingly appropriates* things into bearing a world; it *disclosingly appropriates* world into the granting of things.

The dif-ference is neither distinction nor relation. The difference is, at most, dimension for world and thing. But in this case "dimension" also no longer means a precinct already present independently in which this or that comes to settle. The dif-ference is *the* dimension, insofar as it measures out, apportions, world and thing, each to its own. Its allotment of them first opens up the separateness and towardness of world and thing. Such an opening up is the way in which the dif-ference here spans the two. The dif-ference, as the middle for world and things, metes out the measure of their presence. In the bidding that calls thing and world, what is really called is: the dif-ference.

The first stanza of the poem bids the things to come which, thinging, bear world. The second stanza bids that world to come which, worlding, grants things. The third stanza bids the middle for world and things to come: the carrying out of their intimacy. On this account the third stanza begins with an emphatic calling:

Wanderer quietly steps within.

Where to? The verse does not say. Instead, it calls the entering wanderer into the stillness. This stillness ministers over the doorway. Suddenly and strangely the call sounds:

Pain has turned the threshold to stone.

This verse speaks all by itself in what is spoken in the whole poem. It names pain. What pain? The verse says merely "pain." Whence and in what way is pain called?

Pain has turned the threshold to stone.

"Turned . . . to stone"—these are the only words in the poem that speak in the past tense. Even so, they do not name something gone by, something no longer present. They name something that persists and that has already persisted. It is only in turning to stone that the threshold presences at all.

The threshold is the ground-beam that bears the doorway as a whole. It sustains the middle in which the two, the outside and the inside, penetrate each other. The threshold bears the between. What goes out and goes in, in the between, is joined in the between's dependability. The dependability of the middle must never yield either way. The settling of the between needs something that can endure, and is in this sense hard. The threshold, as the settlement of the between, is hard because pain has petrified it. But the pain that became appropriated to stone did not harden into the threshold in order to congeal there. The pain presences unflagging in the threshold, as pain.

But what is pain? Pain rends. It is the rift. But it does not tear apart into dispersive fragments. Pain indeed tears asunder, it separates, yet so that at the same time it draws everything to itself, gathers it to itself. Its rending, as a separating that gathers, is at the same time that drawing which, like the pen-drawing of a plan or sketch, draws and joins together what is held apart in separation. Pain is the joining agent in the rending that divides and gathers. Pain is the joining of the rift. The joining is the threshold. It settles the between, the middle of the two that are separated in it. Pain joins the rift of the dif-ference. Pain is the dif-ference itself.

Pain has turned the threshold to stone.

The verse calls the dif-ference, but it neither thinks it specifically nor does it call its nature by this name. The verse calls the separation of the between, the gathering middle, in whose intimacy the bearing of things and the granting of world pervade one another.

Then would the intimacy of the dif-ference for world and thing be pain? Certainly. But we should not imagine pain anthropologically as a sensation that makes us feel afflicted. We should not think of the intimacy psychologically as the sort in which sentimentality makes a nest for itself.

Pain has turned the threshold to stone.

Pain has already fitted the threshold into its bearing. The difference presences already as the collected presence, from which the carrying out of world and thing appropriatingly takes place. How so?

> There lie, in limpid brightness shown,
> Upon the table bread and wine.

Where does the pure brightness shine? On the threshold, in the settling of the pain. The rift of the dif-ference makes the limpid brightness shine. Its luminous joining decides the brightening of the world into its own. The rift of the dif-ference expropriates the world into its worlding, which grants things. By the brightening of the world in their golden gleam, bread and wine at the same time attain to their own gleaming. The nobly named things are lustrous in the simplicity of their thinging. Bread and wine are the fruits of heaven and earth, gifts from the divinities to mortals. Bread and wine gather these four to themselves from the simple unity of their fourfoldness. The things that are called bread and wine are simple things because their bearing of world is fulfilled, without intermediary, by the favor of the world. Such things have their sufficiency in letting the world's fourfold stay with them. The pure limpid brightness of world and the simple gleaming of things go through their between, the dif-ference.

The third stanza calls world and things into the middle of their intimacy. The seam that binds their being toward one another is pain.

Only the third stanza gathers the bidding of things and the bidding of world. For the third stanza calls primally out of the simplicity of the intimate bidding which calls the dif-ference by leaving it unspoken. The primal calling, which bids the intimacy of world and thing to come, is the authentic bidding. This bidding is the nature of speaking. Speaking occurs in what is spoken in the poem. It is the speaking of language. Language speaks. It speaks by bidding the bidden, thing-world and world-thing, to come to the between of the dif-ference. What is so bidden is commanded to arrive from out of the dif-ference into the dif-ference. Here we are thinking of the old sense of command, which we recognize still in the phrase, "Commit thy way unto the Lord." The bidding of language commits the bidden thus to the bidding of the dif-ference. The dif-ference lets the thinging of the thing rest in the worlding of the world. The dif-ference expropriates the thing into the repose of the fourfold. Such expropriation does not diminish the thing. Only so is the thing exalted into its own, so that it says world. To keep in repose is to still. The dif-ference stills the thing, as thing, into the world.

Such stilling, however, takes place only in such a way that at the same time the world's fourfold fulfills the bearing of the thing, in that the stilling grants to the thing the sufficiency of staying world. The dif-ference stills in a twofold manner. It stills by letting things rest in the world's favor. It stills by letting the world suffice itself in the thing. In the double stilling of the dif-ference there takes place: stillness.

What is stillness? It is in no way merely the soundless. In soundlessness there persists merely a lack of the motion of entoning, sounding. But the motionless is neither limited to sounding by being its suspension, nor is it itself already something genuinely tranquil. The motionless always remains, as it were, merely the other side of that which rests. The motionless itself still rests on rest. But rest has its being in the fact that it stills. As the stilling of stillness, rest, conceived strictly, is always more in motion than all motion and always more restlessly active than any agitation.

The dif-ference stills particularly in two ways: it stills the things in thinging and the world in worlding. Thus stilled, thing and world never escape from the dif-ference. Rather, they rescue it in the stilling, where the difference is itself the stillness.

In stilling things and world into their own, the dif-ference calls world and thing into the middle of their intimacy. The dif-ference is the bidder. The dif-ference gathers the two out of itself as it calls them into the rift that is the dif-ference itself. This gathering calling is the pealing. In it there occurs something different from a mere excitation and spreading of sound.

When the dif-ference gathers world and things into the simple onefold of the pain of intimacy, it bids the two to come into their very nature. The dif-ference is the command out of which every bidding itself is first called, so that each may follow the command. The command of the dif-ference has ever already gathered all bidding within itself. The calling, gathered together with itself, which gathers to itself in the calling, is the pealing as the peal.

The calling of the dif-ference is the double stilling. The gathered bidding, the command, in the form of which the difference calls world and things, is the peal of stillness. Language speaks in that the command of the dif-ference calls world and things into the simple onefold of their intimacy.

Language speaks as the peal of stillness. Stillness stills by the carrying out, the bearing and enduring, of world and things in their presence. The carrying out of world and thing in the manner of stilling is the appropriative taking place of the dif-ference. Language, the peal of stillness, is inasmuch as the dif-ference takes place. Language goes on as the taking place or occurring of the dif-ference for world and things.

The peal of stillness is not anything human. But on the contrary, the human is indeed in its nature given to speech—it is linguistic. The word "linguistic" as it is here used means: having taken place out of the speaking of language. What has thus taken place, human being, has been brought into its own by language, so that it remains given over or appropriated to the nature of language, the peal of stillness. Such an appropriating takes place in the the very *nature*, the *presencing*, of language *needs and uses* the speaking of mortals in order to sound as the peal of stillness for the hearing of mortals.

Only as men belong within the peal of stillness are mortals able to speak in *their own* way in sounds.

Mortal speech is a calling that names, a bidding which, out of the simple onefold of the difference, bids thing and world to come. What is purely bidden in mortal speech is what is spoken in the poem. Poetry proper is never merely a higher mode (*melos*) of everyday language. It is rather the reverse: everyday language is a forgotten and therefore used-up poem, from which there hardly resounds a call any longer.

The opposite of what is purely spoken, the opposite of the poem, is not prose. Pure prose is never "prosaic." It is as poetic and hence as rare as poetry.

If attention is fastened exclusively on human speech, if human speech is taken simply to be the voicing of the inner man, if speech so conceived is regarded as language itself, then the nature of language can never appear as anything but an expression and an activity of man. But human speech, as the speech of mortals, is not self-subsistent. The speech of mortals rests in its relation to the speaking of language.

At the proper time it becomes unavoidable to think of how mortal speech and its utterance take place in the speaking of language as the peal of the stillness of the dif-ference. Any uttering, whether in speech or writing, breaks the stillness. On what does the peal of stillness break? How does the broken stillness come to sound in words? How does the broken stillness shape the mortal speech that sounds in verses and sentences?

Assuming that thinking will succeed one day in answering these questions, it must be careful not to regard utterance, let alone expression, as the decisive element of human speech.

The structure of human speech can only be the manner (*melos*) in which the speaking of language, the peal of the stillness of the dif-ference, appropriates mortals by the command of the dif-ference.

The way in which mortals, called out of the dif-ference into the dif-ference, speak on their own part, is: by responding. Mortal speech must first of all have listened to the command, in the form of which the stillness of the dif-ference calls world and things into the rift of its onefold simplicity. Every word of mortal speech speaks out of such a listening, and as such a listening.

Mortals speak insofar as they listen. They heed the bidding call of the stillness of the dif-ference even when they do not know that call. Their listening draws from the command of the dif-ference what it brings out as sounding word. This speaking that listens and accepts is responding.

Nevertheless by receiving what it says from the command of the dif-ference, mortal speech has already, in its own way, followed the call. Response, as receptive listening, is at the same time recognition that makes due acknowledgment. Mortals speak by responding to language in a twofold way, receiving and replying. The mortal word speaks by cor-responding in a multiple sense.

Every authentic hearing holds back with its own saying. For hearing keeps to itself in the listening by which it remains appropriated to the peal of stillness. All responding is attuned to this restraint that reserves itself. For this reason such reserve must be concerned to be ready, in the mode of listening, for the command of the dif-ference. But the reserve must take care not just to hear the peal of stillness afterward, but to hear it even beforehand, and thus as it were to anticipate its command.

This anticipating while holding back determines the manner in which mortals respond to the dif-ference. In this way mortals live in the speaking of language.

Language speaks. Its speaking bids the dif-ference to come which expropriates world and things into the simple onefold of their intimacy.

Language speaks.

Man speaks in that he responds to language. This responding is a hearing. It hears because it listens to the command of stillness.

It is not a matter here of stating a new view of language. What is important is learning to live in the speaking of language. To do so, we need to examine constantly whether and to what extent we are capable of what genuinely belongs to responding: anticipation in reserve. For:

> Man speaks only as he responds to language.
> Language speaks.

Its speaking speaks for us in what has been spoken:

A Winter Evening

> Window with falling snow is arrayed.
> Long tolls the vesper bell,
> The house is provided well,
> The table is for many laid.
>
> Wandering ones, more than a few,
> Come to the door on darksome courses.
> Golden blooms the tree of graces
> Drawing up the earth's cool dew.
>
> Wanderer quietly steps within;
> Pain has turned the threshold to stone.
> There lie, in limpid brightness shown,
> Upon the table bread and wine.

INTRODUCTION TO TILLICH'S
"THE MEANING AND JUSTIFICATION
OF RELIGIOUS SYMBOLS"

Undoubtedly, Paul Tillich is the most important theological thinker to have lived and written in the United States. Tillich has shaped a generation of religious thinkers in America. Because of his immigration to the United States, Tillich was less well known in his native Germany than he otherwise would have been. In Europe, his potential influence was overshadowed by the debates between Barth and Bultmann, by other important theological discussions, and by the intellectual energy that surrounded the later writings of Heidegger.

The influence of Tillich's theological thought is destined to grow, not wane, however, both in the United States and Europe. For Tillich, more than Barth or even Bultmann, came to grips with the impact of historical and rational criticism on theological and metaphysical thinking. And Tillich, more than the later Heidegger, was able to place his command of the principles of postmodern thinking into systematic form. In his *Systematic Theology,* Tillich addressed and solved the central problem of postmodern theology—namely, how can a thoroughly critical thinker talk about *God* at all? Seeing how many theologians still have not faced this central problem, but must inevitably do so if they wish to be honest about what it means to think at this time, Tillich's solution to this problem will yet become more widely known and appreciated. But before I discuss this problem and Tillich's solution, I should like briefly to describe his biography.

Born August 20, 1886, in Starzeddel, Brandenburg (today Starosiedle, East Germany), Tillich was the son of a Lutheran pastor. In 1891, the family moved to Schönfliess, a small and secure town with charm and character. For Tillich, the town, with its gates and walls, church at the center, and efficient central management, represented the spirit of the nineteenth century—one of "self-sufficient finitude." The structure of the town seemed to convey the confidence and optimism of a thinking process that found everything needed for the life of thought within thought itself. In 1901, however, Tillich's family moved to Berlin; the contrast was dramatic. Berlin was exciting, open to innovations in cultural expression, and it came to represent for Tillich the forsaking of the familiar in the drive toward openness. Here thought was presented with the possibility of responding to otherness, and thereby transcending itself concretely.

Tillich's elementary school years were spent in Schönfliess in a church school. He was extraordinarily receptive to the Lutheran religious teachings and practices as well as to aesthetic presentations of religious feeling and thought. During those years, the symbols of religion communicated their meaning directly to Tillich; their truth was unquestioned. In the Friedrich Wilhelm Gymnasium in Berlin, however, Tillich saw the conflict between such naive reception of religious image and belief and the critical approach to life. Tillich experienced first hand how critical questioning of symbols drives out the truth of the symbol. For example, a religious symbol such as the image of Jesus ministering to the poor may be held as truly representing the will of God for humanity, until the question is posed: On what grounds do I *know* that the symbol expresses the will and intention of God? Lacking an answer, the symbol loses the immediacy of meaning it once had and sheds the self-evidence of truth. This conflict between religious meaning and critical thinking preoccupied Tillich in his career as a theologian.

Tillich's theological education was at the University of Halle, under Martin Kähler, from 1905 to 1907. In 1911, he earned his doctorate in philosophy from the University of Breslau; in 1912, he received his theological degree from Halle. Both doctoral dissertations dealt with problems in the philosophy of Friedrich Wilhelm Joseph von Schelling. When the war broke out, Tillich became a chaplain in the army and was sent to the western front. He was eventually decorated with an Iron Cross I and Iron Cross II for his courage on the front lines. Tillich displayed a courage to be in face of the most extreme onslaught of nonbeing—the encounters with fate and death, guilt and condemnation, and emptiness and meaninglessness. The war experience nearly shattered him, however, and he recorded his anguish at the loss of hope among the soldiers. One night in particular, during the Battle of the Marne, Tillich felt the complete end of the world as he had known it and was transformed from a philosophical idealist to an existentialist. For a time, his courage was reduced to the courage expressed in the affirmation and acceptance of despair.

At the end of the war, he served as *privatdozent* (instructor) at the University of Berlin (1918–1924), then as *extraordinarius* professor (assistant professor) in theology at Marburg (1924–1925), and finally as *ordinarius* professor (tenured professor) at Dresden and Leipzig (1925–1929). In 1929, he was called as *ordinarius* professor of philosophy and social thought in Frankfurt. In 1933, he was the first German professor to be forced to leave his post by the National Socialist government under Hitler. Tillich immigrated to New York City and Union Theological Seminary at the invitation of Reinhold Niebuhr. At Union, Tillich learned English for the first time and turned his attention to theological questions. Facing incomprehension among Americans who were not familiar with German thought, Tillich began the task of simplifying his thought for a new audience. *Systematic Theology* is one result of that labor.

In 1955, Tillich became university professor at Harvard where he served until 1962. From 1962 until his death in 1965, Tillich was the John Nuveen Professor of Philosophical Theology at the Divinity School of the University of Chicago. By the time of his death, he was legendary. The seriousness of his thought was one of the central reasons why a revival of interest in theological questions occurred among philosophers in the United States. Tillich made it possible for religion and theology to live again for many people who had lost their childhood precritical faith to critical thought and who sensed the possibility of recovery of meaning through the interpretation of religious symbols.

One cornerstone of his theological system is the theory of religious symbols. The upcoming essay, "The Meaning and Justification of Religious Symbols" (1961), presents the skeletal structure of this theory. I now briefly comment on Tillich's idea of the religious symbol and its role in Tillich's hermeneutical method—the method of correlation. Then I turn to the theological accomplishment of Tillich's hermeneutics—his proposal of an answer to the problem of asserting an absolute reality in the context of historical and rational criticism.

The paper "The Meaning and Justification of Religious Symbols" was written after the conclusion of the proceedings of the fourth annual New York University Institute of Philosophy, held at Washington Square, New York, October 21–22, 1960. Tillich presented a paper called "The Religious Symbol" for critical comment by ten philosophers. "The Meaning and Justification of Religious Symbols" was written after Tillich had thought through the criticisms.

Notice that Tillich begins by spelling out the characteristics of representative symbols in general, in contrast to arbitrary and conventional signs. Symbols point beyond themselves, participate in the reality that they symbolize, cannot be created at will, open up dimensions of reality in correlation to opened dimensions of spirit, and have both integrating and disintegrating power for individuals and groups.

Religious symbols are a special set of representative symbols. Rather than pointing to the power of a nation, the performance of a baseball team, the desirability of a commercial product such as an automobile, or some other historical reality, the religious symbol points to the unconditioned— the ultimate, and hence nonobjectifiable, reality. But this is very strange. For in that event, the religious symbol must do the impossible: some conditioned image or material must point to unconditioned reality. It must point beyond the "ontological difference" between being and beings to what Tillich calls "the power of being-itself." Unconditioned being must appear in a finite symbol, yet the unconditioned is precisely what can never be objectified. To the extent that the unconditioned appears, it appears as conditioned. All appearances are conditioned by historical circumstances of understanding. Hence, to the extent that anyone says that "This (symbol) manifests the divine," one can know that he or she is wrong. No symbol can be adequate to the divine ground of being.

Nonetheless, paradoxically, in the real world representative symbols do indeed convince people that they manifest the unconditioned; religious communities have formed around those manifestations. But how, the critical thinker might ask, would we ever know if the symbol in question really does express the unconditioned? How can we locate the referent of the symbol other than through the symbol itself? Tillich mentions three possible methods. One of them, the inductive, he rules out immediately. In it, one lines up the symbols that might be understood as religious and abstracts what is common. The problem is that whatever is abstracted will belong to conditioned reality, to the finite universe. "But the intention of every religious symbol is to point to that which transcends finitude."[1]

The other two methods, the *phenomenological method* and the *ontological method,* corroborate each other. In the former, the religious quality of the symbol is located in the identifiable experience attached to the symbol. Rudolf Otto describes this experience as "the holy." "The experience of the holy transcends the subject-object structure of experience. The subject is drawn into the holy, embodied in a finite object which, in this encounter, becomes sacred."[2] Understood in terms of my proposal of hermeneutical types, this is a description of a theological "overturning" of the subject of symbolic understanding. In face of the holy, which breaks into the structure of being, "I" am dust and ashes; yet "I" am enabled to understand because of the numinous presence to which I am answerable. The object of the experience of the holy becomes a symbol of God.

The ontological method locates the referent of the religious symbol through Heidegger's analysis of Dasein as the being who is open to being-itself. Dasein has an awareness of being-itself in its open moods and their understanding: in anxiety, for instance, I am aware of being-itself as the hidden agent of the event. This is a description of a theological "overturning" of the agent of understanding through a manifestation of the one in the many. The unconditioned here breaks in through the prereflective awareness of being-itself. In anxiety, normal understanding is overturned by the presence of the unconditioned.

Tillich's *method of correlation* utilizes both the phenomenological and ontological ways to the religious reality. The results of ontological analysis are correlated to those of phenomenological analysis. This is possible because the two approaches are two different descriptions of the same experience. Both approaches refer to the unconditioned.

[1] Paul Tillich, "The Meaning and Justification of Religious Symbols," p. 167 below.
[2] Ibid.

The ontological method proceeds by analyzing the structure of everyday human being. It discloses there a religious dimension of depth—the unconditioned, being-itself. Volume 2 of this collection includes a section from *Systematic Theology,* which presents Tillich's version of a hermeneutics of existence. Clearly, this method is indebted to Heidegger's analysis of Dasein in *Being and Time.* Tillich's analysis of existence shows human being as openness to being-itself through the moods of disclosure: joy, anxiety, and courage. But being-itself cannot be thought; it is a presupposition of the subject-object structure of being. It cannot itself be objectified. Thus Dasein is the being who must ask about the meaning of her or his own being, but who cannot expect an answer to come through the method of interpreting the meaning of everyday existence.

The phenomenological method proceeds by identifying and describing the manifestations of the holy in religious experiences. This approach does not grasp the meaning of Dasein by analyzing the structure. It involves situating oneself properly so that one can be grasped by the meaning that appears in the symbol of the holy. The approach is that of responding thoughtfully to what shows itself in the symbol. This method is indebted to Heidegger's later thought on language as address and understanding as listening.

Tillich grounds both approaches, the grasping relation of the ontological method and the responding relation of the phenomenological method, in the structure of *logos,* reason. *Logos* is the middle, the dif-ference in Heidegger's sense, between grasping through thought and responding meditatively with symbols. The grasping function of thought appears in science with its emphasis on formal properties. The responding to symbols appears in art with its emphasis on thematic significance or import. The manifestation of the depth of grasping and responding appears in myth. Correlation between the ontological and phenomenological is possible because *logos* is both a conceptual grasping and a responding to symbols.

As a hermeneutical method, the method of correlation allows for a placing of the meaning of religious symbols with respect to the structure of existence into which they speak. Tillich correlates religious symbol and human existence by reference to the grasping and responding functions of reason. He draws an analogy between grasping and responding on one side and questioning and answering on the other. The human effort to grasp meaning in existence is resolved into the analysis of the basic existential questions implicit in being, existence, and life. The human experience of response to meaning in texts and events is resolved into the interpretation of the answers presented to human existence through primary Christian symbols. The method of correlation becomes one of correlating existential question with religious answer.

For example, if we analyze the structure of being as the relatedness of subject and object or self and world, the question implicit in this neutral and abstract structure is: What is beyond this structure as its ground and goal? Correlatively, if we describe the religious responding to the symbol of God, we receive an answer to that question: God is beyond the structure of being as its ground and goal.

The structure of being is the neutral keyboard on which all human life is played. Lived existence presents concrete disruptions within the structure of being. In existence we find destructive experiences of estrangement, in which self and world are in opposition to each other, having lost their ground. If we analyze the structure of existence as a distortion of the finite structure of being, the implicit question is: How may I regain my authentic being, grounded in God? Correlatively, if we describe the religious responding to the symbol of Jesus as Christ, we receive an answer to the question: Jesus as Christ presents the enabling power to be oneself authentically. In both examples, the religious symbol is correlated with a question implicit in human being by taking it as an answer to the question. The question-answer correlation makes understanding the meaning of the symbol possible.

Through Tillich's method of correlation, "God" is the answer to the question "What is being-itself?" By the same token, "being-itself" is the answer to the question "What is God?" The most basic statement of theology is that "God is being-itself." But we must be clear that this is the correlation of a concrete symbol (God) as answer with a universal question, and is neither a defining of a term nor an attributing of a property to a subject.

But beyond the question of meaning, can theological reflection determine that any religious symbol is *true* in its manifestation of God? This is to ask whether there is an absolute reality that can survive dislodging by critical thought. Can historically-conscious, critical thought assert that any religious symbol is true, that it actually is the expression of God? Historically-conscious thought is profoundly aware that symbols live and die; they are finite and conditioned entities, hence inadequate to represent the infinite or unconditioned reality. Nonetheless, Tillich discovers a solution to this problem and expresses it in the essay "The Meaning and Justification of Religious Symbols."

Tillich's answer is that there are two criteria to apply to symbols of God to test their truth. First, and subjectively, the symbol must be adequate to the religious experience it expresses. This is the "authenticity" of the symbol—the actual ability of the symbol to evoke the experience of the holy. This criterion is a necessary starting point, for symbols should be rooted in experience if they are to be considered living symbols at all. But what about those who do not respond to the holy in that symbol, even if they once did, and do not find the divine there?

This leads to the second criterion: Objectively speaking, the symbol in question must be composed of material that can signify the whole of reality, and only human beings as symbols are able to do so. No other symbolic material can encompass every level of reality, for only in human thought are these levels grasped. But even more importantly, on the objective side, the true symbol is the one that negates itself with respect to the holy itself, the unconditioned. A human symbol of the divine that does manifest the depth of being-itself as the holy to some people, but which on its own denies that it is the manifestation of the holy, is a true symbol of God. Why? Such a symbol is aware of its own limitation and conditionedness and anticipates its loss of expressive power. By accepting its own finitude and anticipating its own demise as a symbol, the true religious symbol truly manifests the symbolic character of religious symbols. Such a symbol is true both for the one who stands in symbolic relation to it (for whom the symbol is God-as-there) and for the one who does not stand in symbolic relation to it (for whom the symbol is not-God-as-there). The symbol supports both interpretations.

In his *Systematic Theology*, Tillich interprets the symbol of Jesus as the Christ to be such a symbol. Jesus is the Christ because he manifests what it means for God to be God, and he does so by denying himself any special status. In its self-negation, the "Cross of Christ" is both the symbol of God and the warning against idolatrous misuse of the symbol of God. Hence Tillich's interpretation of the symbol of the cross of Jesus implies the reconciliation of those who affirm and those who deny that it is the very presence of God. The true symbol of God allows both affirmers and deniers of the symbol of God to be what they fully choose to be.[3]

[3]See Robert P. Scharlemann, *Reflection and Doubt in the Thought of Paul Tillich* (New Haven: Yale University Press, 1969), pp. 173–82, for a thorough analysis of the symbol of the cross.

THE MEANING AND JUSTIFICATION OF RELIGIOUS SYMBOLS
(1961)
Paul Tillich

Religious symbols need no justification if their meaning is understood. For their meaning is that they are the language of religion and the only way in which religion can express itself directly. Indirectly and reflectively religion can also express itself in theological, philosophical, and artistic terms. But its direct self-expression is the symbol and the united group of symbols which we call myths.

I

In order to understand religious symbols we must first understand the nature of symbols generally. And this is a difficult task, because the term symbol is being applied to things which should not be called symbols at all, e.g., signs, symptoms, metaphors, etc. But since the linguistic development can hardly be reversed, one can save the genuine meaning of "symbol" only by adding an adjective whenever "symbol" is meant. Symbols which deserve the name shall be called "representative symbols," following a suggestion by John Randall, in contrast to the symbols which are only signs, such as mathematical and logical symbols—which one could call "discursive symbols." The realms in which representative symbols appear are language and history, the arts and religion. They show common characteristics which must be presupposed if one speaks of symbols in each of these groups. The common characteristics in all realms of representative symbols are the following:

First and most fundamental is the character of all symbols to point beyond themselves. Symbols use "symbolic material": the ordinary meaning of a word, the empirical reality of a historical figure, the traits of a human face (in a painting), a human catastrophe (in a drama), a human power or virtue (in a description of the divine). But this symbolic material is not meant in its proper and ordinary meaning. When it is used as symbolic material, it points to something which cannot be grasped directly but must be expressed indirectly, namely, through the symbolic material. This "something" can be the connotations of a word which transcend the empirical reality of this person, or it can be a dimension of reality which is not open to an ordinary encounter with reality as the artistic forms, or it can be ultimate reality, expressed in symbols whose material is taken from finite reality.

The second characteristic of all representative symbols is to participate in the reality of that which they represent. The concept of representation itself implies this relation. The representative of a person or an institution participates in the honor of those whom he is asked to represent; but it is not *he* who is honored, it is that which or whom he represents. In this sense we can state generally that the symbol participates in the reality of what it symbolizes. It radiates the power of being and meaning of that for which it stands.

This leads to the third characteristic of the representative symbol: it cannot be created at will. It is not a matter of expediency and convention, as signs are. Therefore, one can metaphorically say that a symbol is born and may die. Even if individual creativity is the medium through which it comes into existence (the individual artist, the individual prophet), it is the unconscious-conscious reaction of a group through which it becomes a symbol. No representative symbol is created and maintained without acceptance by a group. If the group ceases to accept it, it may, like the ancient gods, become a metaphor or maintain its poetic-symbolic value, but, as a religious symbol, it becomes lost.

The fourth characteristic of a representative symbol is its power of opening up dimensions of reality, in correlation to dimensions of the human spirit, which otherwise are covered by the predominance of other dimensions of spirit and reality. The historical symbols show historical potentialities which are covered by the everyday historical events and activities. Artistic symbols—in fact, all artistic creations—open up the human spirit for the dimension of aesthetic experience and they open up reality to the dimension of its intrinsic meaning. Religious symbols mediate ultimate reality through things, persons, events which because of their mediating functions receive the quality of "holy." In the experience of holy places, times, books, words, images, and acts, symbols of the holy reveal something of the "Holy-Itself" and produce the experience of holiness in persons and groups. No philosophical concept can do the same thing, and theological concepts are merely conceptualizations of original religious symbols.

One may add a fifth characteristic of representative symbols: their integrating and disintegrating power. This function of symbols refers both to individuals and groups. The history of religion gives an endless number of examples for the elevating, quieting, and stabilizing power of religious symbols. In the larger, and sometimes even narrower, sense of the word, one can speak of the "healing" power of religious symbols. All this is equally true of the three other groups of representative symbols. But in contrast to their integrating function, symbols can also have a disintegrating effect: causing restlessness, producing depression, anxiety, fanaticism, etc. This depends partly on the character of that to which they point, partly on the reaction of those who are grasped by them. Symbols have the same creative or destructive effect on social groups. Symbols are the main power of integrating them: a king, an event, a document in the political realm of representative symbolism, an epic work, architectural symbols, a holy figure, a holy book, a holy rite in religion. But here also are disintegrating possibilities as in some political symbols such as the Führer and the swastika, or in religious symbols such as the Moloch type of gods, human sacrifices, doctrinal symbols producing a split consciousness, etc. This characteristic of symbols shows their tremendous power of creation and destruction. By no means are they harmless semantic expressions.

II

In the preceding general analysis of the nature of symbols, we frequently have mentioned religious symbols. They must now be considered in their particular character. In the language of religion a problem is intensified which appears in every kind of expression, the problem of the "referent." To what does a religious symbol refer, one asks? How can it be reached? And if it can be reached by symbols only, how can we know that something is reached at all? Such questions are certainly justified. One can sum them up by asking: Is there a nonsymbolic statement about the referent of religious symbols? If this question could not be answered affirmatively the necessity of symbolic language for religion could not be proved and the whole argument would lead into a vicious circle. The question then is: what is the referent of religious symbolism and how can it be known except by symbols—known namely in the one and only respect that it is the referent for religious symbols.

There are two ways which lead to the same result, a phenomenological and an ontological one. Excluded by the very nature of the subject matter is the inductive way. For it can lead only to a finite part of the universe of finite objects through observation and conclusion. But the intention of every religious symbol is to point to that which transcends finitude. Nothing finite, no part of the universe of finite relations can be the referent of religious symbols, and, therefore, no inductive method can reach it.

The phenomenological approach describes the holy as a quality of some encounters with reality. The holy is a "quality in encounter," not an object among objects, and not an emotional response without a basis in the whole of objects. The experience of the holy transcends the subject-object structure of experience. The subject is drawn into the holy, embodied in a finite object which, in this encounter, becomes sacred. An analysis of this experience shows that wherever the holy appears it is a matter of ultimate concern both in attracting and in repelling, and of unconditional power, both in giving and in demanding. The phenomenological analysis of the experience of the holy has been carried through in an excellent way by Rudolf Otto and others. It shows what is meant, if religious symbols are used. But it cannot go beyond the description. Phenomenology cannot raise the question of the validity of the phenomena it makes visible.

The other way of reaching the referent of religious symbolism is the ontological one. It analyzes the kind of being man is, in interdependence with his world. It analyzes the finitude of the finite in different directions, it points to the anxiety which is connected with the awareness of one's finitude, and it raises the question of being-itself, the *prius* of everything that is. This approach tries to find the referent of religious symbolism not in a particular experience, that of the holy and of the ultimate concern implied in the holy, but it tries to find it in the character of being as such, in everything that is. The ontological method, as indicated here, does not argue for the existence of a being, about which religion makes symbolic statements, but it gives an analysis of the encountered world with respect to its finitude and finds through this analysis its self-transcending quality, its pointing beyond its finitude. That to which this analysis leads is the referent in all religious symbols. One can give it metaphoric names, like "being-itself" or "power of being" or "ultimate reality" or "ultimate concern" (in the sense of that about which one is ultimately concerned). Such names are not names of a being but of a quality of being. If religious symbols express this quality in divine names, classical theology has always asserted that the referent of these names transcends their nonsymbolic meaning infinitely.

The two ways of finding the referent of symbolic language, the phenomenological and the ontological, corroborate each other. That which is the implication of the phenomenological description is also the focal point of the ontological analysis and the referent of the religious symbols.

III

There is an almost endless amount of religious symbolism in the history of religion. This is not so by chance. It follows from the fact that in a particular encounter with reality everything can become a bearer of the holy. Nothing is prevented from becoming a sacred thing. Only historical contingencies prevent it. But they have not prevented exemplars of almost every class of things from actually becoming sacred things. This produces the impression that the history of religion is a mere chaos of incoherent imaginations. But this is not the case; there are many keys for the understanding of the dynamics of this large realm of human experience. There are also keys for an understanding of the immense amount of religious symbols. Without considering their historical dynamics I want to distinguish certain basic kinds of religious symbols in order to overcome semantic as well as material confusions.

The first distinction needed is that between primary and secondary religious symbolism. The primary symbols point directly to the referent of all religious symbolism. In order to do so they establish a "highest" being, attribute characteristics to him the symbolic material of which is taken from human or cosmic experiences and extended *via eminentiae* to that which to the religious intention transcends all such characteristics. This refers to qualities like personality, power, love, justice, etc. It has been asked whether qualities like being, becoming, essence, existence, can be attributed nonsymbolically to God. It seems to me that such an assertion makes out of that which transcends all beings a being of higher order. The rejection of this attempt agrees with the contention of classical theology that God is "beyond" the split between essence and existence, as well as beyond being (in a static sense) and becoming. This "beyond" is an expression of a symbolic use of these terms.

A second level of primary religious symbolism is the way in which religion speaks of divine actions like creation, providence, miracles, incarnation, consummation, etc. It is especially important to emphasize the symbolic character of these symbols, because they often are understood literally, with the consequence that they fall into insoluble conflicts with the scientific interpretation of reality. In all these symbols the religious imagination subjects that which is ultimate reality to the categories of time, space, substance, and causality. This is unavoidable and without danger as long as the symbolic character is being recognized. But if this is not done, the whole relation between God and the world becomes a nest of absurdities, as, e.g., God's "predestining" or his "almighty" actions.

The third level of primary symbols lives in the realm of divine manifestations in finite reality, divine incarnations in holy things or objects. In the dynamics of the history of religion this level must be considered as the "oldest" one. For the basic religious experience is that of the presence of the holy in concrete things, persons, or actions here and now. The "sacramental presence" of the holy is the lasting basis of all religious experience, and the radical transcendence into which the divine was elevated is a later development, the result of the fight of the higher religions against the demonic distortions of the sacramental religions.

These three basic levels of primary religious symbolism are permeated by a host of secondary religious symbols. Secondary are supporting symbols like water, light, oil, or poetic symbols in which a primary religious symbol is artistically resymbolized, or metaphoric expressions as they appear in parables or are used in poetry. They should not be raised to the rank of primary symbols. In the Psalmist's phrase "The Lord is my shepherd," the word "Lord" is a genuine and primary religious symbol, the word "shepherd" is a poetic metaphor. It must be added that the distinctions made here are neither exclusive nor static. The levels are mixed with each other and, often symbols of one level originate on another level, e.g., secondary religious symbols had once an independent standing as primary religious symbols and vice versa. But the distinction itself is valid.

IV

If one asks about criteria of religious symbols we must state generally that the measure of their validity is their adequacy to the religious experience they express. This is the basic criterion of all symbols. One can call it their "authenticity." Nonauthentic are religious symbols which have lost their experiential basis, but which are still used for reasons of tradition or because of their aesthetic value. The criterion of authenticity is valid but not sufficient. It does not answer the question of the amount of truth a symbol possesses. The term "truth" in this context means the degree to which it reaches the referent of all religious symbols. The question itself can be answered in two ways, a negative and a positive one. The negative quality which determines the truth of a religious symbol is its self-negation and transparency to the referent for which it stands. The positive quality which determines the truth of a religious symbol is the value of the symbolic material used in it. Both statements need interpretation.

It is the danger and an almost unavoidable pitfall of all religious symbols that they bring about a confusion between themselves and that to which they point. In religious language this is called idolatry. The term does not express (or should not express) the arrogant and indirectly idolatrous judgment of one religion over all the others, but it expresses an implicit tendency of all religions to elevate themselves to ultimacy in power and meaning. On the other side, all religions live from the system of symbols by which they have been created and which they continue recreating. They live as long as a whole of symbols is the expression of their particular character. With the end of the power of its symbols a religious group comes to its own end. When, however, the symbols are in power their idolatrous misuse is almost unavoidable. The symbol of the "Cross of the Christ," which is the center of all Christian symbolism, is perhaps the most radical criticism of all idolatrous self-elevation. But even it has become again and again the tool of idolatry within the Christian churches. This consideration is the answer to the question of the truth of religious symbols from the negative point of view. The measure of their truth is the measure of their self-negation with respect to what they point to, the Holy-Itself, the ultimate power of being and meaning.

The other criterion is the quality of their symbolic material. There is a difference whether they use trees and rocks and stones and animals or personalities and groups as symbolic material. Only in the last case do the symbols comprise the whole of reality; for only in man are all dimensions of the encountered world united. It is therefore decisive for the rank and value of a symbol that its symbolic material is taken from the human person. Therefore, the great religions are concentrated on a personal development in which ultimate concern appears and transcends the personal limits, through remaining in a person. The positive criterion for the truth of a symbols (e.g., creation) is the degree in which it includes the valuation in an ultimate perspective of the individual persons.

The negative and positive criteria of the truth of a religious symbol show that their truth has nothing to do with the validity of factual statements concerning the symbolic material. However problematic the symbolic material in its literal meaning may be, its symbolic character and its validity as a symbol are not determined by it.

It seems to me that an understanding of the language of religion in the line developed in this paper is the precondition for an adequate interpretation of religion and for a creative interpenetration of the theological and the philosophical task.

INTRODUCTION TO GADAMER'S "THE UNIVERSALITY OF THE HERMENEUTICAL PROBLEM"

Hans-Georg Gadamer, more than anyone else, is responsible for intensifying and enlivening hermeneutical discussion since 1960. In that year, Gadamer published his monumental integration of hermeneutical philosophy, *Truth and Method*. The impact has been enormous. As professor of philosophy at the University of Heidelberg in West Germany, where he had taught since 1949, he spent the next decade in debate with critical thinkers in Europe, refining and clarifying his thought. Since retiring from the active faculty at Heidelberg, Gadamer has spent a great deal of time at various universities in the United States and Canada. The breadth of his knowledge in the humanistic disciplines and his claim that hermeneutic inquiry raises a universal problem have led to the serious study of his thought in many disciplines and on both continents.

Gadamer was born in 1900 in Marburg. He grew up in the pre-World War I spirit of the late nineteenth century, and his education was grounded in the study of Greek and Latin classics. As a doctoral student in philosophy at Marburg under Paul Natorp, he was at the center of the excitement that surrounded the early lectures of Heidegger and the theological appropriation of Heidegger by Bultmann. Gadamer was a regular participant in evening discussions with Bultmann; Heidegger supervised his *Habilitationsschrift* on Plato's ethics.

As Heidegger turned to issues of language and art in the years after World War II, Gadamer found in Heideggerian ontology the organizing image for a full-blown hermeneutical program: the image of the play-like performance of being in language. *Truth and Method* is a work of integrative philosophy built on Heidegger's insights. Gadamer's work is much more accessible than Heidegger's, however; and it touches the disciplines of art criticism, literary criticism, historiography, jurisprudence, and theology, as well as the history of philosophy. Consequently, Gadamer's hermeneutics commands the attention of many who would not feel obliged to take seriously Heidegger's more cryptic and poetic formulations.

In the essay to follow, "The Universality of the Hermeneutical Problem," we have an eloquent synopsis of the argument developed at length in *Truth and Method*. The central ideas of this essay are basic to current hermeneutical discussion. I shall therefore point out the crucial elements.

Gadamer questions the assumption that modern methodologies provide access to undistorted reality. This is not a polemic against a particular methodical stance on behalf of another, however. Gadamer is not challenging the claims of the explanatory methods employed in the natural sciences from the standpoint of an alternative methodology based on understanding in the human sciences. He is not, in other words, merely perpetuating Dilthey's version of hermeneutical inquiry. Gadamer's questioning of the methodical approach to life takes aim at the methods of Dilthey's hermeneutics as much as it does the methods of modern science. He is convinced that both modern hermeneutical theory and scientific theory, in different ways, cover up an original experience of reality, an experience of the truth of being.

Gadamer's basic point, hinted at in the title of *Truth and Method,* is that modern methods of explanation and understanding lose sight of our experience of the whole of life. Methodical consciousness necessarily abstracts certain definable regions of our relations with the world from the whole of experience. Methodical consciousness then submits the abstraction to preconceived rules of analysis.

Hermeneutical consciousness, by contrast, sees what is questionable in unquestioned method. Modern faith in method carries an ontological presupposition that shapes our attitudes, expectations, and technological applications. Methodologism assumes that our human mode of being is one of *alienation* and distance from being itself. It thereby obliterates the primary human *belongingness* to the whole of being. The strength of Gadamer's hermeneutical philosophy lies in its disclosure, through various disciplines, of the original human belongingness to the truth of being. Three such disclosures of truth are paramount for Gadamer. They are those in art, history, and language.

Before we look briefly at each of the three spheres through which Gadamer shows a primordial human belongingness to being, let us be very clear about the connection Gadamer makes between truth and method. I think Gadamer is misunderstood when his title is taken to mean "truth, and not method." Gadamer is not arguing against the use of method. He is arguing that the applications of methods presuppose a "whole human experience of the world."[1] Application of method is secondary to and derived from the experience of a "world already interpreted, already organized in its basic relations."[2] Disciplines of thought become myopic when they lose sight of the secondary and derivative character of their methodical approaches. Such partial blindness results in a distorted relation to the social, natural, and spiritual worlds. But Gadamer's pointing out of the groundedness of method in a more primordial truth does not warrant the

---

[1]Hans-Georg Gadamer, "The Universality of the Hermeneutical Problem," p. 188 below.
[2]Ibid.

elimination of method or weakening of methodological consciousness. On the contrary, hermeneutics concedes a relative legitimacy to science, and it also discloses its connection to the everyday experience of the world. In this way, hermeneutics contributes to the grounding of science.

Thus, Gadamer's appeal to a truth more basic than method does not set itself in opposition to method. It does oppose dogmatic methodologism that presumes autonomy. Gadamer relativizes such a claim by referring method to its grounding in the truth manifest in our whole experience of the world. His hermeneutics thus invites the working out of methods by a hermeneutical consciousness that is open to the basic experience of truth on which method is founded. But Gadamer himself does not attempt to clarify the reciprocal relations between truth and method. He restricts himself largely to disclosing of the experience of truth that underlies method.

What is this fuller truth that Gadamer says underlies the results of methodically gained knowledge? Gadamer traces a path to it in three steps, beginning with the experience of truth in art. Like Hegel, Gadamer finds the essential matter of thought in art. But unlike Hegel, Gadamer does not claim that the conceptual form of thought supersedes the imagistic form of art. Absolute knowledge in Hegel's sense does not exist. But hermeneutical experiences of the truth in art do. We experience truth in art when art unveils the truth of our everyday life to us. When a work of art allows me to see what was previously hidden about my everyday world, truth appears. What happens is that the artwork provokes a feeling or apprehension of the whole that enables me to recognize it. If the artwork allows me to say "That's the way it is," so that I have something to say about the world as it actually is, or as it should be ideally, truth appears.

Gadamer likens the experience of truth in art to the experience of play in games. In both, the participants are drawn into the sphere of a disclosure, an event with its own life. The subjectivity of the participants responds to a deeper subjectivity that presents itself through the game or artwork itself. The subject-object structure of methodical awareness is transcended in belonging to the event, and the form-content structure of the game or artwork is likewise transcended in responding to the claim to truth made in the event.

Aesthetic methods abstract from this primordial experience. They methodically distinguish subject from object as well as form from content. These objectifications permit the viewer to assume the position of external judge, free to accept or reject the artwork on formal terms, apart from what the work says and presents. Such aesthetic judgments are not so much false as they are forgetful of the truth. They can be rehabilitated by contact with the process of understanding by which we are open to disclosures of truth in art.

A similar structure of alienation is evident in historical consciousness. We can detect it in the methods of the historical school of Leopold von

Ranke, the hermeneutics of Schleiermacher and Dilthey, and more recent historiographies. Each claims to acknowledge the special difficulties in attaining knowledge of history. And each proposes methodical means by which to reconstruct historical reality in its own terms. But the claims to historical objectivity made by modern scholars fail to take their own historical standpoint seriously enough. And those who abandon claims for objectivity in historical study do so without seeing the truth that has been covered up by the methodical study of the past.

Citing Nietzsche, Gadamer says that a trained person can unfailingly reconstruct the historical situation of the author of an "objective" history by referring to the author's interests in the subject matter. What does it mean that the interpretation of history is inevitably directed and colored by one's own social, political, economic, religious, and other interests? And what does it mean that the practices of the historian, through which he or she participates in the whole of the world, have an intelligible history through which they have been handed down? For Gadamer, it means that understanding of the historical world is itself historical. Consciousness of history stands within the stream of history itself. The interests and standards, horizons of understanding, with which we approach the past, are themselves part of the current of history.

Gadamer speculates that perhaps the great works of history are those that mirror back to us the questionability of the interests and standards directing our historical study, while making the past come alive. Rather than attempting to neutralize the author's historical situation and the questions about the whole of things that are part of it, great historical scholarship might be marked by the "splendid magic of immediately mirroring the present in the past and the past in the present."[3] In such cases, understanding would not be thought of as the act of a methodically detached subject but rather as an insertion into a process of tradition, in which past and present constantly adjust themselves.

Prior to any laboriously won critical distance from the past, we participate in ongoing effects of history. Our consciousness of what is continuously influential provides us with prejudices, standpoints or orientations from which we open ourselves to the world. We are open to the other, the new, because we have always already understood. The measure of understanding is the measure of our openness to the other, the not-I. Through such openness, the truth of historical being may appear: we discover the meaning of history not so much in autonomous historical judgments as in taking hold of our own prejudices through the otherness of history.

This brings us to the third sphere of hermeneutical experience of truth—language. This, however, is not so much a distinct sphere as the common medium of both art and history, indeed, of our entire experience of the

[3]Ibid, p. 181.

world. All understanding is language-bound. Only through language does being come to stand as being for us. As Gadamer puts it, "Being that can be understood is language."[4] Language allows being to show itself. And being shows itself only in language. So language says something about what is not language, but being. Yet being is accessible only through our finite and historically conditioned language.

If language is the medium in which our understanding of being takes place, then a hermeneutical philosophy of language becomes speculative ontology, a "first philosophy" for postmodern thought. What is true about linguistic understanding must be true about being as such. When our words bespeak the linguistic conditions under which we experience a meaningful world at all, they disclose truth. Hermeneutic ontology does not thereby elevate itself above the flux of history. Hermeneutic ontology acknowledges the historicity and linguisticality of its own formulations. But according to Gadamer, this acknowledgement does not entail linguistic relativism. Although historical prejudices and linguistic horizons are finite, they are open to the infinity of meaning. Language is not the prison house of understanding, but the universal performance of the dialogical openness of the self to the other.

[4]Hans-Georg Gadamer, *Truth and Method* (New York: The Seabury Press, 1975), p. 432.

THE UNIVERSALITY OF
THE HERMENEUTICAL PROBLEM
(1966)

Hans-Georg Gadamer

Why has the problem of language come to occupy the same central position in current philosophical discussions that the concept of thought, or "thought thinking itself," held in philosophy a century and a half ago? By answering this question, I shall try to give an answer indirectly to the central question of the modern age—a question posed for us by the existence of modern science. It is the question of how our natural view of the world—the experience of the world that we have as we simply live out our lives—is related to the unassailable and anonymous authority that confronts us in the pronouncements of science. Since the seventeenth century, the real task of philosophy has been to mediate this new employment of man's cognitive and constructive capacities with the totality of our experience of life. This task has found expression in a variety of ways, including our own genera-tion's attempt to bring the topic of language to the center of philosophical concern. Language is the fundamental mode of operation of our being-in-the-world and the all-embracing form of the constitution of the world. Hence we always have in view the pronouncements of the sciences, which are fixed in nonverbal signs. And our task is to reconnect the objective world of technology, which the sciences place at our disposal and discretion, with those fundamental orders of our being that are neither arbitrary nor manip-ulable by us, but rather simply demand our respect.

I want to elucidate several phenomena in which the universality of this question becomes evident. I have called the point of view involved in this theme "hermeneutical," a term developed by Heidegger. Heidegger was continuing a perspective stemming originally from Protestant theology and transmitted into our own century by Wilhelm Dilthey.

What is hermeneutics? I would like to start from two experiences of alienation that we encounter in our concrete existence: the experience of alienation of the aesthetic consciousness and the experience of alienation of the historical consciousness. In both cases what I mean can be stated in a few words. The aesthetic consciousness realizes a possibility that as such we can neither deny nor diminish in its value, namely, that we relate ourselves, either negatively or affirmatively, to the quality of an artistic form. This statement means we are related in such a way that the judgment we make decides in the end regarding the expressive power and validity of what we judge. What we reject has nothing to say to us—or we reject it because it has nothing to say to us. This characterizes our relation to art in the broadest sense of the word, a sense that, as Hegel has shown, includes the entire religious world of the ancient Greeks, whose religion of beauty experienced the divine in concrete works of art that man creates in response to the gods. When it loses its original and unquestioned authority, this whole world of experience becomes alienated into an object of aesthetic judgment. At the same time, however, we must admit that the world of artistic tradition—the splendid contemporaneousness that we gain through art with so many human worlds—is more than a mere object of our free acceptance or rejection. Is it not true that when a work of art has seized us it no longer leaves us the freedom to push it away from us once again and to accept or reject it on our own terms? And is it not also true that these artistic creations, which come down through the millennia, were not created for such aesthetic acceptance or rejection? No artist of the religiously vital cultures of the past ever produced his work of art with any other intention then that his creation should be received in terms of what it says and presents and that it should have its place in the world where men live together. The consciousness of art—the aesthetic consciousness—is always secondary to the immediate truth-claim that proceeds from the work of art itself. To this extent, when we judge a work of art on the basis of its aesthetic quality, something that is really much more intimately familiar to us is alienated. This alienation into aesthetic judgment always takes place when we have withdrawn ourselves and are no longer open to the immediate claim of that which grasps us. Thus one point of departure for my reflections in *Truth and Method* was that the aesthetic sovereignty that claims its rights in the experience of art represents an alienation when compared to the authentic experience that confronts us in the form of art itself.

About thirty years ago, this problem cropped up in a particularly distorted form when National Socialist politics of art, as a means to its own ends, tried to criticize formalism by arguing that art is bound to a people. Despite its misuse by the National Socialists, we cannot deny that the idea of art being bound to a people involves a real insight. A genuine artistic creation stands within a particular community, and such a community is always distinguishable from the cultured society that is informed and terrorized by art criticism.

The second mode of the experience of alienation is the historical consciousness—the noble and slowly perfected art of holding ourselves at a critical distance in dealing with witnesses to past life. Ranke's celebrated description of this idea as the extinguishing of the individual provided a popular formula for the ideal of historical thinking: the historical consciousness has the task of understanding all the witnesses of a past time out of the spirit of that time, of extricating them from the preoccupations of our own present life, and of knowing, without moral smugness, the past as a human phenomenon. In his well-known essay *The Use and Abuse of History*, Nietzsche formulated the contradiction between this historical distancing and the immediate will to shape things that always cleaves to the present. And at the same time he exposed many of the consequences of what he called the "Alexandrian," weakened form of the will, which is found in modern historical science. We might recall his indictment of the weakness of evaluation that has befallen the modern mind because it has become so accustomed to considering things in ever different and changing lights that it is blinded and incapable of arriving at an opinion of its own regarding the objects it studies. It is unable to determine its own position *vis-à-vis* what confronts it. Nietzsche traces the value-blindness of historical objectivism back to the conflict between the alienated historical world and the life-powers of the present.

To be sure, Nietzsche is an ecstatic witness. But our actual experience of the historical consciousness in the last one hundred years has taught us most emphatically that there are serious difficulties involved in its claim to historical objectivity. Even in those masterworks of historical scholarship that seem to be the very consummation of the extinguishing of the individual demanded by Ranke, it is still an unquestioned principle of our scientific experience that we can classify these works with unfailing accuracy in terms of the political tendencies of the time in which they were written. When we read Mommsen's *History of Rome*, we know who alone could have written it, that is, we can identify the political situation in which this historian organized the voices of the past in a meaningful way. We know it too in the case of Treitschke or of Sybel, to choose only a few prominent names from Prussian historiography. This clearly means, first of all, that the whole reality of historical experience does not find expression in the mastery of historical method. No one disputes the fact that controlling the prejudices of our own present to such an extent that we do not misunderstand the witnesses of the past is a valid aim, but obviously such control does not completely fulfill the task of understanding the past and its transmissions. Indeed, it could very well be that only *insignificant* things in historical scholarship permit us to approximate this ideal of totally extinguishing individuality, while the great productive achievements of scholarship always preserve something of the splendid magic of immediately mirroring the present in the past and the past in the present. Historical science, the second experience from which I begin, expresses only one part of our actual experience—our actual encounter with historical tradition—and it knows only an alienated form of this historical tradition.

We can contrast the hermeneutical consciousness with these examples of alienation as a more comprehensive possibility that we must develop. But, in the case of this hermeneutical consciousness also, our initial task must be to overcome the epistemological truncation by which the traditional "science of hermeneutics" has been absorbed into the idea of modern science. If we consider Schleiermacher's hermeneutics, for instance, we find his view of this discipline peculiarly restricted by the modern idea of science. Schleiermacher's hermeneutics shows him to be a leading voice of historical romanticism. But at the same time, he kept the concern of the Christian theologian clearly in mind, intending his hermeneutics, as a general doctrine of the art of understanding, to be of value in the special work of interpreting Scripture. Schleiermacher defined hermeneutics as the art of avoiding misunderstanding. To exclude by controlled, methodical consideration whatever is alien and leads to misunderstanding—misunderstanding suggested to us by distance in time, change in linguistic usages, or in the meanings of words and modes of thinking—that is certainly far from an absurd description of the hermeneutical endeavor. But the question also arises as to whether the phenomenon of understanding is defined appropriately when we say that to understand is to avoid misunderstanding. Is it not, in fact, the case that every misunderstanding presupposes a "deep common accord"?

I am trying to call attention here to a common experience. We say, for instance, that understanding and misunderstanding take place between I and thou. But the formulation "I and thou" already betrays an enormous alienation. There is nothing like an "I and thou" at all—there is neither the I nor the thou as isolated, substantial realities. I may say "thou" and I may refer to myself over against a thou, but a common understanding [Verständigung] always precedes these situations. We all know that to say "thou" to someone presupposes a deep common accord [tiefes Einverständnis]. Something enduring is already present when this word is spoken. When we try to reach agreement on a matter on which we have different opinions, this deeper factor always comes into play, even if we are seldom aware of it. Now the science of hermeneutics would have us believe that the opinion we have to understand is something alien that seeks to lure us into misunderstanding, and our task is to exclude every element through which a misunderstanding can creep in. We accomplish this task by a controlled procedure of historical training, by historical criticism, and by a controllable method in connection with powers of psychological empathy. It seems to me that this description is valid in one respect, but yet it is only a partial description of a comprehensive life-phenomenon that constitutes the "we" that we all are. Our task, it seems to me, is to transcend the prejudices that underlie the aesthetic consciousness, the historical consciousness, and the hermeneutical consciousness that has been restricted to a technique for avoiding misunderstandings and to overcome the alienations present in them all.

What is it, then, in these three experiences that seemed to us to have been left out, and what makes us so sensitive to the distinctiveness of these experiences? What is the *aesthetic* consciousness when compared to the fullness of what has already addressed us—what we call "classical" in art? Is it not always already determined in this way what will be expressive for us and what we will find significant? Whenever we say with an instinctive, even if perhaps erroneous, certainty (but a certainty that is initially valid for our consciousness) "this is classical; it will endure," what we are speaking of has already preformed our possibility for aesthetic judgment. There are no purely formal criteria that can claim to judge and sanction the formative level simply on the basis of its artistic virtuosity. Rather, our sensitive-spiritual existence is an aesthetic resonance chamber that resonates with the voices that are constantly reaching us, preceding all explicit aesthetic judgment.

The situation is similar with the historical consciousness. Here, too, we must certainly admit that there are innumerable tasks of historical scholarship that have no relation to our own present and to the depths of its historical consciousness. But it seems to me there can be no doubt that the great horizon of the past, out of which our culture and our present live, influences us in everything we want, hope for, or fear in the future. History is only present to us in light of our futurity. Here we have all learned from Heidegger, for he exhibited precisely the primacy of futurity for our possible recollection and retention, and for the whole of our history.

Heidegger worked out this primacy in his doctrine of the productivity of the hermeneutical circle. I have given the following formulation to this insight: It is not so much our judgments as it is our prejudices that constitute our being.[1] This is a provocative formulation, for I am using it to restore to its rightful place a positive concept of prejudice that was driven out of our linguistic usage by the French and the English Enlightenment. It can be shown that the concept of prejudice did not originally have the meaning we have attached to it. Prejudices are not necessarily unjustified and erroneous, so that they inevitably distort the truth. In fact, the historicity of our existence entails that prejudices, in the literal sense of the word, constitute the initial directedness of our whole ability to experience. Prejudices are biases of our openness to the world. They are simply conditions whereby we experience something—whereby what we encounter says something to us. This formulation certainly does not mean that we are enclosed within a wall of prejudices and only let through the narrow portals those things that can produce a pass saying, "Nothing new will be said here." Instead we welcome just that guest who promises something new to our curiosity. But how do we know the guest whom we admit is one who has something *new* to say to us? Is not our expectation and our readiness to hear the new also necessarily determined by the old that has already taken possession of us?

[1]Cf. Hans-Georg Gadamer, *Wahrheit und Methode: Grundzüge einer philosophischen Hermeneutik* (Tübingen: J. C. B. Mohr, 1960), p. 261. The English translation of this book is: Hans-Georg Gadamer, *Truth and Method*, trans. Garrett Barden and John Cumming (New York: The Seabury Press, 1975). The note is found on page 245.

The concept of prejudice is closely connected to the concept of authority, and the above image makes it clear that it is in need of hermeneutical rehabilitation. Like every image, however, this one too is misleading. The nature of the hermeneutical experience is not that something is outside and desires admission. Rather, we are possessed by something and precisely by means of it we are opened up for the new, the different, the true. Plato made this clear in his beautiful comparison of bodily foods with spiritual nourishment: while we can refuse the former (e.g., on the advice of a physician), we have always taken the latter into ourselves already.

But now the question arises as to how we can legitimate this hermeneutical conditionedness of our being in the face of modern science, which stands or falls with the principle of being unbiased and prejudiceless. We will certainly not accomplish this legitimation by making prescriptions for science and recommending that it toe the line—quite aside from the fact that such pronouncements always have something comical about them. Science will not do us this favor. It will continue along its own path with an inner necessity beyond its control, and it will produce more and more breathtaking knowledge and controlling power. It can be no other way. It is senseless, for instance, to hinder a genetic researcher because such research threatens to breed a superman. Hence the problem cannot appear as one in which our human consciousness ranges itself over against the world of science and presumes to develop a kind of antiscience. Nevertheless, we cannot avoid the question of whether what we are aware of in such apparently harmless examples as the aesthetic consciousness and the historical consciousness does not represent a problem that is also present in modern natural science and our technological attitude toward the world. If modern science enables us to erect a new world of technological purposes that transforms everything around us, we are not thereby suggesting that the researcher who gained the knowledge decisive for this state of affairs even considered technical applications. The genuine researcher is motivated by a desire for knowledge and by nothing else. And yet, over against the whole of our civilization that is founded on modern science, we must ask repeatedly if something has not been omitted. If the presuppositions of these possibilities for knowing and making remain half in the dark, cannot the result be that the hand applying this knowledge will be destructive?

The problem is really universal. The hermeneutical question, as I have characterized it, is not restricted to the areas from which I began in my own investigation. My only concern there was to secure a theoretical basis that would enable us to deal with the basic factor of contemporary culture, namely, science and its industrial, technological utilization. Statistics provide us with a useful example of how the hermeneutical dimension encompasses the entire procedure of science. It is an extreme example, but it shows us that science always stands under definite conditions of methodological abstraction and that the successes of modern sciences rest on the fact that other possibilities for questioning are concealed by abstraction. This fact comes out clearly in the case of statistics, for the anticipatory character of the questions statistics answer make it particularly suitable for propaganda purposes. Indeed, effective propaganda must always try to influence initially the judgment of the person addressed and to restrict his possibilities of judgment. Thus what is established by statistics seems to be a language of facts, but which questions these facts answer and which facts would begin to speak if other questions were asked are hermeneutical questions. Only a hermeneutical inquiry would legitimate the meaning of these facts and thus the consequences that follow from them.

But I am anticipating, and have inadvertently used the phrase, "which answers to which questions fit the facts." This phrase is in fact the hermeneutical *Urphänomen*: No assertion is possible that cannot be understood as an answer to a question, and assertions can only be understood in this way. It does not impair the impressive methodology of modern science in the least. Whoever wants to learn a science has to learn to master its methodology. But we also know that methodology as such does not guarantee in any way the productivity of its application. Any experience of life can confirm the fact that there is such a thing as methodological sterility, that is, the application of a method to something not really worth knowing, to something that has not been made an object of investigation on the basis of a genuine question.

The methodological self-consciousness of modern science certainly stands in opposition to this argument. A historian, for example, will say in reply: It is all very nice to talk about the historical tradition in which alone the voices of the past gain their meaning and through which the prejudices that determine the present are inspired. But the situation is completely different in questions of serious historical research. How could one seriously mean, for example, that the clarification of the taxation practices of fifteenth-century cities or of the marital customs of Eskimos somehow first receive their meaning from the consciousness of the present and its anticipations? These are questions of historical knowledge that we take up as tasks quite independently of any relation to the present.

In answering this objection, one can say that the extremity of this point of view would be similar to what we find in certain large industrial research facilities, above all in America and Russia. I mean so-called random experiment in which one simply covers the material without concern for waste or cost, taking the chance that some day one measurement among the thousands of measurements will finally yield an interesting finding; that is, it will turn out to be the answer to a question from which someone can progress. No doubt modern research in the humanities also works this way to some extent. One thinks, for instance, of the great editions and especially of the ever more perfect indexes. It must remain an open question, of course, whether by such procedures modern historical research increases the chances of actually noticing the interesting fact and thus gaining from it the corresponding enrichment of our knowledge. But even if they do, one might ask: Is this an ideal, that countless research projects (i.e., determinations of the connection of facts) are extracted from a thousand historians, so that the 1001st historian can find something interesting? Of course I am drawing a caricature of genuine scholarship. But in every caricature there is an element of truth, and this one contains an indirect answer to the question of what it is that really makes the productive scholar. That he has learned the methods? The person who never produces anything new has also done that. It is imagination [*Phantasie*] that is the decisive function of the scholar. Imagination naturally has a hermeneutical function and serves the sense for what is questionable. It serves the ability to expose real, productive questions, something in which, generally speaking, only he who masters all the methods of his science succeeds.

As a student of Plato, I particularly love those scenes in which Socrates gets into a dispute with the Sophist virtuosi and drives them to despair by his questions. Eventually they can endure his questions no longer and claim for themselves the apparently preferable role of the questioner. And what happens? They can think of nothing at all to ask. Nothing at all occurs to them that is worth while going into and trying to answer.

I draw the following inference from this observation. The real power of hermeneutical consciousness is our ability to see what is questionable. Now if what we have before our eyes is not only the artistic tradition of a people, or historical tradition, or the principle of modern science in its hermeneutical preconditions but rather the whole of our experience, then we have succeeded, I think, in joining the experience of science to our own universal and human experience of life. For we have now reached the fundamental level that we can call (with Johannes Lohmann) the "linguistic constitution of the world."[2] It presents itself as the consciousness that is effected by history [*wirkungsgeschichtliches Bewusstsein*] and that provides an initial schematization for all our possibilities of knowing. I leave out of account the fact that the scholar—even the natural scientist—is perhaps not completely free of custom and society and from all possible factors in his environment. What I mean is that precisely *within* his scientific experience it is not so much the "laws of ironclad inference" (Helmholz) that present fruitful ideas to him, but rather unforeseen constellations that kindle the spark of scientific inspiration (e.g., Newton's falling apple or some other incidental observation).

The consciousness that is effected by history has its fulfillment in what is linguistic. We can learn from the sensitive student of language that language, in its life and occurrence, must not be thought of as merely

---

[2]Cf. Johannes Lohmann, *Philosophie und Sprachwissenschaft* (Berlin: Duncker & Humbolt, 1963).

changing, but rather as something that has a teleology operating within it. This means that the words that are formed, the means of expression that appear in a language in order to say certain things, are not accidentally fixed, since they do not once again fall altogether into disuse. Instead, a definite articulation of the world is built up—a process that works as if guided and one that we can always observe in children who are learning to speak.

We can illustrate this by considering a passage in Aristotle's *Posterior Analytics* that ingeniously describes one definite aspect of language formation.[3] The passage treats what Aristotle calls the *epagoge*, that is, the formation of the universal. How does one arrive at a universal? In philosophy we say: how do we arrive at a general concept, but even words in this sense are obviously general. How does it happen that they are "words," that is, that they have a general meaning? In his first apperception, a sensuously equipped being finds himself in a surging sea of stimuli, and finally one day he begins, as we say, to know something. Clearly we do not mean that he was previously blind. Rather, when we say "to know" [*erkennen*] we mean "to recognize" [*wiedererkennen*], that is, to pick something out [*herauserkennen*] of the stream of images flowing past as being identical. What is picked out in this fashion is clearly retained. But how? When does a child know its mother for the first time? When it sees her for the first time? No. Then when? How does it take place? Can we really say at all that there is a single event in which a first knowing extricates the child from the darkness of not knowing? It seems obvious to me that we cannot. Aristotle has described this wonderfully. He says it is the same as when an army is in flight, driven by panic, until at last someone stops and looks around to see whether the foe is still dangerously close behind. We cannot say that the army stops when one soldier has stopped. But then another stops. The army does not stop by virtue of the fact that two soldiers stop. When does it actually stop, then? Suddenly it stands its ground again. Suddenly it obeys the command once again. A subtle pun is involved in Aristotle's description, for in Greek "command" means *arche*, that is, *principium*. When is the principle present as a principle? Through what capacity? This question is in fact the question of the occurrence of the universal.

If I have not misunderstood Johannes Lohmann's exposition, precisely this same teleology operates constantly in the life of language. When Lohmann speaks of linguistic tendencies as the real agents of history in which specific forms expand, he knows of course that it occurs in these forms of realization, of "coming to a stand" [*Zum-Stehen-Kommen*], as the beautiful German word says. What is manifest here, I contend, is the real mode of operation of our whole human experience of the world. Learning to speak is surely a phase of special productivity, and in the course of time we have all transformed the genius of the three-year-old into a poor and meager talent.

---

[3]Aristotle, *Posterior Analytics*, 100a 11–13.

But in the utilization of the linguistic interpretation of the world that finally comes about, something of the productivity of our beginnings remains alive. We are all acquainted with this, for instance, in the attempt to translate, in practical life or in literature or wherever; that is, we are familiar with the strange, uncomfortable, and torturous feeling we have as long as we do not have the right word. When we have found the right expression (it need not always be one word), when we are certain that we have it, then it "stands," then something has come to a "stand." Once again we have a halt in the midst of the rush of the foreign language, whose endless variation makes us lose our orientation. What I am describing is the mode of the whole human experience of the world. I call this experience hermeneutical, for the process we are describing is repeated continually throughout our familiar experience. There is always a world already interpreted, already organized in its basic relations, into which experience steps as something new, upsetting what has led our expectations and undergoing reorganization itself in the upheaval. Misunderstanding and strangeness are not the first factors, so that avoiding misunderstanding can be regarded as the specific task of hermeneutics. Just the reverse is the case. Only the support of familiar and common understanding makes possible the venture into the alien, the lifting up of something out of the alien, and thus the broadening and enrichment of our own experience of the world.

This discussion shows how the claim to universality that is appropriate to the hermeneutical dimension is to be understood. Understanding is language-bound. But this assertion does not lead us into any kind of linguistic relativism. It is indeed true that we live within a language, but language is not a system of signals that we send off with the aid of a telegraphic key when we enter the office or transmission station. That is not speaking, for it does not have the infinity of the act that is linguistically creative and world experiencing. While we live wholly within a language, the fact that we do so does not constitute linguistic relativism because there is absolutely no captivity within a language—not even within our native language. We all experience this when we learn a foreign language, especially on journeys insofar as we master the foreign language to some extent. To master the foreign language means precisely that when we engage in speaking it in the foreign land, we do not constantly consult inwardly our own world and its vocabulary. The better we know the language, the less such a side glance at our native language is perceptible, and only because we never know foreign languages well enough do we always have something of this feeling. But it is nevertheless already speaking, even if perhaps a stammering speaking, for stammering is the obstruction of a desire to speak and is thus opened into the infinite realm of possible expression. Any language in which we live is infinite in this sense, and it is completely mistaken to infer that reason is fragmented because there are various languages. Just the opposite is the case. Precisely through our finitude, the particularity of our being, which is evident even in the variety of languages, the infinite dialogue is opened in the direction of the truth that we are.

If this is correct, then the relation of our modern industrial world, founded by science, which we described at the outset, is mirrored above all on the level of language. We live in an epoch in which an increasing leveling of all life-forms is taking place—that is the rationally necessary requirement for maintaining life on our planet. The food problem of mankind, for example, can only be overcome by the surrender of the lavish wastefulness that has covered the earth. Unavoidably, the mechanical, industrial world is expanding within the life of the individual as a sort of sphere of technical perfection. When we hear modern lovers talking to each other, we often wonder if they are communicating with words or with advertising labels and technical terms from the sign language of the modern industrial world. It is inevitable that the leveled life-forms of the industrial age also affect language, and in fact the impoverishment of the vocabulary of language is making enormous progress, thus bringing about an approximation of language to a technical sign-system. Leveling tendencies of this kind are irresistible. Yet in spite of them the simultaneous building up of our own world in language still persists whenever we want to say something to each other. The result is the actual relationship of men to each other. Each one is at first a kind of linguistic circle, and these linguistic circles come into contact with each other, merging more and more. Language occurs once again, in vocabulary and grammar as always, and never without the inner infinity of the dialogue that is in progress between every speaker and his partner. That is the fundamental dimension of hermeneutics. Genuine speaking, which has something to say and hence does not give prearranged signals, but rather seeks words through which one reaches the other person, is the universal human task—but it is a special task for the theologian, to whom is commissioned the saying-further (*Weitersagen*) of a message that stands written.

INTRODUCTION TO EBELING'S "GOD AND WORD"

In my introduction to the essay by Bultmann earlier in this collection, I mentioned the impact that Bultmann's program of demythologizing the New Testament had on theology: the issues raised by Bultmann concerning interpretation dominated the theological discussion after 1941, eclipsing even the thought of Karl Barth. By approximately 1955, Bultmann's program was in turn superseded as the cutting edge of German theology. By then, the debate had produced a new version of hermeneutical theology.

The "new hermeneutic," as it came to be called, was thoroughly immersed in the thought of Bultmann and Heidegger. But the thinkers belonging to this movement departed from specific elements in Bultmann's approach, while retaining his focus on the hermeneutical problem for theology. The leading figures of the new hermeneutic include Gerhard Ebeling, Ernst Fuchs of Marburg, and, less closely related, Heinrich Ott of Basel. Of the three, Ebeling has been central. His work is crucial to the formation of a hermeneutical theology schooled in the later Heidegger and then Gadamer's *Truth and Method*.

Ebeling should not be mistaken as a mere theological spokesman for hermeneutical philosophy, however. Theological interests move Ebeling. He is clearly committed to the Lutheran tradition; his schooling in Heidegger and Gadamer serves his purpose of letting Luther's statement of faith be heard again. Hermeneutical philosophy allows Ebeling to focus on the theological dimension of language. Luther, before Heidegger, had uncovered the fundamental relation between word and faith. Ebeling's task is like Luther's: to interpret the relation between word and faith within one's own time and world.

Bultmann, of course, was also firmly entrenched in the Lutheran tradition. And in many ways, Ebeling's work is an important moment in the reception of Bultmann's reappropriation of that tradition. But Ebeling's "new hermeneutic" moved beyond Bultmann on at least two key points.

First, Bultmann regarded the kerygma as placing something extralinguistic into language, in the manner in which one places a marble in a glass jar where it can be seen. Thus reality and language are quite clearly distinct for Bultmann. Subsequent hermeneutical inquiry moved beyond Bultmann's philosophical home in Heidegger's *Being and Time*, however, with the driving principle of the "linguisticality of being." It states that reality is always already interpreted in language. Reality presents itself linguistically; we have no nonlinguistic grasp of reality. This principle is not found in Bultmann, who lacked an adequate reflection on language.

Second, Bultmann was not willing to carry out his demythologizing program fully. He stopped short of demythologizing the image of an "act of God." He understood the resurrection as the ontological transformation that occurs as faith awakens on hearing of "God's act" of raising Jesus from the dead. But the act of God remains dangling as a remnant of mythology that is otherwise interpreted existentially. Ebeling tried to repair Bultmann's program in both those places.

Ebeling is also open to insights from the dialectical theology of the 1920s, especially those of Barth. Afterimages of Barth's vision of the inbreaking of the "wholly other" God may be caught in Ebeling. Moreover, Ebeling never loses sight of the problem Barth faced as a preacher of God's word. Barth, called upon to communicate the word of God to his congregation in Safenwil, Switzerland, asked himself: How can I, a mere human (that is, if understood correctly, a "godless" sinner) say anything that may be heard as word of God, and not merely as a human word? As a preacher, Barth found himself duty-bound to do the impossible: to utter the word of God in a convincing way. The essay by Barth called "The Word of God as Task of the Ministry" records his answer: one acknowledges the necessity of uttering God's word along with the impossibility of doing so, and one thus gives God the glory if and when the word is heard as God's word. Ebeling takes up a similar question in "God and Word" and universalizes it. The same problem faces any user of language today: we must speak of God, for "God" designates the depth or center of language—the point in language where language transcends itself and is open to reality beyond it. Yet we cannot speak of God, because our technical civilization is closed to that linguistic center or depth. Thus Ebeling, in this essay, is still working with the problem of how speaking and hearing the word of God are possible. But whereas Barth decided not to consider the hermeneutical problem directly, Ebeling gives it his full attention.

The following essay by Ebeling, "God and Word," provides an excellent introduction to his version of hermeneutic theology. Ebeling brought his theological program to completion in his 1979 three-volume magnum opus *Dogmatik des christlichen Glaubens*. The relation between "God and Word" and his dogmatic system is much like the relation between Schleiermacher's *Speeches on Religion* and his theological system, *The Christian Faith*. Both were addressed to a secular audience for whom God-talk had become unintelligible or uninteresting, yet both were actually heard largely by theology students; and both were written prior to a work interpreting the contents of faith for the church community.

"God and Word" was first presented as a series of three lectures in

Berkeley, California, at the Pacific School of Religion, in 1966. The line of inquiry through the three lectures runs as follows.

First, Ebeling characterizes the linguistic situation as *godless* and claims that reflection on that situation demands that we understand the word *God*. The word *godless* names a situation in which we both inherit a language that once sustained "God" as its living center and yet can say nothing about that vanished center or in its name. Ebeling reviews some of the historical reasons for the secularization of the modern world and the inability of the critical thinkers any longer to speak of God. Peculiarly, however, this situation of alienation from God-talk, the situation of critical detachment, accords with the self-understanding of religious consciousness. The Western religious tradition calls all humans "sinners," that is, godless. So the perennial human situation is that of alienation from God-talk. After all, if God is God, no human and thus godless word can define or represent God. Strictly speaking, we cannot talk about God. Silence about God is perhaps the best means to manifest God. But that tactic abandons word. Hence the impasse: the language we receive obliges us to speak about God, yet that language does not permit us to do so.

Second, more careful reflection on language will dispel this false dilemma of either word and not-God or God and not-word. Typically, the Western tradition thinks of words as signifying things. But words do not merely belong to a system of signification. When sentences are uttered, events take place in time. Our words are answerable to the situations in which they occur. In "answerability" we have a more fundamental trait than signification (although it does not dispense with the latter). We open up this deeper dimension of language when we ask, "What happens through word?" and "What end is served by such use?"

If we ask about the answerability of our use of language at all, we discover that what happens through language is the opening of future and the granting of freedom. And if we ask what end is served by language as such, we answer that telling the truth, putting reality into words, is the purpose of language. These two go together: telling the truth makes a person free; it authenticates and makes that person "true." The central point is that our answerability to situations in using language indicates that futurity, freedom, and truth all depend on our relation to language. They are words we receive that call forth or enable the realities they describe.

Words that call forth or enable the realities they describe—words like *freedom, future*, and *truth*—draw their power from an ability to show forth what is already part of the human situation but hidden from view. Enabling words uncover elements of our basic human existence. And the word in our Western languages that manifests the basic human situation as a linguistic situation is the word *God*. The word *God* does not signify a metaphysical being. It evokes and manifests essential human openness as openness through word. *God* means the basic human situation as one in which we are given a language, called upon to speak, and made answerable to the situation in which we find ourselves. As such, it is the "word of words." So it functioned for our predecessors, who dwelt in the Bible as a linguistic home.

Furthermore, the word *God* is irreplaceable in our language. So some talk of God is necessary. Yet who is authorized to speak of God? Can anyone claim nonironically to utter the "word of words" and be understood? This question of authority leads to the final lecture.

Third, authorization for use of the word *God* can only come from the word of God. By this Ebeling means that no human can speak in the name of God and thereby open up the basic human situation. Any claim to speak of God can be met by criticism. No words will be understood as bespeaking God simply because someone, some institution, or some text says it presents the word of God. Today, the word of God may be authorized only in the hearing and recognition evoked by it. Ebeling says, "Authority is now a question of the authorship of evidence and respect."[1] Some words present the reality of "God." They manifest the basic human situation of openness, reversing its apparent closure. If those words break into the world of the hearer so as to illuminate the openness that was there but hidden because unspoken, they are heard as coming not only from a human speaker but also from "God"—the hidden agent of the word-event. In such a case, God appears through the word *God*.

For Ebeling, *God is God as the word that brings our own situation to light*. Any word that brings our situation to light participates in the "word of words," although the word that, as part of the language, traditionally calls attention to our situation as "answerable" is *God*. Experience of the living word of God creates a "healthy modesty" that exercises restraint in uttering the word *God*. The meaning of the word *God* "compels us to acquire a faculty of discrimination and to learn when it is the right time—and that means, when it is necessary—to speak of God."[2]

[1] Gerhard Ebeling, "God and Word," p. 216 below.
[2] Ibid.

GOD AND WORD
(1966)
Gerhard Ebeling

I. THE WORD OF THE GODLESS

The subject "God and Word" is of my own choosing, but I must confess that it involves me in a presumptuous, hazardous, and yet also a necessary project.

The presumptuousness of the project becomes clear to us the moment we recognize that the brief monosyllables "God" and "word" point us into the realm of the boundless. When we deal with God, we deal with the immeasurable, whether it is then said that "God lives" or that "God is dead." And when we enter into the question of the nature of "word," the question of language as the point at which all dimensions of our experience of reality intersect, then we find ourselves in the realm of the inexhaustible, whether that be interpreted as a sign of our power or our impotence. How are we ever to do justice to these two overwhelmingly complex problems? And how are we to consider them together?

The project is, furthermore, hazardous. Between the two principal terms there stands the word "and," simultaneously joining and separating those terms. The impression is of a harmless juxtaposition of two factors, as if each of the two, God and word, was already established in itself and there remained only our inquiry into their relationship. It seems self-evident to us that it is the language which we command as human beings that gives us the standard by which we even talk of God, and also, on the contrary, that God, insofar as he really exists, is independent of our talk of him. But what if the facts are otherwise, and there prevails between God and word a tension which the particle "and" is inadequate to bear? What if the "and" which links them breaks down, so that God is left without word and our word without God, a wordless God and godless word—and thus the place of God is taken by a silence that renders us speechless, smothering every sound and even every thought, while our word ultimately fails and falls silent? Or what if an all too close contact between God and word results in a melting of the "and" which separates them, so that we read, "the Word was God" (John 1:1), and consequently what is to be expected of the word is no less than God? This, too, could be extremely hazardous—provided that familiarity with the language of the Bible does not keep us from thinking about it. Let us only try to realize what it means that God actually comes to grips with us through a word and to understand that we are expected to represent God to the world by means of our word! It is understandable that even a man like Isaiah was appalled: "Woe is me! For I am lost; for I am a man of unclean lips, and I dwell in the midst of a people of unclean lips" (Isaiah 6:5).

And yet I do believe that despite all our misgivings the subject "God and Word" is necessary, in fact vitally necessary. For, although this may be surprising, we threaten to die of language poisoning. This is not because God has completely vanished from our language, but because God is festering in our language.

Our language—it is vastly more than familiar vocabulary or rules of usage. Language is the body of our spirit. The life of language goes on as we receive tradition and convert it again into words for which we ourselves can answer. Two factors—on the one hand, all that we have been taught by parents, by those about us, and by earlier generations, all that has thus entered into us or lies ready for us in a vast warehouse of printed matter; and on the other hand, all that we then can say from personal knowledge and experience, whether publicly, privately, or in the secret places of the heart—these two factors are the poles between which the life of language takes place, grows or wastes away.

Our linguistic tradition is full of references to God. But what *we* are able to say in this respect is little or nothing. It is not merely a question here of the vocable "God," but rather of the entirety of what is to be said of all things in the light of God and before God: how the world and history, my fellows and my own self, my whence and whither, life and death are given expression before God. The Bible was the linguistic home of our forefathers—albeit in various degrees of intensity and understood in conflicting ways—and consequently God was more or less their linguistic center, though not by any means to the exclusion of hypocrisy and blasphemy. That this is the tradition from which we come, no one can deny. But now, in our day, it looks as if talk of God, and all that goes with it, is nothing more than just a tradition, a mere form of speech, a dead relic of the language of the past.

If we do not see this shift in the situation, then there will in fact be a danger of what I have called language poisoning—a sepsis in our spiritual life. This is why the subject "God and Word" is vital, essential to the continuance of life. We must not irresponsibly stop doing so. Yet to a disquieting extent both things are happening today. And both are poisonous, albeit in different ways.

Talk of God that lacks authenticity, that has become empty and powerless, spells disintegration to faith and thought. On this, whether pious or not, all are fundamentally agreed. And hopefully the non-believers will not be the sole advocates of thought. Whoever takes the holiness of God seriously should make certain that no one is more conscientious than he in the use of words. That has always been so, but it has also always been questioned. Talk of God is word at its most demanding, because it demands pure faith. For this reason such talk is always in danger of becoming presumptuous and incredible.

Now, however, we find ourselves in an age in which responsible talk of God has to satisfy extreme demands. Never before was there so great a gulf between the linguistic tradition of the Bible and the language that is actually spoken. Hence, never before was it so easy to suspect that God is merely a matter of tradition. Never before was the task of answering for God in our word put before us so radically. The problem today, seen as a whole, is indeed not that there is any lack of institutions and publications which provide possibilities for speaking of God. On the contrary, the problem is how a genuine word of God is to be asserted in the midst of this tremendous inflation of existing possibilities.

For that reason, is reflection on the relationship between God and word necessary only for those who have an interest in talking of God or who still expect something from this talk? Is this reflection necessary in order to sharpen the responsibility of those men for such talk, or is it necessary in order to support them, since the burden of such responsibility is too great for them? Even when the circle of those who are immediately concerned is described in such narrow terms, the scope of our subject yet extends far beyond to the widest circles of the public. Whoever ascribes no significance to talk of God will in any event have to take seriously the effects of stale and decaying talk of God upon the surrounding world. Even from the standpoint of radical secularism it would be shortsighted to expect anything from the inner self-disintegration of belief in God, for it is also in secularism's own interest to be confronted with genuine talk of God and not merely with stale, putrefied language. The struggle concerning God and word must be fought out with all possible clarity. Far more than is normally realized, our customary talk of God—dull sermons and pious words which have no bearing on reality and cause us no further thought—has become empty, producing a slow disintegration. The consequences of this are not by any means to be found only in the religious realm, but also are considerable outside of it—namely, in the devaluation of words in general, the debilitation of the responsible use of language. Hence the subject "God and Word" has an urgency for all who consider themselves responsible for our age.

But we must go still a step further. It would poison our language—so I have said—not only if we irresponsibly continued to speak of God, but also if we irresponsibly stopped doing so. The superficial and flippant way in which talk of God is today widely regarded—explicitly or implicitly—as a thing of the past, stands in inglorious contrast to the depth and richness of that tradition from which our age has severed itself but from whose heritage it nevertheless is still nourished. To recognize such a difference of level is of course not to remove the obstacles which today stand in the way of speaking of God. But to reconcile ourselves to that difference as our destiny, without reaching a settlement with the great linguistic tradition in which "God" was the word of all words, means cultural collapse, the danger of spiritual barbarism. If it is really to be our lot that we must live with a language without God, then we ought at least to do so as decent and cultural men, i.e., not in forgetfulness, but with a respect for our own linguistic tradition. Otherwise we carry along with us an unexamined heritage which, even though we do not speak of God any more, nevertheless has about it the decaying stench of what is dead but not buried.

I now go still further and declare that not only does the linguistic tradition from which we have come oblige even those who consider themselves free of all responsibility for speaking of God to reflect nevertheless on the relation of God and word. I declare also that the thought of our own linguistic responsibility obliges us to reflect on the relationship in question. How do I do justice to the fact that I am enabled to use words and called upon to use words? What is my duty where words are concerned?

If it is really true that thinking about word as such drives us to think about the relation of God and word, then the usual understanding of our subject is turned the opposite way round. Our immediate reaction to the relation of God and word is of course the idea that it is precisely the examination of the linguistic aspect of faith in God that causes embarrassment. Our talk of God allegedly cannot stand being taken strictly at its word. A critical use of words appears to be dangerous for God. I counter this customary view by making the following assertion, which points the direction for the rest of our reflections: it is precisely the consideration of the nature of word that leads to an understanding of what "God" means.

Yet we would not simply set aside the view that comes readiest to mind. It, too, contains some truth, and thus it cannot be disregarded with impunity. I confine myself to one or two aspects which make it clear why a sober evaluation of word appears to have critical, if not disastrous, consequences for the relation to God.

Faith itself knows that it becomes vain when we stop at pious words, at mere talk of God, and do not go on to corresponding deeds which give realization to the word in life. It is not saying "Lord, Lord" that counts, but doing the will of God. This is one of the strongest impulses for that piety which is given classic expression by, for example, Thomas à Kempis in *The Imitation of Christ*, one of the most widely known works in world literature: "Whosoever would fully and feelingly understand the words of Christ, must endeavor to conform his whole life to Christ. What will it avail you to dispute sublimely the Trinity, if you be void of humility and are thereby displeasing to the Trinity? Sublime words surely make a man neither holy, nor just; but a virtuous life makes him dear to God. I had rather feel compunction, than understand the definition thereof. If you did know by heart the whole Bible and the sayings of all the philosophers—what would all that profit you, without the love of God and without grace?"[1]

Understandably enough, unbelief, too, and it in particular, has a keen eye for this. It even supposes that piety is essentially nothing but hypocrisy, an ideological froth that contradicts and destroys real life. It is no accident that the slogan of "practical Christianity" easily changes into the emancipation of practice from Christian doctrine. And out of mistrust of religious words there grows contempt for words as such.

Of course contempt for words stands in sharpest contradiction to Christian faith, especially as understood by the Reformers. This faith lives, as it confesses, from the word of God, and indeed from the word of God as uttered with final validity, from word become flesh. To be sure, even theology cannot shut its eyes to the fact that here the term "word" is used in a way that breaks the bounds of normal linguistic usage. It even seems to be in the proper interest of theology to turn one's back on the literal understanding of word as an utterance of human speech, in order that God should not be made finite and God's word not confused with the letter. The problem threatens, however, to become the still more acute question of whether the concept of the word of God is not, strictly speaking, altogether self-contradictory since the fact of the matter is that "word" exists for us only as human word. Do we not in all honesty have to choose between meaning "word" but then not claiming God for it, or meaning "God" but then not ascribing a word to him?

This brings us into the wide field of the problems of religious language as such. Under the influence of general philosophic views of language, these problems are being intensively discussed today, in Europe mainly from the point of the hermeneutic approach, in the Anglo-Saxon realm primarily from the standpoint of linguistic analysis. In the one case the terms are those of the cultural or historical sciences; in the other case the terms are those of natural science and logic. The typical leading concepts are "understanding" on the one side and "verification" on the other. How these two strands of contemporary philosophy of language are interrelated, how far they contradict, overlap, or supplement each other, cannot be discussed here.[2] Today, in any event, our subject "God and Word" is normally conceived in terms of those linguistic problems which are characteristic of the man of our time, for he is the victim of linguistic estrangement from his tradition and linguistic confusion among his contemporaries.

[1]*The Imitation of Christ*, chap. I.

[2]For an orientation to these issues, see the following: E. Fuchs, *Hermeneutik* (2nd ed.; Bad Cannstatt: Müllerschön, 1958); M. Heidegger, *Unterwegs zur Sprache* (Pfullingen: Neske, 1959); H.-G. Gadamer, *Wahrheit und Methode: Grundzüge einer philosophischen Hermeneutik* (Tübingen: Mohr, 1960); J. O. Urmson, *Philosophical Analysis: Its Development Between the Two World Wars* (Oxford: Oxford University Press, 1956); F. Ferré, *Language, Logic and God* (New York: Harper and Row, 1961); and, K. O. Apel, "Wittgenstein und das Problem des hermeneutischen Verstehens," *Zeitschrift für Theologie und Kirche* 63 (1966): 49–87.

The problem is then: How can we understand and verify statements describing that which, as it seems, lies outside the realm of experience? Insofar as such statements are not discarded altogether as meaningless, they require laborious reflection if they are to be translated into terms of the present understanding of reality. This threatens to rob them of their original immediacy and force. For in relation to God, talk seems today to be condemned from the start to impropriety. Only silence would seem to be appropriate for God. At this point the atheistic secularism of the modern age, for all its profound difference, is strangely close to mysticism. This experience of the incompatibility of God and word must be kept in mind when it comes to assuming responsibility for speaking of God today.

What is the source of this experience? Why are we finding it so difficult, if not indeed impossible, to speak of God today? What has happened to make us and our age different from the men of earlier times?

Our reflections very soon lead us to the observation that our subject has to do with history, or, to be more precise, with our historical situation in which the relation to tradition has become so problematic. Thus "God and Word" is not by any means a timeless subject, as one might suppose. To be sure, we might well say: what is there about the relationship of God and word that should change and make this question so immediately dependent on the situation? God is surely always God, and word always word! Experience, however, contradicts abstract reflections of this kind. And this is eminently significant for our thinking about God and word. Here time, experience, and history also come into play.[3] They lurk, as it were, in the harmless little word "and." For if we would learn more precisely how God is expressed in language, and thus how God and word unite in such a way that we are dealing not with an empty word but with a word that causes God to be with us and us with God, then we are brought to the important insight that the time is not always right for a word of this kind. And this word is not available at will. Nor by any means does everyone have the right and the power to speak such a word. The "and" between God and word thus marks the place of man in our subject. For it is surely in man that the time and the capacity for such a word must come about. Where else should talk of God take place, and where else should the right to such talk be determined, save in the man who ventures to assume responsibility for such talk?

But our question was not in the first place so general. We did not ask under what conditions it is time to speak of God, or even under what conditions it is at all right to have the vocable "God" on our lips—if our speaking of God is to be at all appropriate to God. Rather, our question was occasioned by a particular experience of history: the experience that although our linguistic tradition was abundantly able to speak of God, our own

---

[3]See my essay, "Zeit und Wort" in *Dankesgabe an R. Bultmann zum 80. Geburstag*, ed. E. Dinkler (Tübingen: Mohr, 1964), pp. 341–356.

age has largely lost the courage—many even believe it has altogether forfeited the possibility—to speak of God. What is the significance of this change in the situation?

Some lament the increasing apostasy of the modern age from God. They blame both individuals and social conditions and see the culpable cause in the age's struggle for autonomy, in its limitation to the things of this world, and in its materialistic outlook. Others celebrate as a sign of progress the fact that man has grown up and freed himself from the darkness of religious superstition and has adopted with fascinating success the path of a purely rational, strictly scientific approach to reality. Both views are superficial.

The optimistic interpretation of our emancipation from God as "enlightenment" suppresses problems which now exist not only as they always did but more intensely than ever. A sober contemplation of the modern age combines an amazement at the triumphs of reason with a horror at the abysmal depths of unreason. In our day we have experienced the frightful reality of unreason, and we must continue to reckon with this possibility as an abiding menace.

The denunciatory interpretation, on the other hand, narrows the matter down to one of morals—as if it all depended on the good will of the individual and as if the greater part of mankind had deteriorated, or even as if the transition to the modern age had been accompanied by something like a second Fall, that both makes the first Fall look like nothing and causes earlier ages to appear in a glorified light. In actual fact, however, we have here a destiny which cannot be altered—much less reversed—at will. We must avoid over-simplified judgments.

On the one hand it has to be emphasized that estrangement from God as a fact in the atheism of modern times—and as interpreted by Friedrich Nietzsche as the death of God, or, to be more precise, as the murder of God by men—is by no means a process which has introduced godlessness into the world for the first time.[4] The phenomenon of godlessness is as old as the phenomenon of religion—not only in the form of manifest violation of the religious law, but also in pious disguise as the veiled and unrecognized hypocrisy of religious self-justification before God. Speech about God does not rule out godlessness; it can itself be abysmally godless. And contrariwise, silence about God is not in itself a sure mark of godlessness.

On the other hand we must recognize that the phenomenon of godlessness has become extraordinarily aggravated in modern times, because in contrast to earlier ages it now appears more in the open. Godlessness presents itself unveiled, confesses itself in atheistic terms, and considers itself justified as an allegedly radical honesty. At the same time, however, the situation has also become more complicated. The modern age has produced

---

[4]See my essay, "Die Botschaft von Gott an das Zeitalter des Atheismus," *Monatschrift für Pastoraltheologie*, 52 (1963): 8–24.

in the course of the process of secularization a completely legitimate and methodologically restricted atheism. This consists in excluding in principle all talk of God wherever we deal with the things that can be calculated, planned, manufactured and controlled by man. Why it was that on the threshold of the modern age man began to explore methodically and consistently all dimensions of the realm of what can be calculated, planned, manufactured and controlled, and to make himself the master of that realm, is a question to which various partial historical answers could be given, which do not solve the riddle or explain the mysterious depths of this historic turning point as such.

This vast process of secularization could ultimately assume the form of atheism only because talk of God had already been deeply blended into the world experience and world order of the former age. In contrast to the modern, secularized age we can call the former age the Christianized age. It was the age in which Christian talk of God was regarded as the precept which dominated all else. Because it was understood as the law of a particular age, Christian talk of God was barely distinguishable from the form of that particular age of the world. Consequently the things of God and the things of man became confusingly tangled. When man awoke to a methodical examination of reality and a systematic exploitation of his own capabilities, his opponent only seemed to be Christian talk of God; in actual fact his opponent was a whole world condition which was imbued with Christian colors. This gave rise to tragic misjudgments. In the name of faith but actually for the protection of an age that was in the process of passing away, false prohibitions were set up. And in the name of unbelief boundaries were overstepped that had been laid down by men of little faith, men who in so doing actually first brought about the understanding and embracing of such defiance as an act of unbelief. This unbelief, to be sure, had no clear understanding of itself.

These references impress on us the duty of avoiding over-simplified judgments when we deal with the question of talk of God. "The Word of the Godless"—this heading which has pointed the way for the first part of our reflections on "God and Word" has accordingly not given us occasion to expose the whole threatening arsenal of so-called atheist propaganda in order that we may now construct against that propaganda a defense which is a match for the attacker. An attitude of this kind would not do justice to our task at all. "The Word of the Godless" leads us, on the contrary, to consider where the real difficulties in the relationship of God and word actually lie.

Can our word be anything other than the word of the godless, if indeed it is the word of men who, precisely according to the verdict of faith, are without exception sinners before God, and who are thus godless in the strict sense of the term? How can a godless man speak of God? What is the experience that drives him to do so and gives him authority to do so? Why must the godless speak of God? It must, it would seem, be a contradictory experience—on the one hand having to speak of God and on the other hand being unable to speak of God. To be sure, this contradictory experience is usually veiled: the godless man does indeed speak of God without sensing the contradiction, be it that as a religious man he makes himself gods after his own image, or be it that he says in his heart, or even with his lips: "There is no God" (Psalm 14:1). The truth of this contradictory experience of having to speak of God while not being able to speak of God, appears to be manifest only where it is given to the godless man to recognize himself as godless even though he is at the same time authorized by God to speak of God. True talk of God, then, would be that in which the godless man receives from God the word which contradicts him, the godless—contradicts him so completely that, godless as he is, it imparts God to him.

These possibly enigmatic-sounding formulations describe provisionally the mystery to which the subject "God and Word" would lead us. They stand on a deeper level than that on which we secularized men usually localize the problem. To us the real problem seems to be how traditional talk of God is to justify itself before the bar of our allegedly unequivocal experience of reality. This experience concentrates itself on the impression of the inhumanity, or non-humanity, of God. That may be seen in two respects. For one thing, the modern age's understanding of reality, which takes its bearings on experience, radically eliminates all anthropomorphism from the idea of God. It thereby makes for a dehumanizing of God which does away with the very idea of God. In the second place, the incomprehensible catastrophes in the history of modern times seem to be irreconcilable with the idea of God as the Father who loves men as his children. The old question of theodicy has become so acute that God has turned into a dark, distorted "X" and in such a form can no longer be addressed as God at all. The death of God would then be due to the fact that God is non-human and appears only in inhumanity—precisely thus does he disappear as God,[5] for only on the ground of his humanity can he be addressed as God.

Speaking of God would in actual fact be meaningful and necessary today if this paradoxical experience of God by secularized man, the experience of the God who has disappeared, only obscures, but does not do away with, the other experience of which we have spoken—namely, the contradiction in man himself of having to speak of God and yet being unable to do so.

Thus the question is: Is the word of man today still the word of the godless? Or have man and his language become so radically secularized that they have ceased even to be godless any more? But is it not the case that the man who in this way has ceased to be godless would have ceased to be human? Would the language which no longer stretches to the phenomenon of godlessness, which no longer shows the deep hurt of the contradiction of

[5]This formulation has been suggested in J. Hillis Miller, *The Disappearance of God: Five Nineteenth Century Writers* (Cambridge, Mass.: Harvard University Press, 1963).

having to speak of God and yet not being able to—would it not be a dehumanized language? For then the experience of the inhumanity of God would correspond to the inhumanity of man himself, which consists in the fact that man is resigned to the idea that God is inhuman.

So long, however, as our word is still a word of the godless, it is, precisely in virtue of his self-contradiction, witness to God.

II. THE WORD "GOD"

In our reflections we are dealing with the conjunction of a known factor and an unknown one. What we have to understand by "word" is considered self-evident, it is held that what we must understand by the term "God" is problematic if not indeed unintelligible. When we now give special attention to the word "God," it is customary to distinguish between the word's known and unknown aspects, i.e., that the vocable as a mere linguistic form is certainly familiar to us, but that God as the content designated thereby is an entirely open question.

On such a presupposition as this, it is certainly pointless to expect that reflection on the nature of word will lead to an understanding of what "God" means. On the contrary, the conception of language here, naively presupposed as self-evident, necessarily makes the term "God" and therewith all talk of God meaningless. This understanding of language, however, also proves to be inadequate, quite apart from the question of God. It is a constriction which, consistently applied, strangles the life out of language.

The prevailing view of language is oriented towards the significatory function of words. The word is regarded as the sign—the spoken or written sign—with a concrete referent. This significatory view, based on the distinction between *signum* and *res*, comes from classical times. It determines the traditional form of grammatical and metaphysical thinking and has also become a standard factor in the tradition of theological thought. The modern age has not eliminated this approach to the understanding of language; on the contrary it has sharpened it. Classical philosophy itself, but more especially the biblical tradition, had long prevented a one-sided development of this significatory concept of language. By this means it was modified—though to be sure also obscured—so that its dubiety was not consciously recognized. With the dawn of the modern age, the corrective function of these counter-forces was increasingly eliminated. Thus the path was clear for an unrestricted development of the mere sign-function of language. The logical result is that words are reduced to ciphers and functions, and syntax to a question of calculus.

The traditional view of language, and also the consistent mathematical treatment of it, doubtless contain elements of truth which cannot be abandoned. Their successful application in dictionaries and grammars, and now most recently in computers and in the science of cybernetics, is undeniable.

This aspect of language, and the possibilities embraced in it, are not, however, the key to the essence of language. We are dealing here with an abstraction—to a certain extent a justified and necessary abstraction—from the humanity of language. To regard language exclusively as a technical instrument is to cut it off from that which is the constant source of its life—namely, the element of time.

Time, the very factor which is constitutive for the living event of language, is of secondary importance for the significatory understanding of language. However true it is that in formalized language temporal things can become the object of calculation, for the mathematical understanding of language as such, time is irrelevant. The constitutive significance of time for the reality of language can nevertheless be shown as follows. From the standpoint of the use of language, the basic linguistic phenomenon is not the vocable as an isolated sign for an equally isolated thing. The individual vocable certainly does designate something, but when spoken it does not yet say anything. The basic unit of meaning in language is the sentence, which pieces together a subject in the medium of time. Word as spoken is always temporal word. Furthermore, the relation between the time stated and the time of the speaker himself is one of perspective. Yesterday I spoke of that which is happening today in the future tense, and tomorrow I shall speak of the same thing in the past tense. Thus not only what is stated is temporal, but also the statement itself. It is no accident that the genuine organ of language is the audible sound. The very fleetingness of the sound suits its purpose.

Word takes place as a temporal event. Thus to word there belongs the situation from which it arises, into which it comes, and which it changes. Accordingly, speaking also undergoes concrete modifications in a variety of ways—as address or promise, as instruction or conversation, as questioning or calling for help, as complaining or accusing, as cursing or praying.

The word situation parallels responsibility for the word.[6] The man who wishes to say something must have something to say and must allow himself to be taken at his word. Every word has its time. The man who says something must know whether it is the time for it. And in every case the word comes from the experience which has been given through time and which is based on the experience of time itself. Indeed we can speak only because language has been handed down to us and taught us and because only thus has experience of the world been opened up to us. The necessity and power of human language is ultimately determined by the fact that the world is experienced as time. I do not merely in a factual sense *have* a past and a future like all temporal things, but I also *know* of this. It is solely through language that I can have a relation to past and future, that past and

[6]See my essay, "Theology and the Evidentness of the Ethical," trans. James W. Leitch, "Translating Theology into the Modern Age," *Journal for Theology and Church* 2, Robert W. Funk, ed., (New York: Harper & Row, 1965), pp. 96–129, esp. pp. 117 ff.

future are present to me, that I can go back behind my present and stretch out ahead of it. Indeed, I not only *can* do this, I *must* do it. Because I am knowingly delivered over to time, I must take up my position towards past and future and answer for myself in my relation to time. It is not the concept of signification, but far more profoundly the concept of answerability that points us to that which is fundamental in language. Here we are provided with important points for the rest of our study.

When we speak of "word," we normally mean not the vocable—the atom of a specific linguistic system—but the totality of a statement. But by this is meant not the abstract linguistic constructions which grammar and logic are accustomed to use as model sentences. On the contrary, we have in mind word as an event, and thus word as inclusive of its relationship to its historical contexts, i.e., to the situation in which it is answered for. We must not by any means hastily reduce word to mere talk as distinct from action. According to the particular circumstances, conduct can be a decisive ingredient of the word, as a sort of sounding board for the word or a commentary on it. Conduct, moreover, can itself be acted word. In fact, a deed can be more eloquent than any word. And contrariwise, a mere word can be a deed. Let us therefore beware of a primitive antithesis between word and reality!

We are really on the track of the phenomenon of word, however, only when we pass over superficial answers and insist on asking: What happens through the word? In view of the everyday use of language the answer might be, understanding in human relationships. On the other hand, in view of the use of language in the exact sciences one could say, information and the processing of information. Yet both answers compel us to ask further: What end is served by such use of language? In the second case a comprehensive answer appears to be simple, namely, that the collecting and processing of information should make it possible to calculate the future and hence to manipulate it. But what is that future over which we seek power?[7] This

---

[7]The idea of cybernetics logically culminates in the technical manufacture (*Herstellung*) and programming of human nature, that is, in a "grasping at the future" which has complete control over the man who is oriented towards the future. But what would be accomplished if this were achieved? Cf. K. Steinbuch: *Automat und Mensch: Kybernetische Tatsachen und Hypothesen* (3rd ed.: Berlin and Heidelberg: Springer, 1965). The cybernetician still looks with a mixture of amazement and envy upon nature's advance over technology: "For an engineer it is simply astonishing what abilities nature could pack into the small space of the human skull. Measured by the number of gearing elements, the human brain is far superior to the greatest of contemporary computers" (Steinbuch, p. 23). But the goal is clear: "For our considerations it would be of incalcuable value if a technical system comparable to the size and complexity of the human nervous system (etc.) could be manufactured. Would such a system then have psychic experiences, memory, emotions, etc.? Or, more precisely stated, would these questions credibly be answered with 'Yes?' The experiment is still several decades off; nonetheless we can expect that—*cum grano salis*—it will be made within the next two hundred years. It is, then, an *experimentum crucis* for or against the thesis of cybernetics" (Steinbuch, p. 10). Fantasy concerning the power of cybernetics to determine the future, may be stimulated by an observation such as the following: "To me the difference between programming a machine

question brings us inevitably back to the first case where the question is that of understanding among men. Why is understanding among men necessary? Here, too, we go straight to the heart of the matter: Men in their thinking and willing are incalculable and therefore become each other's adversaries. The attempt can of course also be made to make men calculable and tractable. But to the extent that such an attempt succeeds, it destroys the human thing about man—namely, his freedom. This corresponds exactly to the question of the future; i.e., to the extent that we succeed in getting the future securely in our grip, it loses its character as future.

And now, it is this that ultimately and properly speaking must happen, and can only happen, through our word: that future is granted, that freedom is granted. To be sure, in a provisional sense future and freedom can be granted by means of specific measures—as, for example, by rescuing a drowning man or liberating a prisoner. In this context the cybernetic use of language which intends to establish specific living conditions certainly also has an important function in the granting of future and freedom. Nevertheless, the establishment of specific living conditions is not by itself a guarantee of future and freedom. By saving a man from drowning, I do not save him from the despair of the future which drove him to attempt suicide. On the contrary, unless something else happens I merely maintain him in his futureless state. Likewise, I do not bestow freedom on a man who is thirsting for murder by letting him loose and so abandoning him to the force of his frenzy. Future and freedom are not things we possess like an object— such as money in our purse—or like an inborn or acquired capacity—such as the use of our senses and limbs. The time that still remains for me to live does not in itself mean I am granted a future, and the elbow-room that is open to me does not as such mean I am granted freedom. The crucial thing is the attitude I adopt towards these things, the use I made of the time and space apportioned to me, whether I let the future be future and freedom be freedom, whether I truly acknowledge them to be what in truth they are.

Is this merely a matter of protection from the loss of future and the loss of freedom through external threats? Is it not rather a question of the fact that the very future and freedom which we possess are themselves the source of that which threatens our future and our freedom? Indeed, to put it still more plainly, is not what we usually call future merely the liquidation of our already lost future, and what we usually call freedom merely the liquidation of our already forfeited freedom? This does not cancel the fact that as long as he lives man does in fact have a future and has it so securely that death, that radical loss of future, is always felt to be a road into the dark and is thus itself understood under the category of the future. It is only on the ground of this

---

(*Automaten*) for a highly skilled activity and training an apprentice is purely an external one" (Steinbuch, p. 4). See also *Der Griff nach der Zukunft: Planen und Freiheit*, ed. R. Jungk and H.J. Mundt (Munich and Basel: Kurt Desch, 1964).

indestructible relation of man to the future that the concept of a "lost future" has any meaning. Likewise, the concept of "lost freedom," rightly understood, does not exclude but includes the fact that freedom belongs to man as a thing that cannot be lost. Such loss is therefore something that cannot be forgotten; it continues to pain like an open wound. But when the loss of future and freedom is no longer a mere possibility but already an accomplished fact, then and only then does what can give future and freedom to the man who has lost future and freedom become a really burning question.

Only word can do this. That is already indicated by our compulsion to inquire about the truth of future and freedom and about their true realization. Truth is the realm of language. It is only because man has the gift of language that the question of truth arises for him. And at the same time to be sure, the question of falsehood also arises. A beast, or certainly a stone, cannot lie, because for it the question of truth does not arise. It is only because man can speak that there is any question of whether he tells the truth or whether he lies. The most elementary answer to the question of the purpose served by word is that it serves to tell the truth. Falsehood is misuse of language, corrupt and corrupting word. Truth is sound and healing word.

But what does it mean to tell the truth? In the first instance it manifestly means to set reality into words. This process could be compared, say, with the fact that a precious stone shows to full advantage only when it is properly cut and set. Truth is reality set in words, and thus the making known of that which—as command and promise—is the mystery of reality. This does not cause the mystery to disappear, rather it causes it to emerge precisely as a mystery, i.e., as something which gives men food for thought and for faith, for hope and for love. These are the basic human forms of conduct, the forms of reverence for the mystery of reality. To be sure, human existence also involves, seemingly first and foremost, the effort, either crude or subtle, to lay hold of unveiled, immediate reality, to plan and dominate, possess and enjoy, press on and break records. But this effort to lay hold of naked immediacy misses reality unless it is bridled through our being grasped by that which can only be a matter of hearing and waiting, and is thus a matter of word.

Telling the truth is therefore something more than the stating of correct facts. This is, of course, also important; but it does not provide the standard, so that everything else would, according to individual taste, be a fine but not determinative superstructure. The correct stating of limited facts which settles individual questions is related to telling the truth, which as such gives us an openness towards the mystery, as a special activity is related to life. The task of word therefore consists in attacking the root of its own misuse and making man himself true.

The criterion of the truth which makes man himself true is that it makes him free. For freedom, too, is dependent upon language. As the rational animal who has the gift of language, man is given the freedom of being able to decide, is released from the compulsion of his instincts and the pressure of the immediate present, and is given space in which to choose—not indeed to choose as he pleases, however. He *must* take responsibility for his freedom, even if only to throw it away and thereby lose himself. And he *must* take responsibility for his freedom, even if only by means of irresponsible evasions. Lies are the perverse attempt to gain back by means of word the lost elbowroom of one's freedom. This merely underlines the fact that freedom is dependent on word—and all the more so when it is a case of helping the man who has lost his freedom back to freedom. It is true that the use of force can to a certain extent destroy freedom, but it cannot create freedom. Freedom can only be *called* into being as one literally "speaks freedom" to his neighbor, i.e., speaks to him in such a way that freedom is passed to him and he is enabled to enter into the field of freedom.

To be sure, the question is now thrust compellingly upon us: What sort of word has this kind of liberating power, this authority to make man true? But let us be patient and continue to persevere with our prior question: What is it that happens through the word? What is it that makes word, and word alone, suited to make man true and to make him free?

Let us give an even sharper edge to the insights already gained by now observing that it is the business of word to make present what is not at hand, what is absent. To be sure, this is in a way also accomplished by a picture, a symbol, a momento, or a relic. But in all these instances there is the danger of an illusion, namely, of the mediated presence being confused with immediate presence. Moreover, in such cases the absence of the thing represented is only of an accidental and temporal kind, and it is only the added interpretation through the word that can make clear what is really meant. For it is the business of words alone to make present what is even utterly hidden.

Everything that is expressed in language is dependent on language only to the extent that hiddenness is involved in one respect or another. However true it may be that our language cannot say everything, because many things are beyond its reach and call for silence, there is nevertheless all the more need to underline the experience, banal and trite as it has become, that language can say infinitely more than is perceived by the senses. From this point of view the convenient distinction between nature and history (in the strict sense of human history) is made more sharp in that reality is deeply hidden in space and time and is therefore abundantly rich in language and strains ever anew towards language.

The primary experience of the hiddenness of historic reality is the remembrance of decisions that have been made and the awaiting of decisions as yet unknown. The former is the field of thankfulness and remorse, the latter that of anxiety and hope. Although the hiddenness of the future is more oppressing, and the desire for a word that grants a future more burning than the need to lighten the darkness of the past and to become free from it, we ultimately have here a single interwoven mystery that embraces past and future and knocks at the door of the present. The word that makes us true and makes us free and therefore grants us a future will in no case lead us on a flight into illusion; but from the truth of what has happened in the past it will invest us with an assurance for that future which is superior to all dwindling and disappointing futures.

Where have our reflections on language and word brought us? I answer: into the realm of the experience of what we mean when we say "God." That sounds like a daring remark and requires some explanation.

The purpose of our undertaking was not to set up a general theory of language in order then to apply it as a special case to our talk of God. Rather, our concern has been to characterize the situation in which man finds himself in virtue of the fact that he has the gift of language. That is to say, since man is rightly called the being who has the gift of language, we have been concerned to take the nature of language as the ground on which to define his basic situation. This has brought us into the situation which is addressed as and intended by the word "God."

The shocking thing about this is, first of all, the suspicion that here the fatal attempt is being made to renew the absurd enterprise of proving God. To have shown the absurdity of that enterprise is generally held to be the one thing which despite all hostilities still unites the theology and philosophy of modern times. Our project does in fact bear a formal resemblance to the way in which Thomas Aquinas answers the question of the existence of God.[8] He radicalizes our experience of the world in various ways, until he finally claims to have reached that which is generally addressed as "God." Whatever the critic may have to say of this, it is hardly possible to understand even Thomas's undertaking as being in the usual sense a proof of the existence of God. But it does seek to show what the word "God" means. This attempt would have to be submitted to a searching interpretation if it is to be rightly understood. It may be criticized as misleading. Yet whoever takes the word "God" upon his lips cannot possibly refuse to give an account which points to an area of universal human experience. The present-day crisis in regard to the word "God"—if indeed it is a crisis at all and not an already concluded death-agony—can be surmounted only when the meaning of the word "God" is verifiable.

But that which is suggested by the claim to verify the word "God" may be even more shocking. The meaning of the word "God," we might venture to say in review, is the basic situation of man as word situation.[9] By normal

---

[8]See my essays, "Der hermeneutische Ort der Gotteslehre bei Petrus Lombardus und Thomas von Aquin," *Zeitschrift für Theologie und Kirche* 61 (1964): 283–326, and "Existenz zwischen Gott und Gott. Ein Beitrag zur Frage nach der Existenz Gottes," *Zeitschrift für Theologie und Kirche*, 62 (1965): 95–110.

[9]This statement necessarily becomes false when it is construed as a definition. For the traditional metaphysical doctrine of God it was axiomatic that God is indefinable: "It is clear

standards it is offensive to assert that God is a situation, and not only that but
the basic situation of man. There arise at once the familiar objections that
ontological statements are here actually dissolved and theology reduced to
anthropology. Whoever measures and sharpens his responsibility for talk of
God on the unaltered present, however, will not easily be content with or
give in to schemes of this sort.

Our suggestion concerning the proper understanding of the word "God"
calls us, in the first instance, to consider the fact that there is no question at
all here of understanding "God" in the usual sense of a content distinct from
the word itself—a sort of speechless thing that has to be brought into the
language by being named, that is, designated by a vocable. On the contrary,
it is here a question of God himself as Word. That is to say, the vocable
"God" points to a word event that is always already in full swing. Pious
mistrust of such statements could be countered by observing that according
to the Trinitarian faith the Word is the Second Person of the Godhead, that
God himself is thus intrinsically word and not something which, in itself
wordless, must first be placed by external means in the field of language in
order to become an object of word. Yet this role of the word in the doctrine
of the Trinity, though highly important, must not now make us flee from the
open field in which we have been moving in order to seek refuge behind the
sheltering walls of ecclesiastical dogma.

If the word "God" means the basic situation of man as word situation,
then by speaking of God one perceives man at the point of his linguisticality.
And indeed the word "God" shows us that man in his linguisticality is not

---

. . . that God has neither genus nor differences, and that there is no definition of God, nor any way
of demonstrating him through his effects. For definition is by means of genus and difference, and
definition is the means of demonstration" Thomas Aquinas, *Summa Theologica* I, Q. 3, Art. 5.
Nature and Grace—Selections from the Summa Theologica of Thomas Aquinas, ed. and trans.
A.M. Fairweather (*The Library of Christian Classics*, Vol. XI [Philadelphia: Westminster, 1954]),
p. 65. Today the logician would base the indefinability of God on the ground that "God" is not
an *Autosemantikon* but a *Synsemantikon*, a word which received meaning through the way it is
used. (For this allusion I am indebted to Professor Paul Lorenzen of Erlangen with whom I met
in Austin, Texas, in connection with these lectures.) My attempts to formulate the above sentence
through the non-use of the copula led, unfortunately, to the weakening of its scope. I request that
the sentence be read as a direction (*als eine Wegweisung*) for the use of the word "God." See
Ludwig Wittgenstein's famous statement that "the meaning of a word is its use in the language"
("Die Bedeutung eines Wortes ist sein Gebrauch in der Sprache") in *Philosophical Investigations I*, trans. G. E. M. Anscombe (Oxford: Basil Blackwell, 1958), No. 43, p. 20. As far as the rest
is concerned, let one free himself from the prejudice of an actualistic understanding of "situation"
as well as from an isolationistic speaking of man. On the basis of the biblical witness concerning
God as creator and redeemer, or of dogmatic speaking of God as *principium* and *finis* (Cf. Thomas
Aquinas, *Summa Theologica* I, Q. 1, Art. 7), or of Luther's use of the formula *coram Deo* (Cf. my
Luther: Einführung in sein Denken [Tübingen: Mohr, 1964] especially pp. 227 ff.), the intention
of the above statement is confirmed. The application of the situational concept corresponds to the
sense of the formula, "between God and God" (see above, p. 26, note 3).

master of himself. He lives from the power of a word that is not his own, and at the same time he thirsts after the power of a word that likewise cannot be his own.

This fact, that man precisely in his linguisticality is not essentially self-sufficient, is illustrated by his dependence on his fellow man. No one can speak independently. And no one can be content to speak alone. Man speaks because he has received the gift of language as taught to him by others, and because he longs to hear in turn an echo, an answer to his own speaking.

This fact, that man as the being who has the gift of language is entwined in an immeasurably vast network of human events, has countless aspects which we cannot here define or even indicate. But it is obvious that the total word event, in which the participation of the individual is like a drop in the bucket, cannot be adequately interpreted from the standpoint of co-humanity. To be sure, the dimension of the individual cannot be excluded from anything that has to do with language, either from the mysterious transformations of language on the large scale or from the hidden conversation of the heart with itself. Yet precisely these two perspectives, the macroscopic and the microscopic aspects of the word event, bring to our attention the fact that in every word event there is present a depth dimension which is indicated by the word "God"—not, so to speak, as a prolongation of the causal series into the adjacent realm of the hyper-macrocosmic and the hyper-microcosmic, but as a hidden and tacit word event to which every word owes its existence.

That it is precisely in that which is the sign of his power—namely, his language—that man reveals himself not to be his own master, is a lesson which we can never learn thoroughly enough. It is a lesson which may be primarily taught to us by answering these two questions: What empowers us to use word? And, what is the power of word?

The question of what empowers us to use word forces us to realize that man participates in word, so that his word is always only an answer. And he in turn has to answer for this answer: he has to await a judgment to which he can add nothing. But summons and judgment derive their power from bestowal and acceptance. How little man in his linguisticality is his own master is experienced most impressively in his dependence on the gift of word, on the permission, the freedom to speak a good, right, helpful, salutary word. It is wholly legitimate to illustrate this by the fact that responsible speaking comes from the silence of listening, and that finding the right word has the character of a sudden bright idea or a happy inspiration. And it may be illustrated further by the fact that man cannot by his word compel understanding, but must wait to see if and when the scattered seed springs up.

The second question, concerning the power of word, recalls once more what we have already said—namely, that it is the business of word to make present what is not at hand. The fact that word brings to us what is past and future, and us to it, is only an illustration of the way in which man is dependent on confrontation by a word that comes his way, that liberates him both from the frightening restrictions that bind him to what is present and from the anxiety of his own heart, and that thus frees him for the things which are outside his power to command but are offered to him to believe. Man needs language more for hearing than for speaking, for believing than for acting. For this reason the extreme situation which man is absolutely unable even slightly to change—namely, bondage to sin and death—puts word to the test: whether man is abandoned to that which renders him speechless, or whether even in muteness he can still cling to a word that sets him outside himself.

The word situation as the basic situation of man makes it plain that because he lives by the word man is ultimately not a doer but a receiver. Although he is able to objectify all things from a neutral distance, he himself cannot escape into neutrality. However much he is and in all respects remains at the mercy of the world and his fellowmen, yet in all these relations he is nevertheless himself, a responsible individual, a person come of age, called to assert and maintain by a right use of the word that mystery of reality which surrounds him and constitutes his true situation. If we said before that the word "God" means the basic situation of man as word situation, then we can now also say: "God" is the mystery of reality.

Yet what right have we to call this "God"? It is true, in any event, that what we finally said about the basic situation of man certainly harmonizes with the fact that the word "God" addresses man and demands that he be a receiver, tolerates no neutrality, and expects from man a responsible account of all that concerns him. But do not the traditional representations of God prevent us from using this word—a word which can be rightly used only with a good conscience, and which insincerity misuses? I do not refer merely to pagan or childish representations of God as an animal or as bearded, or to the Trinitarian picture of two men with a dove, but also to the metaphysical concept of God as *ens realissimum* and *causa sui*, and indeed even to Jesus' talk of God the Father, and to the church's talk of the Father of Jesus Christ.

Representations of God, to be sure, give expression to that which is meant by the word "God" only to the extent that they *present man to God*, and thus awaken man to his basic situation. The moment the word situation of which we have spoken is abandoned and God is regarded in one way or another as reality, rather than as the mystery of reality which lays exacting hold upon us, then God is murdered

Yet what can the vocable "God" do to prevent this? Is it not in any case so ambiguous and so unclear that it no longer means anything to the man who is seeking clear concepts and precise definitions? The classical Christian doctrine of God, it is true, has always declared the indefinability of God to be in accordance with the nature of God. But it has also always seen in this

the reason why the word "God" gives endless food for thought. The apparent
lack of sharply defined meaning is a thing this word shares with all terms
which are not labels for finished products, but are rather summonses which
require of man an inner movement for which the word in question only
points the direction. The movement thus required of man by the word
"God" is known in that situation in which the genuine use of "God" is that
of the vocative, of address.

To be sure, the warrant to use the word "God" in order to call upon God
cannot be derived from the vocable "God." For this, it is necessary that God
becomes audible in the word. The meaning of the word "God" is not to be
believed apart from the word of God.

III. The Word of God

The meaning of the word "God" is determined by its use, or to be more
precise, by the necessity of using the word "God." To use a vocable means
to make use of it along with other words to form a coherent statement. A
necessary use of the word "God" is accordingly one which takes place in a
connected statement, in a word event, for the clarity of which is required that
God be named as that to which the word event in question relates, to which
it refers, to which it appeals, from which it derives its truth. The vocable
"God"—so far as it has any meaning at all—belongs to a verbal whole which
necessarily belongs to God. In short, the word "God" requires the word of
God, as the word of God requires the word "God."

The way we have indulged almost in a verbal play on the two expressions "the word 'God' and "the word of God," together with the pregnant
brevity in which we have stated the fact of their belonging together, can
easily delude us into overlooking the long and arduous path from the one to
the other. An account of this constitutes the last stage of our reflections on
God and word.

In the context of the language of our day, "word of God" seems to be
traditional language, and it is problematic whether and how far it can still be
the language of today. The sense of alienation affects not merely the vocable
"God," nor the concept "word of God"; it affects the whole complex of what,
with the claim to be word of God, has been handed down the form of
scripture and continues to be handed on in the form of preaching. To a
certain extent there is indeed a rising curve of alienation—from the use of the
vocable "God" to the claim of a man to speak in the name of God. Yet we
must ask what is the source of this alienation from what was once an obvious
matter of course. Has preaching lost its authority because the word "God"
has become unintelligible, or has the word "God" become an empty term
because preaching turned empty? The impression that we are using a
foreign language when it comes to the word of God certainly does not arise
from the fact that God is taken seriously as the one who is "wholly other" and

therefore foreign to man. On the contrary, the alienating element is interpreted without more ado as the sign of a false claim. Accordingly, as the case
may be, we emphasize that we have here an antiquated, or inexact, prescientific language, or a group language—namely, a church language which
is of importance only for the initiated.

In this assessment of the situation right and wrong elements are
confusingly entangled. It is certainly right that we have our talk of God from
the tradition. Had we never heard any talk of God—an absurd hypothesis!—
we could hardly conceive it on our own. It is therefore understandable that
the impression arises that our concern with the word "God" and the word of
God is nothing but an expression of the fact that we have not yet overcome
the hampering bonds of tradition, and that this concern results in an
allegorical dislocation—the painful attempt to combine two fundamentally
different languages and artificially to harmonize their contradictions.

It is, moreover, unfortunately true that Christian proclamation has
largely become a ghetto language. Seen superficially, to be sure, it has not by
any means been driven out of public life; but in actual fact it has assumed the
character of a group language for private use. The language of public life on
the other hand, the language of the workaday world of politics, economics
and industry, of science and culture, has been secularized and has become
on the whole so technical that the word of God is entirely out of place in it.
Apart from noncommittal forms of speech, talk of God is confined to specially
reserved, institutional places and occasions—Sunday worship, religious
education, marriages and funerals, religious papers or the religious column
in the daily press, particular hours on radio and television, and so on. Amid
the plurality of languages in modern society, talk of God occupies only one
narrow sector, and is itself in turn split into many dialects. In consequence
of this multiplicity such talk is made into a technical instrument for the
cultivation of particular special traditions, and thus scarcely can it any longer
profess unreservedly to be the word of God—unless this claim, too, has
shrunk to the status of a traditional label. Outside of the appointed reserves
it is extraordinarily difficult even in intimate circles to use the word "God"
at all. Even there talk of God has often degenerated into a scanty element of
custom, say, in the form of grace before meals, or as a part of the conventional
style for congratulation or condolence. As for how much the word "God" is
used in prayer and the word of God read and mediated upon in the privacy
of individual life, here there are—I hope!—no statistics to divulge the facts.

The problems arising out of this situation cannot really be solved by
modernizing our vocabulary, or by calling for a courageous confession of the
faith. Both are in a limited sense right enough. But they are only treatments
of the external symptoms. To expect too much from them is only to cause
trouble. Coloring our language with splashes of alluring jargon underlines a
lack of confidence in the word, which is fatal to Christian proclamation. And

the word of God—prohibiting as it does all self-assertion by man in the face of God—can only be falsified by the activities of the propagandist.

The difficulties which are involved today in the use of the word "God" and in the proclamation of the word of God are not external, but belong intrinsically to the subject itself. And this indeed is most closely bound to the question of the appropriate situation. Much more than we generally admit, our life is strongly determined by the conditions of the age of technology and the masses. Consequently, the basic situation of man, which we have characterized as word situation, is on the one hand very largely pushed into the background; on the other hand and for that very reason it stands out all the more sharply when we are forced to notice it. The technical approach to reality depends on the toning down both of the mystery of reality and of man's involvement in it. Because the basic situation of man is abandoned to silence, which in turn creates further silence, the increasing technical use of our language brings its increasing impoverishment. Similarly, mass society causes the stunting of individual responsibility. The expressing of life in routine patterns can of course lead to a greater isolating or atomizing of existence. Man is then left helpless and speechless.

The word which is to bring help into this situation, however, must submit to the most stringent test of its guarantee of certainty. In the days when Christian faith was publicly recognized as a matter of course, existing principles of thought and established conditions of authority vouched for the legitimacy of the claim of the word of God. Now, however, our talk of God must secure for itself the recognition which it claims. Authority is now a question of the authorship of evidence and respect. And our assent to and agreement with such a demanding word depends on whether the basic situation described above is convincingly expressed in contrast to the situation of the technical approach to the world.

The examination of these relationships enjoins us to prudence. The rationalization and technification of public and largely also of private life, has created an abundance of situations which have been sterilized, so to speak, against a germinating of the basic situation of man, and have thus been made unfruitful for talk of God. This process we have to recognize as a fact, and we must even allow it a certain legitimacy. The reality of human life is not such that the basic situation of man is or could be constantly exposed. At least part of the reason for the disappearance of talk of God lies in a not unjustified sense of shame which is sensitive towards the trivializing of what is extraordinary and tremendous. Hence it is a healthy modesty that compels us to acquire a faculty of discrimination and to learn when it is the right time—and that means, when it is necessary—to speak of God.

At the same time, the reserving of separate occasions for the word of God, or even the forcing of it into the private sphere, are not by any means only to be discredited as reprehensible signs of decay. In light of the results of the comprehensive change in the public situation, we should recognize gratefully and modestly that amid the manifold phenomena of modern life these results do in any event grant us the existence of a form of Christian tradition. A sober evaluation of this kind could free us from much that is constricting in our efforts at proclamation as well as in the form of the church and of the Christian life. Christianity in its historical existence participates also in worldliness, precisely because Christian word, Christian community, and Christian existence are not by any means, if I may say so, word of God in fixed form. Simply and naturally, they are on standby duty in readiness not for any and every eventuality, but, whenever validly required, for the service of the word of God. For that very reason, to be sure, this involves the readiness to assume responsibility before the public and for the public, namely, the readiness to say plainly why it is necessary to use the word "God" and what the word is which authorizes us to do so.

Of course, this can happen only when we discard an idea which falsifies the whole picture—that is, the notion that a particular interest has to be supported in public life, that the cause and the continuance of a particular party has to be propagandized, that a uniformity of language has to be sought. Whoever, therefore, has grasped what is meant by "word of God" cannot be ridden by any sort of anxious concern for the word of God and ultimately therewith for God himself; he can only be driven to concern for man and for the world. It is so easy, of course, to believe that humanity maintains itself indestructibly in history, whereas the word of God is a rare and sensitive plant which belongs to tradition and must be preserved from extinction. The questions concerning the relationship of God and word accordingly appear to constitute a linguistic problem of a special kind, which concerns only those interested in the word of God. Indeed the phrase "word of God" itself appears to be such a linguistic problem. In contrast to this idea, which does in fact readily suggest itself, the very criterion of a right understanding lies in whether God's word is understood as assurance-giving language which has a saving effect in history, as the constant granting of the gift of language, as an authority for the word which is superior to the powers that render us speechless.

We look in the first instance simply to the historic fact of what comes to us from the biblical tradition. To be sure, there is here to a very great extent a conservative element at work—the reverent preserving and maintaining of a language whose original utterances are now two to three thousand years behind us. But this fact of astonishing linguistic continuity cannot be explained by conservatism—that disposition to let the past relieve one of one's own responsibility.

To be sure, the original word event which has taken fixed form in Holy Scripture appears to be a finished production which itself has become the object of further tradition. Yet it is in itself already a traditional event containing an extraordinary variety of movement. The twofold Christian canon of the Old and New Testaments confronts us with the acutely challenging question of its unity and its difference. It is precisely this transition from the Old to the New, with all its inexhaustible implications for thought, that constitutes its canonicity. But even the two parts taken separately do not represent handy units of tradition which would allow simple verbal repetition. Both Testaments embrace an abundance of historic statements. They cannot simply be added together to form a single system, but they are certainly related to each other as elements in a coherent tradition-event. The Old and New Testaments manifest a peculiar conformity with each other in that both are processes of the successive conferral of authority to proclaim the word to new situations, processes which ever grant and renew the gift of language. Neither is in itself simply that which is to be transmitted. On the contrary, the real object to be transmitted is that which remains the source of the word event, not allowing enclosure in merely one, exclusive, invariable linguistic form. The source of authorization can in both cases ultimately be indicated only by a name—in the Old Testament, Yahweh, in the New Testament, Jesus. And they have something else in common, that is, that both processes of tradition—to express it in a precise way, the traditions of the prophets and of the apostles—point beyond their own day to a continuing responsibility for proclamation which the word that has gone before us does not take off our shoulders, but rather opens to us. There is one difference however. It is only through the New Testament that the Old Testament is also incorporated into a universal traditional event, which enters into all languages in order to prepare them for the saving word event, that which is necessary for redemption.

Word of God, according to the biblical tradition, thus seeks to be understood as a word event that does not go out of date but constantly renews itself, does not create closed areas of special interest but opens up the world, does not enforce uniformity but is linguistically creative. Of course it is startling—but only because it reveals what was hidden. Certainly it is tradition, yet tradition of a kind that sets us free for our own present. Whatever is put forth as word of God is certainly changed into an antiquated, constricting word that enslaves us, and thus becomes the opposite of what the word of God is, whenever it is denied responsible participation in the word event.

Naturally, a thing is not a word of God simply because it claims to be so. Yet it would be misleading to say that God's word requires verification—if by that we are thinking of an additional, externally given confirmation and evidence of its truth, as, for example, is given a witness's statement by an inspection of the scene of the crime, or a promise by its actual fulfillment in due course. On the contrary, God's word is itself verification. It verifies itself by verifying man.

In order to grasp the meaning of this, we must proceed from a simple point of hermeneutics: word is a means of understanding. That is to say, the linguistic utterance normally mediates understanding itself and does not first have to be made understandable. It is only when the normal function of word is disturbed that interpretation is required. The aim of such interpretation cannot, however, be anything other than the removal of the obstacle which prevents the word from mediating understanding by itself.

But now, here it is that the matter of *how* word mediates understanding is first brought properly to our attention. Briefly put, one could say that word brings about understanding by announcing in a familiar context something that is hidden. Two points are important. First, word always presupposes word, understanding always understanding. If instead of this we were to say, as would be perfectly correct, that word appeals to experience, then the experiential character of understanding and the linguistic character of experience is only emphasized. Hence, the field of experience into which a word is spoken can appropriately be designated as its context. That is one important point. The second is, word adds to what is familiar the announcement of what is hidden. Whatever the concrete way in which this relationship may present itself, understanding through word in any event involves something hidden coming to linguistic expression. Thus word also always presupposes something that has not been said, and understanding always presupposes something that has not been understood, in order, of course, to say it and understand it to the extent that this is possible. Yet this happens in such a way that what is merely announced in the word is understood as altering the context through the presence of what is hidden. If this is a matter of a change which is not to violate the context but rather to rectify and verify it, then that which is hidden, that which is spoken into the context and added to it, must correspond to that which is already hidden in the context and which is now identified as such and thereby brought to light. Thus there are two elements of hiddenness that correspond to each other—one arising in the context itself and one which is added to the context. That is also why the more fruitful form for disclosing the word's power to awaken understanding is not to spew forth platitudes but rather to allude to something that provokes reflection.

Furthermore, the Bible's word and the proclamation arising from it are obviously addressed to an appropriate context. Only in this way can what is said come to understanding. Thus the word which claims to be God's word always presupposes a corresponding word. And the understanding awakened by the word of God always refers to a corresponding understanding. At the same time, of course, there is also presupposed a lack of word and understanding—and because this happens "at the same time," it must give to the word and understanding already existing in the context the character of an antithetical correspondence, or a contradiction, provided that it is not a matter of supplementary word but of decisive word in the strict sense. God's word is in essence not that which merely supplements the context into which it enters. On the contrary, it renders a decision concerning it. And accordingly the hidden factor which is announced into the context by the word of God does not concern some aspect or other of the context, but rather the whole context itself. It renders a life and death decision.

Here theology seems to find itself in a dilemma. It may emphasize that the word of God always finds a previously given analogue, a "natural" knowledge of God, as it is then called, with which the revealed knowledge of God connects, a presupposed understanding to which the word of God relates. The simplest, and at the same time most effective argument for this consists in asking how God's word is to be proclaimed where the word "God" is not understood at all. Yet the inevitable consequence of this point of view appears to be that it diminishes the wonder of God's word, its indisposability, its power to make all things new, its character of grace. It becomes a word which only supplements its context and therefore, strictly speaking, does not deserve to be called word of God at all.

Or theology may emphasize the opposite pole. All forms of natural knowledge of God are bluntly rejected, and the use of the word "God" is held to be possible solely by virtue of the word of God. Any other procedure is condemned as a transformation of theology into anthropology, as a vain attempt to penetrate into the orbit of the word of God from without. Only when theology is securely established, so it is said, can we also address ourselves—and on that basis—to the theme of anthropology. The consequence of this view, however, is to render problematic the relation of the word of God to experience, to the reality that concerns man as man, to the world, and to history. We are threatened with a positivistic view of revelation which makes the word of God more of a supplement—and an unmotivated one at that—than ever. Or else we are faced with a *salto mortale* and, as a consistent way of eliminating natural theology in favor of Christology, we are urged to renounce the word "God" altogether.[10]

Good theology does not submit to the schematism of these positions, schematisms which suffer from false antitheses and the choice of mistaken battlegrounds. They have also, in point of fact, always been championed only to the accompaniment of auspicious inconsistencies—which, to be sure, have demanded the price paid in the unhappy course of the discussion.[11] The theologian's passion is more easily devoted to talking than to hearing, and expends itself in the impatience in which we talk past each other rather than in the patience with which we must listen to each other.

What is transmitted as word of God can thus be understood as word of God only when it finds in man and his world the context into which it announces something hidden; nor can this be just anything that happens to be hidden, but must be that which, hidden and announced as such—in short,

[10]See Paul van Buren, *The Secular Meaning of the Gospel* (New York: Macmillan, 1963), especially pp. 81 ff.

[11]I am of the opinion that the disagreements which caused the break up of the circle around *Zwischen den Zeiten* ought to be critically re-examined.

as the truth—renders a decision concerning the humanity of man. The tradition of the word of God is thus not added to our experience in an unrelated juxtaposition or as a supplement to it, as something that supplants or embellishes our reality. Rather, the tradition of the word of God seeks to verify us where our being in the world is concerned—that is, according to the basic meaning of this Latin compound from *verum* and *facere* it seeks to "make true," to bring to the truth our being in the world. This is no mere wordplay; it rather takes seriously what is meant by *identification* in relation to the humanity of man. Where man is concerned, identification is verification.

The word of God verifies itself as *God's* word precisely by addressing man with a recognition of his basic situation as word situation, that is, with a recognition of the fact that man as man is always one who is already being approached by God. However man may interpret his encounter with the mystery of reality, the word of God charges him with the concealment, in one way or another, of his basic situation; it declares that he is not identical with himself, thus not in the truth, and that he is therefore lacking the freedom to be in harmony and peace with the mystery which has power over him. Otherwise, he would conform to that mystery with undivided heart, in faith, love, and hope, and so answer for all things by praising God. But man does not exist as the word that conforms to his basic situation—namely, as affirmative answer to God. Because he is not at one with God, he is not at one with himself. As one who is godless, he is man existing in contradiction.

The basic situation of man cannot be regarded in abstraction, in separation from the concretions beneath which it is concealed, ignored, or forgotten. On the contrary, the word of God brings this basic situation to expression precisely in its concretions. That is why the language of the Bible is so rich and so close to reality. This is felt even by those who do not perceive the word of God in the Bible. Above all, however, that this is the Bible's way of speaking results in the fact that the announcement of what is hidden takes place not as theoretic enlightenment or as an appeal for the realization of an ideal, but in such a way that man is transposed into his basic situation as word situation. The Bible's way of saying this is to place man before God; that is to say, the word of God alters the situation decisively. It does so by placing man in a concrete word situation which makes him open to his basic situation; it does so through a word of faith that testifies to love and therefore awakens hope. This is why the word of God is uttered historically and is inseparable from narrative, appearing in its fullness as man, as the man Jesus. To believe in him means to be transposed in him into our own basic situation. This is no artificial substitute, but a promising fulfillment. For the truth that makes man true lies outside himself—that is his basic situation.

Why is it that this word which makes man true, and is therefore a saving word necessary for redemption, must be called "word of God?" To what extent is the word "God" essential to the clarity of this word event? Is it not, on the contrary, hindrance to it? Are we not compelled first of all laboriously to make clear what really ought to serve the purposes of clarity but manifestly does not do so, or at all events no longer does so? It appears in fact as though the word "God" was able to advance the clarity of the saving word as long as it belonged to the things generally accepted as a matter of course. It does indeed have such an overwhelmingly strong hold on the language of the Bible and of church tradition that many find the very question before us to be itself sacrilegious. Yet no one can deny the fact that the word "God" is not simply a biblical or even a Christian word. It refracts all kinds of religious colors. Claims made for the word to which the Bible testifies as word of God involve a never-ending battle for the word "God." The word of God understood in that way is the constant de-idolization of the word "God." Precisely this process caused the word "God" to advance the clarity of the word of God. The historical context of the biblical message was, of course, from the very outset the factual misuse of the name of God.

But must we not draw the consistent conclusion from the changed situation in regard to the word "God"? Does the use of it not restrict Christian proclamation to the circle of those who are still familiar with the word "God" today? Does not that proclamation automatically shut itself off from the vast number to whom the word "God" has become so foreign that faith seems to them a demand for submission to the law of a bygone age? We must take very seriously the question of whether the word "God" does not today bar the way of the word of God to the world. We must even go on to ask still more critically: Does the traditional use of the word "God" not carry with it from its sources in general religion a force of its own, against which the word to which the Bible testifies as gospel has been able only exceptionally, but not permanently, to assert itself purely and savingly? Did not the Christian tradition in some ways grow up in danger because of its use of the word "God"?

Fully aware of such dangers, as they have always existed, we address ourselves once more to the problem which especially concerns our age. We must at all times beware of shortsighted distortions. What causes the traditional understanding of the word "God" to appear obsolete today is partly the result of defective interpretation. If the vocable "God" with its customary associations is set immediately in the context of modern thought, without regard to the thought forms of an earlier age, then the result is a caricature which must not be described as the genuine view of the tradition. Yet even when allowance is made for the change of context, there still remains the difference that formerly the word of God had to rescue the word "God" from idolization, whereas today the word of God has to rescue God himself from anonymity and pseudonymity. If what we have said concerning the basic situation of man as word situation and concerning the indication this provides for the meaning of the word "God" is true, then our task is to take what has subsided into speechlessness, or has been suppressed in superficial talk, and help it anew to linguistic expression. It would be senseless to renounce the use of the vocable "God" for this task. Not for its own sake should it be used, but in order to save man from choking on his own self because he no longer has any word with which to cry out of the depths of his self-contradiction and call upon the mystery that surrounds him. The vocable "God" is therefore by no means to be replaced by another, but it does have to be intensively interpreted within the field of experience and thereby be brought back again to the situation in which its use is essential.

This, to be sure, is not a matter of forming and executing a well-aimed plan of action. What we can do to effect this has at best the character of a standby service which is ready for an event that is not in our power. The enormity of the task dawns upon us when we consider the fullness of tradition in which we have to immerse ourselves, when we also hold ourselves open to the tempestuous vehemence of our age, which is the place of present responsibility, and when we bring both together in the truthfulness which respect for the profound mystery of reality demands of us. The standby service of which we have spoken consists in concentration upon the biblical word of God, not by withdrawal into a comfortable linguistic shell, but by stepping out into the world in confident reliance upon a new authority to speak. When it comes to the inevitable reduction to things that are few but genuine, this authority does not spare us shock and pain—but it is also not without the liberating experience of certainty.

Preparing to regain the word "God" from the word of God is at all meaningful and necessary only because we are concerned with the world. As ecclesiastical traditionalists or religious individualists we could content ourselves with the customary understanding of the word "God"—or indeed we could also manage without this vocable. Responsibility before the public and for the public, however, makes it a duty clearly to identify by name—and by a single name at that—the truth of that power which drives man and holds him in the restlessness of his self-contradiction, and the truth which promises eternal peace.

The word of Holy Scripture discloses that which on a thousand occasions man may experience as his situation:

This is, first, a divided reality which in its dichotomy does, to be sure, assume the most varied configurations, but which possesses its unity and its gravity in the fact that it is the "*one*" reality, whose signature is the tension of the enigmatic and the mysterious.

Secondly, it is a reality of a verbal kind which surges in all directions in inexhaustible multiplicity, but is directed as it were towards man, laying hold of him at the point of his verbal responsibility and causing him—amid the fullness of what is unspeakable, or in the straits of what makes him speechless—to cry out to Him whom he entreats and from whom he receives—even in the midst of the annihilating challenge of that which is incomprehensive—the grace of a word that grants life.

Thirdly, it is a reality which demands faith—a faith about which there are confused interpretations that lead men astray and falsify its concealed truth—the bringing of which to truth and reality is promised to the word which receives its authority from Jesus.

To be able to call this situation of man by a name—to be able to use a single word to indicate both its enigmatic obscurity and the light that shines in it and is not swallowed up by the darkness—is necessary for life itself. For only so is the saving word to be proclaimed as word of God, and that means, as word for the godless. And only so is language in general to preserve its humanity. But then even in the word of the godless there is to be heard a hidden word of God.

INTRODUCTION TO RICOEUR'S "WHAT IS A TEXT?"

Paul Ricoeur is one of the more important thinkers in the current cross-disciplinary debate over the methods and theories of interpretation. The systematic cast of his thought, his elegant prose style, and his ability to mediate the substance of continental thought into an American context have made his works widely read and appreciated. Moreover, the scope of Ricoeur's thought is amazing. A glance at the bibliography of his writings reveals the array of topics about which he has written. Ricoeur offers original and constructive suggestions within several different fields of thought. He has made major contributions to recent discussions in the history of philosophy and religion, philosophy of history and religion, Marxist theory, Freudian theory, behaviorist psychology, social ethics, political theory, philosophical anthropology, the study of symbol and myth, biblical criticism, philosophy of language, structuralism, literary criticism, theory of metaphor, philosophy of action, and theology. In a world of increasing specialization coupled with neglect of what lies outside the immediate boundaries, Ricoeur's manifold achievements are particularly extraordinary.

Ricoeur's broad interests do not lack a unifying focus, however. A single question, the question of philosophical anthropology, guides his intellectual quest: What does it mean to be human? By following the line of thought opened up by this question, Ricoeur has been led to the many disciplinary worlds he has entered—worlds largely composed of interconnecting texts.

The permanent horizon of Ricoeur's work is the ontology of human finitude. Although focused on the being of the "I" as it relates to the totality of its world, Ricoeur is not tempted to pretend that he has a metaphysical standpoint available to him, from which he could articulate the meaning of being as "I" in abstract categories. Descartes took that privilege from his standpoint in self-reflection: "I think, therefore I am. . . . I am a thinking being." Struck by the inability of modern philosophy to define the self as a being, whether thinking or otherwise, Ricoeur holds that self-reflection is always already interpretation: the "I" must interpret the meaning of its own being in its actions and self-understandings by interacting with the world, the other, and the self.

At best, the "I" can catch indirect glimpses of its being, as it enacts its being and recollects its enactments. What the "I" sees in self-reflection is always an expression of the "I"—a "word" in the broadest sense (which

includes "deed" and even "mood"). No other access to the "I" is possible.
Descartes, in fact, erred, as Heidegger reminds us, in deducing "I am a
thinking being" from "I am thinking." I cannot deduce a definition of my
being from the sheer activity of thinking. The being of the "I" is accessible
only in the situated act of interpretation: the "I" is always already implicated
in the problems of language in use in any effort to spell out the meaning and
structures of its own being. Hence for Ricoeur the inquiry into the nature of
language is a key for the ontology of human being. We shall see presently
how the problem of "text" pertains to this general concern.

Given the limitations of language on the work of philosophical anthropology, Ricoeur is wary of making ontological assertions about the being of
humans that would appear to rise above the involvement with language,
which refracts our view of human being. Thus Ricoeur, the French translator
of Husserl and philosophical commentator on the Husserlian corpus, is
critical of some elements of pure phenomenology in its descriptions of
human being. Specifically, Ricoeur criticizes Husserl's method of founding
a phenomenology of human being on perceptual rather than linguistic
experiences. In addition, he argues against Husserl's apparent lapse into
idealism that posits an ahistorical absolute "I" behind all phenomena.

But Ricoeur is just as cautious about the tendency, which he sees in
Heidegger and in even more exaggerated form in Derrida, to make assertions about the being of humans that substitute poetic for philosophic
expressions. Thus Ricoeur, who explicitly acknowledges Heidegger's profound influence on his work, criticizes some components of "hermeneutical"
philosophy in its swift move to give voice to the language of being through
poetry. Ricoeur wants to counter the move by the later Heidegger to blur the
difference between poetic-religious and speculative languages—for this
leads to loss of rigor, clarity, and eventually to loss of meaning as the newly
coined "absolutes" (such as "language speaks") fail to resonate in changing
contexts of intelligibility.

Ricoeur thus places himself between the rationalizing tendencies of
Husserl and the poeticizing tendencies of Heidegger. He argues for clear
lines of distinction between the philosophic and poetic-religious realms of
discourse. Only in their difference can they cross-fertilize each other.
Speculative thought has its origins in myth and symbol, yet rises above it,
eventually to detach itself from it, only to return and recover itself in it. No
Hegelian absolute offers itself at the end of the dialectic, however. The
unraveling of absolute ideas is as timely in the movement of thought as the
generation of absolute ideas. In Ricoeur's vision, hermeneutics plays the
intermediary role between the poetic-religious and the philosophic. Thus
one of Ricoeur's important strategies is to distinguish even more basic
components of language, which make poetic or philosophical language

possible. I shall return to this topic shortly. But first let me say a few words about the life and work of Paul Ricoeur and how he came to hermeneutics.

Born in 1913, in Valence (France), Ricoeur studied philosophy at the Sorbonne under Gabriel Marcel. Marcel gave Ricoeur his philosophical theme—the ontology of human finitude. But Ricoeur found his methodological mentor in Edmund Husserl. During the Second World War, Ricoeur served in the French army in 1936–37 and from 1939 to 1945. Most of these years, 1940–1945, were spent as a prisoner of war in Germany. His German captors allowed Ricoeur to read the works of Husserl, Heidegger, and Jaspers; so his years of internment by the German army were spent studying German philosophy. Following the war, Ricoeur established himself as a leading Husserl scholar, and he wrote book-length studies on Jaspers and Marcel. In 1948, Ricoeur was called to the philosophy faculty at the University of Strasbourg. Each year, he immersed himself in the collected works of one great philosopher and taught a seminar on that thinker. In this way, he worked through the tradition from Plato to Nietzsche.

In 1950, Ricoeur published *Freedom and Nature*, the first volume of a *Philosophy of the Will*, which was conceived as a comprehensive and systematic study of the volitional and affective core of human existence. The reception of *Freedom and Nature* made Ricoeur's name as a leading figure in French phenomenology. In 1957, Ricoeur moved to a position in philosophy at the Sorbonne. Shortly thereafter, in 1960, the second volume of the *Philosophy of the Will*, called *Finitude and Guilt*, appeared in two separate books.

Fallible Man, the first part of *Finitude and Guilt* can be called an "existential" phenomenology in contrast to the "pure" phenomenology of *Freedom and Nature*. *Fallible Man* describes the discontinuities that exist in human being between perceiving and conceiving, between the situatedness of character and the open horizon of the drive for happiness, and between the vital drives toward possession, power, and worth and the spiritual feelings or "open moods" of joy, anxiety, and courage.

The second book of *Finitude and Guilt* focuses not on general features of existence that make humans fallible, but on concrete expressions of fallen and disrupted existence. Ricoeur's hermeneutic turn was necessitated by this part of his study, which he called *The Symbolism of Evil*. For phenomenology, in either its pure or existential forms, cannot trace an intelligible line from the possibility of evil to its actual occurrence. Evil intentions and actions are inscrutable to reflection. The actuality of evil requires interpretation of the avowals of evil. The evil will is not accessible directly, but only indirectly through its expressions. In *The Symbolism of Evil*, Ricoeur thus develops a hermeneutical methodology for interpreting religious texts.

The third volume of *The Philosophy of the Will* will offer a poetics of the will. It has not appeared. The expectations awakened by the first two volumes cause its readers to look for a study of the redemptive possibilities in language. What are our linguistic resources for reappropriating the authentic human stance in the world? To answer this, Ricoeur has undertaken an encyclopedic study of language. He has consequently published a number of works on different reflective approaches to language.

The first of his studies preliminary to the poetics of the will was *Freud and Philosophy*, published in 1967, the year following Ricoeur's move to a chair in philosophy at the University of Paris, Nanterre. His *Conflict of Interpretations: Essays in Hermeneutics* was published in 1969. In both works, Ricoeur tries to mediate among the competing theories of interpretion. He does so by clarifying the levels on which linguistic interpretation operates. Ricoeur's view is that psychoanalysis, structuralism, and other objectivist programs of interpretation theory are not incompatible with hermeneutics conceived as either practical philosophy or even ontology. Interpretation theory can be reconnected to practical philosophy and ontology by showing how language as discourse involves both objective sense and existential appropriation. Since these take place at different levels, the formalism embedded in hermeneutical theory need not be incompatible with either hermeneutics as practical philosophy or as indirect ontology of finitude.

In 1973, Ricoeur began a joint appointment at the University of Paris, Nanterre, and the University of Chicago, where he succeeded Paul Tillich as John Nuveen Professor of Philosophical Theology. The appointment in the Divinity School at Chicago has been a boon for religion studies in the United States. Since his tenure at Chicago, Ricoeur has both given greater consideration to the theological dimension of hermeneutics (see "Philosophical and Theological Hermeneutics" and "Biblical Hermeneutics" in the bibliography) and has broadened his cross-disciplinary studies of language (see *The Rule of Metaphor* [1975], *Interpretation Theory* [1976], and *Time and Narrative* [1981]). For the purpose of reading Ricoeur's essay, "What Is a Text?" which follows this introduction, let me present a scandalously brief overview of some central points in Ricoeur's recent language theory. From there, I shall summarize his main intentions in "What Is a Text?"

First, following the well-known distinction between *parole* and *langue*, Ricoeur differentiates two levels of language, each the proper object of a different inquiry. (1) At the abstract level of formal linguistic relations, languages display a system of signs. Each sign is defined by its internal relation to other signs in the system. The presence of such a significatory system engenders semiotics as the inquiry into the ways signs constitute systems on the basis of formal codes. (2) At the concrete level of discourse, languages are employed for the purpose of communication. An individual says something about something to someone within a situation. Semantics is the discipline that inquires into the ways sentences in discourse convey meanings to a hearer. In Ricoeur's view, neither level of language can be reduced to the other. Each side of language may be developed in different ways and related to the other side in different ways. In a global reflection on language, neither side should be exalted to the exclusion of the other.

Second, Ricoeur draws a distinction within the level of language he calls discourse (*parole*): Discourse has a subject-object structure. On the subject side, "someone speaks" and intends to convey understanding of that intention. On the object side, someone "says something" and the utterance bears a meaning that may not coincide with the utterer's meaning. The subject-object structure of discourse appears in two basic features of discourse. (1) Discourse is both event and meaning. By this Ricoeur means that discourse is an act in time with illocutionary and perlocutionary dimensions (the author does something in the utterance and evokes a response); yet discourse communicates an objective meaning that can be separated from any perlocutionary doings. (2) The meaning or intention of a sentence has both sense and reference. Loosely following Frege, Ricoeur means that sentences carry a formal sense, a thought, that in turn refers to a real object, state of affairs, and so forth.

Third, Ricoeur distinguishes between literal discourse, which reduces to a single meaning, and figurative discourse, which exploits plurivocity in words and sentences to create new meanings. As anyone might guess, scientific discourse is the paradigm of the literal use of language and poetic discourse is the model of the figurative use. In *The Rule of Metaphor*, Ricoeur goes to great lengths to account for both sense and reference in figurative language. He intends to show that we misunderstand poetic discourse if we think either that it has sense but not reference or that it breaks away from the sense-reference structure of meaning found in literal language. For Ricoeur, metaphor (by which he means "figurative language" generally speaking) carries double meaning, which makes possible "split reference." Figurative expressions carry a literal sense that refer us to some nonlinguistic reality. But they also carry a surplus of meaning. By "surplus," Ricoeur means that metaphor is a matter of semantic innovation, a creating and discovering of new sense and reference through the overturning of efforts to determine a literal sense and referent. He explains it as follows.

We read a figurative expression and attempt to follow the literal meaning. Thus in the Trakl poem "A Winter Evening," which is the subject of Heidegger's essay "Language," the line "Golden blooms the tree of graces" leads us to follow the sense of the sentence (perhaps just the image suggested by the line) to a referent. In the literal reading, the "is" of the metaphoric copula connects images in the poem and depicts reality. As the image invites thought, however, the self-sufficiency of the literal meaning breaks down. Poetry thrives on the failure of such literal signification, however. The literal "is" gives way to an "is not" in the inability to conceive or locate the literal referent. Thus the metaphoric "is" comes to signify, for Ricoeur, both an "is not" and through it an "is like." In the collapse of literal sense and reference, metaphor rises again to project its figurative meaning. This second meaning refers not to literal reality but to modes of being in the world. "Golden blooms the tree of graces" refers not to a physical tree, nor to nothing, but to a way of existing in the world that is manifest only through the words of the poem. Thus in Ricoeur's view, poetic texts open new worlds, the worlds of possible modes of being for appropriation and actualization.

For Ricoeur, hermeneutics proper begins with the problem of the text conceived as a work. The reason Ricoeur privileges the text in hermeneutics is that texts actualize the distinctions that determine discourse, whereas in spoken language or other direct modes of communication, the distinctions remain as mere possibilities. With texts, we are distanced from speech and have the time to consider both semiotic and semantic approaches. Texts also manifest the subject-object structure of discourse: "utterer's meaning" and "utterance meaning" more easily diverge in texts than in spoken discourse. The event of speaking and the objective sense of what is said are in the nature of the case separated once language is produced as a text. Moreover, texts are more capable of displaying subtle exchanges between literal and figurative senses, because texts are marked by the telling relation they bear to their genre, their construction as thematic compositions, and their unique presentation of styles. Subtle differences latent in all language are made explicit in texts, for the benefit of interpretation.

In "What Is a Text?" Ricoeur draws the implications of his theory of text for hermeneutics. His point of reference is the dichotomy, inherited from Dilthey, between interpretation and explanation. Dilthey's hermeneutical theory holds that linguistic expressions, which demand understanding and interpretation, are the subject matter of the human sciences. The natural sciences, whose sensory or mathematical objects are external to language, engage in a different mode of knowing—that of explanation. Thus interpretation and explanation are different methods for use in different domains of inquiry.

Ricoeur argues that developments in linguistics and philosophy of language have made that dichotomy obsolete. He proposes a mediation between interpretation and explanation based on the various dualities present in language. Linguistics routinely objectifies language as a system of signs that displays an objective structure. But language cannot be reduced to a system of signs—it remains the medium of the communication and reception of a message. Explanatory methods, such as those practiced by structuralist critics, are not alien to the human sciences, whose aim is understanding. But neither can they methodologically exhaust the human sciences. Because both are rooted in a distinct level of language, explanation and interpretation should be viewed as two different kinds of reading. Thus Ricoeur writes, "As readers, we can remain in the suspense of the text and treat it as a worldless and authorless text, in which case we explain it by means of its internal relations, its structure. Or else we can remove the text's suspense, accomplish it in a way similar to speech, returning it to living communication, in which case we interpret it. These two possibilities both belong to the act of reading, and reading consists in a dialectical interplay of these two attitudes."[1]

The first attitude can result in determination of an objective sense through structural analysis. Ricoeur presents us with an example of structural analysis of myth from Lévi-Strauss. The first attitude is "explanatory" in Dilthey's sense. But it is no longer the polar opposite of interpretation; it does not represent the invasion of the humanities by the methods of the natural sciences. Explanatory procedures and methods aimed at the objective sense of a text are warranted by the distance between texts and living speech.

The second attitude is "interpretive" in Dilthey's sense. It follows the direction opened for thought by the objective sense carried by the structured relations in the text. Texts, like sentences, have a sense that signifies a referent. The sense of a text is its structure. To interpret the text is to work out the referential design indicated by the structure of the text itself. In the case of fictional, poetic, or religious texts, reference might be made to "possible worlds" or "modes of being in the world" rather than to dimensions of the literal world. But Ricoeur does not spell that out in this essay. For more on the referential power of fictional texts, see "Existence and Hermeneutics" in the second volume of this collection.

Moreover, proper understanding of the nature of text opens the way, neglected by Gadamer and Heidegger, to return from hermeneutics as ontology of language and practical philosophy to the other problems bequeathed by Dilthey and Schleiermacher and not yet solved: namely, how to develop methods of interpretation and how to form standards of evaluation in interpretation. In Ricoeur's estimation, if we understand both what a text is and how we actually interpret texts, we will draw near to the answers. A text is like a musical score, a structural whole with clues for its performance in life: its structure is its sense through which it refers to the world. If this is so, then methods in interpreting texts ought to conform to the theory of text. We should first read with open imagination, then analyze the structure of the text, so we can critically follow the direction of the text in pointing to its referent. Interpretations of texts can likewise be tested—a hypothesis concerning the referential design of the text can be tested against an analysis of its structure. Correspondence between the two is one criterion for truth in

---

[1]Paul Ricoeur, "What Is a Text?", p. 236 below.

interpretation. The theory of text thus paves the way for a return from truth as unverifiable disclosure to method and back again to verifiable truth. This step toward theory of text thus remains for Ricoeur a crucial element in the working out of an authentically critical hermeneutics.[2]

[2]For a more complete account, see David E. Klemm, *The Hermeneutical Theory of Paul Ricoeur* (Lewisburg, Penna.: Bucknell University Press, 1983).

WHAT IS A TEXT?
EXPLANATION AND INTERPRETATION
(1970)

Paul Ricoeur

This essay will be devoted principally to the debate between two basic attitudes which one can adopt in regard to a text. These two attitudes were summed up, in the time of Wilhelm Dilthey, by the two words "explain" and "interpret." Dilthey called *explanation* that model of intelligibility borrowed from the natural sciences and extended to the historical sciences by the positivistic schools, and he took *interpretation* as a derived form of *understanding* in which he saw the basic approach of the "human sciences" (*Geisteswissenschaften*), the only one which can do justice to the basic difference between these sciences and the "natural sciences." I would like here to examine the outcome of this opposition in the light of the conflicts between contemporary schools. The notion of explanation has, indeed, shifted positions; it no longer stems from the natural sciences but from strictly linguistic models. As for the notion of interpretation, it has, in modern hermeneutics, undergone deep transformations which set it off from the psychological notion of understanding, in Dilthey's sense of the term. It is this new situation of the problem perhaps less contradictory and more fruitful, which I would like to explore. But before entering into the new concepts of explanation and interpretation, I would like to devote some time to a preliminary question which in fact will determine all the rest of our investigation. The question is this: What is a text?

I. WHAT IS A TEXT?

Let us call a text every utterance or set of utterances fixed by writing. According to this definition, the fixation by writing is constitutive of the text itself. But what is fixed by writing? We have said: every utterance or group of utterances. Is this to say that these utterances must have been previously enunciated physically or mentally, that all writing has been, at least in a potential way, first of all speech? In short, how does it stand with the relation of the text to speech?

The psychological and sociological priority of speech over writing is not in question. *Psychological priority*: if by speech we mean the production of a particular discourse by a particular speaker addressing himself to a hearer who may or may not understand what the first speaker means, this kind of human experience precedes that of writing. *Sociological priority*: the need for a preservation of spoken language by the means of some kind of fixation, inscription or recording may be assigned to a rather late stage of economical and political development. One can however wonder if the late appearance of writing has not provoked a radical change in our relation to the very utterance of our discourse. That which is fixed by writing is a discourse which certainly one could have spoken but *which one writes precisely* because one does not speak. The fixation by means of writing occurs in the plan of speech itself, that is, in the plan where speech could have arisen. One can then wonder whether a text is not truly a text when it is not just limited to recording a prior speech, but when it invites directly in written words the meaning of the utterance.

That which could give insight to this idea of a direct relation between writing and the meaning intended by the utterance is the function which reading plays in regard to that which is written. Indeed, a written text calls for a reading which later will allow us to introduce both concepts of explanation and interpretation as specific kinds of reading. For the time being, let us say that the reader takes the place of the listener, just as writing takes the place of speaking. Indeed, the writing-reading relation is not just a particular instance of the speaking-answering relation. It is not an instance of dialogue. Whereas dialogue is an exchange of questions and answers, there is no exchange of this sort between the writer and his reader; the writer does not answer the reader. Rather, the book introduces a shift between the act of writing and the act of reading, between which two acts there is no communication: the reader is absent from the writing of the book, the writer is absent from its reading. In this way the text produces a double effacement (occulation) of reader and writer. It therefore replaces the relation of dialogue which immediately binds together the voice of the one and the ear of the other.

This substitution of reading in the precise place of a dialogue which does not occur is so evident that when we have the occasion of meeting an author and of speaking with him (about his book, for instance), we experience a kind of disturbance in that very special relation which we have with the author in and through his work. I like to say sometimes that to read a book is to consider its author as already dead and the book as posthumous. Indeed, it is when the author is dead that the relation to his book becomes complete and, in a way, intact. The author can no longer respond; it only remains to read his work.

This difference between the act of reading and the act of dialogue confirms our hypothesis that writing is a process similar to speech, parallel to speech, an operation which takes its place and in a way intercepts it. This is why we were able to say that writing is a direct inscription of this intention, even if, historically and psychologically, writing began as a graphic transcription of speech signs. This liberation of writing whereby it gets substituted for speech is the birth of a text.

At present, what happens now to the utterance itself when it is directly inscribed instead of being pronounced? Emphasis has always been placed on the most striking characteristic of writing, that it preserves discourse and makes of it an archives available for individual and collective memory. Added to this is the fact that the linearization of symbols allows for an analytic and distinctive translation of all the successive and discrete traits of language and thus increases its efficiency. Is this all that it does? Preservation and efficiency still only characterize the transcription of oral language into graphic signs. The liberation of a text from vocal existence results in a veritable upheaval as much in the relations between language and the world as in the relation between language and the different subjectivities involved, that of the author and that of the reader.

Let us call reference or referential relation the relation between language and the reality (whatever it may be) *about* which something is said in a sequence of discourse; to speak is to say something *about* something *to* somebody; let us put aside for a moment this relation of discourse to somebody else, in order to focus on the relation "about" something; this "about" designates the referent of the discourse. This referential relation is, as one knows, borne by the sentence, which is the first and simplest unity of discourse. This referential function is so important that it compensates, so to say, for another characteristic of language which is the separation of signs from things: by means of the referential function language "returns" so to say, to reality, which it tries to grasp, to represent, to express. What we call the symbolic function of language is a kind of balance between a process of *difference* which separates the world of signs from the world of things and a process of *reference*, which "pours back" language into the universe. It is this subtle balance between *difference* and *reference* which speech preserves and which writing destroys.

In speech the function of reference is linked to the role of the *situation of discourse* within the exchange of language itself; in exchanging speech, the speakers are present to each other, but also to the circumstantial setting of discourse, not only the perceptual surroundings, but also the cultural background known by both speakers. It is in relation to this situation that discourse is fully meaningful; the reference to reality is in the last analysis reference to that reality which can be pointed out "around" the speakers, "around," so to speak, the instance of discourse itself. Language is, moreover, well equipped to insure this anchorage; the demonstrative articles, the spatial and temporal adverbs, the personal pronouns, the tenses of the verb, and in general all the ostensive indicators of language serve to anchor discourse in the circumstantial reality which surrounds the instance of discourse. Thus, in living speech, the *ideal* meaning of what one says bends towards a *real* reference, namely to that "about which" one speaks; at its limit this real reference tends to get confused with an ostensive designation wherein speech joins up with the indicative gesture, that of pointing out.

This is no longer the case when a text takes the place of speech. The shifting of references towards ostensive designation (showing) is intercepted, at the same time that dialogue is interrupted by the text. I say indeed intercepted and not suppressed; it is here that I will shortly take up my distance from what I shall call the ideology of the absolute text which is based on an undue hypostasis of the rightful remarks we have just made. A text, we shall see, is not without reference; it will be precisely the task of reading, as interpretation, to actualize the reference. At least, in this suspension wherein reference is deferred, in the sense that it is postponed, a text is somehow "in the air," outside of the world or without a world; by means of this obliteration of all relation to the world, every text is free to enter into relation with all the other texts which come to take the place of the circumstantial reality shown by living speech.

This relation of one text to another, in the disappearance of the world about which one speaks, engenders the quasi-world of text or *literature*. Such is the upheaval which affects discourse itself, when the movement of reference towards designation (showing) is intercepted by a text, words cease to efface themselves in front of things; written words become words for their own sake.

II. Structural Analysis as "Explanation"

We are now prepared to introduce the opposition between explanation and interpretation as a consequence of the autonomous status of the written text as regards speech. What we called masking (occultation) of the surrounding world by the quasi-world of texts gives rise to two possibilities. As readers, we can remain in the suspense of the text and treat it as a worldless and authorless text, in which case we explain it by means of its internal relations, its structure. Or else we can remove the text's suspense, accomplish it in a way similar to speech, returning it to living communication, in which case we interpret it. These two possibilities both belong to the act of reading, and reading consists in a dialectical interplay of these two attitudes.

Let us take them up separately, before considering their connections. We can make the text into a first kind of reading, a reading which acknowledges, so to speak, the text's interception of all the relations with a world which can be shown and with subjectivities who can converse. This transfer into the "place" where the text stands constitutes a special project in regard to the text, that of prolonging its suspension of the referential relation to the world and the reference to the author as the speaking subject. By means of this special project, the reader decides to stay within the "place of the text" and within the "enclosure" of this place. On the basis of this choice, the text has no outside; it has but an inside; it aims at no transcendence, as would speech which is directed *to* someone, *about* something.

This project is not only possible but legitimate. Indeed, the constitution of the text as text and the system of text as literature justifies the interception of this double transcendence of speech towards a world and another person. On this basis an explanatory attitude in regard to the text becomes possible.

Now, unlike what Dilthey thought, this explanatory attitude is in no way borrowed from an area of knowledge and an epistemological model other than that of language itself. It does not rely on a naturalistic model extended only secondarily to the human sciences. The nature-mind opposition is not even operative here. If something is borrowed, it takes place inside the same field, that of semiology or semiotics. It is indeed possible to treat texts according to the explanatory rules which linguistics successfully applied to elementary systems of signs which constitute language (*langue*) in opposition to speech. As is known, the language-speech distinction is the basic distinction which furnishes linguistics with a homogeneous object; whereas speech belongs to physiology, psychology, sociology, language, as the system of rules of which speech is the exception, belongs only to linguistics. As is also known, linguistics considers only systems of entities which possess no absolute meaning and which are divined only by their difference from all the other unities. These unities, which are either merely distinctive like those of phonological articulation or significant like those of lexical articulation, are oppositive entities or unities. It is the interplay of oppositions and their combinations on the basis of an inventory of discrete unities which defines the notion of structure in linguistics. It is this structural model which furnishes the type of explanatory behavior which we are now going to see applied to a text, mainly by French structuralists.

Even before beginning this undertaking, it might be objected that laws which are valid only for language as distinct from speech could not be applied to a text. Is not a text, one might say, while not being speech still in the same position as speech in regard to language (*langue*)? Is it not necessary to oppose in an overall way speech as a succession of utterances, that is, in the last analysis, as a succession of sentences, to language? Is not the speech-writing distinction secondary in regard to this language-discourse distinction, language and speech occupying the same position as discourse? These remarks are perfectly legitimate and permit us to think that that explanatory model characterized as structural does not exhaust the field of possible attitudes in regard to a text. But even before saying what the limit of this explanatory attitude is, it is necessary to grasp its fruitfulness. The working hypothesis of all structural analysis of texts is this: in spite of the fact that writing occupies the same position as speech in regard to language, namely that of discourse, the specificity of writing in regard to actual speech is based on structural characteristics which may be treated as analogies of language within discourse. The working hypothesis is perfectly legitimate; it

consists in saying that under certain conditions the larger unities of language, that is to say, the unities of higher order than the sentence, are
organized in a way similar to that of the small unities of language, that is, the
unities of an order lower than the sentence, those precisely which belong to
the domain of linguistics.

In his *Structural Anthropology*,[1] Claude Lévi-Strauss formulates in the
following way this working hypothesis in regard to one category of texts, that
of myths: "Like every linguistic entity, the myth is made up of constitutive
unities; these constitutive unities imply the presence of those which generally occur in the structure of language, namely phonemes, morphemes,
semantemes. Each form differs from the one which precedes it by a higher
degree of complexity. For this reason we will call the elements which
properly belong to the myth (and which are the most complex of all): large
constitutive unities." By means of this working hypothesis, the large unities
which are at least the same size as the sentence and which, put together,
form the narrative proper to the myth will be able to be treated according to
the same rules as the smallest unities known to linguistics. It is in order to
insist on this likeness that Claude Lévi-Strauss speaks of mythemes, just as
one speaks of phonemes, morphemes, etc. But in order to remain within the
limits of the analogy between mythemes and the lower level linguistic
unities, the analysis of texts will have to operate on the same sort of
abstraction as that practiced by the phonologist. For the latter, the phoneme
is not a concrete sound, in an absolute sense, with its acoustic quality; (it is
a function defined by commutation which resolves itself into its oppositive
value in relation to all the others). In this sense, it is not, to speak like
Saussure, a "substance" but a form, that is to say, an interplay of relations.
Similarly, a mytheme is not one of the sentences of a myth but an oppositive
value attached to several individual sentences forming, in the terminology of
Lévi-Strauss, a "bundle of relations": "It is only in the form of a combination
of such bundles that the constitutive unities acquire a meaning-function."[2]
What is here called meaning-function is not at all what the myth means, its
philosophical or existential content or intention, but the arrangement, the
disposition of mythemes, in short, the structure of the myth.

I would like to recall here briefly the analysis which, according to this
method, Lévi-Strauss offers of the Oepidus myth. He separates into four
columns the sentences of the myth. In the first column he places all those
which speak of an over-esteemed parental relationship (for example, Oedipus weds Jocasta, his mother, Antigone buries Polynices, her brother, in
spite of the order not to); in the second column are to be found the same

---

[1]Claude Lévi-Strauss, *Anthropologie structurale* (Paris: Librairie Plon, 1958) p. 233. The
English translation is Claude Lévi-Strauss, *Structural Anthropology*, trans. Claire Jacobson and
Brooke Grundfest Schoepf (Harmondsworth: Penguin Books, 1968), pp. 210–11.

[2]Ibid., p. 234 (English: p. 211).

relations but affected with the opposite sign, and under-esteemed or deval-
uated parental relationship (Oedipus kills his father, Laios, Eteocles kills his
brother Polynices); the third column is concerned with monsters and their
destruction; the fourth groups together all the proper names whose meanings suggest a difficulty to walk straight (lame, clumsy, swollen foot). A
comparison of the four columns brings out a correlation. Between one and
two what we have are parental relationships by turns overesteemed or
underesteemed; between three and four we have an affirmation and then a
negation of man's autochthony (aboriginal, indigenous): "It would thereby
result that the fourth column holds the same relation with column three as
column one does with column two . . . ; the overestimation of the blood
relationship is, in regard to its underestimation, like the attempt to escape
from the autochthonous situation and the impossibility of therein succeed-
ing." The myth thus appears as a sort of logical instrument which draws
together contradictions in order to overcome them: "the impossibility of
connecting groups of relations is thus overcome (or, more exactly, replaced)
by the affirmation that the two contradictory relations are identical between
themselves to the degree that each, like the other, is self-contradictory."[3] We
will return shortly to the conclusion of the formal analysis; let us limit
ourselves (now) to stating it.

We can indeed say that we have explained the myth, but not that we
have interpreted it. We have, by means of structural analysis, brought out the
logic of the operations which relate the four bundles of relations among
themselves; this logic constitutes "the structural law of the myth under
consideration."[4] It will not fail to be noticed that this law is pre-eminently an
object of reading and not at all of speaking, in the sense of a reciting where
the power of the myth would be actualized in a particular situation. Here the
text is but a text; and reading inhabits it only as a text, thanks to the
suspension of its meaning for us, to the postponement of all actualization by
present speech.

I have just taken an example from the field of myths; I could take another
from a neighboring field, that of folklore narratives. This field has been
explored by the Russian formalists of the school of Propp and by the French
specialists of the structural analysis of narratives, Roland Barthes and
Greimas. The same postulates as those of Lévi-Strauss are to be found in
these authors as well: the unities above the sentence have the same
composition as the unities below the sentence; the meaning of an element is
its ability to enter into relation with other elements and with all of the work.
These postulates together define the enclosure of the narrative; the task of
structural analysis will then consist in operating a segmentation (the hori-
zontal aspect) and then establishing various levels of integration of the parts

[3]Ibid., p. 239 (English: p. 216).
[4]Ibid., p. 241 (English: p. 217).

in the whole (the hierarchical aspect). But the unities of action, which are segmented and organized in that way have nothing to do with psychological traits susceptible of being lived or with behavioral segments susceptible of falling under a behaviorist psychology; the extremities of these sequences are only switching points in the narrative, such that if one element is changed, all the rest are different. One recognizes here a transposition of the commutative method from the phonological level to the level of narrative unities. The logic of action consists then in a linking together of action kernels (*noyaux d'action*) which all together constitute the narrative's structural continuity; the application of this technique results in a "dechronologizing" of the narrative, so as to make apparent the narrative logic underlying narrative time. Ultimately, the narrative is reduced to a combination (*combinatoire*) of a few dramatic unities: promising, betraying, hindering, aiding, etc., which would thus be the paradigms of action. A sequence is thus a succession of action kernels, each one closing off an alternative opened up by the preceding one. These elementary unities fit in with larger unities; for example, the encounter embraces elementary actions such as approaching, summoning, greeting, etc. To explain a narrative is to get hold of this symphonic structure of segmental actions.

To this chain of actions correspond relations of the same sort between the "acting characters" of the narrative. By this we do not at all mean psychological subjects, but formalized roles correlative to formalized actions. The acting characters are defined only by the predicates of action, by the semantic axis of the sentence and narrative: the one who does the act, the one to whom, with whom, etc., the action is done; it is the one who promises, who receives the promise, the giver, the receiver, etc. Structural analysis thus brings out a hierarchy of acting characters correlative to the hierarchy of *actions*.

It remains then to assemble the narrative as a whole and to put it back into narrative communication. It is then a discourse addressed by the narrator to a receiver. But, for structural analysis, the two interlocutors must be looked for in the text and nowhere else; the narrator is designated only by the narrative signs which themselves belong to the very constitution of the narrative. There is no longer anything beyond these three levels (level of actions, level of acting characters, level of narration) which belongs to the semiologist's science; there is but the world of the users of the narrative which itself eventually falls under other semiological disciplines (social, economic, ideological systems), but which are no longer ones of a linguistic sort. This transposition of a linguistic model to the theory of the narrative perfectly verifies our initial remark: explanation today is no longer a concept borrowed from the natural sciences and transferred into a different field, that of written monuments; it proceeds from the same sphere of language, thanks to an analogical transfer of the small unities of language (phonemes and lexemes) to the large unities subsequent to the sentence, such as narrative, folklore, myth. As a result, interpretation will no longer be *confronted* with a model foreign to the human sciences, a model of intelligibility, borrowed from a science, linguistics, belonging to the same field of human sciences. As a result, it will be on the same ground, inside of the same sphere of language that explanation and interpretation will dispute each other.

III. Towards a New Concept of Interpretation

Let us now consider the other attitude which one can adopt in regard to a text, that one which we have called interpretation. It is first of all by opposing it to the preceding one, in a way similar to that of Dilthey, that we can introduce it. But it will be possible gradually to reach a relation more closely complementary and reciprocal between explanation and interpretation.

Let us start off once again from the act of reading. Two ways of reading, we have said, are offered to us. By reading we can prolong and reinforce the suspension affecting the text's reference to the environment of a world and the audience of speaking subjects; this is the explanatory attitude. But we can also bring an end to this suspension and complete the text in actual discourse. It is this second attitude which is the genuine aim of reading. The other sort of reading would not even be possible if it were not first of all apparent that the text, as writing, waits and calls for a reading; if a reading is possible, it is indeed because the text is not closed in on itself but opens out onto something else. By any supposition reading is a linking together of a new discourse to the discourse of the text. The linking reveals, in the very constitution of the text, an original capacity of being reenacted, which is its *open* character. Interpretation is the concrete result of this openness and of this linking together. How?

Our first concept of interpretation will still be close to that of Dilthey. We may characterize it, in general terms, as *appropriation*. Truth to tell, this meaning will not be abandoned, it will only be mediated by explanation itself, instead of being opposed to it in an immediate and rather naive way.

By appropriation I mean several things. I mean first that the interpretation of a text ends up in the self-interpretation of a subject who henceforth understands himself better. This completion of text-understanding in self-understanding characterizes the sort of reflective philosophy which I call concrete reflection. Hermeneutics and reflective philosophy are here correlative and reciprocal: on the one hand, self-understanding provides a roundabout way of understanding the cultural signs in which the self contemplates himself and forms himself; on the other hand, the understanding of a text is not an end in itself and for itself; it mediates the relation to himself of a subject who, in the short circuit of immediate reflection, would not find the meaning of his own life. Thus it is necessary to say just as strongly that reflection is nothing without mediation by means of signs and cultural works and that explanation is nothing if it is not incorporated, as an intermediary stage, in the process of self-understanding. In short, in hermeneutical reflection—or in reflective hermeneutics—the constitution of *self* and that of meaning are contemporaneous.

The term appropriation entails two further characteristics. One of the aims of all hermeneutics is to fight against cultural distance; by cultural distance I mean not only the temporal distance but the kind of estrangement in regard to the system of values to which the cultural background of the text belongs. In this sense, interpretation "brings together," "equalizes,"—all of which is to genuinely render *proper* (one's own) that which was previously foreign.

But, above all, the characterization of interpretation as appropriation is meant to draw attention to the kind of *actuality* which belongs to the process of interpretation. Reading is like the performance of a musical score: it betokens the fulfillment, the actualization of the semantic virtualities of the text. This third trait is the most important; for it is the interpretations with self-interpretation, the overcoming of cultural distance; this character of actualization reveals the decisive function of reading, namely that it achieves the discourse of the text in a dimension similar to speech. Speech too is an event; speech is discourse as event. Speech is the instance of discourse, as Benvenito says; in speech and by speech, the sentences which constitute the discourse as discourse signify *hic et nunc*. Reading—as the actualization of the text—gives to writing a similar achievement: the actualized text finds at last an environment and an audience, a world and an intersubjective dimension. In interpretation, we shall say, reading becomes like speech. I do not say, becomes speech, for reading never equals an exchange of speech, a dialogue. But reading is concretely accomplished in an act which is, in regard to the text, what speech is in regard to language, namely, an event and instance of discourse. In explanation the text had only internal relations, a structure; in interpretation it has now a significance, that is, an accomplishment in the subject's own discourse. By means of its structure the text had only a semiological dimension; by means of the actualization, it now has a semantic dimension.

Let us pause here. Our discussion has reached a critical point: interpretation understood as appropriation, still remains exterior to explanation in the sense of structural analysis. We keep opposing them as two attitudes between which it would be necessary to choose.

I would like now to overcome this non-dialectical opposition and make apparent the inner connections which render structural analysis and hermeneutics complementary. For this it is necessary to show how each of the two attitudes which we have opposed refers back to the other by means of characteristics which are proper to it.

Let us return to the examples of structural analysis which are borrowed from the theory of myth and narrative. We tried to hold ourselves to a notion of sense (or meaning) which would be strictly reducible to the arrangement of the elements within the text. As a matter of fact no one remains with a conception as formal as this of the sense (or meaning) of a narrative or myth. For instance, what Lévi-Strauss calls a "mytheme," and which is in his opinion the constitutive unity of the myth, is expressed in a sentence which has a meaning, in the sense of a referential intention of its own: Oepidus kills his father, weds his mother, etc. Is one to say that the structural explanation neutralizes the meaning proper to these and those sentences as merely to retain their positions in the myth? But the bundle of relations to which Lévi-Strauss reduces the mythemes is still of the same order as the sentence, and the interplay of oppositions which is instigated at this very abstract level is still of the same order as the sentence. If one speaks of "overevaluated" or "underevaluated blood relationships," of man's "autochthony" or "non-autochthony," these relations can still be written in the form of a structure: the blood relationship is not as high as the social relationship, for instance the prohibition of incest, etc. In short, the contradiction which according to Lévi-Strauss the myth attempts to resolve, expresses itself in meaningful relationships. Lévi-Strauss admits it, in spite of himself, where he writes: "the reason for these choices becomes apparent if it is recognized that mythical thought proceeds from the becoming aware (*de la prise de con-science*) of certain oppositions and tends towards their progressive mediation."[5] And again: "the myth is a sort of logical root destined to achieve a mediation between life and death."[6] In the background of the myth there is a question which is a highly meaningful one, a question about life and death: "Is one born from one or from two"? This question expresses anxiety and agony concerning the origin: whence does man come? Is he born of the earth, is he born of his parents? There would be no contradiction, and no attempts to resolve the contradiction, if there were no meaningful questions, meaningful conjectures concerning the origin and the end of man. Is it possible to put within brackets this function of the myth as a narrative of the origins? I do not think so. In fact, structural analysis does not succeed in including this function: it merely postpones it. If the myth is a logical operation, it does not play this role between any propositions whatsoever, but between utterances which point towards border-line situations: birth and death, sexuality and suffering, origin and end. Structural analysis, far from getting rid of this radical questioning, restores it at a level of even higher rationality. Would it not then be the function of structural analysis to put into question a superficial semantics, that of the apparent narrative, so as to make manifest a depth-semantics, which is the latent narrative, or, if I may say so, the live semantics of the myth? I readily believe that if such were not the living function of structural analysis, it would be reduced to a sterile

[5]Ibid., p. 248 (English: p. 224).
[6]Ibid., p. 243 (English: p. 220).

game of combinations; the myth would be robbed even of the function which Lévi-Strauss himself recognizes it to have where he says that mythical thought proceeds from the awareness of certain oppositions and tends towards their progressive mediation. This awareness is that of the enigmas of existence and end which mythic thought generates. To eliminate this meaningful intention would be to reduce the theory of myth to a necrology of the meaningless discourses of mankind. If, on the contrary, one considers structural analysis as a stage—and a necessary one—between a naive interpretation and a critical interpretation, between a superficial interpretation and a depth interpretation, then it would seem possible to locate explanation and interpretation at two different stages of a hermeneutical arch and to integrate the opposed attitudes of explanation and understanding within the unique concrete act of reading.

We will take a step further in the direction of this reconciliation between explanation and interpretation by submitting to a parallel critique our initial concept of interpretation. To interpret, we said, is to appropriate *hic et nunc* for ourselves the intention of the text. In saying that, we remained within the enclosure of Dilthey's "understanding." Now, what we have just said concerning the depth-semantics of the text to which structural analysis refers is an invitation for us to understand that the intended meaning is not the supposed intention of the author, the vivid experience of *the writer*, into which we should have to transport ourselves, but rather that which *the text* wants to say: not the psychological intention of the author, but the *injunction* of the text. What the text wants, is to orient our thought according to it. The sense of the text is the direction which it opens up for our thought.

This concept of sense as direction for thought leads us to a new definition of interpretation which would be less a subjective operation than an objective process; less an act *on* the text, than an act *of* the text. This process of interpretation has something to do with the depth semantics of the text delivered by structural analysis; it is this depth semantics which is to understand in dynamic terms; whereas the structure constitutes the statics of the text, the depth semantics is itself a process of meaning; it requires a fresh interpretation because it is itself an interpretation, this interpretation which I called the act of the text.

I will take an example in the field of biblical exegesis. Werner H. Schmidt has shown the account of creation according to Genesis 1–2, relies on the interplay of two narratives, a *Tatbericht*, in which creation is expressed merely in terms of action: "God made . . . ," and a *Wortbericht*, in which creation proceeds from the word: "God said, and there was . . ." The first narrative plays the role of tradition and the second that of interpretation. Within the same text, therefore, tradition and interpretation constitute the two poles of the meaning as process. To interpret the text is to follow the pattern of thought opened by this process. In that way, interpretation is the act of the text, before being an act of exegesis; it is like an arrow borne by the text itself, indicating the direction for the exegetical work.

This concept of objective interpretation, or, if we may say, of intratextual interpretation has nothing unusual about it—it even has roots in an older tradition than the concept of subjective interpretation which is definitely modern. Aristotle called *hermeneia* (interpretation) the very act of language on things; unlike the hermeneutical technique of the augurs and interpreters of oracles, which announces the hermeneutic of romanticism, *hermeneia* designates the process of language; for Aristotle, to interpret is not what one does in a second language as applied to a first language; it is already what the first language does in mediating by signs our relation to things. Interpretation is thus, according to the commentary of Boethius on Aristotle's *Peri Hermeneias*, the very work of the *vox significativa per se ipsam aliquid significans, sive complexa, sive incomplexa.*

Indeed, interpretation in Aristotle's sense does not cover over concepts of interpretation which imply some kind of dynamic relation between several layers of meaning within the same text (tradition and interpretation in the sense of Werner H. Schmidt); for Aristotle, interpretation means the semantic dimension of the noun, of the verb, of the sentence, in a word, of the discourse as such. Nevertheless, we may retain from Aristotle the idea that interpretation is interpretation *by* language before being interpretation *on* language.

The closest author which we may invoke for founding our concept of "objective" interpretation is Charles Saunders Peirce. According to Peirce, the relation of a "sign" to an "object" is such that another relation, that of a series of interpretants to the "signs" can graft itself onto the first. What is important for us here is that the relation of sign to interpretant is an open relation, in the sense that there is always another interpretation capable of mediating the first relation. This triangular relation between object, sign and interpretant, with the character of openness of the series of interpretants provides us with the best model for rebuilding our initial concept of interpretation. Indeed, it is with a great deal of caution that one should apply Peirce's concept of interpretant to the interpretation of texts. This interpretant is an interpretant of signs, whereas our interpretation is an interpretation of utterances, of sentences, of discourse. Nevertheless this extension of Peirce's interpretant to texts is neither more nor less analogical than the transfer, with the structuralists, of the organized laws of unities from a level inferior to the sentence to unities of an equal or superior order than the sentence. In the case of structuralism, it is the phonological structure of language which serves as model for coding the structures of higher level. In our case, it is a characteristic of lexical unities—the triangular relation between object, sign and interpretant—which is carried over to the order of utterance and texts. If, therefore, one is perfectly aware of the analogical character of the transposition, it can be said: the open series of interpretants which grafts itself onto the relation of a sign to an object brings to light a triangular relation, object-sign-interpretant, which can serve as a model for another triangle at the level of the text. The sign is the depth-semantics, unearthed by structural analysis, and the series of interpretants is the chain of interpretation produced by the interpretative community and incorporated into the dynamics of the text. In this chain the first interpretants serve as a tradition for the last interpretants which constitute the interpretation in the true sense of the term.

Enlightened in this way by the Aristotelian insight of interpretation and above all, by Peirce's concept of interpretant, we are in a position to "depsychologize" as much as possible our action of interpretation and to tie it up with the process which is at work in the text. As a result, for the exegete to interpret is to place himself in the direction initiated by this interpretative relation included in the text. The idea of interpretation, understood as appropriation, is not for all that eliminated; it is only postponed until the end of the process. It is the other end of what we have called the *hermeneutical arch*: it is the last pillar of the bridge, the anchor of the arch in the soil of lived experience. But the entire theory of hermeneutics consists in mediating the interpretation as appropriation by the series of interpretants which belong to the work of the text on itself. The appropriation poses then its arbitrariness to the degree that it is the recovery of what is at work, in labor, in the text. What the reader says is a re-saying which reenacts what the text says by itself.

At the end of this investigation it appears that reading is that concrete act in which the destiny of the text is accomplished. It is at the very heart of reading that explanation and interpretation are independently opposed and reconciled.

INTRODUCTION TO PERRIN'S "HISTORICAL CRITICISM, LITERARY CRITICISM, AND HERMENEUTICS"

New Testament scholarship has made enormous contributions to hermeneutical discussion. Schleiermacher, Bultmann, and many other central figures of hermeneutical thought have approached the problem of interpretation as scholars and exegetes of the New Testament. Indeed, the New Testament scholar receives a tradition of hermeneutical reflection with roots in the New Testament itself. The New Testament, after all, presents itself as an interpretation of the "Old" Testament. Its earliest documents are interpretations of the image of Jesus formulated by the faith experiences of the primitive communities. Later texts in the canon self-consciously interpret earlier texts (for example, Matthew and Luke interpret Mark). New Testament scholarship is permeated with hermeneutics. No wonder the discussion of hermeneutics has reached an extraordinarily sophisticated level among New Testament scholars, since so much attention has been given to the canonical texts of the Christian communities.

Norman Perrin is one of the most interesting of the New Testament scholars to make explicit contributions to hermeneutical inquiry in the last two decades. His essay is particularly well suited for this collection. Exemplary in its clarity, Perrin's essay claims that in dealing with hermeneutical issues, "It is always more helpful to discuss the interpretation of specific texts than it is to discuss general principles, although of course the two necessarily go hand in hand."[1] His texts, the parables of Jesus and the Gospel of Mark, are especially productive of hermeneutical insight.

A major influence on New Testament scholarship in the United States, Perrin was neither born nor educated in this country. English by birth and upbringing, Perrin was twenty years old when he was called to defend his country in the Second World War. He served in the Royal Air Force from 1940 to 1945. After the war he studied theology at Manchester University (B.A., 1949) and London University (B.D., 1952). He focused on the Greek New Testament and apocryphal studies for his master's in theology degree at London (1956). Perrin then went to the University of Gottingen in Germany, where he studied with Joachim Jeremias. The doctorate was conferred in 1959. Perrin embarked on an academic career in the United

---

[1] Norman Perrin, "Historical Criticism, Literary Criticism, and Hermeneutics," p. 253 below.

States, first at Emory University (1959–1964) and then at the University of Chicago Divinity School, where he worked until his death in 1976.

Norman Perrin's hermeneutical inquiry is closely connected with his interest in New Testament theology. Perrin was sympathetic to scholarly studies of the New Testament conducted on purely historical, literary, and other nontheological grounds; his work contributes to a general history of the religion of early Christianity. But he also was convinced that the formulation of a theology of the New Testament was a crucial need for the Christian communities. Highly aware of the diversity of theological expressions in the New Testament, he sought a basis from which to talk about *a* theology of the New Testament. How did Norman Perrin resolve the problem of the one and the many, that is, the unity amidst the differences of New Testament texts? And how did his thought about this question shape the hermeneutical project in "Historical Criticism, Literary Criticism, and Hermeneutics"? These are the questions I want briefly to address by way of introducing Perrin's essay.

Joachim Jeremias, Perrin's great teacher, argued that New Testament theology can be unified around the picture of the historical Jesus as reconstructed by historical criticism of texts. Historical criticism was Perrin's intellectual starting point, *die Heimat* from which he would wander. The following essay by Perrin shows that he would always include historical criticism in his scholarly activity and grant it an important place. But as fundamental a role as historical criticism plays for Perrin, by no means did he assign to it the whole task of the scholarly reading of New Testament texts.

On the other end of the theological spectrum from Jeremias was Rudolf Bultmann. From the beginning, Perrin was impressed by Bultmann's argument for including the irreducibly hermeneutical dimension of New Testament interpretation and the need to hear what claim the text now makes on its hearers. Bultmann argued that the unifying factor in the New Testament was not the historical Jesus but the kerygma of the early Church. The historical Jesus is a presupposition of New Testament theology, not an element within it. The image of Jesus in the New Testament is always the "faith image" of Christ, experienced as risen into the preaching of the early Church. The presence of Christ in the preaching and hearing of Jesus' crucifixion and resurrection is what unifies the New Testament.

Norman Perrin's work toward a theology of the New Testament mediates between Jeremias and Bultmann. Perrin carries on the intentions of Bultmann's New Testament hermeneutics. But he does so by criticizing some shortcomings in Bultmann's program and working out alternative proposals. Perrin builds on Bultmann's work by rethinking Bultmannian scholarship. In so doing, he preserves a significant place for historical criticism, which is linked with hermeneutics by way of literary criticism. Perrin thus constructs his program with the help of the best elements of both Jeremias's historical criticism and Bultmann's hermeneutics. To these twin sources, he adds a literary critical approach. The result is a balanced method for reading texts that can contribute to a New Testament theology. Neither the author's intention/audience's reception nor the claim the text now makes on its readers is neglected or given undue importance. Let me attempt to be more specific about how Perrin moves from historical criticism to hermeneutics by way of literary criticism.

In his Göttingen dissertation, which was published in 1963 as *The Kingdom of God in the Teaching of Jesus*, Perrin reveals his early interest in the historical Jesus as a possible unifying factor for a New Testament theology. Under the training of Jeremias, Perrin had faith in the ability of the critic to penetrate through added layers of text to the core of the New Testament. There, at the core, stands the memory image of the historical Jesus. Given the advances of form criticism (*Formgeschichte*) after World War I, scholarship possessed abundant resources for reconstructing the historical Jesus. Form criticism is concerned with identifying the standard literary forms in the New Testament writings, reconstructing the cultural context (*Sitz im Leben*) in which the forms functioned to communicate a message, and tracing the history of the transmission of traditional forms. Through form criticism, Jeremias had turned up striking results in investigating the parables of Jesus. Jeremias seemed to provide evidence that it is possible to get back to the message of Jesus; Perrin took careful note of Jeremias's arguments.

But alongside his interest in the historical Jesus and approval of the tools of historical criticism, another interest shows itself in Perrin's writings. In *Rediscovering the Teachings of Jesus* (1967), Perrin shifted his assessment of the unifying factor in New Testament texts. Under the influence of Bultmann and his school, Perrin became persuaded that none of the New Testament texts simply preserve the image of the historical Jesus. In every case, the Jesus of the New Testament is interpreted through the faith experience of a Christian community. Later, Perrin put it like this:

> At the beginning of the stream of tradition that eventually forms the basis for the Gospels there stands the historical Jesus, his message and his ministry, the impact he made on his followers, and the memories of him that lived on after his death. With the coming of belief in his resurrection and the growing sense of his presence through his spirit in the experience of the believer and in the life of the believing community, the memory image of Jesus becomes transformed into the faith or perspectival image, an image in which the memory of the historical Jesus plays only a part, however important that part may be.[2]

Bultmann was right that the direct concern of New Testament theology is the "faith-image of Jesus," not the memory image. Perrin came to agree

[2]Norman Perrin, "Jesus and the Theology of the New Testament," *The Journal of Religion* 64 (October 1984): 418.

with Bultmann that the historical Jesus is the presupposition for New Testament theology, not an element within it.

Nonetheless, Perrin held that in many cases, especially in some of Jesus' parables of the Kingdom of God, form criticism can help the scholar retrieve some of the authentic words of Jesus. Perrin used the criteria of dissimilarity (with Jewish and Hellenistic sources), coherence, and multiple attestation to isolate Jesus' own words. Moreover, he postulated a coherence between the message of Jesus and the kerygma of the early church. So Perrin retained a more important role for historical criticism than did Bultmann, who argued on theological grounds that any form of the quest for the historical Jesus was ill advised: Bultmann held that the historical quest is a disguised form of salvation by works and not faith![3]

Perrin expanded his work from historical criticism to literary criticism by way of the insights of redaction criticism. Redaction criticism focuses on how traditional materials, identified through form criticism, were edited by the final author of a text and what theological interest directed the editing decisions. In this phase of his work, Perrin moved beyond Bultmann, who did not give enough attention to the divergent theological viewpoints represented by the editing of traditional materials in the synoptic Gospels and the literature of emerging Catholicism (as Perrin calls the letters of James, Peter, Jude, Timothy, and Titus). Bultmann was satisfied to deal only with Paul and the Gospel of John in constructing his kerygmatic theology of the New Testament. To Perrin, that limitation seemed arbitrary. Perrin's project was to rethink Bultmann, taking the full range of theological viewpoints into account.

The uncompleted sketch for a theology of the New Testament may be discerned in Perrin's next writings: *The New Testament: An Introduction* (1974), *Jesus and the Language of the Kingdom* (1976), and *The Resurrection According to Matthew, Mark, and Luke* (1977). These works are distinguished by increased concentration on literary forms. Once the editors of traditional materials are understood as constructive authors expressing distinct theological viewpoints, and not merely as neutral transmitters of tradition, then literary critical analysis may fruitfully be brought to bear in the task of determining the theological interests more precisely.

In *Jesus and the Language of the Kingdom,* Perrin focuses on the parabolic form of discourse. When Jesus spoke in parables, everyday narratives functioned metaphorically to shatter expectations and to open new perspectives on life's situations. Jesus likened these occurrences to the Kingdom of God. In Perrin's words, the Kingdom of God functions for Jesus as a "tensive" symbol, a symbol that mediates the reality to which it refers: the reality of the inbreaking of God as Lord of history. In the synoptic Gospels, the parables become allegories; the symbol "Kingdom of God" no

---

[3]See Perrin's reference to this in "Jesus and the Theology of the New Testament," p. 417.

longer functions tensively to mediate the reality in the present, but rather points to a future reality that is not presently mediated by the words. The critique of literary forms makes these differences evident.

In *The Resurrection According to Matthew, Mark, and Luke,* Perrin analyzes the literary form and function of the resurrection narratives within the context of each of the synoptics. The intention is not to inquire about what happened behind the text, but to show how the Gospels differently manifest an understanding of the risen Christ in the structures of the text.

In these later writings, literary criticism provides the link to hermeneutics. For a literary analysis of the texts shows how symbol, metaphor, narrative, and so forth can either point away from themselves to some external referent, or can present the power to which they refer. In the latter instance, something happens between reader and text—a claim is made on the reader. At this point, literary criticism gives way to hermeneutics.

In the following essay, given as a lecture in 1971, we have a concise statement of Perrin's theory of interpreting New Testament texts. It illustrates some of Perrin's characteristic moves and serves as an excellent introduction to his other writings.

HISTORICAL CRITICISM, LITERARY CRITICISM, AND HERMENEUTICS:
THE INTERPRETATION OF THE PARABLES OF JESUS AND THE GOSPEL OF MARK TODAY*
(1971)

Norman Perrin

This paper is intended to be both a discussion of the interpretation of particular texts from the New Testament, the parables of Jesus and the Gospel of Mark, and also a contribution to the general discussion of hermeneutics that is so real an aspect of the study of the humanities today. I speak as a New Testament scholar, but I have tried to take some account of the discussion as it is being carried on by philosophers of language, literary critics, and historians of religion. I am going to address myself to the interpretation of the parables of Jesus and the Gospel of Mark because I believe it is always more helpful to discuss the interpretation of specific texts than it is to discuss general principles, although of course the two necessarily go hand in hand. From all the texts within the New Testament, I have chosen the parables of Jesus and the Gospel of Mark because they are both highly original and very important texts. Moreover, their particular nature and the subsequent history of their interpretation and reinterpretation in the New Testament and in the church are such as to make them particularly good vehicles for a discussion of what the Germans call *das hermeneutische Problem*, the problems necessarily involved in any act of interpretation. Let me begin therefore by saying a word about each of those texts.

In speaking of the parables of Jesus, I intend to speak of the parables as Jesus actually taught them, that is, of the parables of Jesus as reconstructed from the gospels by modern New Testament scholarship. This reconstruction is indeed one of the triumphs of that scholarship, and work upon the parables remains a major preoccupation of contemporary New Testament scholars.[1] As originally delivered by Jesus, they were oral texts—they were remembered rather than written down. But they were of course eventually

---

*This paper was delivered as the Waterman Lecture at the University of Michigan on October 11, 1971.

[1] I have had occasion to review aspects of the work twice in the last ten years: N. Perrin, "The Parables of Jesus as Parables, as Metaphors, and as Aesthetic Objects: A Review Article," *Journal of Religion* 47 (1967): 340–46, and "The Modern Interpretation of the Parables of Jesus and the Problem of Hermeneutics," *Interpretation* 25 (1971): 131–48.

written down, and they were transmitted in the tradition of the church, no doubt both orally and in writing, and finally found their present place in the canonical gospels and in the Coptic gospel of Thomas, a Gnostic document from Nag Hammadi. In the canonical gospels, they have usually been reinterpreted as allegories, and this allegorization continued in the church until modern times. The question of the legitimacy of this reinterpretation will concern us later. The parables of Jesus are artistic creations of a very high order, and they embody a distinct and distinctive vision of reality. They represent probably the highest form of verbal art in the New Testament, and they are religious texts of very great importance indeed.

The Gospel of Mark has been traditionally regarded in the church as an abbreviation of the Gospel of Matthew, but modern scholarship has reversed this, viewing Matthew as an expansion of Mark, and regards Mark as the earliest of the gospels. Indeed, the evangelist Mark has created the genre "gospel," and this is the one unique literary creation of early Christianity. In Judaism and Hellenism one can find letters, homilies, tracts, acts of distinguished men, and apocalypses, but the genre "gospel" is unique to early Christianity, and its creator is the evangelist Mark.[2] The Gospel of Mark is therefore a particularly significant work. Like the parables of Jesus, the Gospel of Mark is drastically reinterpreted within the New Testament itself, in this instance by the evangelists Matthew and Luke, and it has been further reinterpreted in modern times. Both the parables of Jesus and the Gospel of Mark offer us, therefore, a good opportunity to come to grips with the problems and possibilities of interpretation, of hermeneutics.

THE ACT OF INTERPRETATION

It is the fundamental claim of this paper that the act of interpreting a text, any text, including the parables of Jesus and the Gospel of Mark, includes three distinct but interrelated aspects. I designate these aspects of the act of interpretation "historical criticism," "literary criticism," and "hermeneutics." To begin with, we have the fact that the text is a historical entity written (or spoken—in the case of the parables of Jesus and the Gospel of Mark, the distinction is immaterial) by one man, in a distinct set of circumstances, and for a definite purpose, intended to have a particular meaning and understood by its addressees in a particular kind of way. As I am using the term, it is the task of "historical criticism" to recover this information, and in the case of the parables of Jesus and the Gospel of Mark this has in fact been done. Then we have the further fact that the text as a text

---

[2]James M. Robinson and Helmut Koester in their book *Trajectories through Early Christianity* (Philadelphia: Fortress Press, 1971) are of the opinion that both the evangelists Mark and John came independently to the genre "gospel" in response to forces at work in the tradition. I find this hard to accept for reasons indicated in an extended review of this book in *Interpretation* 26 (1972): 212–15.

takes on a life and vitality of its own, independent of the historical circumstances of its creation. It is interpreted and reinterpreted in any number of
new and different situations, and therefore takes on new and different
meanings and is understood in new and different ways. But even here, there
are rules to the game. A text has a given form, and this form functions in one
way and not another. A text is written in a certain kind of language, and this
language has a certain force and not another. A text may be and indeed is
open-ended, but it is not inchoate. Its form and language are in no small way
determinative of the manner in which it may be understood and interpreted.
It is this aspect of the act of interpreting the text which I am designating
"literary criticism." Then, finally, we have the fact that a text is read by a
given individual and understood in a certain dynamic relationship between
the text and the individual reader that I am designating "hermeneutics."

Any given text then must be considered from these three standpoints. It
must be considered from the standpoint of historical criticism, as a text
intended to say something and saying something to its first readers or
hearers. We must respect the act of authorship and the intent of the author,
as we must also respect the understanding of a text reached by its intended
readers or hearers. To do anything less than this is to commit an act of rape
on the text. But at the same time, we must admit that something happens
when a text is committed to writing and hence broadcast to the world for
anyone to read who can master the language in which it is written. It is now
no longer a private communication with its potentiality for meaning limited
to the intent of the author and the understanding of its intended reader. It
now exists in its own right, essentially independent of the original author
and intended reader, and its potentiality for meaning is limited only by the
function of its form and its language. In practice, of course, its potentiality for
meaning is not even limited in that way, but it is an argument of this paper
that it should be so limited. Even with independently existing literary
objects, there is a difference between exegesis and eisegesis! Finally, a text
is read and something happens, or does not happen, between the text and
the reader. This is the most difficult area to explore, and yet we must attempt
to explore it. At this point in the discussion, a well-known New Testament
scholar with a special interest in hermeneutics, Ernst Fuchs of Marburg,
normally reverts to his native Schwabian dialect and tells a story about a cow
licking a calf! The French philosopher with a special concern for hermeneutics, Paul Ricoeur, speaks of a "second naiveté." As is well known, that
greatest of modern New Testament scholars, Rudolf Bultmann, thinks
essentially in terms of a dialogue between text and readers, a dialogue
determined on the one hand by the "preunderstanding" (*Vorverständnis*)
which the reader brings to the text and, on the other hand, by the kind of
questions which the text is designed to answer. All are attempting to do
justice to the fact that a text only has meaning when it has meaning for some

readers, when, as I have put it, "something happens" between the text and the reader.

We must therefore concern ourselves with historical criticism, literary criticism, and hermeneutics, and I will now develop this theme by means of a consideration of the parables of Jesus and the Gospel of Mark from each of these standpoints.

HISTORICAL CRITICISM OF THE PARABLES OF JESUS AND THE GOSPEL OF MARK[3]

The parables of Jesus were directed to a specific situation, the situation of men and women confronted by the imminence of the irruption of God into their world to destroy and renew. In this situation, the parables exhort them to have confidence in God's future (the Sower), to respond to the challenge of the imminence of God's action in terms of the reality of their everyday life (the Good Samaritan), to recognize the extraordinary nature of their present situation (the Unjust Steward), and to recognize that the one overpowering reality is the reality of God's love (the Prodigal Son). This was done by means of a particular literary form, the parable. In a parable, two things are set side by side in a comparison: in the case of the narrative parables of Jesus, the situation of the central character in the story, on the one hand, and the situation of a man before the imminent irruption of God into the world's history, on the other. So far, so good. The central thrust of the meaning of the parables of Jesus in their original historical situation has been thoroughly established by modern historical critical scholarship (in this instance particularly, the work of my own teacher, Joachim Jeremias), and there are no serious doubts about the validity of this work. But then the question is not that of the validity of the work of historical critical scholarship, but of its significance for hermeneutics.

The Gospel of Mark was directed to a group of Christians who were living in an intense state of apocalyptic expectation brought on in part by the

---

[3]Throughout the paper, I shall be making a series of assertions about the parables of Jesus and the Gospel of Mark from the standpoint of historical criticism which I shall not stay to argue or justify. As far as the parables are concerned, the justification can be found in modern work on the parables, to which I have made some contribution in my *Rediscovering the Teachings of Jesus* (New York: Harper and Row, 1967) and which I reviewed and interpreted in the articles mentioned in n. 1 above. As far as the Gospel of Mark is concerned, the justification comes from the intensive work on the gospel that my students and I have been doing for the past five years or so: Vernon Robbins, "The Christology of Mark" (dissertation, University of Chicago, 1969); Werner Kelber, "Kingdom and Parousia in the Gospel of Mark" (dissertation, University of Chicago, 1970); John Donahue, "The Trial Narrative in the Gospel of Mark" (University of Chicago dissertation nearing completion); and N. Perrin, "The Christology of Mark: A Study in Methodology," *Journal of Religion* 51 (1971): 173–87, and a manuscript nearing completion, *Towards the Interpretation of the Gospel of Mark*, to be published by SCM Press in their series Studies in Biblical Theology.

Jewish war and the destruction of Jerusalem. Unfortunately, they had accepted a false Christology which paid attention only to the aspects of triumph and glory of Jesus Christ, the Son of God, and this had led them to a false expectation with regard to the nature of Christian discipleship in the interim period between the Passion of Jesus and his coming as Son of Man. The evangelist Mark challenges them to recognize that Jesus as Son of God and Son of Man had to go through suffering to triumph and glory, and that as Christians they will have to follow Jesus in such a way that the disciples represent his readers and their false understanding of Christology and discipleship, while the true understanding is here on the lips of Jesus. So Jesus addresses Mark's readers directly out of the narrative, and they and their concerns are represented directly in the narrative. This is possible because for Mark the time of Jesus and the time of himself and his readers is one and the same time. In many respects the gospel is essentially an apocalypse, and in typical apocalyptic fashion the evangelist sees himself and his readers caught up in a divine-human drama which began with the mission of John the Baptist and will shortly reach its climax with the return of Jesus on the clouds of heaven as Son of Man. All this is one and the same drama, all this is one and the same time. I am stressing this point about the fact that for Mark the time of Jesus and the time of himself and his readers are one and the same time because this helps us to grasp the essence of the Gospel of Mark and at the same time prepares us to recognize how radically the evangelists Matthew and Luke reinterpret the Gospel of Mark.

Such then, all too briefly presented, is a contemporary historical critical understanding of the Parables of Jesus and the Gospel of Mark. In order to obviate any possibility of misunderstanding, let me pause for a moment to point out that in the context of a discussion of hermeneutics it does not matter whether the historical critical understanding of these texts which I have presented is accurate in all its details. I believe it is, and in dialogue with my colleagues in New Testament scholarship I would be prepared to produce evidence and arguments for everything I have said. But in a general discussion of hermeneutics, the important thing is not how correct a particular historical critical understanding of the parables of Jesus or the Gospel of Mark is, but how significant any reputable historical critical understanding of these texts is to their interpretation in the present. To this point I shall return; in the meantime, let us consider the parables of Jesus and the Gospel of Mark as texts with an ongoing life of their own.

LITERARY CRITICISM OF THE PARABLES OF JESUS AND THE GOSPEL OF MARK

One of the striking things about the parables of Jesus is that they were almost immediately and totally misunderstood; they were treated as allegories and not as parables. Jesus himself took vivid pictures from the life and circumstances of the people he was addressing and then by acts of comparison drew lessons from them with regard to the activity of God in the world. Even today, the pictures are so vivid that the parables make an immediate impact upon anyone for whom the circumstances depicted are realistic. The Good Samaritan, for example, has an immediate impact upon anyone who lives in any "inner city"—whereas the Parable of the Sower has surely lost its point for a farmer who operates with tractors, fertilizers, and insecticides! An allegory, on the other hand, is quite different. Now what matters is not the realism of the story but the key to identifying the quite arbitrary references. So, for example, the Pauline allegory of the root and the branches in Romans, chapter 11, makes perfect sense in terms of the relationship between Jews and Gentiles in the purpose of God as Paul understands it, however disastrous the agricultural process actually described might be to any owners of an olive orchard who tried it!

The fact is that to allegorize a parable is not only to lose the original point which the parabolist Jesus intended to make but also to misunderstand the essential nature of the parable as a parable. Now in my view it is the combination of these things that matters. If a text exists as a text with an ongoing life of its own, then subsequent generations of readers cannot be faulted for drawing from that text meanings which its author did not in fact intend. But on the other hand, a text which has an ongoing life of its own has also a distinctive form which the literary critic can recognize, and that form functions in one way and not another—in this instance, as parable and not as allegory—and this fact surely raises a new point. A subsequent reader may be able to understand a text better than the author himself, but is that understanding valid if it does violence to the form and function of the text itself as a literary critic would understand it? Is an allegorization of a parable of Jesus ever valid? The answer is no, it is not. It is not, not because it reads from the text meanings which the author Jesus did not intend—that is the potential fate of any text broadcast to the world—but because it does violence to the form and function of the text as a text; in the jargon of the scholarly discipline from which I come, because it is eisegesis and not exegesis.

I regard this point as extremely important, indeed as crucial. A text is open-ended, capable of many different interpretations in different situations, and the original intent of the author, the original meaning the author gave to the text, is by no means determinative of the possibilities for future interpretation. So far, so good. But when we add to the intent of the author the factor of the form and function of the text *as a text*, then it seems to me we have a different ball game. The parables of Jesus are open-ended and may indeed be interpreted in ever-new ways in ever-new situations, but the moment the interpreter crosses the line from parable to allegory, the interpretation has become invalid, not because it does violence to the intent of Jesus but because it does violence to the integrity of the text as a text. Let me add, therefore, that I welcome the interpretation of the parables of Jesus by Dan Otto Via, Jr., in terms of movement of plot, role of the protagonist, disclosure scene, and so on, precisely because this interpretation takes the text seriously as a text. As my published reviews of, and reflections upon,[4] his work indicate, I have reservations about some aspects of his interpretation, but that he has taken the interpretation of the parables of Jesus a significant step beyond the work of the historical critics is a fact of which there can be no doubt.

Now we turn from the parables of Jesus to the Gospel of Mark. In this instance, what was essentially an apocalypse became a foundation myth. Both Matthew and Luke provide the Gospel of Mark with a beginning and an end. Both provide birth stories as a beginning and resurrection (in the case of Luke, resurrection-ascension) stories as an end. Moreover, both provide means whereby the reader may relate to the time of Jesus—which is now no longer the reader's time—Matthew by the Great Commission (Matt. 28:16–20) and the authoritative teaching church, and Luke by the concept of a *Heilsgeschichte* wherein his readers live in an epoch parallel to and related to the time of Jesus, but not the same time as the time of Jesus.[5] Here we are at a point of very real significance. For Mark, who is in this sense essentially an apocalypticist, the time of Jesus and the time of himself and his readers are one and the same time, whereas for Matthew and Luke the time of Jesus has become a sacred time to which they and their readers must relate. The apocalypse has become a foundation myth.

I want to stress the fact that I am using the term "myth" as Mircea Eliade uses it, to denote the story of how something came into being. "Myth narrates a sacred history: it relates an event that took place in primordial time, the fabled time of the 'beginnings.' Myth . . . is always an account of a 'creation'; it relates how something was produced, began to be."[6] When I

---

[4]Dan O. Via, Jr., *The Parables: Their Literary and Existential Dimension* (Philadelphia: Fortress Press, 1967); reviewed by me in *Interpretation* 21 (1967): 465–69. See, further, the two articles mentioned in n. 1 above.

[5]Here I am simply relying upon recent work on the gospels of Matthew and Luke, especially that of Günther Bornkamm and his pupils in the case of Matthew and of Hans Conzelmann in the case of Luke-Acts. Conzelmann's work on Luke-Acts can be strengthened by observing certain literary factors. The Gospel of Luke and Acts of the apostles are made strictly parallel in their beginnings in that the baptism of Jesus is reinterpreted as a descent of the Spirit and the descent of the Spirit at Pentecost as a baptism (Luke 3:21–22; Acts 1:5). (I owe the observation that Pentecost is a baptism to my former student Werner Kelber). Further, both the gospel and Acts signal their end by means of a mental resolve on the part of the chief protagonist—Jesus in Luke 9:51 and Paul in Acts 19:21—both resolves being followed by a travel narrative which ends in Jerusalem and Rome, respectively. These literary features (and there are many others) testify to the deliberate parallelism of the time of Jesus to the time of the readers of Luke-Acts.

[6]M. Eliade, *Encyclopaedia Britannica* (1968), s.v. "myth."

describe the Gospel of Mark as a foundation myth, I intend to call attention to the fact that the story narrated is the story of the time of Jesus now seen as sacred time, the story of the ministry of Jesus now seen as the event in relationship to which Christian reality is constituted, the story of Jesus wherein he is viewed as Lord and as Christ, as the *fons et origo* of Christian faith. As a foundation myth, the Gospel of Mark separates this sacred time from the time of the reader, and a means now has to be provided whereby the reader can relate to the sacred time. A myth that relates the sacred time of origins has to be accompanied by a ritual by means of which it becomes possible for the hearer or reader to relate to that time. In fact, both Matthew and Luke in interpreting the Gospel of Mark as a foundation myth do provide their readers with the equivalent of a ritual, a point I shall develop in my next section.

In its way, this reinterpretation of the Gospel of Mark by the evangelists Matthew and Luke is as drastic as the church's allegorization of the parables of Jesus. But there is also a difference in that the allegorization of the parables does violence to their nature as texts—as parables—whereas the transformation of the Gospel of Mark into a foundation myth does not do violence to its nature as a text. As a text, the Gospel of Mark is essentially unstable because there is real conflict between its form and its purpose. Its form is that of realistic narrative, and yet its purpose is essentially apocalyptic. But apocalyptic is most naturally expressed in direct discourse, as in the case of I Thessalonians or Mark, chapter 13, or in nonrealistic narrative, as in the case of the apocalypse of John, the Book of Revelation. The realistic narrative of the Gospel of Mark moves quite naturally in a different direction, that of a story by which the readers are affected and into which they are caught up, but from which they are separated in time. The point is that the allegorization of the parables of Jesus does violence to their nature as texts, whereas the interpretation of the Gospel of Mark by the evangelists Matthew and Luke as foundation myth does no such violence to it as a text.

If this point is valid, then I have established a very real hermeneutical principle, namely, that although the reader may understand a text better than the author, he may not do violence to its nature as a text. To stay with the Gospel of Mark, it is well known that in the nineteenth century this gospel was further reinterpreted, by means of the "Markan hypothesis," as essentially a chronicle of the ministry of Jesus. Innumerable "Lives of Jesus" have been built upon this foundation. However, this view of the gospel has to be rejected, because it does violence both to the intent of the author *and* to the essential nature of the text as a text. The Gospel of Mark may be an apocalypse or a foundation myth, but it is not a chronicle of the ministry of Jesus. From the standpoint of interpretation theory, an interpretation of a text may well go beyond anything the author intended, but it may not do violence to the nature of the text as a text.

HERMENEUTICS

We now come to the crux of the matter. The tools of the disciplines of historical criticism and literary criticism can after all be acquired by careful study and applied by a reasonable exercise of intelligence and will. But then there always comes the final moment when a reader is confronted by a text and responds to it: the hermeneutical moment. Professor Ricoeur has described this moment well, as the second, post-critical, naiveté, in his work *Freud and Philosophy*; and in his more recent paper, as yet unpublished, "Interpretation Theory," (now published as a small book by that title—Ed.) he speaks of the world projected in front of the text which the reader appropriates. Let us think of this matter a little more closely with regard specifically to the parables of Jesus and the Gospel of Mark.

The parables of Jesus are highly personal texts. By means of metaphor and of metaphor extended in narrative, they express the vision of reality of their author, Jesus. Now of course they are not alone in this. Many texts are expressive of their author's vision of reality—the plays of Jean-Paul Sartre, for example, or of Tennessee Williams, and the novels of Albert Camus. Nor is this expression of reality limited to verbal texts. Bix Beiderbeck's cornet playing in "Royal Garden Blues" says something abut the reality of life in Chicago in the 1920's, or Louis Armstrong in "Muskrat Ramble" says something about the American Negro in New Orleans. Obviously, also, Picasso's *Guernica* dramatically expresses the reality of the Spanish Civil War as Picasso himself experienced it, just as the prints and paintings of William Hogarth say something ferocious about the London of the eighteenth century. In all of these instances, and the many, many more that could be quoted, the reader-hearer-viewer is being confronted not only by a vision of reality, but by a *particular* vision of reality. One could, after all, find views of London in the eighteenth century decidedly different from those of William Hogarth, as one must remember that from the 1920's comes not only the jazz of Bix Beiderbeck and Louis Armstrong but also the "symphonic jazz" of Paul Whiteman! The point is that there are certain expressions of the reality of life in the world—written, oral, or visual—that are so highly personal that one cannot contemplate them except in dialogue with their creator. The parables of Jesus are like this. One can read the parable of the Prodigal Son in terms of the realities of economic life in first-century Palestine and the opportunities of the Diaspora. One can discuss the agricultural procedures of the Sower; and the Germans are very fond of telling a story about the American preacher who claimed that although the Good Samaritan bound up the wounds of the man on the Jericho road, the Better Samaritan organized a police patrol of the road, and the Best Samaritan went and worked with juvenile delinquents in Jericho! But when all else is done and said, once cannot read the Prodigal Son without realizing that someone once believed that the extravagant welcome to the prodigal was indicative of the reality of the world as it may be experienced; as one cannot read the Good Samaritan without remembering that its author did in fact die for the things he was trying to express. In the same way, I cannot hear Beiderbeck's cornet without realizing that he did not survive the circumstances that called forth his music, nor Armstrong's without the glad realization that he did. This may be romanticism, but it is also reality. There are some artistic creations that are so intensely personal that they cannot be separated from the vision of reality which gave them birth. Let me pose a hypothetical question. Is it not possible that some day after Jean-Paul Sartre dies, one might discover a hitherto unpublished play of his and know immediately that it was genuine, not only because of the language and style, but also because of the unique vision of reality that it breathed?

The question is whether there can in fact be a general theory of interpretation, a general hermeneutics. Are texts not always particular, written in a certain kind of language, belonging to a peculiar genre, reflective or nonreflective of the vision of the author? Since I have been discussing intensely personal texts, let me remind you of the story of Queen Victoria, who so admired Lewis Carroll's *Alice in Wonderland* that she gave orders that the author's next work be made immediately available to her. She received a mathematical treatise!

The point is surely that a text is a text is a text, and that the actual interpretative method, the hermeneutics, used in the case of one text may not always be applicable to another. Let us pursue this matter further in the case of our second text, the Gospel of Mark. In the Gospel of Mark there is one intensely personal element, the use of Son of Man. I believe that I may claim that I have shown in various publications[7] that the particular use of Son of Man in Mark—present authority, necessary suffering, future glory—is *Markan*, that it represents the evangelist Mark's own vision of the reality of Christology and of Christian discipleship in the world. In this respect, the Gospel of Mark is as intensely personal a text as are the parables of Jesus. Moreover, no small amount of the impact of the Gospel of Mark upon subsequent generations of readers was due to the fact that he chose to express a basic aspect of his message by means of the archaic and evocative symbol "Son of Man." At the same time, however, as I noted above in the section on literary criticism, the Gospel of Mark did not maintain its intensely personal character. It was properly and appropriately reinterpreted by the evangelists Matthew and Luke—the apocalypse became a foundation myth—whereas, by contrast, the parables of Jesus were improperly and inappropriately reinterpreted as allegories. But the hermeneutics involved in the case of a foundation myth are quite different from those involved in the case of an apocalypse.

---

[7]N. Perrin, "The Creative Use of Son of Man Traditions by Mark," *Union Seminary Quarterly Review* 23 (1965): 357–65, and "The Christology of Mark" (n. 3 above).

In the case of an apocalypse, the reader is directly involved in the narrative: the drama that is being related is one in which he is directly involved, it leads directly into his own time, it will shortly reach a climax in which he will be directly involved. Now, however unconsciously, the evangelist Mark appreciated this fact and so he addresses his readers directly out of his narrative. The Jesus of the teaching on discipleship which follows each of the passion predictions (8:31; 9:31; 10:33–34) is addressing Mark's readers directly, as is the Jesus who interprets the confession of himself as "Christ" or "Son of God" by a use of "Son of Man" at Caesarea Philippi and in the trial before the Sanhedrin and as is the Jesus of the apocalyptic discourse in chapter 13. Indeed, there are at least three places in which Mark the evangelist addresses his readers directly out of his text: Mark 2:10, where the "you" who "may know" are Mark's readers; 9:9b, where Mark's readers are given to understand their place in the drama; and the most obvious one, 13:16.

Mark increases the involvement of his readers in his text by a number of literary devices, some no doubt unconscious and others quite deliberate. There is, for example, the realism, the mimetic quality of his narrative. The literary critic Eric Auerbach called attention to this in his well-known *Mimesis* and ascribed it to the element of personal (Petrine) reminiscence in the narratives. Well, he was wrong about the cause (the form and redaction critics have shown that no single narrative in Mark is Petrine reminiscence) but not about the effect. The narratives of Mark are realistic, and as realistic narratives they necessarily catch the reader up into the story they narrate. Here, unconscious literary artistry and conscious literary purpose go hand in hand to make the Gospel of Mark an extraordinarily effective text. A conscious literary device is the depiction of the relationship between Jesus and Peter. In the gospel, Peter is the representative Christian disciple; he follows Jesus at once (1:18, with its Markan *euthus*, "immediately"), confesses him correctly and yet misunderstands the meaning of the confession (8:27–33), finally breaks down in the courtyard in a scene Aristotle would have recognized as cathartic, and in a postscript is restored to his proper status as a disciple, as Mark hopes his readers will be (16:7). Another conscious literary device is that of ending every major section of the gospel on a note which looks toward the Passion of Jesus: 3:6, the plot to destroy Jesus; 6:6a, the rejection of Jesus by "his own"; 8:27, the misunderstanding of the disciples, which Mark sees as a rejection leading inevitably to the Passion; 10:45, the ransom saying; and 12:44, the widow's sacrifice of her "all."

All of this has important hermeneutical consequences. It suggests at the very least that we should approach the Gospel of Mark as a drama in which we personally are involved, that we should attempt to hear the words on the lips of Jesus as words addressed directly to us, that we should ask seriously how far the story of Peter in the gospel is the story of Everyman and indeed our own story, and so on. All of this and more is a natural consequence of our accepting the Gospel of Mark as an apocalypse.

But at the hands of Matthew and Luke, the apocalypse becomes a foundation myth, and this fact also has important hermeneutical consequences. Now we have to consider the ritual, the means whereby the reader relates to the sacred time of the myth. Matthew provides for this with his concept of the authoritative teaching function of the church, as deliberately epitomized in the Great Commission. So the careful exegesis of the gospel by a recognized authority in terms of its meaning for faith and morals, the kind of treatment the Gospel of Matthew has in fact received during the long history of the church, is a wholly legitimate hermeneutic. This is not only what the evangelist intended; it is also inherent in the literary form and indeed in the very language he uses. It is no accident that the Gospel of Matthew became the "church's book" par excellence. Luke, on the other hand, provides his "ritual" by structuring a careful parallelism between the time of Jesus and the time of the reader. Then he proceeds to make Jesus a paradigm of Christian piety—going to the synagogue "as his custom was," praying at the great crises of his life and being helped thereby, achieving a final triumph through his sufferings, and so on—and to underscore this by drawing careful parallels between Jesus and the leaders of the church—for example, as the parallels between the passion-ascension of Jesus and the passion-implicit ascension of Stephen—with whom Luke's readers can identify. In a sense, Luke writes the first homiletically conceived life of Jesus, and it is no accident that his gospel did in fact become the basis for the lives of Jesus beyond the counting. The kind of hermeneutics involved in a life of Jesus is a direct development from the literary form and language which Luke uses.

I have spoken only briefly of Matthew and Luke because I want to do no more than indicate the kind of hermeneutical consequences that I see as necessarily involved in their reinterpretation of the Gospel of Mark. Let me now return, in conclusion, to the parables of Jesus and the Gospel of Mark.

The parables of Jesus seem to be of such an essential nature, to be such intensely personal texts, that the vision and intent of the author remain most important hermeneutical considerations. To read a parable of Jesus is ultimately to be confronted by Jesus' vision of reality. As an aid to this, we can and we should consider the nature and function of metaphor and of metaphorical language, we can and we should consider such literary critical aspects of the movement of the plot, the function of disclosure scenes, the Unjust Steward as a picaresque rogue, and so on. But ultimately what matters is the vision of reality of the author and the challenge of that vision of reality to ourselves. But then the parables of Jesus are intensely personal texts.

The Gospel of Mark is not so intensely personal a text as are the parables of Jesus, and the author's personal vision of reality is not therefore so important, although of course it still matters that he is concerned to teach a suffering Son of Man Christology and the consequences for Christian discipleship. What matters most from a hermeneutical standpoint in the case of the Gospel of Mark is its actuality as an apocalypse and its potentiality as a foundation myth. Here, I would claim, are to be found the clues for an appropriate method for interpreting the gospel.

It can be seen that my intended contribution to the discussion of hermeneutics, and to the interpretation of the New Testament, consists of two parts. In the first place, I have argued that the act of interpretation of a text, any text, involves the three aspects I have somewhat arbitrarily designated "historical criticism," "literary criticism," and "hermeneutics." Then, in the second place, I have sought to demonstrate by a consideration of the parables of Jesus and the Gospel of Mark that the emphasis will be placed on different aspects of the act of interpretation in accordance with the actual and specific nature of the text concerned.

INTRODUCTION TO SCHARLEMANN'S
"BEING 'AS NOT'"

It is appropriate that this collection of essays concerned with interpreting texts should conclude with a representative publication of a thinker currently practicing his craft in the United States. Of the many theologians and historians of religion who reflect on what it means to interpret texts, Robert P. Scharlemann stands out as exceptional. One test of the lasting value of his writing is the reward gained from rereadings. The arguments are dense; the interconnection of thought is complex. But the reader will be amply rewarded for his or her efforts. Like any serious thinker, Scharlemann's thought says something original about the way we view the past, present, and future. His work offers profound insight into the tensions and interconnections within the systems of theological and philosophical thought from times past; he carefully assigns present meaning to the theological and philosophical terms crucial to his arguments; and he opens suggestive lines of thought and questions for future theological inquiry.

Robert P. Scharlemann was born in Minnesota in 1929. Educated at Concordia College through the B.A. and B.D. degrees, he went to Germany for his advanced training and received the doctorate in theology in 1957 from the University of Heidelberg. After serving two years as instructor of philosophy at Valparaiso University, in 1963 he was appointed assistant professor of theology at the Graduate School of Religion at the University of Southern California. In 1966, Scharlemann accepted an offer to become professor of theology at the University of Iowa's School of Religion. He remained there until 1981, when he became Commonwealth Professor of Religion at the University of Virginia. As of this moment, he continues to teach and write theology at Virginia.

Scharlemann's first works were interpretations of some especially significant theological thinkers within the Western tradition. But as one may expect from a creative thinker, his interpretations contain a constructive dimension. While respecting historical contexts and intentions in their integrity as expressions of meaning, he brings thinkers of the past into the present through systematic interpretations. And he builds from these proposals a foundation for constructive work of his own in systematic theology.

Scharlemann's first book, *Thomas Aquinas and John Gerhard*, analyzes not only what each of the classic theologians said, but also what they saw through their distinctive systematic forms. His second book, *Reflection and*

Doubt in the Thought of Paul Tillich, placed Tillich's theology in the context of the conflict between idealism (which posits a dimension within the human spiritual life where the division between divine and human is overcome) and historical criticism (which posits the sheer objectivity and temporal distance of the past). But the book is by no means simply a placement of Tillich in the history of ideas. Scharlemann not only showed how Tillich solved the theological problem he inherited, he also proposed constructive changes in Tillich's system that extend the theological discussion beyond Tillich's own vision.[1]

Most impressive, however, is the more recently published *The Being of God: Theology and the Experience of Truth*. This is Scharlemann's first sustained reflection on a single question in theology from the standpoint of his own postmodern system of theology. Here he addresses the question of truth in theology: Does theological thinking reach the being of God? Or does it think about nothing? Scharlemann approaches his answer to this question methodically. In moving through his analysis of types of thinking, his formulation of the conditions under which theologians must think today, his uncovering of the three traditional meanings of the assertion "God is," and his testing the truth of these assertions, the reader is presented with a tour de force in postmodern theology. Peter Hodgson, in a review essay on *The Being of God*, says, "In my judgment this is the most significant book to appear in philosophical theology for at least a decade."[2] Before considering some of the intentions of the upcoming essay, "Being 'As Not': Overturning the Ontological," let me highlight some of the contents of *The Being of God*, namely, his delineation of types of thinking, conception of the conditions of thinking, analysis of three ideas of God, and testing of the truth of theological language.

Scharlemann is more clear than most in determining kinds of thinking, and I shall begin there: First, there is *prethinking*, immediate and dreamy relatedness of subject to the object in which no distinction is made between the two. Thinking and the being about which "I" think are not clearly distinguished in prethought.

Second, there is *mundane, literal, or objective thinking*. At this level judgments are made about empirical or logical objects. An example is "This is a tree," or "This is identical to that." One mark of objective thinking is the direct presence to sight or mind of the object of thought. With objective thinking, subject and object, thinking and being, are now clearly distinct.

Third, there is *reflective thought*, which doubles back upon the results of objective thinking in order to judge those thoughts. An example is "'This

---

[1]See my introduction to Tillich's "The Meaning and Justification of Religious Symbols" in this volume. A synopsis of Tillich's solution to this conflict is spelled out there.

[2]Peter Hodgson, "Thinking the Being of God: The Recent Work of Robert Scharlemann," *Religious Studies Review* 9 (October 1983): 40.

is a tree' is true," or "Your statement of identity accords with the real
situation." The thinker is now one step removed from the original object of
thought—the tree or the identity relation are now indirectly present. Directly present to mind in reflection is the relation between objective thought
and its object. The subject of thought now sees itself as distinct both from the
object of thought and also from the other subject's thinking of that object.

Fourth, there is *reflexive thought*, reflection that doubles back on itself.
In reflexivity, judgments are made about reflective judgments. It is two steps
removed from the original object and is now focused on the depth of thinking
itself. An example is "It is true to say that 'This is a tree' is true." Present to
mind in this reflexive judgment is the truth about truth, the depth of truth.
Remarkable about reflexivity is the recovery of identity between subject and
object, thinking and being. With reflexive thinking, the activity of thinking
and the object of thinking are one and the same: for when the subject thinks
about thinking, thinking and the being about which it thinks are the same.
Thought is the being that is being thought.

Scharlemann notes that the nineteenth-century speculative idealists,
Fichte, Hegel, and the early Schelling, identified reflexive thinking with the
being of God. They saw the being of God mirrored in the identity of being
and thinking embedded in reflexivity. Thus for speculative idealism, to think
reflexively is to enter into the divine life as it thinks itself. It is to participate
in the being of God.

But Scharlemann refuses to identify theological thinking with reflexive
thinking in the manner of the speculative idealists. To account for theological thinking, thinking the being of God, Scharlemann adds a fifth form of
thinking—*afterthinking*. Afterthinking thinks the reflexive thinking of being
not literally as the being of God, but as a symbol of the being of God.
Theological afterthinking is thinking of our reflexive thinking of being as the
being of God *for our thinking*. To use the language of "Being 'As Not',"
theological thinking sees the reflexive thinking of being as an appearance of
the being of God, in the time when God is not being God. In other words, the
sign of God—the identity of being and thinking in reflexivity—is not literally
God but an appearance of God. Appearances are distortions as well as
disclosures. So also with reflexive thought. It is a sign of the being of God in
our thinking, but it is not identical with God's being.

For Scharlemann, at least two crucial conditions of theological thinking
today are set by the basic principles of historical criticism and by those of the
critique of metaphysics. We have already mentioned historical criticism, but
the focus here is on the principle of historical consciousness: Current
theology must reckon with the recognition that all thinking is historically
situated and thus embedded into a set of contexts—linguistic, biographical,
cultural, ideological, political, and so forth. In addition, any attempt at
theological thinking today must take seriously the crux of Kant's critique of
precritical metaphysics and theology. Traditional theology formed concepts

of supernatural objects that lie beyond possible experience. The soul, the world, and God are three such objects. Precritical theology warranted such concepts on the fact that *we must form the thoughts of soul, world, and God.* What is special about these ideas, the precritical tradition held, is that they are necessary thoughts. Logic demands that we form these ideas; thus we know that objects exist that correspond to these ideas. Kant criticized traditional theology and metaphysics for perpetrating an illusion. In effect, Kant said that even if the ideas of the soul, world, and God are logicallly necessary for thought, a necessity of thought does not demand that there be an object corresponding to them. In Scharlemann's view, theology must accept the Kantian critique as the basic condition of thinking. Theological thinking must be thinking about some reality—God—that enters experience so that theological thinking is always thinking in reference to a dimension of experience.

Scharlemann identifies three ideas of God that are candidates for theological consideration. The reader of the general introduction to this volume will already be familiar with Scharlemann's scheme, because I employed it there in discussing theological hermeneutics. Briefly, the three ideas are these: First, when we say "God is," we can mean there is a supernatural entity that possesses the divine properties of omniscience, omnipotence, and the like. Second, when we say "God is," we can intend to name the one whose essential act is "to be," the one agent of the whole action of being—the one in the being of the many. Third, when we say "God is," we can point to the symbol of God as the place where the being of God is shown or appears.

In testing the truth of the three assertions of "God is," Scharlemann rules the first idea—God as supreme being—to be false. Why? It fails to accept the condition of contemporary theology in the light of Kantian critique of metaphysics. The only warrant for the notion of a supernatural being is a necessity of thought, from which it does not follow that such a being exists. Moreover, even if God were to be established by reflection, in that case reflection would have raised itself above God. But this vitiates the claim that the one proved to exist is God. If God is God, and not some lesser being, God is always judge and not the one judged to be or not to be. Reflective judgment places the standards of reflective judgment above the being of God, thus reducing God to what is not God.

The second idea of God is that of the one in the many. In this case, God is thought as the one whose very being is to be. Here, not a supreme being, but the living unity of being-itself, is thought. This idea, which must be disclosed and cannot be defined, may be judged true if a single event in history shows a double agency—a human agent(s) and a divine agent. Here truth is manifest as an event in which some historical occurrence shows, in addition to itself, the one in the many. Just as a certain performance of a game of tennis might reveal both the many actions of the players, and (if it is a classic performance of the game) what tennis is all about—the being of tennis; so a historical event might show the actions of many and, with and through them, the being of the one who is, or God.

But Scharlemann says that the truth of this second idea is experienced at best ambiguously today. No events today call forth in consensus a theological language to describe them, as certain events described in the Bible seemed to call forth a language of God as hidden agent in the event. In other words, in our current technological world we seem not to require the name of God; nothing happens that demands that we speak about the one and only agent in the universe. In the twentieth century the only events that do seem to rivet our attention and to stay in the memory evoke, if anything, a second language testifying not that "God is" but that "evil is."

The third idea of God—the concrete symbol that shows what it means for God to be God—is both ascertainably true and ascertainably false as well. To say "Jesus shows the being of God" can be measured as true by reflection, if it applies criteria to the experience beneath the expression. The criteria could be embodied in questions such as these two: Does the experience of the symbol overcome the subject-object split? Does the symbol embody what is meant in the idea of God? If so, we see truth. But reflection can also judge the symbol to be false. For some others, using the same criteria as those who see truth there, the experience behind any such expression is not one of transcendence, and the symbol does not point to what is meant in the idea of God. For this second group, "Jesus does not show the being of God." Reflection divides on this matter, depending on the standpoint of the person responding to the symbol.

At this point the notion of reflexivity is brought back into the discussion. For reflexivity can bridge the conflict inherent in reflection. If reflexive thought finds a symbol that is effective in showing the being of God both to the believer and to the doubter, then it has found a symbol that is absolutely true as a symbol of God. If one symbol, in the nature of the case a "reflexive" symbol, carries as its primary meaning both the capacity to show the being of God and the denial that it does so; then that symbol undeniably stands as the symbol of God. For Scharlemann, like Tillich, the cross of Christ is one such symbol. The being of Jesus, disclosed in parable and action, can manifest the being of God, the one final reality as grace or love, to those who are receptive to it; but the being of Jesus, as it accepts the cross and denies anything special about him, justifies the disbeliever and the stance of critical distance as well. The point is that reflexive consciousness sees a depth of truth in the symbol: a dimension of meaning that can be affirmed as true from both sides of the split in reflection, both by those who verifiably find an appearance of God in the symbol and by those who verifiably do not.

Moreover, Scharlemann finds the same "doubleness" or unity of affirmation and negation in language itself. A word is a thought and a thing. We can view it first as one and then as the other; both standpoints are validated by the nature of the word. This doubleness of language is caught in the word *God*. As a thought, *God* has no definable meaning, for God belongs in no class. But the word *God* negates that nothingness. It is a word that can carry power by presenting through that nothingness the sheer otherness that is meant by *God*.

Scharlemann claims that the reflexivity found both in language and in the word *God* point to one another, making reflexivity a symbol of God. Language, for Scharlemann, is a signification, a pointing: Words point from thought to things. And within language, the word *God* means and instantiates signification by pointing: "God" points away from anything and any "I" to what is "not-this" and "not-I"; it turns everything into a signifier and does not point out what is signified. Scharlemann says, following hints in the neglected writings of Karl Daub, "What God means and what language is are the same . . . . God means otherness, words are otherness; God signifies the otherness of subject and object; words are the otherness of subject and object."[3] God shows Godself in the deep structure of language ("God is God as word"); and the essence or deep structure of language shows itself as the word *God*.

Let us now see how this structure of thought bears on Scharlemann's topic in "Being 'As Not'." The guiding question of Scharlemann's essay is "What is meant, in the parables of Jesus, by the expression 'the kingdom of heaven'?" The inquiry leads Scharlemann to distinguish a theological reality from an ontological or religious one by referring to the "overturning" it performs on the ontological and religious realms. Moreover, the inquiry turns up an interesting suggestion concerning the formulation of the metaphoric process in language. Let me address these two points in turn.

Scharlemann holds that when we use terms like *religion, ontology,* and *theology,* we are not referring merely to things in the world but also to things in their meaningful relation to human beings, things as they have entered into language and existence. The words *religious* and *ontological* can be understood with relation to the elements of meaning in language and most clearly manifest in texts. In the cases of religious and ontological language, the elements of meaning are differently configured than in ordinary discourse. Whereas in ordinary discourse, sense and reference are clearly distinct (as in both objective thinking and reflective thinking, defined above), in religious and ontological discourse, sense and reference are given together. This means that in these instances of discourse what I am saying and that about which I am speaking are given together in the event of speaking and understanding the words. In ontological discourse, the sense is conceptual; for example, discourse about Dasein, the one I am as myself, presents the referent with the sense of the words *I* or *Dasein*. In religious

[3]Robert P. Scharlemann, *The Being of God: Theology and the Experience of Truth* (New York: Seabury Press, 1981), p. 176.

discouse, the sense is imagistic; for example, the words "the kingdom of God" may present an image that is as real or more so than the physical world. The togetherness of sense and reference described here is the same as the identity of thinking and being that occurs in both prethinking and, at the higher level referred to here, reflexivity.

A theological entity in discourse, by contrast, overturns the togetherness of sense and reference. By this Scharlemann means that the reflexive experience of identity that occurs in reading an ontological or religious text becomes a sign of or appearance of God. But this sign or appearance of God is not literally God—it is the manifestation of God in the time of God's otherness from Godself.

Scharlemann illustrates his scheme through his interpretation of the expression "kingdom of God" as used by Jesus in the parables. The parables are examples of religious discourse for those people who find themselves in the kingdom of God when they read and understand what happens in the story. For many, sense and reference are given together in reading "The kingdom of heaven is like treasure hidden in a field, which a man found and covered up; then in joy he goes and sells all that he has and buys that field." The imagistic sense donates a reality as referent.

How should this redescription of reality through metaphor be understood? Ricoeur's interaction theory of metaphor proposes that the play of "is" and "is not" in the copula of the metaphor engenders an "is like" that redescribes reality in its image. But Scharlemann points out the flaw in this formulation. To say something is like something else assumes we can identify the subject term of the metaphor (here "the kingdom of God" or "the kingdom of heaven") apart from the metaphoric comparison. But in the case of this subject-term, we cannot do so. The kingdom of God, unlike worldly kingdoms, cannot be identified on its own. Consequently, the language of "being like" ("The kingdom of heaven *is like* . . .") reinforces the false impression that the parable speaks about a metaphysical or supernatural kingdom.[4] Scharlemann corrects Ricoeur by pointing out that the term "kingdom of heaven" negates the ordinary sense we have of a kingdom. The term "kingdom" names something we understand, but it is conjoined with "of heaven" which breaks down that understanding. A "denominator" (kingdom) is joined with an "alienator" (of heaven). The effect of the expression "kingdom of heaven" is to show the negation or otherness of worldly kingdoms. This otherness then appears as the event narrated in the

[4]See Dominick LaCapra's criticism of Ricoeur's theory of metaphor as metaphysical in "Who Rules Metaphor?" *Rethinking Intellectual History: Text, Contexts, Language* (Ithaca: Cornell University Press, 1983), pp. 118–44, especially p. 140. See Dominick LaCapra's criticism of Ricoeur's theory of metaphor as metaphysical in "Who Rules Metaphor?" *Rethinking Intellectual History: Text, Contexts, Language* (Ithaca: Cornell University Press, 1983), pp. 118–44, especially p. 140.

parable. The otherness appears *as* what it *is not*. Hence the expression "being 'as not'."

Scharlemann's term "being 'as not'" does not appeal to a metaphysical kingdom; it seems rather to refer us to the religious experience associated with understanding the parable. Theological thinking, with its reflexive or immediate identity of thinking and being, interprets itself with reference to that experience as a sign of the God who is being God in the time (the telling of the parable) of being other than God. This makes sense if the being of God is to be other than God, as it is for Scharlemann.

BEING "AS NOT":
OVERTURNING THE ONTOLOGICAL
(1981)

Robert P. Scharlemann

The overarching theme for this discussion is the relation of religious language to ontology. Like all program themes,* the title leaves some questions to be answered in defining the matter more specifically. Does the title intend to suggest, for example, that ontology is itself a kind of language, so that the comparison is between religious language and this other language? Or does it intend a contrast between language and concepts as well as between religion and being so as to result in a double comparison—of religion in language on one side with ontology in concepts on the other? Finally, is "religious" to be equated with "theological" in this context? All of these possibilities are legitimate understandings of the title, but it will simplify matters if, for the purposes of this paper, we adopt one or another of the possibilities. I shall do so presently, by setting up some definitions at the beginning, and I shall also introduce "theological" as a third term, not identical with "religious." In order to keep the whole from being an exercise in definitions only, I shall take as a guiding question this one: "What is the kingdom of heaven if the term 'kingdom of heaven' refers to a theological entity that is not the same as either an ontological or a religious entity?"

I propose the thesis that, in defining the relations among the ontological, religious, and theological worlds (or among those three kinds of texts), one needs to take account of a certain overturning of the ontological and religious that is effected by the theological. This can be taken, then, as a commentary and elaboration upon an observation that Ricoeur makes in his essay "Philosophische and theologische Hermeneutik."[1] There he writes:

> Mein Interesse ist auf den Doppelsinn der Beziehung von philosophischer und theologischer Hermeneutik gerichtet. Einerseits scheint ja die theologische Hermeneutik ein Sonderfall der philosophischen zu sein, insofern als sich deren wichtigste Kategorien, die der Rede, der Schrift, der Erklärung, der Interpretation, der Verfremdung, der Aneig-

---

*This essay was originally given as a paper to the Interpretation Theory of Paul Ricoeur Group of the American Academy of Religion at the Annual Meeting of 1981, in San Francisco.

[1]*Evangelische Theologie*, Sonderheft, "Metapher: Zur Hermeneutik religiöser Sprache" [Munich: Kaiser, 1974] p. 24

nung, usw., dort wiederfinden: ihr gegenseitiges Verhältnis ist also das einer allgemeinen Hermeneutik zu ihrem Teilbereich. Andererseits besitzt die theologische Hermeneutik spezifische Merkmale, die den Universalitätsanspruch der philosophischen Hermeneutik, wie er zum Beispiel von Hans-Georg Gadamer formuliert wird, in Frage stellen. Hier erscheint das Verhältnis der beiden Hermeneutiken umgekehrt: die philosophische wird Organon der theologischen Hermeneutik.

My interest is directed toward the double meaning of the relation between philosophical and theological hermeneutics. On the one side, theological hermeneutics appears to be a special case of philosophical hermeneutics, insofar as the most important categories of philosophical hermeneutics are found there anew: discourse, writing, explanation, interpretation, distanciation, appropriation, and so forth. Their reciprocal relation is, therefore, that of a general hermeneutics to a regional hermeneutics. On the other side, theological hermeneutics possesses specific characteristics which place in question the claim for universality on behalf of philosophical hermeneutics, as this has been formulated by Hans-Georg Gadamer, for example. Here the relation of the two hermeneutics appears to be reversed: philosophical hermeneutics becomes the organon of theological hermeneutics.**

What is implied about the connection between ontology and theology if the relation of the special to the general can be thus inverted—if, on one side, theological hermeneutics is a special case of general hermeneutics and, on the other side, philosophical hermeneutics turns into an organon of theological hermeneutics?

I. SOME DEFINITIONS

Terms like "religion" and "ontology" do not refer to things, like trees and animals, that can be defined by genus and specific differences. They are not given objects. Hence, they require constructive definitions, which formulate the rule for how a thing is constituted as religious or ontological or theological. When defining things like plants and animals, we have definite entities in view, even before and without the definition, and we ask what their characteristics are—what, for example, are the features that distinguish a dog from a cat or a Persian cat from an Angora cat? In the case of terms like "religion" and "ontology," the perceptible features of a thing do not serve to distinguish the one from the other. Any object can serve as a potential illustration of the terms; for the definition lies in how the entity is constituted. That is to say, constructive definitions take account not only of what a thing is on its own but of what it is in the framework of a certain kind of relation to it. Thus, what distinguishes a certain figure—say, a sculpture of a man on a horse—as an esthetic object, a work of art, from a physical object is

---

**Editor's translation.

the way in which the object is constituted in relation to the one making or viewing it.

The constructive definitions of the terms "ontological," "religious," and "theological" that I offer here will make use of the elements of meaning (or sense) and reference (or significance, or world) in order to show the nature of their constitution: an entity (or word or text) is ontological (religious, theological) if meaning and reference are connected in certain ways. "Sense" refers to what we understand to be carried by a sign (whether a word or an entity); "reference" is what the sense in the sign signifies, or what it is about. Thus, the sense of a proposition is what it *says*, and the reference of that same proposition is what it says it *about*. It does raise problems, admittedly, if we too easily shift from the sense of a word to the sense, or meaning, of a thing. But, assuming that the shift can be made, the sense of an entity is defined as that which we can understand it to say, and the reference is what that meaning is about. A tree in autumn may convey the sense of mortality ("You too are mortal!"), when that is what we understand the browning and falling of its leaves to be saying. The referent of that meaning is the life process of nature as a whole, including our bodily existence, or, at least, of that part of nature to which the tree belongs and which it can signify.

By the different ways in which sense and referent are put together, we can make the following distinctions:

An *ontological* entity (be it a word or a thing or a person) is one in which sense and reference are always given together. The two main examples of ontological entities are *human being* (Dasein, understood as a thinking that is also a being—how we think and how we are are one and the same) and *language* (for a word, in distinction from a mere sound or a mute entity, is a thing—a perceptible sound or sight—that is also a meaning). A human being is a meaning that is a thing, and a word is a thing that is a meaning; both are ontological. Take away either the meaning or the thing, and what is left is not a human being or a word but an animal of a certain kind, or a sound or sight of a certain kind.

A *religious* entity can be, and often is, understood to be identical with an ontological one as just described. But if we make a distinction between the two terms, we can say that a religious thing differs from an ontological one in its embodying a unity of sense and referent when the sense is not a thought-content but an image. Words that bear thoughts (concepts) are different from words that bear images, but both can signify a referent. A word is religious when the image and the referent are given together.

A *theological* entity, as distinct from both an ontological and a religious one, is an entity in which being is overturned. Since this is the matter that I want to explicate further in the course of the paper, I shall add here only that the formula underlying this conception of the theological is not the identity between God and being expressed in the proposition "God is being" but rather the identity and difference expressed in the proposition "God is God

278 Hermeneutical Inquiry

as not God," which has to do with the being of God in the time of not being, or with the being of God when God is not being God. A corollary of this formulation is that worldly existence will also be understood not as "finite being"—being limited by nonbeing—but as being in the time of not being.

In summary form, then, an "ontological" text is a text that both carries a thought-sense and also is the world that that sense signifies; a "religious" text is that same unity of meaning and signified except that the meaning is an image instead of a thought; and a "theological" text is—in a way still to be elaborated—a religious or ontological text that is overturned so as not to be what it is or to be what it is not.

To explicate these definitions, it will be helpful to introduce an additional term, besides those of sense and reference. Ricoeur generally (always?) follows Frege's essay "Über Sinn and Bedeutung" in describing the relation of language to reality by making the two aspects those of sense and reference. In a statement like "The leaf is green," the sense is what the statement says, and the reference (or significance) is what it is about. But we can notice an additional aspect—there is a difference between the *leaf* that the statement is about and the *being of* the leaf that the statement is also about. Usually this difference plays no role at all, and, certainly, in our dealing with things in the world nothing much hinges on our being able to distinguish between a thing and the being of that same thing, between the leaf and the being of the leaf. In hermeneutics, however, when one tries to understand what we routinely understand, or to interpret what is understood, we need to pay attention to this distinction. In order to mark it, let me propose that we speak, threefoldly, of what a statement *says* (that the leaf is green), what it is *about* (the leaf), and what it is *all about* (that the leaf is the leaf it is as the green thing there). This provides a first introduction to the way in which the concept of "being . . . as" comes into interpretation theory.

This triple distinction can be found not only in statements about physical things but also in references to Dasein. The basic assertion of the presence of Dasein is "I am here," or "I am this one here." What it *says* is a unity between the subject "I" and the place "here." What it is *about* is the very person making the statement (though one can abstract from that reference artificially in classroom discussions or in discussion groups on interpretation theory, where "I" means not much more than "one" or "some person"). And what the assertion is *all about* is the mode of being expressed in the statement that I am myself *as* what is here—I am I *as* "here."

For purposes of theological interpretation, and also for purposes of understanding the relation among the religious, ontological, and theological, a key phrase is, then, that of "being . . . as", which has to do with what texts or propositions may be all about in addition to what they say and what they are about.

II. BEING LIKE AND BEING AS

The phrase that Ricoeur has used in order to designate the unity of being and nonbeing involved in the metaphorical process is the phrase "being like": "Metaphor is the rhetorical process by which discourse unleashes the power that certain fictions have to redescribe reality."[2] The place of the metaphor is not the noun or the sentence or the discourse but the copula of the verb "to be": "The metaphorical 'is' at once signifies both 'is not' and 'is like'."[3]

But this phrase occasions certain difficulties when applied to parables about the kingdom of God. Normally, in making comparisons by using the phrase "being like" ("N is like X"), one has to assume that the subject of the metaphorical predication can be shown for what it is before it can be shown as like something else; it must designate something, so that we know what we are talking about and what we are comparing to something else. But the name "kingdom of God," or "kingdom of heaven," does not designate a kingdom which can first be pointed out and then, through the parable, shown to be like something else. With this name we do not know, initially, what we are talking about; the name does not designate in the same way as does "the kingdom of Prussia." For similar reasons, Gadamer has indicated hesitation about using the concept of "metaphor" for the process that is at work in poetic literature. So the question is whether there is not a more accurate way of describing the unity of being and not being which is characteristic of poetic worlds as well as of the world designated "the kingdom of God." I think the answer lies in the difference between "being like" and "being . . . as"; indeed, it seems to me that the being characteristic of such worlds as the kingdom of God is a unity of being and not being that can be exactly formulated with the phrase "being . . . as not." The intention of this wording is, I think, the same as Ricoeur's when, for example, he speaks of the kingdom of God as the "extraordinary" that "is like" the ordinary.[4] But there is a difference in what the two wordings can say.

A simple example will show the difference almost immediately. If we say, "Richard is like Hamlet," we draw a comparison between a Richard who can be named and known independently of the comparison being drawn and Hamlet. Richard is the person we have known for years, have conversed with, played games with, gone to school with, and so on; and we can make non-metaphorical predications of him. But then something happens which occasions the thought "Richard is like Hamlet," in which the biographic and the dramaturgic worlds converge to show a new world. This is—if I

---

[2]*The Rule of Metaphor*, translated by Robert Czerny (Toronto: University of Toronto Press, 1977), p. 7

[3]Ibid.

[4]"Listening to the Parables of Jesus," in *The Philosophy of Paul Ricoeur*, edited by Charles E. Reagan and David Stewart (Boston: Beacon, 1978), pp. 239–245, p. 239.

understand him rightly—the way in which Ricoeur conceives of metaphor, or the metaphorical process. Prior to the expression of this thought, there existed the biographic discourse in which we could speak of Richard—his friendship, his schoolwork, his character, his physical features—and, next to it, the dramaturgic discourse connected with Shakespeare's play "Hamlet." What we said about "Hamlet" (such as: "He was played well by N") and what we said about Richard referred to different worlds. Richard was an actual person in our circle of acquaintances, Hamlet was a dramatic figure played by different actors over time in different places and not identical with any one performance or actor. But when something happens to make us see a connection between the biographic and the dramaturgic, a new horizon likens the two in the metaphor that Richard is like Hamlet. This does not mean that Richard has become an actor and is playing the role of Hamlet; but it does mean that an identity between two orders of personhood (a biographic and a dramaturgic) is opened up and an identity in difference is now expressed in the metaphor. We are not comparing Richard with Hamlet by finding features common to them. We are not saying, for example, that Richard hesitates before decisions and cannot resolve to do what he has decided he should do, just as Hamlet hesitates before the prospect of being or not being and of killing or not killing his stepfather. Instead, the intention of the metaphor is to say that Richard "is" Hamlet in a context of being at which the biographic and dramturgic coalesce. Once the identification between the two is made, a whole range of predicates can accrue to Richard, from the world of "Hamlet," that did not accrue to him before. With the metaphor, a kind of new being is manifested upon the being of Richard as Richard. It is new in comparison both to the biographic world of Richard and the dramaturgic world of Shakespeare's "Hamlet."

It is not difficult to see a difference between the sense of "Richard is (like) Hamlet" and the sense of a second proposition: "Richard is Richard as Hamlet." This proposition, too, combines being and not being and transgresses the biographic world associated with the person of Richard. What it intends to say is, again, not that there are points of comparison between the figure of Richard and the dramatis persona of Hamlet but something else. It intends to say that Richard becomes who he is in playing the role of Hamlet, which implies that, in ordinary biographic terms, the one we know as and name Richard falls short of being who he really is. Now, I don't wish to go into the question of whether such a situation is ever literally possible (though one is reminded of Peter Sellers's thoroughgoing identification of himself with his various roles so that, at the end, he was not sure who, if anyone, he was on his own, biographically). If one were to pursue the matter, one would have to take up such questions as how we recognize that a person is not who he really is. But I think the kind of situation referred to is familiar enough that these further questions do not provide a hindrance. We all know an instance or two, I should think, where it has been said that someone is really himself when playing a certain role. The similarity in difference that is noted in such observations is not that of likeness but that of the way, or the time, in which a person becomes the self he or she essentially is.

"Being as," in this sense, seems to come closer to the kind of unity of being and nonbeing that the metaphorical character of parables involves. But one more consideration must be brought in.

III. BEING . . . AS NOT

The difference between "Richard is like Hamlet" and "Richard is Richard as Hamlet" does not yet take us to the overturning that the theological world effects upon the ontological. Richard, even if he comes into his own in the role of Hamlet, still exists apart from that role; the name of Richard designates, or shows, a subject apart from its identification with Hamlet's role. Hence, we do not need to overturn the identity between Richard and himself, what he is biographically and what he is essentially, in order to say that he comes to himself in the role of Hamlet.

Even in this example, however, there is a hint of the change because what Richard biographically is is *not* what Hamlet dramaturgically is. The complete overturning comes about with the naming of a different kind of subject, one that is *not* shown except through what constitutes the material of the predicate. This is the case with such a term as "the kingdom of heaven" (though one will need to specify more exactly how it is not shown by its name). Unlike Richard, who is a person among persons in a biographical world, the kingdom of heaven is not a kingdom among the kingdoms of the political world. The very title "kingdom *of heaven*" introduces a negation of the existence of the subject. To refer to the kingdom of heaven is to refer to a kingdom that is *not* before us as are the other kingdoms. Hence, we cannot construe a parable about the kingdom of heaven as a comparison between an identifiable subject and some other thing with which it has certain likenesses. The kingdom of heaven does not exist at all *except as* what is shown through that to which, in the biblical parables, it is being likened. This is a way of saying that the kingdom of heaven *is* what it is *as* what is shown in the parable—the kingdom of heaven is the kingdom of heaven as the man who finds a treasure in a field and sells all he has to buy the field. (Matthew 13:44: "The kingdom of heaven is like treasure hidden in a field, which a man found and covered up; then in his joy he goes and sells all that he has and buys that field.")

In the case of such titles as "the kingdom of heaven," therefore, we have to attend closely to how being and not being are intertwined:

1. "The kingdom of heaven" contains a negation of the concept or name "kingdom." To speak of the kingdom of heaven is to speak of a kingdom that does not exist. It is a kingdom that, strictly, is not a kingdom at all. Like the term "God," which instantiates the negation of the "I" upon which it is

shown, the term "kingdom of heaven" instantiates the negation of the world that is designated by the term "kingdom."[5] The kingdom of heaven is, in any case, *not* the kingdom of Israel, or of Egypt, or of Prussia, or of any other nation. Ricoeur adopts the characterizations "enigmatic" and "limiting" for such names. But those terms do not indicate that, in "kingdom of heaven," there is a combination of a *denominator* and and *alienator*. "Kingdom" denominates, and "of heaven" alienates.

2. Hence, to begin a parable by reference to the kingdom of heaven ("The kingdom of heaven is like . . .") is to begin by reference to something that appears only as the negation of kingdoms or, to put it differently, as the otherness that is shown upon any kingdom or a given kingdom; showing the otherness is the function of the alienator, which it performs in conjunction with the denominator.

3. What is designated thus by a negation of some real entity—the kingdom of heaven is the "not" or the otherness that appears upon some kingdom and is actualized there—is, in the course of the parable, shown as something else. What is that kingdom, which is other than kingdoms, like? How does it appear besides as the "not" of any actual kingdom? It appears as the event that is narrated in the parable—as, for example, the man who sold all to buy the field in which he had found a treasure. (We can leave aside the question of whether the happening is the event narrated in the parable or the very telling of the parable. In either case, the relations described will be the same.)

4. Of itself, the event of a man buying a field is not the kingdom of heaven any more than is one of the existing kingdoms. Hence, to say that the kingdom is the kingdom of heaven as the occurrence in that parable is to say that the kingdom of heaven is what it is as something that it is not.

I would propose formulating this relation of being and not being in the showing of the kingdom of heaven by saying: "The kingdom of heaven *is* this occurrence *when* the kingdom of heaven is *not* being the kingdom of heaven." And this is the sense of the "being as not" which I have designated as the overturning of the ontological by the theological. The ontological

---

[5]When one says or thinks the word "I", one becomes the referent of the word. In that sense, the very word "I" instantiates what it means; it is an ontological word with reference to actual thought or speech. In correlation with the word "I", the word "God" instantiates the negation of the self; God means the not-I that is instantiated in the speaking or thinking of the name, the "other" of the I, in the same fashion as the "I" instantiates the subject. In this sense, again, the word "God" is ontological. One cannot really think the meaning, or understand the word spoken, without at the very same time instantiating the negation it means. This is the same relation as that between the name "the kingdom of K" and the name "the kingdom of God," with the exception that the noun "kingdom" does not instantiate what it means in the way the word "I" does. Every intelligible noun, of couse, does show the reality it means to the mind—if someone says the word "kingdom," and I understand what it means, I cannot help thinking of a kingdom. But "I" and "God" present their referent not only to mind but also in reality, at a certain time and place, namely, those of the speaker or thinker.

refers to an identity between the meaning and the reality. In that sense, the ontological dimension of the phrase "the kingdom of heaven" has to do with the extent to which the very meaning shows the negation, the otherness, to which it refers. If, in the telling of the parable, the otherness meant is at hand, the parable itself is ontological. To understand the meaning of the parable is, in such a case, simultaneously to be in the kingdom to which the meaning refers. That occurrence is what the kingdom of heaven is. Yet this is not simply an ontological relation, but a relation in which the ontological is overturned, just because the reality to which the meaning refers is the reality of the kingdom of heaven when that kingdom is not the kingdom it is; it is the kingdom of heaven in the time when the kingdom of heaven is not being the kingdom of heaven. To understand the parable is to understand that what shows the kingdom is not the kingdom, and to be in this kingdom (while understanding the parable) is to be in the world that is not the kingdom of heaven. Hence, the summary phrase for the being of the parable and its referent is "being . . . as not." The kingdom of heaven is the kingdom of heaven as what is not the kingdom of heaven.

IV. An Illustration

I would like to illustrate as well as to test the preceding by reference to a text which makes no mention of the kingdom of heaven but which will show the ontological, religious and theological worlds. (Implicitly it will also show the difference in giving ontological, religious, or theological interpretations of a text.) The text I have in mind is the poem of Robert Lowell entitled "Skunk Hour." No one will be under the illusion that I have any expertise as a literary critic, deconstructionist or other; but I find the text, which Sue Crowley brought to my attention in a seminar, helpful for illuminating the relations and for disabusing ourselves of the notion that a religious text has to be one found in a sacred book, or must mention the subjects that sacred books mention, and that an ontological text must be found—to exaggerate the point—in a work by Heidegger or one of his followers.

The pertinent lines from the poem are these:

> I myself am hell;
> nobody's here—
> only skunks, that
> search in the moonlight for a bite to eat.

and the concluding lines:

> I stand on top
> of our back steps and breathe the rich air—

a mother skunk with her column of kittens swills the garbage pail.
She jabs her wedge-head in a cup
of sour cream, drops her ostrich tail,
and will not scare.

What are the ontological, religious, and theological references in these lines (as they form part of the whole poem)? To approach this question, I shall follow Ricoeur in distinguishing the first and second senses of the lines. The first sense is what we understand as borne by the words, what they directly say. This sense of the four lines does not present any problem, except perhaps in the first line. "Nobody's here—only skunks, that search in the moonlight for a bite to eat" is readily intelligible. "I myself am hell" is somewhat different, since "hell" is not a usual predicate of the self. Let me offer the interpretation that "I myself am hell" says that the self is in a state of internal contradiction. One can support this interpretation by the concept of hell (absolute self-contradiction) as well as by reading "I am hell" as the appearance in meaning of "I am ill, not well," a reading which, obviously, involves more conjecture.

In addition to this first, plain meaning of the words, there is a second meaning, provided by the structure of the verse (not by the sense of the words themselves). Significant for our purposes is the structure of "existential interruption," if I may term it so, in the four lines. Consider that the formulation of the being of Dasein is given in the words "I am here" and that the "I am here" presented in the lines is interrupted by the incursion of the Nichts (hell; nobody): "*I* myself *am* hell; nobody's *here*—." And what follows this interrupted existential assertion is an opening, marked by the dash after "here," a sign of the openness of existence qua existence: I am here—("Where?" "In the world"). What appears there, to show the in-the-worldliness of Dasein is "skunks, searching in the moonlight for a bite to eat."

This second meaning—the meaning of the being of Dasein—is drawn from the structure of the poetic lines. Whereas the "I" of the first sense is read autobiographically, the "I" of the second sense is universal—it is the self of any existent, and the disruption by contradiction is the background of the Nichts against which existence stands out.

The two meanings correspond to two different referents, or worlds. The referent of the first meaning is the self of the poet or the speaker and possibly the reader of the poem. Conceivably, it could be anyone who has found himself or herself on Nautilus Island in the scene the whole poem portrays. The second referent (which Ricoeur calls the "world of the text" made possible by the poem's being able to "redescribe reality") is the being of Dasein, as the self's being the self it is in the midst of Nothing.

Given this interpretation of the lines, brief as it is, we can identify the ontological in the text as the place (or, perhaps better, the time) where what it means and what it is converge. That is to say, the lines are ontological when in the very reading or hearing of the verse, I am the self I am—not only does the structure of "*I* myself *am* hell; nobody's *here*—" show the being of Dasein but it makes it possible for "me," any reader, to be a self in the reading-thinking of those lines. If I cannot read the lines without becoming disrupted and established in doing so, they are ontological—meaning and reality at once. Normally, these lines may not function ontologically in that sense; but they have the potential for being so and, indeed, they may have been so for Lowell himself.

Similarly, the lines are religious if the meaning that the structure signifies is the imagery itself (hell; nobody; skunks) and if this imagery is the very world it imagines. Again, this potential lies in the lines, even it it is not normally actualized in the reading or hearing.

The ontological and religious referents appear in correlation with the second meaning; the first meaning is about the everyday (a scene on Nautilus Island). What of the theological, if the theological is to overturn the ontological and religious? It seems to be absent; the poem contains no alienators in denominators (not even in the "Trinitarian Church" under whose spire the skunks, in a line I've not quoted, "march on their soles up Main Street"). But to show the theological upon the material of the poem, through its ontological and religious meanings and worlds, we might fashion a short parable for the poem's readers, taking "island" as a denominator and "Utopia" as an alienator:

"The Island of Utopia is like a man who breathes the 'rich air' of a column of skunks but does not flee or chase them away."